English G 2000

A4

für das 8. Schuljahr
an Gymnasien

Cornelsen

English G 2000
Band A4

Im Auftrag des Verlages herausgegeben von
Prof. Hellmut Schwarz, Mannheim

Erarbeitet von
Barbara Derkow Disselbeck,
Laurence Harger, Allen J. Woppert
sowie David W. Bygott

unter Mitarbeit von
Wolfgang Biederstädt, Köln; Joachim Blombach, Herford; Helga Estor, Darmstadt; Dr. Jens-Peter Green, Oldenburg; Wolfgang Neudecker, Mannheim; Mervyn Whittaker, Bad Dürkheim; Herbert Willms, Herford *sowie* Karen Carlson-Kreibohm, Berlin; Erich Fleischhack, Ebern; Martina Kretschko, Dresden

in Zusammenarbeit mit der Englischredaktion
Cedric J. Sherratt (Projektleitung), Hartmut Tschepe (verantwortlicher Redakteur), Gareth Evans; Kirsten Bleck, Susanne Döpper, Uwe Tröger;
John Stevens (Redaktionsdienst Context, Bad Münstereifel) *sowie* Katie La Storia, Sandra Schwarz (Assistenz)

Beratende Mitwirkung
Prof. Dr. Peter Bruck, Lüdinghausen; Luis Cass, Sutton, Nebraska; Richard P. Emanuel, Anchorage, Alaska; Angelika Hauß, Weinheim; Albert Rau, Brühl; Wolfram Schnaidt, Schwäbisch Hall; Susanne Schroeder-Thürauf, Erlangen; Dr. Jana Schubert, Leipzig; John Stark, Aurora, Illinois; Sabine Tudan, Erfurt; Markus Vetter, Mühlacker; Harald Weißling, Mannheim; Manfred Wildhage, Braunschweig *sowie* John Eastwood, Street

Illustration
Linda Rogers Associates, London: Roger Fereday, Tony Morris, Gary Rees; Dick Smolinski/Bookmakers Ltd., USA *sowie* Gabriele Heinisch, Berlin; Dr. Hans-Joachim Kämmer, Berlin; Skip G. Langkafel, Berlin; Mark Salwowski, Stanford in the Vale; Katharina Wieker, Berlin

Gestaltung und technische Umsetzung
Gisela Hoffmann, Susanne Meyer, Manuela Tanner

Bild-, Text- und Liedquellen
s. Verzeichnis auf S. 195

Zusatzmaterialien zum vorliegenden Schülerbuch

Workbook (Bestellnummer 350622);
3 CDs zum Schülerbuch (Lehrerfassung 351122) *oder*
3 Cassetten zum Schülerbuch (Lehrerfassung 351327)
Auf weitere Bestandteile wird im Handbuch für den Unterricht (350738) verwiesen.

Cornelsen online
http://www.cornelsen.de

1. Auflage €
Druck 9 8 7 6 Jahr 07 06 05 04

Alle Drucke dieser Auflage können im Unterricht nebeneinander verwendet werden. Aus Rücksicht auf die Ereignisse am 11. September 2001 wurden einige wenige Änderungen vorgenommen.

Druck: CS-Druck CornelsenStürtz, Berlin

ISBN 3-464-35047-9 – broschiert
ISBN 3-464-35048-7 – gebunden

Bestellnummer 350479 – broschiert
Bestellnummer 350487 – gebunden

Gedruckt auf säurefreiem Papier, umweltschonend hergestellt aus chlorfrei gebleichten Faserstoffen.

Contents

∘ fakultativ

◦ fakultativ

Dein Englischbuch enthält folgende Teile:

UNITS	die sechs Kapitel („Einheiten") des Buches
U.S. MAG	eine amerikanische Jugendzeitschrift mit Geschichten, Berichten, Gedichten, Liedern usw.
REVISION	Wiederholungsübungen (zur Vermeidung von Fehlern)
TRANSLATION	Übungen und Tipps zum Übersetzen (Englisch–Deutsch)
INTERPRETING	Dolmetschübungen
LANGUAGE SUMMARY (S)	eine Zusammenfassung der Grammatik jeder Unit
VOCABULARY (V)	das Wörterverzeichnis zum Lernen der neuen Wörter
DICTIONARY (D)	das alphabetische Wörterverzeichnis (der Bände 1–4) zum Nachschlagen
LISTS	Listen: *States/Countries/Continents; Names; Grammatical Terms; Irregular Verbs; Useful Phrases for Discussions in the Classroom*

Jede Unit besteht aus diesen Teilen:

'LEAD-IN'	die erste Doppelseite einer Unit; Einstieg in das neue Thema
▶ A: A-SECTION	der neue Lernstoff mit ersten Übungen
▶ P: PRACTICE	Übungen, Sprachspiele und Aktivitäten
▶ T: TEXT	z. B. eine Kurzgeschichte, ein spannender Bericht oder ein Auszug aus einem Theaterstück
▶ H: HOW TO ...	Hinweise und Übungen zum Training nützlicher Fertigkeiten

In den Units findest du diese Überschriften und Symbole:

▶▶▶ NOW YOU	Hier kannst du über dich selbst sprechen oder schreiben.
ACTIVITY	Aufgaben, bei denen du etwas tust – z.B. eine Collage gestalten
GAME	Spiele für zwei, für eine Gruppe oder für die ganze Klasse – natürlich auf Englisch
ROLE-PLAY	Vorschlag für das Spielen einer Szene mit verteilten Rollen
PROJECT	Hier findest du Vorschläge für ein größeres Projekt, das ihr am besten in einer Gruppe planen und durchführen solltet.
FOCUS ON GRAMMAR	Hier lernst du neue Grammatikstrukturen kennen.
FOCUS ON WORDS	Hier sammelst, ordnest und verwendest du neue Wörter und Ausdrücke.
WORD WATCH	Unter dieser Überschrift geht es immer um Übungen zum Wortschatz.
LISTENING	Hier gibt es Hörtexte auf einer Cassette/CD und dazu Aufgaben im Buch.
REVISION	Hier wird Bekanntes wiederholt – damit du nichts vergisst.
WORKING WITH THE TEXT	Unter dieser Überschrift stehen Aufgaben zum vorangehenden Text.
◆◆	Partnerarbeit
❖	Gruppenarbeit

WELCOME

TO THE UNITED STATES OF AMERICA!

What do you think of when you hear the words 'United States of America'? Famous people and places, films, crime? Collect ideas on the board and talk about them.

2

3

4

5

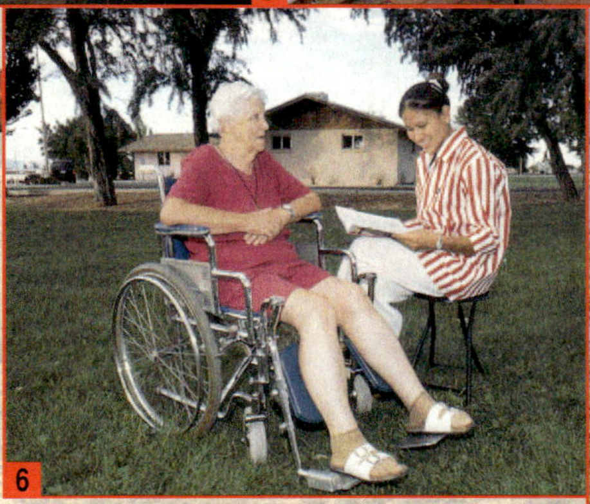

6

7

An American girl chose the seven photos on these two pages. She thinks they give a good idea of life in the USA. Match these captions to the photos.

a) Supermarkets often stay open 24 hours.
b) It's about 5000 kilometres from the east coast to the west coast.
c) Family barbecues are very popular.
d) Lots of kids in cities play streetball.
e) Religion is important for most Americans in their everyday lives.
f) Kids from high schools often do volunteer work in hospitals.
g) Some Americans prefer the life of a traveller to living in one place.

How are your ideas about the USA different from the American girl's?

LISTENING

Listen to the song on the cassette/CD.

- *Write down as many place names from the song as you can. Look for them on the US map at the front of the book.*
- *Say how the singers feel about the USA.*

ACTIVITY

Now start an American album. Collect photos, postcards or maybe souvenirs from the USA. Stick them into your album. You can add more as you go through this book.

UNIT 1 Space Camp Florida

These kids met at Space Camp Florida. Look through the units of this book and find out where they come from.

Conchita Gonzales
14

Kimberley Haynes
13

Margo Blair
14

Glen Oktollik
12

Scott Truong
14

Joshua Brown
13

Nancy Griess
14

about florida

After your stay at Space Camp, why not explore Florida, the Sunshine State? There's so much to see and fall in love with: the sunny beaches of Miami, the Everglades,

where the alligators swim through the water, and the beautiful fruit farms which produce oranges and grapefruit for the whole world!

Don't miss a tour of the Kennedy Space Center. Or visit one of Orlando's many fantastic theme parks – Epcot for science fans and Sea World for dolphin lovers are just two of many and are both in Orlando.

Oh, and you'll find lots of great places where you can eat. Many of them offer wonderful Hispanic food because almost two million Hispanics live here in Florida.

? *What do you know about Florida? Use the information from pages 8/9 and make notes.*

cities	weather	tourist attractions	...

What would you like to do or see in Florida?

ACTIVITY
Collect photos and other material about Florida for your American album.

→ P 1, 5 → U.S. Mag, pp. 92/93

▶ 1

'OK, Mars Team, end of briefing,' said the counsellor. 'We'll let you take a break now: we start mission training back here at twelve.'
Conchita ran quickly to the phones. There was one free. 'Can you let me use the phone first, Conchita?' asked Scott, a kid from her team. 'I need to talk with Mom before she goes to work at nine o'clock.'
'Sorry, Scott,' Conchita smiled at him, 'it's already ringing, and anyway, if my watch is right, it's almost twelve!'
'Not in San Francisco!' he laughed.
'So, you're from Cali… Oh, hi Mamá! Sí, estoy bien … I'm fine … Yeah, our counsellor is neat. He lets us ask as many questions as we want. … OK, Mamá, I'll call again. Hasta luego!'

→ P 6

? *It's 12.05 and mission training has just begun. What time is it in LA (Los Angeles), Denver, Milwaukee, Phoenix, Seattle? (Look at the map at the front of the book.) Then choose a city yourself and ask your partner what time it is there.*

▶ 2

Margo and Glen of the Mars Team wrote home about their first day at Space Camp.

Space Camp
Monday evening

Dear Grandma and Grandpa,
How are you all back home in 'little old England'? When I landed here, I wasn't sure whether I was in the right country – all the signs were in Spanish! (And English, of course).
The people in my team, the Mars Team, are great. I like Conchita most – she's from Chicago. Her family is Mexican and I think they're quite poor. But she won a scholarship to Space Camp. Joshua from New York makes us all laugh – well, everyone except Kimberley from Virginia. She's so serious about science and makes the others feel terrible if they don't understand everything.
Our first day has been very busy: we've been working hard since early morning. First a briefing, then mission training in the afternoon. Tomorrow we're doing a space walk and a tour of Kennedy Space Center.
Time for dinner at the Cosmic Café now. See you soon.
Love,
Margo

September 8

Hi Dad, hi Amy,
Just look – I cut this photo out of the brochure. It's a kid in a space-walk simulator. I'm sending it to you because you may never see me again: tomorrow, at 8 a.m. Eastern Time, I'll be in it!

Love, Glen

And just before the lights went out,
Conchita wrote in her diary:

MONDAY, SEPTEMBER 8
On my first day at Space Camp I saw a real rocket, ate freeze-dried food, had my first briefing and started mission training. I've only been in Florida for one day, but I already feel like a real astronaut – awesome!

→ S 1: 1, 2 (pp. 124/125)
→ P 2, 3

▶ 3

The next morning at breakfast the Mars Team was talking excitedly. 'Gee, Dad never gives us bacon and eggs for breakfast,' said Glen.
'Poor you!' said Nancy. 'Where I come from, in Nebraska, we say it's best to start the day with a big breakfast.'
'Where I come from, in the Bronx, we're too poor to eat breakfast,' said Joshua. Everybody was very quiet. Joshua began to laugh. Soon everyone was laughing, except Kimberley. She looked at Joshua and said: 'That wasn't funny, Josh.'
At eight o'clock the counsellor spoke to the Mars Team in the simulator hall. 'OK, put on your helmets now. And remember, if there's anything you aren't sure about, look it up in the mission manual before you go in the simulator.'
Glen was first and was put in the chair. The space-walk simulator went from side to side and upside down. When Glen came out, he was smiling. 'I was real scared at first. But then it was cool. I can't wait to do a real space walk.'

→ P 7

▶ 4

In the afternoon the Mars Team sat on a tour bus. They watched the Kennedy Space Center come closer. Then the guide started to speak. They listened to her talk about the tour. 'Welcome to KSC,' she said. 'First stop: the Space Shuttle Launch Complex. And I have got some good and some bad news for you. The good news is: you're real lucky. You can see us launch a space shuttle on Thursday. The bad news is: it's at 5 am!'
The kids all laughed.

? *What do you know about the kids in the Mars Team? Look at pages 8–11 and take notes on things like name, family, where they're from, … Fill in more information as you go through this unit.*

→ U.S. Mag, p. 94

5

At the end of her week at Space Camp Conchita wrote in her diary:

FRIDAY, SEPTEMBER 12

My last day at Space Camp: Margo's parents have arrived from England for a vacation in Florida. I heard Mrs. Blair promise to take us to Epcot (Experimental prototype community of tomorrow). I'm real happy because Mamá and Papá said I can go with the Blairs. It will be great!
Tonight we were all a little sad. We sat around and talked a lot. We all looked at Nancy's photos of Nebraska. Then we listened to Glen tell us how cold and dark Alaska winters are. Margo showed us a poster of an alligator she bought for her cousin. And we swapped addresses and phone numbers. Scott is going to send me a letter or call me every week – he says.
I didn't waste my money on too many phone calls home, so I've been able to save some to buy Paco an Apollo T-shirt.

SATURDAY, SEPTEMBER 13

On the way to Orlando today, we stopped at a Mexican restaurant for lunch. The waiter talked Spanish to us and I had to help the Blairs. Mr. and Mrs. Blair were surprised that Spanish is my first language. In the end we all had chicken tacos with rice. I guess the other stuff on the menu was just too strange for them. I wonder what they eat in England! The people at the restaurant were real nice. Mrs. Blair asked how tacos are made – so we all went into the kitchen and watched the cook make them. Then he gave me the menu as a present, so I could put this in my diary.

FOCUS ON GRAMMAR

1 *Look at A4 and A5 again and find the sentences with these verbs of perception:* watch, listen to, see, hear. *Write them down in a table like this:*

	Verb of perception	*Object*	
They	*watched*	*the KSC*	*come closer.*

2 *How would you say these sentences in German?*

3 *What is the form of the verb after the object?*

→ S 1: 3 (p. 125)
→ P 4

▶▶▶ NOW YOU

Think of a time when you had to say goodbye to a group of friends – the end of a class trip, a change of school, etc. Write your diary for that day and describe how you felt.

Our class trip ended this afternoon. When we got back to ..., I was very ... . We ...

FOCUS ON WORDS Space

1 *Collect words and phrases about* space *and* Space Camp *from this unit. Make a network with them.*

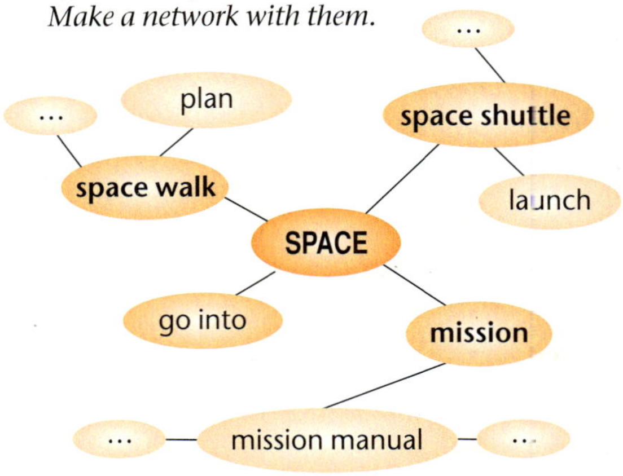

◆◆ 2 *Imagine you are an astronaut. Use your network and tell your partner about the most exciting day of one of your trips into space.*

Monday was the most exciting day of our trip. After the shuttle was launched, we ...

→ P 8
→ How to present an argument, p. 19
→ U.S. Mag, p. 95

1 ▶ **America**

Read this poem about America. Then choose a word from pages 6–9 (Florida, space, …) *and write your own poem. You can put it in your American album.*

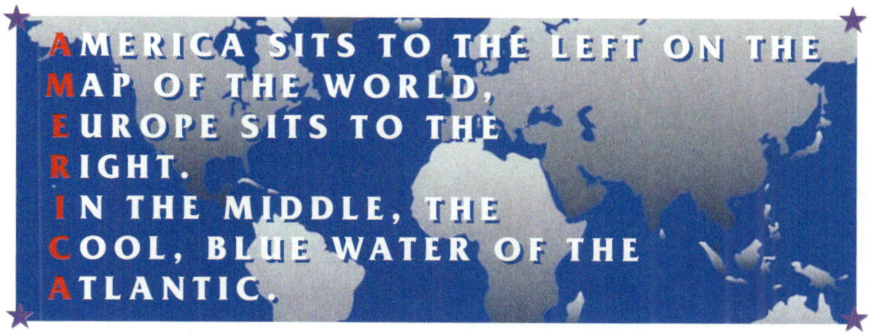

2 **REVISION** Scott's phone call → S 1 : 1 (p. 124)

a *When Scott phoned his mother on his first morning in Space Camp, she was already out. So he phoned again in the evening. Complete what he said with the right form of* let *or* make.

'Yeah, Mom, they let us stay up till 9.30 at night. But then they … us go to bed and it's lights out at ten. – Tomorrow? Oh, we're trying one of the simulators. It looks scary and they (not/…) anyone go in it until the doctor says everything's OK. – Oh yes, they're so careful. They … us check everything three times before we do anything. And they (not/…) us do anything alone. There's always someone from Space Camp there. But they're going to … us go shopping alone at the end of the week.'

don't let

let

◆◆ **b** *What do your parents make you do at home? What do they let you do? Tell your partner and listen to what he/she says. Who has an easier time at home?*

c *Now imagine you could tell your parents what they should do at home. What would you make or let them do?*

I would let my parents go out every evening.

3 **REVISION** What are you doing next week? → S 1 : 2 (p. 125)

a *On a piece of paper, write your name and what you are doing on each day of next week.*

Sophie
Monday: watch videos
Tuesday: meet Micha at club
Wednesday: play tennis
Thursday:

◆◆ **b** *All the pieces of paper are put in a box. Now take one (not your own!), find a partner and tell him/her what your person is doing. Then find out what his/hers is doing next week.*

A My person is watching videos on Monday. What about yours?

B Oh, my person is playing the piano. On Tuesday my person …

Can you and your partner guess who the people are? If not, find another partner and do it again.

4 ▶ Voyager's arrival

Two spaceships, called Voyager 1 and Voyager 2, were launched in 1977 to collect information about Jupiter, Saturn, Uranus and Neptune. They left our planetary system in 1990. They both carried gold discs with sounds and pictures of the Earth.

Jupiter ['dʒu:pɪtə] Saturn ['sætən]
Uranus ['jʊərənəs] Neptune ['neptju:n]

Complete this passage about what happened to Voyager when it entered another solar system. Use the correct verbs from the box.

arrive • bring • call • play (2×) • say • sing • speak

After the satellites discovered the spaceship, scientists from all over the planet saw it *arrive* in their solar system. They sent a space shuttle up. Later a large crowd watched the shuttle … the strange spaceship down to the ground. When the scientists looked in the spaceship, they found a gold disc. They listened to the disc … sounds from another world. They heard strange voices … and orchestras from another planet … music. Pictures showed these strange people from another solar system. They watched the people … to them in a strange language. They heard them … hello and … their planet 'Earth'.

◆◆ 5 ▶ Florida and the USA

Partner B: Look at page 112.

a *Partner A: Look at the table on the right. The Florida information is missing, but your partner has it. Ask your partner questions about Florida and answer his/her questions about the USA.*

A What's the capital of Florida?
B It's …
What's the capital of the USA?
A It's …
How big is …?
B It's …

	USA	Florida
capital	Washington, D.C.	?
size	9.5 million square km	?
population	272 million	?
Hispanics	c. 28.5 million (=10.5%)	?
national bird	bald eagle 	?

b *Write down what you have found out about Florida. You can put the information about the USA and Florida in your American album.*

c *Make a similar table for Germany or your home state in Germany. Compare the facts for Germany with the facts you have for the USA and Florida.*

WORD WATCH

6 LISTENING Telephone calls

◆◆ **a** *Think of as many telephone words and phrases as you can and write them down:*
(to) phone, phone call, (to) leave a message, ...

b *Amy, Glen Oktollik's sister back in Alaska, is trying to phone her friend Tina Jenkins. Listen to the five telephone calls on the cassette/CD. Then match these descriptions to the calls:*

1 Tina is at home – she'll come to the phone in a minute.
2 Amy has got the wrong number.
3 Amy leaves a message with Mrs Jenkins.
4 Mrs Jenkins tells Tina that she should go to her phone.
5 The answering machine is on.

c *What can you say when you hear these questions or statements on the phone?*

1 'Hello?'
2 'Who is this, please?'
3 'Can I give him/her a message?'
4 'You've got the wrong number.'
5 'Please leave a message after the beep.'

Listen again to the phone calls and add the phrases to your list from **a**.

❖ **d** *Everyone writes a message for an answering machine. Swap messages with another group. Choose one message. What would you say if you heard it on an answering machine? Record your messages and answers on cassette or read them out to your class.*

7 ▶ The astronaut's report

a *Choose the correct word from the box and complete the astronaut's report.*

> for • off • on • out (2×)
> through • to • up (2×)

When we were in orbit, I looked ... and saw the Earth. Then I got ... from my seat to start work. I took ... my helmet and went ... the radio. At first we couldn't get ... to NASA but we heard Mission Control after about a minute. I turned ... the volume so I could hear the instructions. 'Turn ... the computer,' they told us, 'and look ... the file "Mission".' That's when we found ... why we were up there.

b *What happened next? Finish the story. Use some of these verbs:*
land on, look after, look for, put on, take off, ...

8 ▶ Money matters

a *What can you do with money? Write down as many sentences as you can. There is some help in the box.*

> ... buy ... • ... give money to ...
> ... pay for ... • ... save money for ...
> ... spend/waste money on ...
> ...

b *A lot of things you want cost money. Where does your money go? What do you have to pay for yourself? How much do you spend on what?*

What do you think Conchita's first day back at school was like? Why? Now read the text.

Little Miss Astronaut

My plane from Orlando arrived at O'Hare Airport at nine o'clock this evening. Papá got time off at the factory to meet me. Mamá and the little ones came to the airport with him. It was great to see them all. It's like I've been away much longer than a week and my whole life has changed. Mamá cried when she saw me come through the gate. She was so happy.

When we got on the bus, I remembered what Margo said: "All Americans have cars, don't they?" Why didn't I say, "Well, we don't have enough money"? On the way home I told Paco and María all about Camp. They both asked lots of questions.

Before María went to bed, I had to tell her about Orlando, too. When I'm an astronaut and have lots of money, I'll take her there.

The wind is cold tonight. I missed it in Florida, but now I'm back home and I miss the warm sun! Here fall has really begun – lots of trees are already red and yellow. I talked to Linda on the phone. I tried to tell her all about Camp, but she wasn't interested. She just said, "See you tomorrow." And she told me some boring stuff about Mike Donovan and the other guys on the football team. I wonder: will Scott really write? School tomorrow. Must sleep ... can't sleep ...

'Look, here comes little Miss Astronaut!' whispered Rita.

'Hi, Linda! Hi, Rita!' called Conchita to her friends.

'Oh, hi, Conchita,' said Linda.

'Well, are you ready for your talk tomorrow?' asked Rita. 'Remember, we "ordinary" kids have to learn all about the great US space programme from you!'

'Here's the bus. Come on!' said Linda

'Space Camp was real exciting,' Conchita told her friends as she sat down behind them on the bus.

'Yeah? Well then your talk will be "real exciting", won't it?' smiled Rita. She got out her magazine and started reading. 'Hey Linda, did you see, there's another competition this week ... you can win a weekend in New York. Maybe one of *us* can win that – more fun than a week at a Space Camp, huh?'

'There was this real nice guy at Camp – he came from New York. If you really went there, maybe he could show you the city ...'

'Sure, Conchita. I couldn't go on a trip to New York without your help!' said Rita

Conchita was quiet the rest of the journey.

At Roberto Clemente High School it was the usual loud Monday morning. José saw the three girls come into the class and called: 'Hey, guys – look who's here! It's little Miss Astronaut ...'

At recess Conchita didn't go outside with the others. She sat alone in the classroom and began to cry. She was so happy and proud when she won the scholarship to Space Camp and the chance to come back with an extra Science credit. It all seemed so great, but now ...

Ms Morrison looked in. 'Why aren't you outside?' she asked Conchita. Then she saw that Conchita was crying. 'Hey, what's wrong?'
'It's like I've come back and no one wants to know me any more,' said Conchita. 'They call me stupid names and ...'
Ms Morrison smiled and sat down.
'It's like this, kid!' she started. 'You can be like everyone else – that's cool, you're one of the clique. Or you can try to do something different. That's cool, too, but the clique may be J - E - A - L - O - U - S.'
'Jealous? You think the others are jealous?'
'Sure they are, Conchita! I was real popular on our block down on the South Side – you know: all poor blacks together – till I was the first girl who went to college. Suddenly the sidewalk was empty when I walked down it! But here I am today with a crowd of new friends and doing what I want to do. So, hang in there, kid!'
Conchita started to smile.
'I'll try, Ms Morrison, thanks.'

Next day, in Science class, it was time for Conchita's talk.
'I know you are all very excited!' said Ms Morrison. 'Here's "little Miss Astronaut"! She's going to tell us all about the glamour of life in space.'
The kids all watched Conchita walk to the board. She smiled.
'Yeah, that's what I thought: one week of glamour as an astronaut. Here's the suit – neat, huh?' Conchita showed the class her spacesuit from Space Camp. 'Until you want to go to the bathroom!'
Conchita laughed. A few of the kids began to laugh, too. Even Rita laughed, but then she saw José. He was in the Fireball Gang on her block. He was looking at the ceiling and yawning. 'Ha, ha, ha!' he said loudly. Rita and Linda began to yawn, too.
Conchita looked across to Ms Morrison. Then she went on, 'Not so glamorous – right? And just wait till you try a freeze-dried space meal! Here, "hamburgers" – I brought one back for each of you.'
Conchita gave everyone in her class some freeze-dried food. Mike Donovan read the instructions.
'Hey, Ms Morrison, we need hot water for this. Can I go and get some, when Conchita finishes her talk?'
'Yeah!' shouted some of the other kids.
'Come on!' shouted José. 'Who wants to eat this sh...?'
'What do you know?' shouted Mike. 'Why don't you just shut up and listen?'
Linda and Rita looked at each other again. José was really angry. He started to shout, 'Boring, boring ...'
'OK,' said Ms Morrison. 'Who thinks Conchita's talk is boring? Hands up!'
Rita watched José and his friend Pedro put their hands up – then she put her hand up, too.
'Put your hand up,' she whispered to Linda. But Linda didn't put her hand up.
'OK,' said Ms Morrison. 'Twenty-eight kids want to hear Conchita, so *you* three can be quiet!'

After school, Conchita met Linda at the bus stop.
'That was nice of you, Linda,' she said.
'Yeah, well, I'm glad not everyone is scared of José. He's a jerk. Great talk. And wasn't it funny when Mike Donovan showed us how to catch a hamburger in the air and eat it when you're at zero gravity?'
'Yes, even José and Pedro had to laugh!'

WORKING WITH THE TEXT

1 ▶ Spot the mistakes

a *Look at these pictures. Put them in the right order. Can you find the mistakes in two of them?*

1

2

3

4

b *Can you say which page and lines go with each picture? Lines ... to ... on page ... go with picture 1. ...*

2 ▶ What people felt

a *Read 'Little Miss Astronaut' again. Make a list of the people and their different feelings during the story. (The adjectives are not all in the text.) Complete the notes.*

Conchita	– *happy, proud, excited; disappointed, ...*
Rita	– *...*
Linda	– *not interested in Space Camp; jealous, ...*
Ms Morrison	– *...*
...	– *...*

◆◆ **b** *Now choose one of the characters in the story and tell your partner the feelings that character has. Your partner has to say when that was in the story.*

A Conchita was happy and proud.
B I think Conchita was happy and proud when she met her family at the airport.

3 ▶ How you feel

How do you feel about the way José, Pedro and Rita acted during Conchita's talk? Why did Linda act differently?

4 ▶ Beyond the text

a *Are there cliques at your school? Do they always stick together or have the same opinions about everything? Is that 'cool'? Could something like this story happen in your class?*

b *Write Conchita's diary entry for her first days at school after Space Camp. What did others in her class do? How did that make Conchita feel?*

◆◆ **ROLE-PLAY** 'Hi, Conchita, how was school?'
Imagine that Scott calls Conchita and they talk about their first day back at school. What do they say? With a partner, record the conversation on cassette and play it to the class. You can write your own role cards or use the ones your teacher has.

HOW TO ... present an argument

1 ▶ What do I think about it?

'Isn't space exploration fantastic? It's one of the greatest achievements of the twentieth century.'

This is what some people think, but others are not so sure, and there are some who think it costs a lot of money that could be spent on other things.

*So, what's **your** opinion about space exploration? Make notes about what you believe and the reasons for your opinion. The picture might give you some ideas.*

2 ▶ This is why I think so

a *Other people may think differently. How can you make them agree with you? Read the 'one-minute talk' on the right. It has five parts – try to find where each part starts. Then say what the main point of each part is.*

Part	Starts with ...	Main point
Introduction	If you ask ...	...
Argument 1	...	...
Argument 2	...	...
Argument 3	...	...
Conclusion	...	...

If you ask me, space exploration is expensive but very important. Why? Because the money the scientists spend has brought people lots of advantages. Just remember – satellites let us phone people all over the world. So space exploration has helped to bring people closer together, hasn't it? Also, space exploration is making the world a safer place, for example big nations are working on projects together, and not fighting to be best. On top of that, there are lots of developments from space programmes that we use in our everyday lives – things like new medicines and materials for motorbike helmets. So all in all, I'd say space exploration means real progress for the people of our world – even if it costs a lot of money.

b *The speaker gives examples to support his/her arguments. Read the talk without the examples. What do you notice? What other examples can you think of?*

c *Find words and phrases in the text that link ideas and speak to the listeners. Add some more that you know.*

Words that link ideas	Phrases that speak to the listeners
because	hasn't it?
...	...

3 ▶ Let me tell you what I think

Prepare your own 'one-minute talk' to tell the class your opinion. Use your notes from **1**. *Arrange your arguments in a sensible order and check that you have supported each argument with facts and examples. Use an introduction and a conclusion – this will make your talk easier to follow. Don't write out the whole talk – people are more interested if you look at them while you're speaking from your notes.*

REMEMBER

1. Be careful you know what your opinion is and what reasons you can give for it.
2. Prepare your opinion as a list of arguments and give facts and examples to support them.
3. Link your ideas and present them in an interesting way.

2 UNIT 2 Alaska – the Great Land

LISTENING

Look at the photo for a minute.

Then close your eyes and try to remember as much as you can about the photo. Listen to the cassette/CD and take an imaginary journey to the Brooks Range, some mountains in the north of Alaska.

▶ 1

After Glen Oktollik had arrived back home from Florida, he found life in Alaska a little boring. He had learned so much at Space Camp and had made a lot of friends there.

Beep, beep, beep.
Glen opened the door of the microwave and took out his supper. He had bought it on the way home from school. When his sister came in, he had just started his meal.
'How can you eat that stuff?' she asked. She had always hated microwave food.
'It's easy, Amy. You just open your mouth and put it in. I know you prefer whale blubber, but the butchers don't have it here in Anchorage.'
'Oh, you're so stupid!'

Later, after Mr Oktollik and Amy had eaten, they were watching TV with Glen. Suddenly Amy asked, 'Dad, can I go up to Barrow for Christmas? Grandma says I should come.'
'How do you plan to get there?' Glen asked.
'I'm going to fly. What else?'
'What about the timeless old traditions of the Inuit, Amy? Real Eskimos would go by dog sled!'
'Don't be stupid, Glen. We can combine old ways and new. Grandma always says that.'

? *Look at the map of Alaska on pages 96/97 of the U.S. Mag. Find the town where Glen and Amy live, and their grandmother's town. How far is it between them?*

▶ 2

As soon as the TV show had finished, Amy completed a letter to her Grandma. She had started it earlier that evening.

Glen has really changed since Space Camp. We're arguing a lot. He's only interested in his silly science projects. He makes fun of our Inuit traditions all the time. I think he's jealous because I visited you in Barrow in April. Now, about Christmas:

At the same time, Glen called a friend and complained about his sister.

You can't talk to Amy about anything ordinary any more. Only Eskimos. She isn't interested in anything else. She's been learning Inupiaq for months but she still can't speak it. At least my science projects aren't useless.

FOCUS ON GRAMMAR

1 *Look for examples of a new tense in A1 and A2:* *had arrived, ...* *How do you form this tense? What do you think it is called?*

2 *Look at the sentences with the new tense in A2. What happened first? Did Amy finish her letter before or after she watched TV? When do you use this tense?*

→ S 2: 1 (pp. 125/126)
→ P 1, 2

▶ 3

★I★G★A★R★A★M★K★I★N★

STUDENT NEWSPAPER OF A.J. DIMOND HIGH SCHOOL, ANCHORAGE

A City Girl Goes Whaling

Dimond's own Amy Oktollik writes about her adventures in Barrow

Amy and an "umiak" near Barrow last spring

As you can probably guess from my name, I'm an Inuit, one of the "blubbers" you see at school. (I've learned to laugh at that word now – but you really shouldn't use it.)

Last spring I visited my grandmother in Barrow. More than half of the 4,100 people there are Inupiat Eskimos. That's what the Inuit there call themselves. It was good to be with my own people and hear them speak their language, Inupiaq. And I was able to learn more about Inupiat traditions. Barrow is great in the spring: everybody is excited to see the sun again after 67 days of endless darkness.

When I was there, we went whaling: yes, we Inuit are allowed to kill some whales – about 60 every year! I know a lot of people are against whaling. But if you want to understand Inuit culture, you have to know how important whaling is for us.

Everyone has a job to do at whaling time. The men look for big holes in the ice. Holes are the best places to find whales. The women cover the "umiaks", the boats we use, with seal skins.

We use snowmobiles to pull our tents and umiaks to an ice-hole. Then the men wait, often for days, for a whale. When a whale comes, they use harpoons to kill it and to pull it onto the ice. It takes a day to cut up a whale. We use every part of the animal.

In June we go out on the tundra in order to celebrate *Nalukataq*, the whaling festival, with family and friends. We eat the whale meat, talk, sing, dance and do Inupiat sports. We Inuit were the first to come to Alaska 8,000 years ago and we have been doing things this way since then.

→ S 2: 2a–f (pp. 126/127)
→ P 3, 4, 5, 8

LISTENING Inuit whaling – for and against

a *Dave, a new boy at Amy's school, saw her article and was shocked. So the class talked about Inuit whaling in Social Studies. Here are two of Dave and Amy's arguments:*
– Whaling is an old Inuit tradition.
– Modern Inuit don't need whale meat to live.
Think of more arguments for or against whaling and write them down in two lists.

b *Now listen to the cassette/CD and find out if any of your arguments are used.*

c *Listen again and collect arguments. Who do you agree with – Amy or Dave? Find others in your class with your opinion and discuss your ideas. Then write to the student newspaper about Inuit whaling. Remember to give reasons and examples for your opinions. Look at page 19* (How to present an argument) *for help.*

▶ 4

When Amy visited Barrow last April, her grandmother took her to a big festival with song and dance. But Amy found it very difficult to understand what was happening. 'That's because you only hear Inupiaq when you're here,' her grandmother told her.
'Yes, I know,' Amy agreed. 'I'd like to speak Inupiaq better.'
'Yes, and I'd like you to speak Inupiaq better, too,' her grandmother went on.
'Well,' said Amy, 'I dated an Inupiat guy in Anchorage for a few weeks. I told him to speak Inupiaq with me – but his was worse than mine!'

'There are plenty of Inupiat boys in Barrow!'
'Yes, Grandma, and I met a cute guy when I was getting our drinks. How can I get to know him? Do you think I can ask him to go on a date with me?'
'You're not in Anchorage now, Amy,' her grandmother answered. 'Don't expect a boy here to act like someone from the city. You might embarrass him. Go in a group. Show him that you want him to sit next to you. That's how I met your grandpa.'
'And what do I do after that?' Amy asked. Her grandmother smiled and told her not to worry. 'You'll know if he's interested. Then you can ask him to visit you here. Maybe he'd even like you to meet his family.'
'Wow!' Amy said quietly. 'Dating sure is easier in the city.'

FOCUS ON GRAMMAR

1 *Look at these two sentences from A4:*
I'd like to speak Inupiaq better.
I'd like you to speak Inupiaq better.
What's the difference between them?

2 *Now write down the other infinitive constructions with the verbs* ask, expect, tell, want *and* would like *in A4.*
I told him to speak Inupiaq with me, ...

What sort of sentences do you use to say these things in German?

▶▶▶ NOW YOU

Sometimes we would like other people to do something. Say what you would like to happen:
– at Christmas (my parents)
– in our next English lesson (our teacher)
– at the weekend (my best friend)

At Christmas I'd like my parents to take me to Spain.
In our next English lesson I'd like our teacher to ...

Think of one or two more ideas.

→ S 2: 2g (p. 128)
→ P 6, 7, 9

FOCUS ON WORDS Old and new

1 *On pages 22–24 find examples of words and phrases for old ways and new in Alaska. Write them down in a table like this:*

old ways	*new ways*
prefer whale blubber/ fresh food	*eat microwave food*
speak Inupiaq	...

2 *Write a few sentences about old and new ways in Alaska. You could write about:* food, language, transport, dating, ...

A long time ago the Inuit in Alaska only travelled by dog sled or boat. Now they use snowmobiles, all-terrain vehicles and planes.

→ Ancestor Song (p. 28)

▶ 5

Denali

National Park Alaska

Denali, the "High One", is the name the Indians gave North America's highest mountain, Mount McKinley. Denali is also the name of the huge national park around the mountain. With its 9,420 square miles (24,395 square kilometers), Denali National Park is larger than the state of Massachusetts.

? *How big is your home state in Germany? Compare it with Denali National Park. Find out about a national park in Germany. Look for information like its name, where it is, what animals you can see there, etc. Then tell your class about it.*

→ How to use a dictionary, p. 33

ACTIVITY

Partner B: Look at page 113.
Partner A: You and your partner have different information about four of the animals in Denali. Read your information, shut your book and tell your partner what you know about the animals. Then listen to what your partner tells you about the animals and take notes. Use your information and notes and write in your American album about one of the animals.

Some animals of Denali

◀ Caribou
Caribou travel in groups and move a long way from south of the Alaska Range and northwest of Mount McKinley to the northern parts of the park in winter. Caribou may be seen from the park road.

Moose ▶
Moose, the deer family's largest members, are not herd animals. The young are born in May and will stay with the mother one or two years. In spring, the mother and young eat young plants.

◀ Grizzly bear
Grizzly bears eat plants, small animals, and young, old, or sick moose, sheep and caribou.

Wolf ▶
Wolves are not seen often, but they play an important role in the park. They keep Denali healthy because they catch the weak, old and very young animals. And only a healthy park can support wolves.

→ P 10, 11 → U.S. Mag, pp. 96/97

1 ▶ They had been busy

a *Glen wasn't very happy when he returned home from Space Camp. It seemed everything was different. Try and guess who had done what. Use the past perfect.*

1 Glen wasn't able to find anything in his bedroom.
Maybe his sister had taken his stuff. Or perhaps ...
2 His computer was turned on.
3 His favourite CD was in Amy's player.
4 His pencil-case was empty.
5 There was a fax with a party invitation for yesterday.
6 His room looked all tidy and clean.
7 He couldn't find his pet mouse.

b *Describe a situation where you were angry because somebody had done something you didn't like.*

2 ▶ When Glen had finished his homework

a *Read the pairs of sentences below and decide what happened first and what second. Then connect the two sentences with words like* after, because, but, so, when, *etc. Always use the simple past and the past perfect.*

1 Glen finished his homework. He called his friend Cora and asked her to go to a movie.
When Glen had finished ..., he called ...
2 Cora's bike was stolen. She forgot to lock it.
3 She arrived at the movie theater late. Glen went in.
4 Glen sat down near the door. Cora soon found him.
5 The movie was a thriller. Glen saw it on the plane from Florida.

b *Now try to finish these sentences.*

1 I was only allowed to watch TV after ...
2 My brother couldn't come on the trip because ...
3 My sister had already tried on eight sweatshirts before ...
4 ... because he had seen the film before.
5 ... after I had learned to swim.
6 ... I bought the group's new CD.
7 As soon as I had heard the news, ...
8 All my friends arrived before I ...

◆◆ **c** *Write sentence halves like the ones in* **2b** *for your partner. He/She has to finish them.*

3 REVISION What Amy was able to do in Barrow → S 2: 2a (p. 126)

a *Fill in the right verb forms from the list on the right.*

1 When Amy was in Barrow, she ♦ learn a lot about Inupiat life.
2 She ♦ go whaling with some people from the town.
3 The Inuit ♦ pull their tents and umiaks by dog sled – they had snowmobiles.
4 For many years Inuit ♦ kill some whales.
5 In the old days they ♦ kill whales to live.
6 Now they ♦ do it because it is part of their culture.
7 When Amy returned to Anchorage, she ♦ write about her trip for the school newspaper.
8 She ♦ write anything she wanted.
9 She didn't know if she ♦ make Inuit whaling sound OK.

was able to (2×)
are allowed to
was allowed to (2×)
have been allowed to
had to (2×)
didn't have to

b *Write four or five sentences about what Glen was able to/was allowed to/had to do at Space Camp.*

4 REVISION Here's what to do! → S 2: 2c (p. 127)

a *When Rob has got a problem, he always turns to other people for help. But they are fed up with him and tell him he should find out for himself. What do they say to Rob?*

dictionary			
instructions			
manual	can	show	how to …
street map	should	tell	what to …
teacher	will	…	…
timetable			
Yellow Pages			

1 My computer has crashed! What shall I do now?
Don't ask me! Why don't you look in the manual? It will tell you what to do next.
2 Where's the town library?
3 Where can I get a new watch?
4 How do I go on with my project?
5 Where's the Maths lesson?
6 How do I say this silly word?
7 What do I push for 'record'?

◆◆ **b** *What do you do when you have a problem at school? Tell your partner.*

A When I …, I often use/ask/look at/ … . He/She/It tells me where to …/ how to …/…
B Oh, I usually … . He/…

5 ▶ The place to live

a *Amy loves Barrow but Glen prefers the Anchorage area. Here is part of a brochure he sent to the Space Campers. Add the verbs from the box in the right places.*

come • do
get to know • live
look at • miss • move to
see • visit

If you want a change of address, Anchorage is the city *to move to*. For tourists, it's a great place … and for its population of 250,000, a beautiful place … . There are thousands of things … and endless sights … . The Aviation Museum is the place … old planes. And a trip into the beautiful Chugach Mountains is a great way … the countryside. Portage Glacier is not a place … on your trip. You can watch ice fall from the end of the glacier into the lake below. March is the time … if you want to see the famous Anchorage-to-Nome Dog Sled Race. See you in Anchorage, everybody!

b *Now write about your town or village. Try to use infinitive constructions as you explain why it is a great place to live.*

◆◆ **6 ▶ They want her to listen to them all!**

Partner B: Look at page 112.
Partner A: Everybody wants the girl in the picture to do something. Ask your partner what the people in the box want/would like/are asking her to do. Then your partner will ask you about the people in the picture on the right.

A What does her friend want her to do?
B She'd like her to go to … What is her mother asking her …?
A She's asking her to come to the phone.

friend • music teacher
little sister • man

7 ▶ A fax from Dad

a *When Glen and Amy get home from school, they find a message from Mr Oktollik in the fax machine. What does he want/tell/ask them to do?*

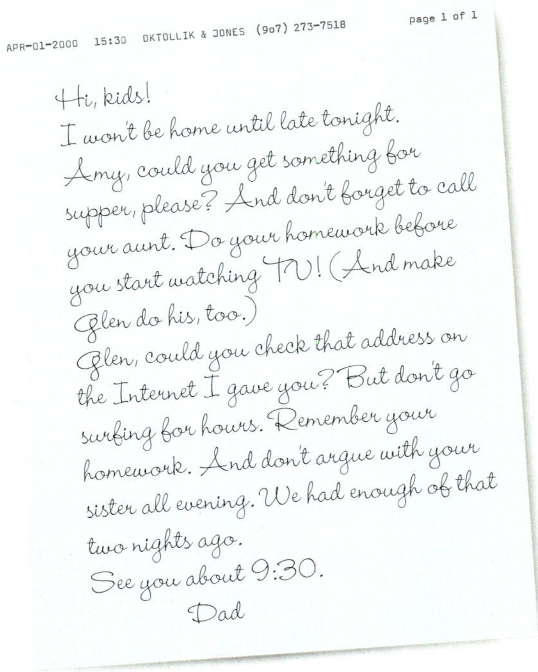
APR-01-2000 15:30 OKTOLLIK & JONES (907) 273-7518 page 1 of 1

Hi, kids!
I won't be home until late tonight.
Amy, could you get something for supper, please? And don't forget to call your aunt. Do your homework before you start watching TV! (And make Glen do his, too.)
Glen, could you check that address on the Internet I gave you? But don't go surfing for hours. Remember your homework. And don't argue with your sister all evening. We had enough of that two nights ago.
See you about 9:30.
Dad

1 He asks Amy to get …
2 He tells her not to …
3 He wants her to …
4 …
5 He asks Glen …
6 He tells him …
7 …
8 …

b *Think of three or four things you would like people in your family to do for you. Write them a message.*

"I sometimes think Peter's a little too hard[1] on the child ..."

[1] hard on *streng zu*

° ANCESTOR SONG

To our elders
Who teach us of our creation and our past,
So we may preserve Mother Earth
For ancestors yet to come:
We are the land.

To our brothers and sisters
And all living things across Mother Earth:
Her beauty we've destroyed
And denied the honor
The Creator has given each individual.

The truth lies in our hands,
All my relations.

ancestor ['ænsestə] *Vorfahr* elders ['eldəz] *ältere Leute, Stammesälteste* creation [kri'eɪʃn] *Schöpfung* preserve [prɪ'zɜːv] *erhalten* beauty ['bjuːti] *Schönheit* deny [dɪ'naɪ] *leugnen, bestreiten* honor ['ɒnə] *(AE) Ehre* the Creator [kri'eɪtə] *der Schöpfer* individual [ˌɪndɪ'vɪdʒuəl] *Einzelne(r), Individuum* truth [truːθ] *Wahrheit* relations [rɪ'leɪʃənz] *Verwandte*

WORD WATCH

8 WORD BUILDING The suffix *-less*

The suffix -less *usually means 'without something'. Add* -less *to the nouns in the box to make adjectives, e.g.* hopeless. *Then put the adjectives in sentences 1–8.*

clue • end • head • hope • job
life • sleep • time

1 It's *hopeless*! We'll never find the place without the right address.
2 Barrow is OK in summer but it's quite a ... place in winter. Just dead.
3 I'm so worried. It's giving me ... nights.
4 If they don't open new oilfields, thousands of people will be ...
5 You don't understand a word I'm saying. You're really ... sometimes.
6 Please stop, you two! I'm fed up with your ... arguments.
7 You like the ... traditions of the Inuit, but I think their time is over.
8 What's the problem? You're running around like a ... chicken.

9 WORDS AND PHRASES Arguments

Describe the situation in the photo. The words on the right can help you.
What do you think the boy and the girl might say to each other? You can use the list below.

angry • argue • complain • fight
hate • have an argument • love
jealous • shout • unhappy • ...

Useful expressions:
At least I/my ...
Don't expect me to ...
Have you ever thought about ...?
How can you ...?
I want you to ...
The difference is ...
Why can't you ...?
You'll just have to ...
You may not believe this, but ...

◆◆ ROLE-PLAY

What do you argue about with other people? Think of a situation that made you feel angry. Write a role card and act out the situation. Or take a role card from your teacher.

Here is a suggestion:
You think you have made a good friend on holiday, until you find out he/she has organized a party but hasn't invited you.

10 TROUBLE SPOT Which word is right?

1 OK, so Barrow might not be the (biggest/greatest) city in Alaska. But it's a (big/great) place for a holiday!
2 So killing that whale (had/made/was) a lot of fun, you say? Is that right? You (had/made/was) great fun?
 – Don't (have/make/be) fun of Inuit traditions!

11 WORD LINK

Choose a verb from the box for each group of words below.

get • give • have
hurt • spend • teach

... an argument, supper, tea, time
... History, a lesson, oneself
... someone's feelings, oneself, one's leg
... angry, cold, a letter, lost, dressed
... blood, reasons, someone a message, up
... money, time, one's holidays

Imagine you are going on a walking trip in the cold north of Alaska. Decide what the five most important things are that you will take with you.

Alone on the North Slope

Lester Swenson was woken up by the sound of an all-terrain vehicle. He heard the ATV move away and he felt cold – but he didn't know where he was.

He shut his eyes again and thought about it. Of course! He and his friend Henry Serkoak had come here on a camping and hunting trip. 'Here' was on the North Slope of Alaska, 45 miles from Atqasuk. Why had he gone on this trip with Henry? 'I could be in my big office back in Barrow now – all nice and warm,' he said to no one. Henry had wanted to show Lester this place – 'before you destroy it,' Henry had said.

But Lester had told Henry, 'The project won't destroy anything. The pipeline didn't hurt the environment and the new oil wells won't hurt it either!' But Henry never listened.

* * *

Lester and Henry had always been good friends. They had grown up together in Atqasuk, both the youngest sons of poor Inupiat families. Lester had been more interested in school than Henry. So when the Native Regional Corporation got all that money from the oil companies and decided to send young Inuit to college with it, Lester went to college in Seattle. Henry stayed at home. Lester had come back to Barrow and started work with the Corporation. He had worked hard, and now, at 39, he was president. As president, Lester helped to make a lot of decisions for the Inuit people: Who gets money to go to college? Which towns or villages can kill a whale this year? Should a new hospital be built? And now: Can the oil companies build their new oil wells on Native land? Meanwhile, Henry had become a guide: he took groups of city people out to hunt or fish and led a life that was completely different from Lester's. '*My* office is the North Slope,' Henry often joked. But Lester and Henry had stayed friends.

* * *

'Where's Henry now?' Lester thought. 'And why did he take the ATV? Why did he leave me alone out here?'

There was only one way to find out. Still in his sleeping-bag, Lester put on his new super-warm jacket and trousers. This wasn't easy: it took almost five minutes. Then he got up. 'Man, that's cold!'

Lester opened the tent and went outside. He looked around: no Henry, no ATV, no equipment, nothing. Henry had taken everything!

Three hours later, Lester thought, 'Henry isn't coming back.' He had thought about it the whole time: Was Henry trying to kill him? Was he trying to teach him a lesson? Or had he just gone for a ride when something happened to him?

'Does it matter?' Lester asked himself. 'I'm a dead man. If the cold doesn't kill me, the bears will.'

Lester was hungry – and cold – and 45 miles from the nearest town. He had to walk the whole way. But not today. The sun had risen three hours before. He had only two more hours of light.

The next morning Lester woke up a little before the sun. His whole body was cold. 'Got to make a fire,' he said and looked around. There was still some oil in the lamp in the tent, but he had no matches to light it. Then he remembered that the early Inuit knew how to make fires: they hit two stones together to make sparks. Lester found some paper, some dry leaves and some wood. Then he poured a little oil from the lamp on them. It didn't take long until he had a nice fire. He sat down next to it and waited until he felt a little warmer. Then he tied the tent and sleeping-bag together and threw them over his back. He put the lamp over his arm and started to walk.

'Got to go east. Sun's in the south. I must keep the sun to my right,' he said again and again.

When he couldn't walk any more, Lester began to look for a new camp-site. He stopped on some flat ground near a frozen stream because he needed water. 'Starting to think like a real Inuit,' he laughed. He put up the tent quickly, then looked for wood. When his fire was burning nicely, he thought about water. As a boy he had read that the Inuit had melted snow in their hands to get water, but that was in a white man's book. His grandmother had laughed when he had told her that. 'If you used your hands, you would freeze,' his grandmother had said. 'We made little bottles out of animal skins, put snow in them and hung them near the fire.'

But Lester didn't know how to make little bottles, and the idea of animal skins only made him hungrier than he already was. 'What about the tent?' he said loudly. The sound of his voice made him feel less alone. He tried to tear off a piece of material from the tent, but the nylon was too strong for him. 'Need a knife. No knife ... What did the early Inuit do? – They had knives, stupid!'

Lester sat down on the cold ground. He wanted to cry. Then he remembered something his grandfather had told him. 'We used what we could find. And the right tool is always there. Always.'

'That's where you're wrong, Grandpa!' But when Lester looked around, he found the right tool: fire. He took a piece of wood from the fire and blew out the flame. The wood was still very hot – hot enough to melt the nylon of the tent! Lester used his fire-knife to cut a round piece of nylon. He pulled the edges together and tied his little bottle with a piece of rope from the tent. It was easy to find a tool to break the ice: a large stone worked well, and soon Lester had his first bottle of water. He drank five bottles before the thirst went away. He felt stronger, but he needed food to survive. Lester remembered that he had seen animal tracks in the snow: some were bear tracks, but there had been smaller ones, too. 'Probably rabbit,' he thought. 'But without a gun ...?' *The right tool is always there.*

Lester went back to where he had seen the tracks. When he found them, he followed them to a hole in the ground. The animal's warm body had melted some of the snow around the hole.

Slowly Lester moved towards the hole. But what could he use to catch the rabbit? He looked down at his hands and knew that they – and his brain – were his best tools. With one quick movement Lester had the rabbit in his hands. The animal was frightened and fought hard. Lester didn't want to kill it, but he knew that one of them had to die.

And Lester didn't want to die. He had to stay strong. He had to survive and get back to Atqasuk. He had to find Henry.

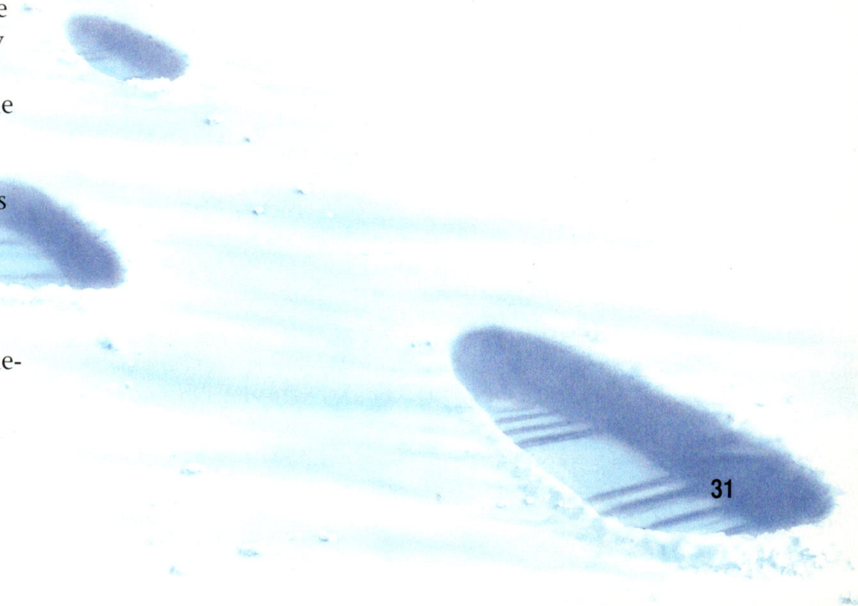

WORKING WITH THE TEXT

1 ▶ What is the story about?

In no more than three sentences, write what the story Alone on the North Slope *is about. Use the present tense.*

◆◆ 2 ▶ Right or wrong?

Look at these two statements. Which one is correct?

1 Lester Swenson and his friend Henry went on a camping and hunting trip.
2 Henry wanted Lester to build oil wells on the North Slope.

Now write four more statements about the story, two right and two wrong, for your partner. He/She must correct the wrong ones.

3 ▶ Lester and Henry

Copy and complete this table about Lester and Henry's lives. What's the same? What's different?

	families	education	jobs	where they work
Lester				
Henry				

4 ▶ The old ways to survive

How did old Inuit traditions help Lester to survive? Copy this network and complete it.

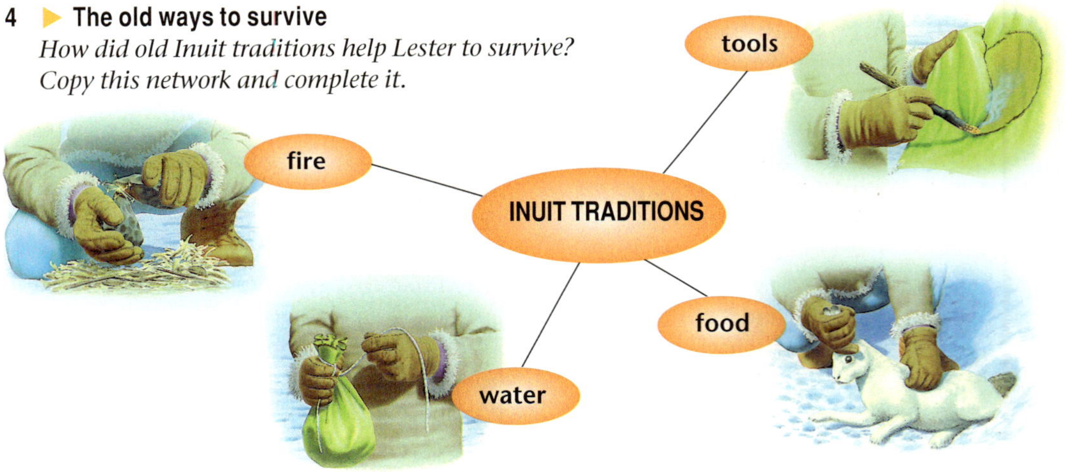

❖ 5 ▶ Beyond the text

Why do you think Henry left his friend alone on the North Slope without any food or equipment? Does one of Lester's ideas (p. 30, ll. 61–64) seem right to you? Discuss this in your group and then report back to the class.

◆◆ 6 ROLE-PLAY 'Where were you, Henry?'

a *If Lester survives and finds Henry, what will their meeting be like? With your partner, write role cards for their conversation. Your ideas from* **5** *might help you. Or look again at exercise 9 on page 29. Don't forget to make a list of useful phrases.*

b *Now use your role cards and act out the conversation. Or swap your role cards with another pair and act out the conversation with their role cards.*

→ Revision, p. 116
→ Translation, p. 120

HOW TO ... use a dictionary – Part 1: German-English

1 ▶ Looking up a word

When you do the project on the next pages, you'll probably need some words that you don't know yet in English. Imagine you want to look up the English word for Decke *in a dictionary. How does the dictionary help you to find the page the word is on? Would you look at page 401 or page 402?*

Now try this to become faster at finding words: Write down ten German words that start with different letters and see how quickly you can find them all in a dictionary. Write down the page numbers.

dazu 401 **Demokrat(in)**

dazu 1 with it/them **Es gibt Würstchen und dazu Senf.** There are sausages and mustard to go with them. | 4 (*schützen*) cover /'kʌvə(r)/; (*Gegenspieler*) mark /mɑ:k/

Demokratie 402 **derselbe**

Demokratie democracy /dɪ'mɒkrəsi/
demokratisch democratic /ˌdemə'krætɪk/ (*Adv* demo- | 3 *wenn „denn" zur Verstärkung gebraucht wird, wird es oft nicht übersetzt* **Wo steckt sie denn?** Where has

2 ▶ The entry

Look at this dictionary entry for Decke *and find out what it tells you. What help does **your** dictionary give you when you look up* Decke*?*

Decke 1 (*Woll-*) blanket /'blæŋkɪt/; (*Stepp-*) duvet /'du:veɪ/ **Er zog sich die Decke bis über den Kopf.** He pulled the covers up over his head.
2 (*Tisch-*) tablecloth /'teɪblklɒθ; *AE* 'teɪblklɔ:θ/
3 (*Zimmer-*) ceiling /'si:lɪŋ/

the headword
the correct translation for your context
how to use the word in a sentence
how to pronounce the word

3 ▶ Test yourself

a *Find the correct English words for the underlined German words in these sentences:*

1 Das Lager am Fluss war gut geschützt.
2 Das Lager im Fort enthielt genügend Gewehre.
3 Sie jagten den Mörder des Häuptlings.
4 Die Krieger beschlossen den Wolf zu jagen.
5 Der Rat beschloss den Krieg zu beenden.
6 Die Kranken befolgten den Rat des Medizinmannes.

Lager 1 store /stɔ:(r)/, warehouse /'weəhaʊs/ **etwas auf Lager haben** have sth in stock
2 (*Quartier*) camp /kæmp/ **Die Bergsteiger schlugen da ihr Lager auf.** The climbers set up camp there. **im Lager der Opposition** in the opposition camp

jagen 1 (*Tiere*) hunt /hʌnt/
2 (*Verbrecher etc*) chase /tʃeɪs/
3 (*Wolken, Puls*) race /reɪs/

Rat 1 advice /əd'vaɪs/ (*kein Plural*) **Ich möchte Ihnen einen guten Rat geben ...** Let me give you some advice ...
2 **jdn/etwas (wegen etwas) zu Rate ziehen** consult /kən'sʌlt/ sb/sth (about sth) **einen Arzt zu Rate ziehen** consult a doctor
3 (*Versammlung*) council /'kaʊnsl/

◆◆ **b** *Find German words with two or more meanings, e.g.* Karte, handeln, faul. *Then write at least two sentences with each of the German words. Let your partner find the correct English words. If you aren't sure which translation is right, check the English words in the English-German part of your dictionary.*

REMEMBER

1 Use the words at the top of the page to find the entry faster.
2 Study the entry carefully and find the meaning you need for the context of your word. Notes in brackets will help you.
3 Example sentences and phrases show you what constructions the word is used in.
4 If you aren't sure, check the translation in the English-German part of your dictionary.

○ PROJECT 1 Native Americans

❖ *Would you like to learn more about Native Americans? Why don't you do a project about them? It is usually best to work in groups of four or five. Here is some help with the steps for project work. You might like to look at the 'HOW TO ...' pages 49, 77 and 91 for more help.*

1 Choose a topic
Choose a topic from these two pages or find a different one you are interested in. Make sure[1] you know exactly what you want to do before you start.

2 Get information
Ask teachers, go to the library, look on the Internet, write letters/e-mails to organizations[2], ...

3 Use audiovisual[3] materials
You could use models, maps, PC printouts[4], music, video, a poster, a display on the board, handouts, ...

4 Do your project
Decide how you are going to organize your information. Who is going to do what?

5 Check it
Check your English. Use a dictionary and the language summary on pages 124–139. Ask your teacher for help.

6 Practise and present
Decide who presents what. Make sure you have everything you need (OHP[5], cassette recorder, etc.). Use visuals and handouts – don't just read out what you have written. Explain important new words.

Native houses
Alaska's Inuit didn't usually live in igloos, and most Native Americans didn't live in tepees[6]. Find out about:
- hogans[7]
- wigwams[8]
- longhouses
- pueblos[9]
- sweat[10] houses

The different tribes
There are many different 'nations' or 'tribes' of Native Americans.
- What are the main groups and how do they live?
- Where did they live before the first Europeans came? Where do they live now?
- What has happened to the numbers of Native Americans since Europeans arrived? Why?

1 make sure *darauf achten (, dass)*
2 organization [ˌɔːɡənaɪˈzeɪʃn] *Organisation*
3 audiovisual [ˌɔːdiəʊˈvɪʒuəl] *audiovisuell („Hören und Sehen ansprechend")*
4 printout [ˈprɪntaʊt] *Ausdruck*
5 OHP (overhead projector) [ˌəʊvəhed prəˈdʒektə] *Tageslichtprojektor*
6 tepee [ˈtiːpiː]
7 hogan [ˈhəʊɡən]
8 wigwam [ˈwɪɡwæm]
9 pueblo [ˈpwebləʊ]
10 sweat [swet] *Schweiß, schwitzen*

From 'Red Indians' to 'Native Americans'

How have things changed between whites and the Native Americans? How do they feel about each other?
Find out about:
- Plimoth Plantation
- the 'Trail[1] of Tears'
- citizenship[2]
- Wounded Knee[3] (1890 and 1973)

Native art

Art played an important role in everyday life and celebrations. Find out about:
- rock painting[4]
- totem-poles[5]
- jewellery[6]
- masks and baskets
- quilts[7] and blankets[8]
- songs and poems

Famous Native Americans

Find out about:
- Sitting Bull
- Jim Thorpe
- Chief Joseph
- Sacajawea
- Buffy Sainte-Marie
- Geronimo

How Native Americans see the world

Native Americans see the world in many different ways – but often very differently to European Americans.
Find out about:
- their feelings about the land
- their religion
- shamans[9]
- social life
- wealth[10] and property[11]

1 trail [treɪl] *Weg, Spur*
2 citizenship ['sɪtɪznʃɪp] *Staatsbürgerschaft*
3 Wounded Knee [ˌwuːndɪd 'niː]
4 painting ['peɪntɪŋ] *Malerei*
5 totem-pole ['təʊtəm pəʊl] *Totempfahl*
6 jewellery ['dʒuːəlri] *Schmuck*
7 quilt [kwɪlt] *Steppdecke*
8 blanket ['blæŋkɪt] *(Woll-)Decke*
9 shaman ['ʃæmən] *Schamane*
10 wealth [welθ] *Reichtum, Vermögen*
11 property ['prɒpəti] *(Grund-)Besitz*

Colonial Williamsburg

From 1699 to 1780, Williamsburg was the capital of Great Britain's largest and richest colony, Virginia.

Inside a colonial store

Hard at work in the James Anderson Blacksmith Shop

Every year, nearly three million people visit Colonial Williamsburg, America's biggest living-history museum. Why don't you join them on a journey into America's past? The many programs, walks, tours and plays will take you inside the lives of people who lived here more than two hundred years ago: black or white, rich or poor, famous or unknown.

Colonial Williamsburg

A Williamsburg shoemaker

At the end of the day

A colonial wedding

Descendants of the Carter family

1 John 'Colonel' Carter c. 1620 - c. 1669
+Sarah Ludlow ? - c. 1670
2 **Robert 'King' Carter** 1663 - 1732
+Judith Armistead 1680 - c. 1708
3 Elizabeth Carter c. 1695 - c. 1750
+Nathaniel Burwell 1680 - 1721
4 Lewis Burwell c. 1721 - c. 1747
+Mary Willis c. 1723 - 1746
5 Mary Burwell 1744 - 1809
+Lewis Hail 1742 - 1802
6 William Hail 1771 - 1847
+Lucy Stone 1778 - 1848
7 Susan Hale 1800 - c.1828
+Rev. Morgan Bryan 1795 - c. 182
8 Lucy Bryan 1818 - 1905
+Henderson Cheek 1804 - 1897
9 Caroline Cheek 1864 - 1912
+Wiley P. Maxwell 1865 - 1959
10 Lucy Jane 'Lula' Maxwell 1
+Thomas Gwyn Choate 1888 -

Marching for liberty

Your ticket is also good for Carter's Grove, an 18th-century plantation on the James River, eight miles south-east of Williamsburg.

A house slave chases her master's supper

❖ ACTIVITY

The brochure, the postcard and the list of descendants have been collected for an entry for a history competition.

Form seven groups. Each group chooses a picture from the brochure. In your group, imagine you are 'in' one of the pictures. It might help if you try to 'walk' through the picture from left to right and from the foreground to the background. What can you hear, smell, see, feel? What are the people doing, saying and thinking, and why? What questions would you like to ask the people in your picture? Make notes. (You may have to look up some words in a German-English dictionary.)

Now use your notes and present your picture to the class. Introduce the character(s) in it and answer any questions.

→ U.S. Mag, pp. 98/99

▶ 1

'Is this *all* the stuff you got while I was at Space Camp, sis? Just this one brochure?' Kimberley Haynes asked her twin sister Mariah. The brochure was for their entry for the Virginia History Day Competition: *Everyday Life in Colonial Virginia*.
'Yeah, Kimbers,' answered Mariah.
'Well, I was looking at this family-tree program on my computer when I found this,' said Rebecca Maxwell and put a printout on the desk. She was working on the project with the twins.
'What is it?' the two sisters asked.
'Some of my ancestors. This Lula Maxwell here is my great-great-aunt, so I think I'm a descendant of "King" Carter.'
'You mean you're, like, a descendant of a real king? Well, it's an honour to have you here in our house, Your Majesty.'
'Ha, ha, very funny!' Rebecca said. 'This "King" Carter was some really rich guy when Virginia was still a British colony.'
'We could check him out in that huge encyclopedia of Virginia that grandpa has,' said Kimberley. 'Come on. Let's go.'

▶ 2

Robert "King" Carter (1663–1732)

In 1722 about 1,000 slaves worked on the tobacco plantations of Carter, the richest planter in Colonial Virginia. His family became so large and important that people said, "Shake any tree in Virginia and a Carter will fall out". Three descendants of "King" Carter signed the Declaration of Independence and two became U.S. presidents. Other famous descendants are General Robert E. Lee (1807–1870) and the country singer June Carter Cash.

'Gee, they forgot Rebecca in the list of famous descendants,' said Kimberley when she had read the entry on 'King' Carter. 'But listen: it says this Carter was the richest colonist in Virginia, so maybe we'll find out more about him in Colonial Williamsburg. Perhaps he even lived there.'
'Yeah, my mom says we should go there, too,' Rebecca agreed. 'And it's only a few miles away.'
'I don't know, Kimbers,' said Mariah. 'Dad always says Williamsburg is just a place for white people to feel good about US history.'
'Well,' her sister replied, 'the brochure says that they have programmes on blacks there, too. Why don't we just go and find out for ourselves?'

ACTIVITY

Rebecca Maxwell's family history might go back to 'King' Carter. How far can you get back in your family history? Which of your relatives had or has had the most interesting or exciting life? Write about this person and then tell the class. (You can invent a relative if you want to.)

→ S 3: 2a (p. 130), 2e (p. 132)
→ P 1, 2, 10

Indirekte Rede

▶ 3

The next weekend Mariah, Kimberley and Rebecca went to Colonial Williamsburg.

Afterwards Kimberley wrote about their visit in her diary.

When we got off the bus, a guide told us that it was May 15, 1776 – the day Virginia declared independence. I was surprised: not July 4 – Independence Day!
A lot of the people who work in Williamsburg are dressed in 18th-century clothes. We visited the Governor's Palace and the Capitol, but we didn't find out much about "King" Carter. One of the guides – a soldier at the Palace – said that Carter hadn't come to Williamsburg very often. But the guide thought we would get more information on Carter at Carter's Grove, an old plantation eight miles away. Then he explained that a lot of other famous Virginians had lived or worked in Williamsburg: people like George Washington and Thomas Jefferson. We heard Jefferson – well, an actor – speak in the Palace Gardens. He talked about the war with Britain and said that he would die a free man before he lived like a slave. Of course, Jefferson was a slave-owner. He even had children with a slave!
Rebecca wants us all to go to Carter's Grove tomorrow. Dad promised he would take us there.

FOCUS ON GRAMMAR

1 *Look again at the four speech bubbles above. Then find the sentences in Kimberley's diary where she reports what the people said.*
A guide told us that it was May 15, 1776 ...

2 *Look at the reporting verbs* (tell, say, think, *etc.) that Kimberley uses. What tense are they in?*

3 *Compare what the people say with how Kimberley reports what they said. What happens to the tenses in indirect speech?*

4 *Find the two other examples of indirect speech in the diary. Write down what the people said in direct speech.*

→ S 3: 2b (pp. 130/131)
→ P 3, 4, 5, 6

▶ 4

Early the next morning, Mr Haynes dropped his daughters and Rebecca at Carter's Grove. They walked through the Visitor Center and followed the signs towards the plantation house. A black man in simple old clothes was coming their way.

GUIDE Good morning, young ladies.

KIMBERLEY Are you one of the guides, sir?

GUIDE I work on the plantation, miss.

REBECCA What can you tell us about 'King' Carter?

GUIDE Well, I don't know much about the Carter family. They'll know more about them up at the house. I work at the slave quarter. Have you been there yet?

MARIAH The slave quarter? No, where is it?

GUIDE Well, when you've learned all about the slave-*owners* up at the house, just follow this path here and go and see how their *slaves* lived.

On our way to the plantation house at Carter's Grove, we met a black guy in old clothes. I asked him if he was one of the guides. He was, so Rebecca wanted to know what he could tell us about "King" Carter. He couldn't really tell us anything but he asked us whether we had been to the slave quarter yet. That was where he worked. When we asked him where it was, he told us to follow the path and to go and see how the slaves had lived.

Rebecca fell in love with the plantation house, but we thought it was pretty boring – just lots of rooms full of old furniture. So we went down to the slave quarter. Our black guide asked us why we were so interested in the Carters. When we told him about our project, he wanted to know why we weren't writing about our real ancestors – the slaves.

When we met Rebecca again, she said she wanted to work on the life of her ancestors, the Carter family, the richest planters in Colonial Virginia. But we wanted to find out about our ancestors – the slaves on the Carter plantations.

The slave quarter, Carter's Grove

FOCUS ON GRAMMAR

1 *In her diary Kimberley reports what the guide asked the girls and what they asked him. Write down all the examples:*
I asked him if he was one of the guides.
Rebecca wanted to know ...

2 *Now write down what the guide's and the girls' questions were.*
Are you one ... ?

3 *How does Kimberley report the questions? What happens ...*
... to the word order?
... to the question words?
... in yes/no questions?

4 *What did the guide say when Mariah asked him the way to the slave quarter? How does Kimberley report what he said?*

→ S 3: 2c, d (p. 131)
→ P 7, 8, 9

▶▶▶ **NOW YOU** and a partner

a *On a piece of paper, write down*
- *something important/interesting/funny that someone said to you,*
- *a question someone asked you that you couldn't answer,*
- *something silly/... someone told you to do.*

Also write down who said these things.
'Old photos make me feel young again.' – my grandmother
'What is Thomas Jefferson famous for?' – teacher
'Put some coffee in my milk, please.' – my dad

b *Swap with your partner. Now report your partner's sentences to the class.*
Antje's grandmother said old photos ...

▶ 5

Ten days later Rebecca was at the Haynes' house again. When the three girls were upstairs in Mariah's room, she smiled and said, 'I've finished my part of our entry!' 'Well, we have, too – almost. Take a look,' Mariah said and pointed at the computer. 'And we've got a song that could go with it,' added Kimberley. 'I'll play the CD while you're reading. Then you can tell us if you like it.'

Colonial Virginia.doc

TERROR on the plantations of Colonial Virginia

It is often said that many Virginians are descendants of people like Thomas Jefferson and Robert "King" Carter – the rich white men whose tobacco plantations made Virginia Britain's richest colony in the 18th century. This is true, but a lot more are descendants of the people who had to work for them – black slaves.

The life of Virginia's plantation owners was made easy by the work of black slaves. Slaves had no rights – they were just the property of their owners and could be bought and sold like animals.

Large plantations produced nearly everything the people needed: tobacco and other crops were grown for sale. They were taken down the rivers to the sea and then to Europe. Corn, fruit and vegetables were grown for food. Farm animals were kept for food and work. Who did all the work? Black slaves: house slaves, field slaves and skilled slaves. Man, woman or child, they all worked from morning till night from the age of ten till they died.

Plantation slaves always lived in fear. Would they be beaten because their master was angry? Would they be sold to another plantation and separated from their family? How would they survive another 16-hour day in the hot sun? Should they try to run away and be beaten or even killed if they were caught? The feelings that best describe a slave's life in Colonial Virginia are FEAR and TERROR.

LISTENING Ol' Man River

Listen to the song. What is it about? Do you think it goes well with the girls' project? Explain why. You could think about the type of music, style, words, feelings, etc.

? *What are the most important facts that you have found out about the lives of blacks and whites in Colonial Virginia? Write four or five facts down and compare them in class.*

FOCUS ON WORDS Life on a plantation

1 *Find words and phrases in the unit about life on colonial plantations. Think of the places* (the plantation house, the fields, ...) *and who did what.*
Then use your imagination and draw a plan of a plantation on a large piece of paper and list your words and phrases on it. Or connect them in a network or another way.

2 *Imagine you lived on a colonial plantation. Decide who you were and then write what you did on a typical day.*

→ P 11, 12, 13
→ How to organize information, p. 49
→ U.S. Mag, pp. 100–102

1 REVISION At grandpa's house → S 3: 1 (p. 129)

Complete what Kimberley wrote in her diary. Put the verbs in brackets in the simple past, past progressive or past perfect.

When we (arrive) at grandpa's house, he (sleep) outside in the sun. He (wake up) at once when Mariah (call) his name. He (be) very pleased to see us because we (not visit) him for some time. While we (wait) outside, he (go) in and (get) us the encyclopedia. There (be) a short article about Robert "King" Carter in it. While we (read) the encyclopedia, grandpa (disappear) into the house again.
When we (finish) the article, we (talk) a bit and then (decide) to go to Williamsburg to get more information.
Grandpa still (not come) back outside, so I (go) in to see what he (do). He (be) in the kitchen. He (make) us some real lemonade. So then we all (sit) in the sun and (talk) for an hour.

2 ▶ Colonial Williamsburg information

A tourist from Washington, D.C., phones the Colonial Williamsburg Visitor Center and listens to the recorded message. How does she report to her family what she hears? Be careful with the words in green. How do you need to change them?

1. This message will help you to plan your stay in Colonial Williamsburg.
   It's a recorded message. It says it will help us to plan our stay in Colonial Williamsburg.
2. More than three million people visit Williamsburg every year, so you should book your hotel or motel rooms early.
   It says that more …
3. You might like to stay at one of our hotels – the *Williamsburg Inn* is one of the finest in the country.
4. It's very hot in Virginia in the summer, so you should wear the right clothes and bring your hats.
5. If you would like information about tickets, press '1' now.
6. We look forward to seeing you here in Colonial Williamsburg soon.

3 ▶ Who said what?

Look at the speech bubbles. Decide who said what and then report what that person said.

Kimberley Mariah Rebecca The soldier	said told them explained …	that	…

Mariah said that the tickets were really expensive and that their dad …

4 ▶ What did they say?

'That was funny when he said he'd get his big brother.'

What did the little penguin really say to the bear? (Begin: 'I ...'*)*

'I told you if we didn't tie him up he'd follow us.'

What did the woman say to her husband before they left? (Begin: 'If we ...'*)*

5 ▶ But you told me ...

Complete the answers with the words in brackets. Be careful with the tenses.

1 'I didn't see you at Jane's party on Friday.' – 'But you told me ... (be on Saturday).'
'But you told me it was on Saturday.'

2 'Suzy has fallen in love with Mark.' – 'Oh, I thought ... (hate him).'

3 'Mom and Dad are going to the movies tonight.' – 'But they said ... (help me with my homework).'

4 'I played tennis here with Joe once.' – 'You told me ... (never come to this part of town before).'

5 'Shall we both pay half?' – 'Didn't you say ... (going to buy me dinner)?'

6 'I'll meet you after the game at 8 pm.' – 'But you said ... (finish before seven).'

6 ▶ June said ...

Often when you report something someone has said, you do not remember the words exactly. So you just report the meaning. Match the sentences on the left to the statements on the right.

1 June said she was going to Spain in the summer.

2 Jim told me he'd seen – oh, what's her name?

3 Dad said it would take longer by car.

4 Did you hear about that terrible accident on the east coast? At first they thought over 200 people had died.

5 She said she'd come early.

a) 'Guess who I met at the club yesterday. Lisa. You remember her, don't you?'

b) 'I'll be there no later than 8 am.'

c) 'My next holiday is going to be in Mallorca.'

d) 'You'll get there faster by train, you know. Much faster.'

e) 'The ship hit the rocks and people jumped into the sea. First reports spoke of over 200 deaths.'

7 ▶ At Carter's Grove

Read the speech bubbles and report what Rebecca asked the guides at Carter's Grove.

When did the Carter family live here?

Can I walk there through the gardens?

What are the buildings I can see down near the river?

Is the furniture from the 18th century?

When was the house built?

Why was the kitchen outside the house?

Did 'King' Carter live here himself?

Does anybody live here now?

How many rooms are there in the house?

Is it far to the slave quarter?

a Rebecca asked the guides when …
She wanted to know why …
…

b Rebecca asked the guides if …
She wanted to know whether …
…

8 ▶ Difficult questions

Questions sometimes make Joe think that life is very hard. Report what these people asked him.

His girlfriend asked him …

best friend: Why don't you talk to me when your girlfriend is around?

girlfriend: Where were you when I phoned last night?

father: Have you tidied up your room yet?

little brother: Can I come to the party with you on Saturday?

teacher: Where's your homework?

mother: When are you going to throw that old jacket away?

9 ▶ Have a great time in Colonial Williamsburg

Report what the guide told or asked the girls to do.

Follow the path to the end of the gardens to see Thomas Jefferson.

1 *The guide told the girls to follow the path to the end of the gardens to see Thomas Jefferson.*
2 'Could you wait here for the next tour of the Governor's Palace, please?'
The guide asked the girls to …
3 'Don't miss the reading of Virginia's Declaration of Independence at the Capitol.'
4 'Have lunch at Chowning's Tavern. The food is great.'
5 'Could you show me your tickets, please?'
6 'You should see the movie *Williamsburg – The Story of a Patriot*[1] before you leave.'
7 'You must visit the Archaeology Museum.'

[1] patriot ['pɜɪtriət]

WORD WATCH

◆◆ 10 ▶ Make a crossword

Partner B: Look at page 113.

a *Partner A: Read clues 1–4 to your partner. He/She must find the right words for the clues.*

Clues for partner B
1 someone who had a plantation in old Virginia
2 a sort of big farm
3 land that a country takes in another part of the world
4 a very rich British colony that later became a US state

Answers: 1 *planter* 2 *plantation* 3 *colony* 4 *Virginia*

Now listen to B's clues 5–8, choose the right words from the list and write them down.

colonist • descendant • family tree
governor • master • slaves • tobacco

b *With your partner try to make a crossword with the eight correct words. (Letters next to or above each other must all be part of a word.) Which team can make the crossword first?*

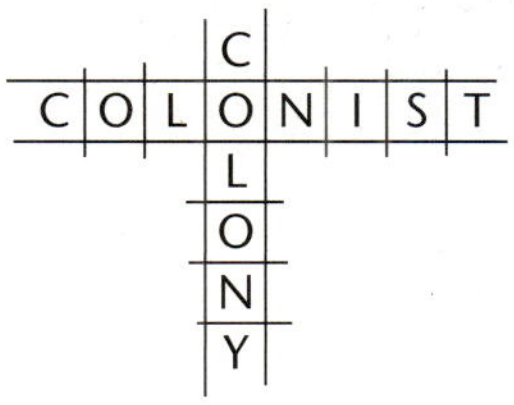

11 WORD BUILDING Word families

You can often understand new English words because you know other words from the same word family. When you know the word colony *for example, it is easy to understand the words* colonist, colonial *and* colonize. *Find the missing words in this table. A lot of them are in the sentences on the right.*

noun (thing)	noun (person)	adjective	verb
colony	colonist	colonial	colonize
Virginia	?	?	—
history	?	?	—
?	planter	—	?
printout	?	—	?
declaration	—	—	?
?	?	—	report
?	—	dead	?

1 Tobacco was first planted in Virginia in 1612 and made the colony rich.

2 The printer William Parks started the *Virginia Gazette* in 1736. At first, he was its only reporter.

3 The newspaper printed reports on the life of the colony.

4 Today historians study the *Virginia Gazette* as a historical document.

12 TROUBLE SPOT Expressions of time

Which of the words on the left can go with the phrases on the right?

at	a fine day • lunch Monday morning
in	month • night one o'clock
on	Saturday night • Sunday
next / last	the future • the morning the past • the weekend week • weekdays • year

13 ▶ Violent lives

Slaves in the old British colonies of North America had a terrible life. Use as many words as you can from the box below to write a paragraph about them.

beat • buy • catch • crops
dangerous • disappear • death
die • fear • field • grow
house • kill • hot • master
property • punish • sell • skilled
terror • work • ...

– What do you think of when you see this flag?
– What do you know about pirates in the past? And what about today?

The Drinking Cup

It was 1717. The last boat left the ship and returned towards the plantation. With the tobacco on board, Captain Keene could take the *Dolphin* down the James River and into Chesapeake Bay. From there they would sail south to the Atlantic and then east towards England. He would spend Christmas at home in Bristol.

Two hours later, as the *Dolphin* reached the end of the James River, another ship appeared from behind Point Comfort. Captain Keene saw the ship's black flag and his whole body went cold. Pirates! The planters had told him at dinner the night before that pirate ships had been seen in the bay. Keene had said he couldn't wait for the convoy later in the month. Now he wished he had. He wondered if he would ever see Bristol or his wife and children again. The pirate ship came closer until Keene could see there was a skeleton on the black flag. Yes, pirates – and not just any pirates, but Blackbeard himself!

The captain of the *Dolphin* knew at once that he could not fight Blackbeard's ship, the *Adventure*. It was faster and carried eight cannon – the *Dolphin* had only two. There was only one thing to do. He told his men to put the boats in the water. If they worked fast, they could escape before the pirates came on board.

Boom! He heard the sound of the cannon as the shot flew across the *Dolphin* and hit the water. It was just a warning. Blackbeard would not want the *Dolphin* to sink. There was no profit in that.

The last boat, with Captain Keene, hit the water just in time. Moments later pirates began to climb on board. As Captain Keene's boat moved away, he looked back at the *Dolphin*.

Blackbeard appeared on deck. Many sailors thought that Blackbeard was the devil himself, and Keene could almost believe it. The tall pirate had wild eyes. He wore a black hat and his long black beard hung down over a black coat. Smoke from matches in his hair and beard rose into the air around him. He looked as if he had just come up from hell.

Blackbeard had taken one more English ship, but at least the crew would be safe, Captain Keene thought. Then he saw that the pirates had turned the two cannon on the *Dolphin's* deck towards them. With terror in his eyes, Captain Keene shouted at his men: 'Faster!' At the same time he heard Blackbeard's terrible voice cry: 'Fire!'

On an October evening 11 years later, the Raleigh Tavern in Williamsburg was already quite full when an Englishman came in. He had arrived in town the day before and sat down now at a table in the corner of the room. He ordered food, ate quietly and seemed not to notice anything or anyone else in the room. At the next table two men from the town were smoking and drinking as they talked.

'Mr Walker was in town today,' said one of them. 'He said that Captain Maynard had been murdered by two of his slaves.'

'What, Thomas,' asked the other, 'you mean the brave Captain Maynard who killed Teach? The man who saved the colonies from that devil?'

'The same, George.'

'My God! What a tragedy! We must drink to his memory. Mary, let's have the Drinking Cup,' George shouted to the waitress.

A few minutes later Mary brought the Drinking Cup. The Englishman could see that the cup was, in fact, a skull. As Thomas and George drank from it, he asked them, 'Is it Edward Teach, the pirate, that you speak of?'

'It is, sir,' replied Thomas. 'And this is the butcher's skull we're drinking from now. Drink with us, sir, to Captain Maynard's memory.'

'I shall drink only too gladly, sir,' the Englishman answered, 'but first tell me how Teach died.'

And while George told the story, the Englishman sat and smiled.

'As you must know, sir, ten years ago, the Chesapeake Bay was full of pirates, and the worst pirate of them all was Edward Teach, also known as Blackbeard. No ship was safe from him. Blackbeard attacked the ships that brought goods from Britain or slaves from Africa, and he attacked those that carried tobacco from Virginia back to Britain.

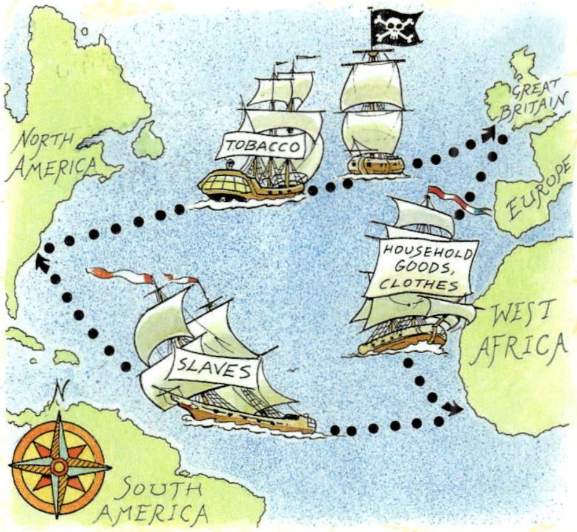

In 1718 trade in Virginia and North Carolina stopped completely. The life of the colonies was in danger. So planters in Carolina asked Governor Spottswood of Virginia for help. He sent two ships under Robert Maynard out of Chesapeake Bay to an island in North Carolina, where he had heard that Blackbeard was hiding. They soon discovered Blackbeard's ship, the *Adventure*. One of Maynard's ships was almost destroyed at the start of the battle. So Maynard had to sail on with the other ship, the *Ranger*, to meet Blackbeard.

As Maynard had no cannon, he decided to try to beat Blackbeard with a trick. He told his sailors to hide below deck and hoped that the pirates would then come on board. Blackbeard did just that. When the pirates climbed on board, they were at once attacked by Maynard's men. Soon the sea was red with blood.

Suddenly Blackbeard stood before Maynard. Maynard shot him, but he didn't kill the pirate. Then Blackbeard broke Maynard's sword. Just as he was lifting his own sword to kill the captain, another sailor came from behind and cut Blackbeard's throat. But still Blackbeard continued fighting. When, at last, he was dead, Maynard cut off Blackbeard's head and threw the rest of his body into the sea. With the pirate's head on board, Maynard returned to Virginia.'

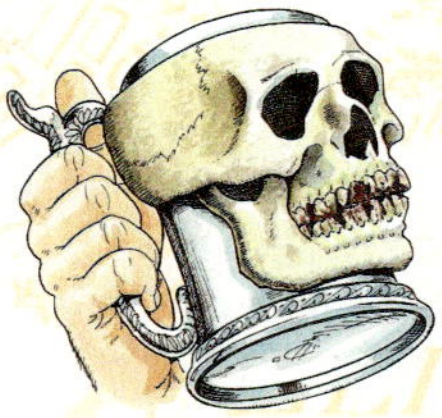

George sat back in his chair. 'That is how brave Captain Maynard saved us from the terrible pirate Teach. And now Maynard is dead, too,' he said.

'Let us drink together to his memory,' Thomas said. 'But first let us know the name of the man we are drinking with.'

The Englishman smiled: 'My name is Keene. Captain Joseph Keene.'

The three men drank together for the rest of the evening until George and Thomas fell asleep at the table.

The next morning, Captain Keene and the Drinking Cup were gone. They were never seen in Williamsburg again.

WORKING WITH THE TEXT

1 ▶ What do you think?

Did you like reading the story? Explain why or why not. Perhaps these words will help:

(un)believable • (un)clear
exciting • great • hard to put down
silly • slow • violent • …

2 ▶ Reading between the lines

Explain the meaning of the following:

1 Keene had said he couldn't wait for the convoy later in the month. (p. 46, ll. 17–19)
2 Blackbeard would not want the *Dolphin* to sink. There was no profit in that. (p. 46, ll. 37–41)
3 And while George told the story, the Englishman sat and smiled. (p. 47, ll. 52/53)
4 In 1718 trade in Virginia and North Carolina stopped completely. The life of the colonies was in danger. (p. 47, ll. 62–64)

3 ▶ Blackbeard's attack

What did Blackbeard write in his logbook on the night after his attack on Keene's ship?

❖ **4 ROLE-PLAY** After Blackbeard's attack

Imagine that Captain Keene's wife and children ask him what happened after Blackbeard attacked his ship. Act out what they say during their first meal together. You can write role cards for Captain Keene, his wife and two children, or use the ones your teacher has. If you write your own, decide first how Keene escapes, how he gets back to Bristol, and what happens to him on the way.

5 ▶ Keene's letter home

What happened after Keene left the Raleigh Tavern? Imagine that he writes a letter to his wife. Write the letter and read it to the class. You should decide first

– *why he takes the Drinking Cup,*
– *where he goes,*
– *what happens to the Cup.*

→ Revision, p. 117

HOW TO ... organize information

1 ▶ Collecting information

For a project in English you get this task: Write a short report about the life of slaves in Colonial America. You have collected information from a number of different sources and have written down the notes on the right. What next? How are you going to make a report from the notes?

The life of slaves in Colonial America

- jobs: repairing shoes / making clothes / working with wood
- many tried to escape, some successful
- small farms: whole family worked (had few slaves)
- big plantations: >100 slaves
- punishment: beating
  salt in wounds
- some saved money / bought liberty
- a few worked in the house (house slaves), did cooking + cleaning for master's family, looked after children
- some fought as soldiers / set free afterwards
- simple clothes
- slave quarters: one-room huts for families
- most worked in fields – grew corn / tobacco ...
- some had little gardens (looked after in free time)
- runaways: tied up in sun all day

2 ▶ Grouping ideas

a *On page 41, the information about life on a colonial plantation has been organized in paragraphs. Read Mariah and Kimberley's text again and look carefully at the sentences that form each paragraph. Try to find headings that summarize the topics of each paragraph:*

1 Descendants of colonial Virginians
2 ...

Also write down words that connect the facts:
like, and, that, ...

b *Now have another look at the notes above. Which facts belong together? Put them in groups and find headings that describe the topic of each group.*

Slaves' tasks —> notes 1, 7, 11
...

3 ▶ Ordering sentences and paragraphs

a *Decide on the best order for your topics and for the sentences in each paragraph. Think about a beginning and an ending. Before you write your report, read all the notes again.*

b *Now write out the report in paragraphs. While you are writing, remember to use a number of linking words to connect the ideas. Here are some examples:*

as a result	although
so	even if
that is why	it is true that ... but
	some ... but others
in fact	
of course	especially
on top of that	first(ly), second(ly), third(ly)
	for example (e.g.)

REMEMBER

1. Before you present information, you need to organize it.
2. Find headings that summarize pieces of information that belong together.
3. Put the headings in a sensible order and write a paragraph for each one.

New York – Gateway to America

For millions of immigrants, New York Harbor was the gateway to the USA. They saw the Statue of Liberty when they sailed to the immigration offices on Ellis Island. As they got off the boats, they could see – and almost touch – Manhattan. But first they had to go through the immigration process.

Ellis Island – Great Hall, 1909
About 12 million people came to the USA through Ellis Island between 1892 and 1924. They came because there was religious or political persecution, hunger or poverty in their own countries. They all hoped for a better life in America.

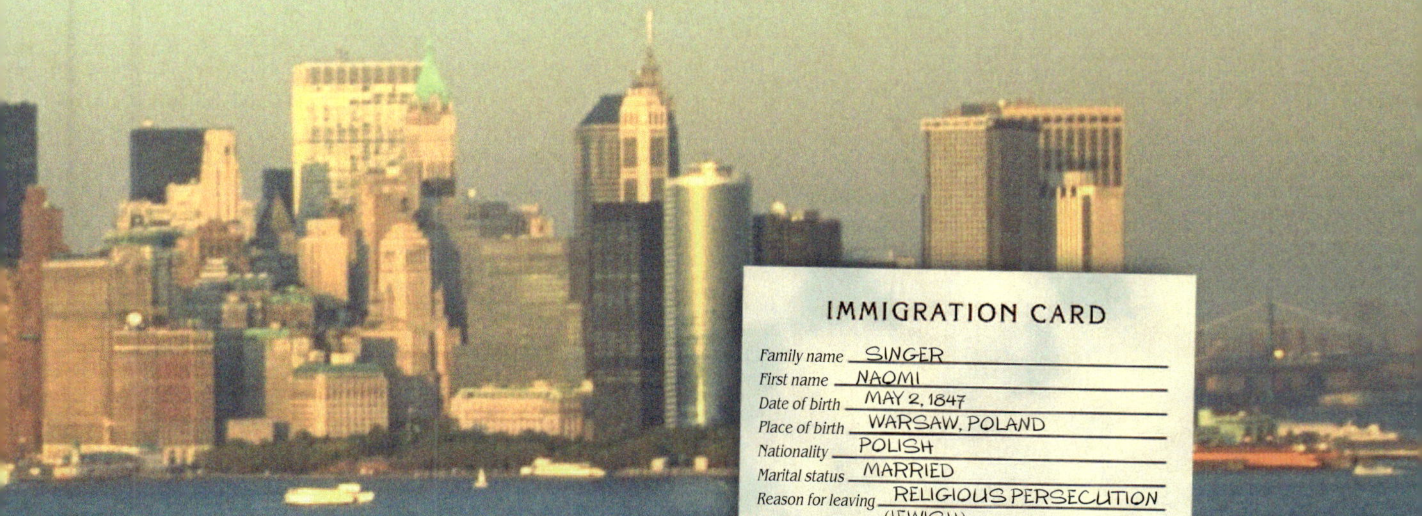

IMMIGRATION CARD

Family name SINGER
First name NAOMI
Date of birth MAY 2, 1847
Place of birth WARSAW, POLAND
Nationality POLISH
Marital status MARRIED
Reason for leaving RELIGIOUS PERSECUTION (JEWISH)

IMMIGRATION CARD

Family name LUCARELLI
First name FEDERICO
Date of birth NOVEMBER 3, 1875
Place of birth NAPLES, ITALY
Nationality ITALIAN
Marital status MARRIED, 2 CHILDREN
Reason for leaving OUT OF WORK

IMMIGRATION CARD

Family name FEDOROV
First name ALEXEI
Date of birth JULY 7, 1884
Place of birth MOSCOW, RUSSIA
Nationality RUSSIAN
Marital status SINGLE
Reason for leaving POLITICAL PERSECUTION

Look at the three immigration cards from 1909 and try to match them to people in the photos on the left. (Who has no card?) Discuss your answers with other students in your class.

LISTENING

Copy an empty immigration card into your exercise book or American album. Then listen to the cassette/CD and fill in the card for the person who is talking.

▶▶▶ NOW YOU

Choose one card and imagine you are that person. Write five or six sentences about 'yourself'. Start with the facts and then say what you think life in the USA will be like.

• new books • new books • new books •

Shalom, U.S.A.!

This sad but funny book looks at the history of the Jews in the time between 1880 and 1930, when over three million of them immigrated to the U.S. *Shalom, U.S.A.!* shows that, over time, the lives of most Jewish Americans have been quite ordinary, but also describes some of the most famous Jewish Americans, from Levi Strauss to Steven Spielberg. A wonderful view of Jewish history and life in America.

▶ 1

Daniel Schwarz's father looked up from his newspaper. 'Here's a review of a book you could read before your bar mitzvah,' he said. 'And don't forget to mail your invitations.'
But how could Daniel forget? He was really worried about his big day. He would have to know about Jewish history, recite something in Hebrew from the Torah, speak in front of lots of people …
He put the letters in his school bag. One had no stamp on it, just a name: MR. JOSHUA BROWN. 'I hope Josh can come,' he thought. Josh was his best friend at school.
Then Daniel's mother called out, 'Say, honey, come here a minute. I've found your great-grandfather's prayer shawl – the one he brought from Russia in 1905. You can wear it for your bar mitzvah!'

▶▶▶ NOW YOU

Have you ever felt nervous before a 'big day'? What was the event? Why were you nervous?

▶ 2

Daniel met Josh in the school cafeteria.
'Hey, Dan! I just saw Al Pacino!'
'Al Pacino! What, here?'
'No, in this brochure about our school,' Josh laughed. 'He was a student here.'
'Great joke,' Daniel said and gave Josh the invitation. 'This is for you. My bar mitzvah is soon. You know, when a boy …'
'Oh, yeah, ... becomes a man. Right? Tell me more. And can you pass me the sugar?'
'You don't usually take sugar in coffee.'
'No, but the coffee tastes different today. Now, about this religious party, Dan …'

FIORELLO H. LaGUARDIA HIGH SCHOOL OF MUSIC & ART AND PERFORMING ARTS
100 Amsterdam Avenue
New York, New York 10023

LaGuardia High is one of four special high schools in New York. It offers young people training in art, music, dance and drama, as well as the usual school subjects.
Students of all races and cultures and from all five boroughs of New York City come to the school. This year we chose just 650 from the 15,000 young people who wanted to come.
Many of the students who come here have a good chance of becoming famous. Since 1936 Liza Minelli, Al Pacino, Pinchas Zuckerman, Keith Haring, Erica Jong, Eartha Kitt, Suzanne Vega,

FOCUS ON GRAMMAR

1 *The word* sugar *appears twice, in two phrases, in A2. Which phrase refers to sugar* <u>*in general*</u> *and which to some* <u>*specific*</u> *sugar?*

2 *Find more nouns that appear twice in A2, in the school brochure, and in the book review above. Put the nouns into two groups: general – specific. What do you notice about the definite article?*

→ S 4: 1a, b (p. 133)
→ P 1, 2

3

Two English girls stopped Josh and Daniel on the sidewalk outside their school. 'Excuse me, please. Can you tell us how to get to the Bronx? We want to visit the zoo.'
'Sure,' Daniel said. 'Walk past Lincoln Center to the subway station on Broadway. You need to catch an uptown 2 to East ...'
'But the zoo closes in an hour,' interrupted Josh. 'You wouldn't get there, even if you ran. Why not stay in Manhattan today and go to the zoo tomorrow? Go downtown to Fifth Avenue or uptown to a museum.'
'Or take a walk in Central Park,' added Daniel, 'and check out Times Square later.'
'Actually,' said Josh, 'I think we're going your way. Dan?'
'Sorry,' Daniel said. 'I have to learn more Hebrew for my bar mitzvah.'

? *Look at the street map of Manhattan at the back of the book and find the places from A3. What do New York's avenues have in common? And what about the streets?*

◆◆ **ACTIVITY**

Partner B: Look at page 114.
Partner A: Here is some information about New York City. Look at the map and read the text below. Find out:
- *What are the names of the five boroughs and where are they?*
- *How many people live in each borough?*
- *What special things can you see there?*

For the things you can't find out, ask your partner.

New York City is made up of five boroughs. Queens and Brooklyn are east of Manhattan. Brooklyn has the largest population: 2.4 million people live there. Its most famous sight, the Brooklyn Bridge, links Brooklyn to Manhattan (where 1.5 million people live). Nearly 2 million people live in Queens. It's the first borough many visitors see, as Kennedy Airport is there. The noise is quite bad for people who live near JFK.

→ S 4: 1b, c (p. 133)
→ P 3, 8
→ U.S. Mag, p. 103

FOCUS ON WORDS Immigration to the USA

1 *As you go through this unit (up to page 55), collect 'immigration' words and phrases under the headings* ***transport*** (come by boat, ...), ***reasons*** (religious persecution, ...) *and* ***nationalities*** (Polish, ...). *Add more words and phrases you already know.*

2 *Write a few paragraphs about why and how people immigrated to the USA.*

▶ 4

'Man, those English girls!' Josh told Daniel on the phone that evening. 'Weird! Not like that girl I met at Space Camp.'
'If they had looked in their guidebook,' said Daniel, 'they would have known when the zoo closed. What did they do instead?'
'They stayed in Manhattan,' said Josh. 'Went to Chinatown. If they'd asked me, I'd have gone too. They were weird – but cute!'
'So they didn't ask you?' said Daniel.
'No. It might have been different if you'd been there. You know, two and two.'
'Of course. My good looks, my charm …'
'Yeah, too bad you didn't come.'
'I'd have come if I hadn't been so busy with my Hebrew – and the speech I'm making.'
'A speech? I knew you'd be a star someday!'
'Well, I have to say a special thank-you to my guests – for the presents and all.'
'Oh. So everyone has to give you a present? If I'd known that, I wouldn't have accepted the invitation!' Josh laughed.

Chinatown

? *What do you know about bar mitzvah so far? Try and find more information (ask an RE teacher, look in an encyclopedia, …).*

▶▶▶ NOW YOU

What is done where you live to show that a teenager has come of age? (confirmation, birthday parties, …)

FOCUS ON GRAMMAR

1 *Find all the sentences with* if *in A4 and write down the verb forms from the* if-*clauses and from the main clauses like this:*

If-clause	*Main clause*
had looked	*would have known*
'd asked	…
…	…

2 *What tense is used in the* if-*clause? What verb forms are used in the main clause?*

3 *Explain the difference in meaning between these sentences:*
If they asked me, I would go with them.
If they had asked me, I would have gone with them.

→ S 4: 2 (pp. 134/135)
→ P 4, 5, 6, 9, 10

▶ 5

An hour later Josh called back.
'Listen, Dan. You should have told me about your "thank-you speech" at the party earlier. But I may have had a good idea anyway.'
'What sort of idea?'
'Uh, well, it might be a good one or a bad one – I'm not sure. Listen.'
Daniel listened with wide eyes …

When the big day came, Daniel welcomed his 120 guests. After they had all eaten a wonderful meal, he and Josh went to the microphone together.
'Ladies and gentlemen,' they said, 'your attention, please.'
Everyone looked at them.

LISTENING

Listen to the cassette/CD and find out what happened next.

→ S 4: 3 (p. 135)
→ P 7
→ U.S. Mag, pp. 104/105

PROJECT 2 An American timeline

This page shows the beginning of an American timeline. Make your own timeline – it doesn't have to be about immigrants.

Use dates and facts from American history. You'll know some already and you can find more in this book. Or use other English and German books or magazines, talk to your history teacher, look on the Internet, etc. Collect texts, pictures, charts, songs, etc. or write your own texts and make your own drawings.

You could put your timeline on a long piece of wallpaper. Then, over the weeks, whenever you find more information at school or at home, you can add it to your timeline.

→ How to use a dictionary, pp. 33/63
→ Project 1, pp. 34/35

The USA: A Land of Immigrants

c. 10,000 BC

People cross from Asia into North America.

c. 8000 BC

As early stone tools show, Native Americans have spread[1] to all of North and South America.

c. 6000 BC

First Inuit live in Alaska.

1492 AD

Columbus lands in the New World.

1607 AD

English settlers[2] found[3] Jamestown in Virginia.

[1] (to) spread [spred] – spread – spread *(sich) ausbreiten* [2] settler *Siedler/in* [3] (to) found [faʊnd] *gründen*

New York traffic

Ice skating in Central Park

1 ▶ **Life in New York City**

Who is talking here? Add the *where it is needed.*

'1 … money is a problem for my family – and for lots of families in the Bronx. Without my scholarship I just wouldn't have … money to go to LaGuardia High. 2 We have to work hard, but it's great. My main subject is … music, and jazz is … music I play most. 3 We have to do all … work that kids in regular schools do, too. For us … work starts at 8.10 and ends at about 3 pm. 4 … traffic is a big problem in cities today, but not for me – I take the subway to school. Other kids say … traffic into Manhattan is terrible. 5 … air in the city often gets bad in summer, so we go to Central Park during the lunch break to fill up with … fresh air.
6 Winters are cold, and the water in the lake changes into … ice – and … ice in Central Park is great for skating! 7 I have often dreamed of going into space – even more since Space Camp. But my main dream is to be in a Broadway show one day: dancing, singing, making music – … stuff like that. Broadway shows are better than all … stuff you see on TV.'

2 ▶ **The things that I like**

How do you feel about these things?

fashion • homework
music • religion • school
science • crime • …

general	specific
I'm good at/interested in/ …	… we do at school …
I usually enjoy/hate/love/ quite like …	… that my parents …
I (don't) think …	…

First give your general opinion, then write another sentence with more specific information. The table on the right will help you.

Example:
I'm good at science. The science we do at school is really interesting.

◆◆ 3 ▶ **A tour of New York**

Partner B: Look at page 114.
Partner A: When Daniel or Josh have visitors from out of town, they usually show them the sights. Complete sentences 1–6 about Daniel's tour of New York. Ask your partner.

1 First Daniel goes to …
2 Next he shows his visitor …
3 They always have lunch in …
4 They sometimes sit in …
5 They usually walk through …
6 In the evening they see a show on …

A Where does Daniel go first?
B …
A What does he show his visitor next?
B …

Now look at the list on the right and answer your partner's questions about Josh's tour. Be careful – some place names need the definite article, some don't. Finally, find all the places on the Manhattan street map at the back of the book.

Where Josh takes his visitors
1 Rockefeller Center
2 Brooklyn Bridge
3 Chinatown
4 Central Park
5 Fifth Avenue
6 Times Square

4 REVISION If you enjoy a good joke → S 4: 2 Remember (p. 134)

a *Match these four captions to the cartoons A–D and put in the right forms of the verbs in brackets.*

1 'But if I (not wait) for him to phone, how (I/can/tell) him to get lost[1]?'
2 'If I (be) you, I (keep) the oil and change the car.'
3 'If the boat (start) sinking, who (you/save) first? Me or the children?' – 'Me!'
4 'Come on, junior[2], Daddy (get) angry if you (not play) with your food.'

A

[1] (to) get lost *(infml.)* *abhauen, verduften*
[2] junior ['dʒu:niə] hier: *Junge*

B

C

D

b *Tell the class:*
What would or wouldn't you do …
1 … if you went to New York?
2 … if you moved to the USA?
3 … if you lived in a skyscraper?
4 … if you fell in love with an American?
5 … if you were robbed on the subway?
6 … if you could visit any place in the world?

5 ▶ Friday 13th, my unlucky day

a *Read sentences 1–5. Then say how things would have been different if it hadn't been Friday 13th.*

1 My parents forgot to wake me up, so I got up too late.
If my parents hadn't forgotten to wake me up, I wouldn't have got up …
2 Our dog was in my way, so I fell over her. *If our dog hadn't been in my way, …*
3 The toast was hot, so I dropped it. *If the toast hadn't …*
4 I missed the bus and walked to school. *If I …*
5 I arrived late and the teacher was angry. …

◆◆ **b** *Make three more sentences like the ones in* **a** *and give them to a partner. He or she must say what wouldn't have happened if it hadn't been Friday 13th.*

6 ▶ I'm happy that …

a *You are probably very happy about some things in your life. Write down four.*
1 *I am happy I met my friend Pat at kindergarten.*
2 *I am happy I wrote a story for a competition.*
3 *I am happy …*
4 …
5.
6.

b *Now imagine what life would have been like if you hadn't done these things.*
1 *If I hadn't met Pat, I wouldn't have …*
2 *If I hadn't written a story, …*
3 …
4 …
5
6.

7 ▶ She may have forgotten me

John was hoping to meet a girl outside the cinema. Complete what he is thinking.

1 'Did she miss the bus? Yes, she may have missed …'
2 'She probably started late. Yes, that's right. She might …'
3 'Did I tell her the right place? I'm not stupid, I must …'
4 'Maybe she forgot to look at her watch. Yes, she must …'
5 'Why hasn't she arrived? She should … by now.'
6 'It was silly to ask her. Yes, I'm stupid. I shouldn't …'

8 LISTENING Tell us a joke

a *New York jokes are famous. Listen to the cassette/CD and find the correct last sentence – the punch-line – for each joke.*

1 'I know, you just take me back the part of the way that cost two eighty.'
2 'Shut up, or we'll *all* lose our jobs!'
3 'You want *me* to win this – or the lion?'
4 'It's the last scene in the movie anyway.'
5 'I *began* as a millionaire.'

b *Listen again and check your answers. Then think of a joke you know and try to write it in English. Tell it to the class.*

WORD WATCH

9 WORD LINK Phrases with *make* and *have*

Make a diagram like the one here. Then look at the words in the list next to it and decide where in the diagram you should put them.

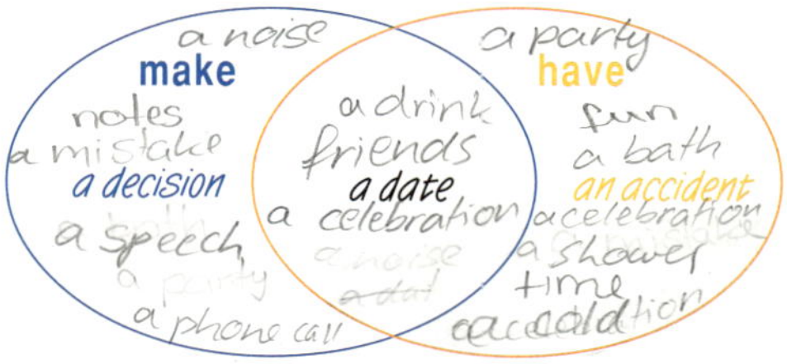

an accident	a drink	a party
a bath	friends	a phone call
a celebration	fun	a shower
a cold	a mistake	a speech
a date	a noise	time
a decision	notes	trouble

10 ▶ The people game

a *'Weird – but cute' is what Josh thought of the two English girls in New York. Cut out four pictures of people you do not know (all male or all female) from old magazines. Now imagine you meet and talk to one of these people at a party. How would you describe him/her to a friend the next day?*

Make notes first. You could think about:
- *what he/she looks like (size, hair, eyes, …)*
- *his/her character (funny, serious, quiet, …)*
- *what he/she does (job, school, …)*
- *why you liked or didn't like him/her (talked too loudly, laughed at your jokes, was really interesting, …)*

◆◆ **b** *Now show your four pictures to your partner. Use your notes to tell him/her about the person you met. Can your partner guess which person it is?*

I met this boy at a party yesterday. He goes to Goethe Gymnasium and is really interested in music. He's quite small and has blond hair. He didn't look interesting at first – but when I talked to him, he told me some really funny jokes. He's got a beautiful smile. I haven't met anyone as cute as that for a long time.

A Knight in New York

– What is unusual about the title 'A Knight in New York'? What could the story be about?
– Do you know any songs about New York City or films that take place there?

→ How to use a dictionary, p. 63

'On Broadway' – the first time I walked down Broadway, I really wanted to sing this song out loud.

Ray walked south down Broadway, away from Times Square and toward the Empire State Building. He couldn't believe it. The huge skyscrapers, the colourfully-dressed people from every part of the world, the endless river of noisy traffic. Was he really in this city he had seen in so many movies? Was he really in Manhattan? On Broadway?
He waited for the lights where Broadway met 34th Street and the Avenue of the Americas. Broadway! The home of so many songs that people knew all over the world! Was it Frank Sinatra who had sung 'New York, New York, it's a hell of a town'? Ray felt Sinatra was right. He had only been in the city for an hour, but already he felt at home. He had never been here before in his life, but he knew more about New York than any place back in Tennessee. Ray had his cousin Jim's address in his pocket. But he wasn't a hundred per cent sure he would find his way around the Lower East Side, the area of Manhattan where Jim lived. Ray could even get lost in his own home town!

* * *

'So you found it OK, Ray,' Jim said two hours later.
'Yep, no problem,' answered Ray.
'Well, it's good to see you. I hope you have a great week and, for a start, we're going to a party tonight.'

Most of the people at the party worked for the same company as Jim and were much older than Ray. But there were a few who were about his own age. Ray wanted to speak to a tall girl in a blue dress, but he was nervous.
'You OK, Ray? Can I get you something to drink?' his cousin asked him.
'Uhuh. Yes, please. But tell me, Jim, who's that girl over there?'
'The blonde girl? She's Tom's younger sister. You know, the guy who was talking to you earlier about baseball. Pretty, isn't she? Come on, I'll introduce you. But careful, now. She's made of ice. All the guys fall in love with her and they line up outside her house, but she breaks their hearts. She has a different boyfriend every week. Her name is Josie.'
As they walked across the room, a foot came from nowhere and Ray almost fell. His arm flew up and most of his drink flew through the air toward Josie's face and hair. Splash!
'S-s-sorry,' Ray said.
Jim said, 'I'd like you to meet my cousin. He arrived today. He's from out of town.'
'Swam here, huh?' Josie said.

you break my heart

Bestimmter Artikel Diktat
Vokabel von 4 if Sätze
Conditionalsätze

After that terrible introduction, they talked a little and laughed a lot. Josie had a quick sense of humour and spoke much faster than people in Tennessee, but he usually got the joke in the end. Although she acted tough, Ray guessed she had a softer side. When he said he had no plans for the week and asked for her phone number, she smiled and said, 'Like a challenge? OK, try this. Phone numbers have seven digits, right? But I'll only give you the first two, not the last five. If you can find out what they are, you can call me tomorrow night at about 6.15.'
'OK. I'll call at exactly 6.15,' Ray said. He thought, 'Huh, she calls this a test? I'll just ask Jim for her brother's phone number.'
But Josie went on, 'By the way, I won't be home tomorrow night. I'll be at a friend's house. It's her phone number you'll need.'
'Oh,' Ray said. 'What's her name?'
Josie smiled a beautiful smile. 'Hey, not that easy. But I'll give you three clues. Go to the Metropolitan. Find my favourite painting – *Dance Class* by Degas – and get the number of the floor that it's on. That's the first digit you need. For the next two digits, go to a place on 89th Street and find out how much it costs to rent a horse for an hour in Central Park. And the third clue is ...'

That night, Ray dreamed Josie was a princess who lived in a castle made of ice. Ray was a knight on a white horse. To win the hand of the princess, he had to find the answer to a difficult riddle. In the dream, it didn't seem too hard ...

* * *

When Ray woke up the next morning and went into the kitchen, he found a note from Jim:
SORRY. HAD TO FLY TO CHICAGO. BACK TOMORROW, I HOPE. IF YOU NEED HELP WITH ANYTHING, ASK MR. AND MRS. GOMEZ, MY NEIGHBORS IN APARTMENT 2C. THEY'RE GREAT.
After a quick breakfast, Ray ran to 2c. Mr and Mrs Gomez were at work, but their daughter, Maria, was home. She was about Ray's age and, like him, had no school that week. Ray asked if she had a street map with details of the city's museums. 'Sure,' Maria said. She even showed him which subway to take for the Metropolitan Museum of Art.

At the museum, Ray hurried across to the information desk and said to the woman there, 'Hi. I'm looking for a *Dancing Lesson*. I'm trying to work out this number, you see. And I need the right floor. Can you help me, please?'
The woman put down her pen and spoke very slowly. 'I'm sorry, this isn't a dance studio. It's a museum of art. We don't teach dance here. OK? Have a nice day.'
'Err, ... it's a painting by Degas.'
'Oh, you mean *Dance Class*. It's on Floor 2.'

Next, Ray had to hurry north along Fifth Avenue and then find the place on 89th Street where horses could be rented. He hurried along East 89th Street, but he couldn't see any horses anywhere. Just then a police officer got out of a car, so Ray asked him for help.
'You can't find what? A horse?' the man said. 'Hey, is this a joke? You got a hidden camera somewhere? Am I going to look stupid on TV tonight?'
Ray said he was doing a school project and the officer was friendlier. He used his car radio and said: 'You want *West* 89th Street, kid, on the other side of Central Park.' Then, 'You sure you don't have a camera?'
Central Park was bigger than Ray had thought, but he felt at home. He knew so much about it from a movie. In fact, he felt as if he was in a movie. He kept thinking, 'Hey, world, I'm in New York!'
He found the horses, heard the price was $33 for an hour and wrote down: 33.

Then he got into a taxi. 'To the American Museum of Natural History, please,' he said to the driver.
Ray soon found the last two digits: the whale in the Hall of Ocean Life was 94 feet long.

At 6.15 Ray phoned. Nobody answered at first, so he wondered if he had the wrong number. Then he got through. Josie wasn't there and Laura, her friend, was surprised Ray had called. But she seemed to know about him because she said, 'OK. Do you have a pen, so I can give you the second part of Josie's challenge?'
'What second part?' Ray said.
'You don't have to do it,' Laura said. 'But it will give you a phone number where you can reach Josie at about 3.15 tomorrow.'
Ray was starting to get angry. But he wanted to see Josie again. So he wrote down the first digit of the new phone number and Josie's clues for the last six. 'Six this time!' he thought. And he'd have to go all over the city, too. He went back to Jim's apartment, depressed and angry.

As he was opening the door, he saw Maria.
'Did you have a nice day?' she asked.
'Well, yes and no,' Ray said.
'My parents say you can eat with us if you want. We're having a Puerto Rican meal and you'd be welcome.'
'Thanks, I'd like that.'
The food was good, and Mr and Mrs Gomez showed a lot of interest in Ray's trip around their city and his plans for tomorrow.
'Do you have any plans for tomorrow night, Ray?' Mr Gomez asked. 'We have three tickets for a show tomorrow – at the Gershwin Theater – but I can't go. Would you like to go instead?'
'That's real nice of you, but, um, I don't know about tomorrow night yet,' said Ray. 'Maybe,' he thought, 'Josie will ...'

* * *

The next day Ray left early, and Maria went with him. She knew how many floors the Chrysler Building had – 77 – so they went straight to the Brooklyn Bridge to look for a plaque about the immigrants from Germany who had designed the bridge. They enjoyed the view.
'Awesome!' Ray said. 'I've seen this bridge a million times on TV, but being here is something else!'
Maria was quiet at first, but slowly she began to talk more. She told Ray why her parents had left Puerto Rico and come to the USA. They had been poor and had both had two jobs: full-time by day and part-time in the evening. Maria was very proud of them.
Suddenly Ray said, 'You know, I've had enough of Josie's game. For her next digit we'd have to go to the Bronx. But I'd prefer to see more of Manhattan.'
Maria smiled again. 'How about the Songwriters' Hall of Fame at Times Square? There's lots to see, and you can play some of the instruments.'
'Sounds cool,' Ray said.
That evening, as Ray and Maria got out of the elevator back on the Lower East Side, they met Jim. 'Hi, Ray, I'm back,' he said. 'I

hear from Mrs Gomez you've been busy.'

'Sure,' Ray said. 'We had a great day.'

'Oh, by the way, there's a message for you on the answering machine. It's from Josie. She says you passed the first part of her test at least, and she'd like to meet you tonight. How did you melt the heart of the ice queen?' Jim laughed.

Ray looked at Maria, then said to Jim, 'I can guess what she'd say if I agreed to see her. She'd ask me to meet her somewhere – like the top of the Empire State Building. But you know what would happen if I went up there to wait for her? I'd wait there and wait there, and in the end I'd have to go down: alone. Josie wouldn't come. No way. I have better things to do.'

Maria smiled.

'Can you call Josie for me, Jim?'

'Sure, Ray, if that's what you want. What should I say?'

'Tell her your cousin just swam away.'

WORKING WITH THE TEXT

1 ▶ Following the story

a *Look at the map of Manhattan at the back of the book and try to follow Ray's movements.*

b *Read between the lines and explain the meaning of the following:*
1. The woman put down her pen and spoke very slowly. (p. 60, ll. 57/58)
2. 'You sure you don't have a camera?' (p. 60, ll. 84–86)
3. 'Tell her your cousin just swam away.' (p. 62, l. 25)

c *Explain the title of the story. What other titles for this story can you think of?*

2 ▶ Understanding the characters

a *What sort of person is Ray? What sort of things is he interested in and how does he feel about New York? (How do you know?)*

b *Imagine you are Ray. Would you have accepted Josie's challenge? Why?/Why not?*

3 ▶ Beyond the story

a *Imagine Ray writes to Maria when he gets back home. What does he write? (sights they visited together/feelings about New York/feelings about Maria/...?)*

b *Find out more about one of the places Ray visits (use the Internet, go to a library/tourist office/travel agent, ...). Then give the class a short talk on it.*

→ How to give a presentation, p. 91

◆◆ 4 ROLE-PLAY 'How was your week?'

Act out one of these scenes. You can write your own role cards, or use the ones your teacher has:
- *Ray is talking to a friend in Tennessee about his time in New York.*
- *Maria is talking to her best friend about her time with Ray.*

I ♥ NY

→ Revision p. 118
→ Translation p. 121

HOW TO ... use a dictionary – Part 2: English-German

1 ▶ Understanding new words

When you are doing your American timeline, you may find information (in English) with words you don't know. You can often guess the meanings of these words from the context or because you know part of a new word, or the word is like a German word, or even like a word you know in another language (French, Latin, ...). Pictures might also help.

Located a few hundred yards north of the Statue of Liberty in New York Harbor, Ellis Island is a monument to the great tradition of freedom in America. Immigrants commenced their new lives in a free country here.

2 ▶ Looking up the meaning of words

a *If you can't guess the meaning or want to check if you guessed right, you will need a dictionary. On page 33, you learned about some of the information that dictionaries give. What information does the entry below give?*

primary[1] /ˈpraɪməri; *AE* ˈpraɪmeri/ *Adj* Haupt-, grundlegend, primär **of primary importance** von höchster Wichtigkeit **primary colours** Grundfarben
ˌprimary eduˈcation *Nomen* Grundschulerziehung
ˈprimary school *Nomen (BE)* Grundschule

primary[2] /ˈpraɪməri; *AE* ˈpraɪmeri/ (auch **primary eˈlection**) *Nomen* (**primaries**) *(AE)* *(Politik)* Vorwahl

b *Look at the dictionary entry again and decide what* primary *means in these sentences.*

1. During the primary inspection, doctors screened the immigrants for dangerous illnesses, and some people were not admitted on these grounds.
2. Candidates for US President are chosen after a large number of state primaries.
3. Which school does your brother go to? – He's only 8, he's still at primary.

c *Your dictionary might use abbreviations like* Obj., Sing., v./t., fig., umgs, mil., pol. *to give you extra information about grammar, style and meaning. Find the list of abbreviations in your dictionary.*

3 ▶ Test yourself

a *Look at the dictionary entries for* admit, ground *and* screen *and find the correct translations of these words in* **2b** *(sentence 1) on the left.*

admit /ədˈmɪt/ *Verb* (admi**tt**ing, admi**tt**ed, admi**tt**ed)
1 admit (to) sth etwas zugeben **He refused to admit to the theft.** Er weigerte sich, den Diebstahl zuzugeben. **She admitted having broken the toy.** Sie gab zu, das Spielzeug kaputtgemacht zu haben.
2 *+ Obj* **admit sb/sth (into/to sth)** jdn/etwas (in etwas) hineinlassen **He was admitted to hospital.** Er wurde ins Krankenhaus eingeliefert.

ground /ɡraʊnd/ *Nomen* **1 the ground** *Sing* die Erde **We sat down on the ground.** Wir setzten uns auf die Erde. **He slipped off the ladder and fell to the ground.** Er rutschte von der Leiter und fiel auf den Boden.
2 *kein Plural* Boden **stony ground** steiniger Untergrund
3 Platz **a sports ground** ein Sportplatz
4 grounds *Plural (eines Gebäudes)* Anlagen, Gelände
5 *meist Plural* Grund **She retired on medical grounds.** Sie ging aus gesundheitlichen Gründen in den Ruhestand. **grounds for divorce** Scheidungsgründe
6 *meist Sing* *(AE)* *(in Elektrogeräten)* Erde

screen[1] /skriːn/ *Nomen* **1** Bildschirm
2 Trennwand, Wandschirm
3 Leinwand
4 the screen *Sing* der Film **a star of stage and screen** ein Film- und Bühnenstar

screen[2] /skriːn/ *Verb + Obj* **1 screen sb/sth (off) (from sb/sth)** jdn/etwas (von jdm/etwas) abschirmen, jdn/etwas (vor jdm/etwas) schützen
2 screen sb (for sth) jdn (auf etwas) überprüfen, jdn (auf etwas) untersuchen **screen for cancer** auf Krebs untersuchen
3 zeigen; *(im Fernsehen)* senden; *(Film)* vorführen

b *Find the best translation for the underlined words from the context or in a dictionary:*

1. They were often allowed in if somebody assumed their financial support.
2. They had to stay in the immigrant hospital until they recovered.

REMEMBER

1. Don't look up every word. When possible, use the context to guess the meaning.
2. Read the whole dictionary entry. Don't just use the first word you see.
3. Look at the abbreviations (or symbols) to decide which meaning is right or best.

UNIT 5 Nebraska – the Middle of Nowhere?

A

B

Sutton High School Student Handbook

Grading system

A Excellent
B Very good
C Average
D Poor
F Failure

D

C

SUTTON HIGH SCHOOL

Nancy Griess, Grade 9
Locker number 142

	Monday	Tuesday	Wednesday
PERIOD 1 8:15 - 9:04	WEIGHT TRAINING Room 22 Mr. Leininger	WEIGHT TRAINING Room 22 Mr. Leininger	WEIGHT TR Room 22
PERIOD 2 9:07 - 9:57	SOCIAL STUDIES Room 24 Mr. Stark	SOCIAL STUDIES Room 24 Mr. Stark	SOCIAL S Room 24
PERIOD 3 10:00 - 10:50	ENGLISH I Room 02 Ms. Kucza	ENGLISH I Room 02 M	ENGLISH I Room 02 Ms. Kucza
PERIOD 4 10:53 - 11:41	STUDY HALL Room 5	STUDY HAL Room 5	
PERIOD 5 11:44 - 12:31	ALGEBRA I Room 20 Mr. Engler	ALGEBRA Room 20	
	LUNCH	LUNCH	
PERIOD 6 1:01 - 1:49	HEALTHY LIFE Room 22 Ms. Ochsner	HEALTH Room 2	
PERIOD 7 1:52 - 2:40	PHYSICAL SCIENCE Room 11 Ms. Sullivan	PHYSI Room	
PERIOD 8 2:43 - 3:30	COMPUTER APPLICATION I Room 17 Mr. Atkins	COMF Room	

E

LISTENING

1 *Look at the photos. What do they show?*
2 *Listen to the cassette/CD and match pictures A–G to the students' comments.*
3 *Listen again and take notes on as many things as you can that you find surprising, interesting, or different from German schools.*
❖ 4 *Collect all your ideas, make a group list and report back to the class. Add to the list as you go through the unit.*

❖ ACTIVITY

What would American high school students find different if they spent a year at a school in your part of Germany? In your group, discuss what they should know.
Then you could record a cassette, collect photos, or write short articles to send to the American students.

→ How to brainstorm, p. 77

F

G

▶ 1

During the second period, Nancy Griess's class had to take a quiz on Nebraska. Nancy was usually good at remembering facts. But today she kept thinking back to the day before, when she had walked hand in hand with her boyfriend along the road between the endless fields of soy beans. She loved being with him, but it was nearly always the same – a slow walk past bean fields! You just couldn't avoid them here.
Unlike most of his friends, he had no car, and that was a real problem. There was no movie theater in Sutton, not even a shopping mall, and the nearest big town – Hastings, with a population of 25,000 – was 30 miles away.

▶▶▶ NOW YOU

What do people dream of doing if they live in small places? And if they live in big cities? What about you?

→ S 5: 1 Remember (p. 136)
→ P 1, 2, 3, 4, 13

▶ 2

'Well? Think you'll get another "A"?' asked her friend Debbie Nuss, as the students gave their quizzes to the teacher.
'Uh, I don't think so,' Nancy replied. 'The time seemed to go kind of quickly today, Deb. How did you do?'
Debbie felt she had passed the test, but she was worried about the big exam at the end of the semester. It would be harder and she was afraid she might fail it. 'You'll be OK,' Nancy told her.

When the girls went to get their books for the next period, they saw a note on Nancy's locker. Without saying a word, Nancy took it off. It said: *Usual place, 3:30? – J.D.* After reading the note, Nancy smiled.
On seeing this, Debbie asked, 'So who's it from, Nancy?'
Nancy thought for a few seconds before answering. Then she said, 'Oh, no one, Debbie. Er, I mean ... Look, I have to go now or I'll be late for English. OK?'

▶ **3**

At lunch-time Nancy called her mother at work. Her mother's voice sounded friendly but formal. 'Sutton Foods. How may I help you?'
Nancy tried to hide the fact that she was nervous by speaking quickly. 'Hi, Mom, it's me. I forgot to tell you …' She stopped. Then, after looking around to see if anyone was listening, she went on: '… that I have band practice after school today. So I'll be home late.'
'That's OK, honey,' Mrs Griess said. 'I'm not cooking dinner tonight – remember? I've got a real important meeting at church after work.'

FOCUS ON GRAMMAR

1 *Look for the prepositions* after, before, by, on, without *in A2 and A3. Find examples where they are followed by verbs.*

2 *What forms are the verbs in?*

3 *Translate the examples of 'preposition + verb form' that you have found into German. What do you notice?*

→ S 5: 1 (p. 136)
→ P 5, 6

? *What do you think Nancy is really doing after school?*

▶ **4**

It seemed half of the town had come to Mrs Griess's meeting, including several neighbours and also teachers from Sutton High. Most people in Sutton went to one of its five churches, but so many at one church was unusual.
Mrs Griess didn't feel nervous, however. The topic was too important to her. She knew that people loved their cars and trucks, but she also knew how dangerous cars could be. Although Sutton was only small, too many local families had lost someone they loved.
'As you all know from the notices around town,' Mrs Griess began, 'we're here to found a local group of *Mothers Against Drunk Driving*. You may have heard of the group by its shorter name – *MADD*. Well, I have some information here that'll tell you …'

MADD's History

MADD
Mothers Against Drunk Driving

MADD was founded in 1980 after a 13-year-old girl was killed in a traffic accident. The driver had drunk too much alcohol and didn't stop to help the girl. He was found a few days later but was then just sent to a "half-way house" for two years, not to prison. He had to sleep there, but he went to his old job during the day and could see his friends. That's when the girl's mother got mad and founded MADD.

? *Do you know any groups in your home town that are trying to make the world safer for people or better in some way? What are the aims of these groups?*

→ P 7

FOCUS ON WORDS Dangers

→ How to use a dictionary, p. 33

1 *Collect words and phrases for things that are or may be dangerous for young people. Use a dictionary. Think of:*

- **traffic** (drive too fast, ride a bike with no lights, …)
- **drugs** (drink alcohol, take pills, smoke, …)
- **food** (eat the wrong things, eat too little, …)
- **free-time activities** (go inline skating without a helmet, climb without a rope, …)

2 *Imagine that parents want to warn their children about some of these dangers. What would they say?*

▶ 5

The next morning at breakfast, after Mr Griess had said grace, Mrs Griess began, 'Nancy, a teacher of yours was at our meeting last night. She directs the school band, I understand. But she wasn't at band practice yesterday.'
Nancy didn't know what to say. Mrs Griess went on: 'You didn't have band practice, did you? You must have lied to me, Nancy.'
'Yes, Mom. I'm sorry.'
'So where were you after school yesterday?'
'I was ... er ... with some friends of mine from school. Bobbie has a car now and she drove us over to Hastings.'
'And who were these "friends of yours"?' her father wanted to know.
'Mmmhhh ... Betsey Wagner, Scott Jones and, er, Jimmy,' Nancy answered.
'Jimmy who?' asked Mr Griess.
'Jimmy Domeier.'
'Nancy, you know you mustn't have anything to do with the Domeiers!' Mrs Griess said. 'Phil Domeier – Jimmy's uncle – drank and drove, and killed my brother. Avoid that Domeier boy!'
'But Mom, that accident was years ago. And, anyway, Jimmy's dad was ... '
'That's enough, young lady,' said Mr Griess. 'You won't see the boy again. End of story.'

▶▶▶ **NOW YOU**

Can you understand Nancy's parents? Why?/Why not?

FOCUS ON GRAMMAR

1 *The phrase* a teacher of yours *is made up of a noun +* of *+ what?*
2 *Find two more phrases like this in A5.*
3 *Compare these two phrases:*
a teacher of yours – your teacher
Try to work out a rule for when you use a teacher of yours.

→ S 5: 2 (p. 137)
→ P 8

▶ 6

On the way to her first class of the day, Nancy pushed a note inside J.D.'s locker: *Usual place. Usual time. Must talk. – N.*
At 3.30, when school was over at last, J.D. hurried off to the ice-cream place. He had a feeling something was wrong.
'I got your note, Nance. What's the matter?'
'Trouble, J.D. My mom found out about us. She says I can't see you any more. I guess it's over.'
'You mean – us?' J.D. asked slowly, as if he hoped her words could possibly have a different meaning. 'But Nance ...'
'We'll still see each other around school,' she offered.
'Yeah, sure,' J.D. said. He looked as if he might cry.
'I'm real sorry, J.D. But you know what my parents are like. And you know how hard it's been for me. I just hate telling them lies.'
'Yeah. I know. Yeah, well ...'

▶▶▶ **NOW YOU**

What would you have done in Nancy's place? How would you have reacted if you had been J.D.?

→ P 9, 10

▶ 7

A week later Mrs Domeier said, 'You've been very quiet the last few days, Jimmy. You know, if anything's wrong, you can always talk to us.'
J.D. said nothing, though there was a lot he would have liked to say. His mother didn't seem to notice. 'OK,' she went on. 'Now, there's something your dad and I would like to discuss with you. Here, read this: it's a kind of contract. I think we should all sign it. What do you think? Can we discuss it?'
His father nodded. 'Yeah, read it and see what you think, Jimmy.'

CONTRACT FOR LIFE

Student I promise to avoid putting my health or safety in danger. I promise that I will try to stay away from alcohol and drugs. By signing this contract, I agree that I will never drive under the influence of alcohol or drugs. I will not accept a ride from someone who is under the influence. Finally, I agree to call you if I am ever in danger.

Signed .... (Student)

Parent I promise that I will arrange safe transportation home for you if you are ever in a dangerous situation – and I agree to wait with any discussion of the situation until we are both calm. I also promise that I myself will not drive under the influence of alcohol or drugs.

Signed .... (Parent)

J.D. couldn't believe his eyes. 'But this is from MADD, isn't it?' he said. 'Isn't that the group Mrs Griess started?'
'That's right. And I'm a member now too,' his mother said.
'But the Griesses don't want anything to do with us! You know – since the accident.'
'That's history now, son,' his father said. 'It had gone on long enough.'
His mother continued, 'If Mrs Griess and I can go to the same church and pray together, we ought to be able to get along together. Now – what about this contract?'

? *In the USA lots of students and their parents sign the 'Contract for Life'. Why do they call it a 'Contract for Life'? Can a contract like this stop drunk driving? Why?/Why not?*

▶▶▶ NOW YOU
Would you sign the 'Contract for Life'? What sort of contract might make your life safer? Discuss.

◆◆ ROLE-PLAY 'It's all different now'
Imagine that J.D. calls Nancy at once after the news from his parents. Act out their conversation. You can write your own role cards, or use the ones your teacher has.

→ P 11, 12
→ U.S. Mag., pp. 106/107

◆◆ 1 **GAME** A quiz on Nebraska

Partner B: Look at page 115.

a *Partner A: Ask your partner questions 1–4 about Nebraska. Your partner will offer several answers. Guess the correct one.*

A What's the population of Nebraska?
B It's 1.66 million or 2.66 million or 3.66 million. Which is correct?
A I think it's 2.66 million.
B No, try again.
A Is it …?

1 population – Nebraska?
2 biggest town – Nebraska?
3 three movie stars – born – Nebraska?
4 two of Nebraska's important industries?

Now your partner will ask you questions 5–8. Give him/her these answers to choose from. (The correct answers are underlined.)

5 a) under 30% b) 40% to 60% c) <u>over 65%</u>
6 a) 270,000 b) <u>370,000</u> c) 470,000
7 a) <u>Gerald Ford</u> b) Bill Clinton c) George Washington
8 a) Harriet Tubman b) <u>Malcolm X</u> c) Martin Luther King

Malcolm X, black American leader, murdered 1965

b *Write all the correct answers into your American album.*

2 **REVISION** Who is it? → S 5: 1 Remember (p. 136)

Think of a girl or boy in your class (or a famous person that you know about). Write down five sentences about 'your' person (with a gerund in each sentence). Read the sentences out (but don't say his/her name). Can the others in your class guess who it is?

Example:
1 She hates *sitting quietly*.
2 She likes *wearing jeans*.
3 She is good at *dancing*.
4 One of her hobbies is *taking photos*.
5 She dreams of *working for a magazine*.

3 **REVISION** Old ways and new → S 5: 1 Remember (p. 136); S 2: 2a (p. 126)

Use the gerund or the to-*infinitive of the verbs in brackets.*

Over 95% of the land in Nebraska is used for (farm) and there are 55,000 farms in the state. 'I couldn't imagine (live) in a city,' says Sam Nuss. 'Our nearest town has a population of only 3500 but I don't enjoy (go) there. It's too busy.'

More and more people are deciding (move) to Nebraska. 'My high school had a drug problem, so Mom suggested (come) to this little town on the prairie, and Dad and I agreed (try) it for a year,' Sue Hill explains. 'We hoped (lead) a quieter life here. But maybe it's too quiet. I miss (go) to the movies with my friends. Mom and Dad would like (stay) here, I know, but I plan (go) back to Detroit one day. I already mentioned (go) back and they promised (think) about it.'

In fact, half of all Nebraskans live in or near two big cities, Omaha and Lincoln, and many have started (work) in a new industry: telemarketing. They sit at phones and call people all over the USA. They hope the people they phone will decide (buy) the things they are selling.

4 REVISION Nancy's grandfather

→ S 5: 1 Remember (p. 136); S 2: 2a (p.126)

Translate these six sentences into English with the help of the correct pair of verbs from the box.

1 Nancys Großvater beschloss als junger Mann, von New York nach Nebraska zu ziehen.
2 Er bat seine Freundin, mit ihm zu gehen.
3 Sie konnte sich aber zuerst nicht vorstellen, in Nebraska zu leben.
4 Sie meinte, dass ihr das Leben in der Großstadt fehlen würde.
5 Daher schlug sie vor, nach einem Jahr wieder darüber zu reden.
6 Nach einem Jahr erklärte sie sich bereit, ihren Freund zu heiraten.

ask/go
agree/marry
decide/move
imagine/live
miss/live
suggest/talk

5 ▶ Tornadoes

Read this text about tornadoes. Complete parts 1–3 with a preposition from the box and a following gerund.

before • by (2×) • instead of • on • without

The Midwest of the USA is tornado country – and tornadoes are very dangerous. So should you avoid the Midwest? No. But be careful, and don't forget that tornadoes kill about 100 people every year in the USA.

1 Unfortunately, some people take photos of a tornado ... (try) to find a safe place – and then find they don't have time. ... (go) out and (take) photos, you should look for a safe place at once.
2 You can usually avoid serious danger ... (listen) to the radio regularly. There are tornado reports at least every hour during the tornado season. Some Nebraskans don't like to go for a picnic in the tornado season ... (take) a radio.
3 Tourists can find a safe place ... (follow) special signs on many buildings. As a tourist, ... (hear) that a tornado is near, go to a public shelter.

6 ▶ Not thinking about school

a *Make two sentences into one. Use a preposition + gerund.*

1 J.D. didn't phone Nancy. He put a note on her locker.
Instead of phoning Nancy, J.D. ...
2 Nancy saw the note. She felt excited.
On ...
3 Nancy read the note. She felt happy.
After ...
4 Debbie walked away. She didn't say anything.
... without ...
5 Nancy went to English. First, she wrote a note for J.D.
Before ...
6 Nancy put the note on J.D.'s locker. Then she hurried to English.
7 Nancy didn't listen to Ms Kucza, her English teacher. She thought of J.D. all the time.
8 Ms Kucza read a poem. She asked Nancy if she liked it.
9 Nancy heard her name. She woke up.
10 Ms Kucza was angry and told Nancy, 'You should listen to me. You shouldn't sleep in class.'

b *Can you remember a journey that you enjoyed (or hated)? Write 4–5 sentences with* before/after + *gerund.*
Last summer my family and I went to ... Before leaving home, I ... After visiting the castle, we ...

7 **REVISION** Some Sutton facts → S 3: 1 (p. 129)

Put the verbs in brackets in the simple present or past. Use the passive where necessary.

The town of Sutton (found) in 1871. It (call) 'Sutton' after Sutton, Massachusetts. In 1873 lots of German-Russians (come) to live in Sutton. The first houses in the town (make) of earth, but today most of the houses (make) of wood. The first school in Sutton (open) in 1884. However, the people of Sutton (build) a new school in 1964 and it is this later building that (use) today.

8 ▶ **Party talk**

Your family is having a barbecue. One of the guests asks you about other people at the party. Answer with the help of the information in brackets.

1 GUEST Who's that man near the table?
YOU *(You have several uncles – so you say:)* He's an uncle of mine.

2 GUEST Who's that woman near the pool?
YOU *(You have one grandmother.)* She's my grandmother.

3 GUEST Who's that boy in the red jeans?
YOU *(You have lots of cousins.)* He's a …

4 GUEST Who's that girl with the mobile phone?
YOU *(You have lots of friends.)* …

5 GUEST Who's the DJ?
YOU *(You have one father – of course!)* …

6 GUEST Who's that woman in the long yellow dress?
YOU *(Your mother has lots of friends.)* . .

7 GUEST Who's that girl with the camera?
YOU *(You have one sister.)* …

8 GUEST Who's that big guy in the blue shorts and pink shirt?
YOU *(Your family has lots of neighbours.)* …

9 **LISTENING** Sylvia's Mother – a Country & Western song

a *The song 'Sylvia's Mother' might remind you of the trouble that J.D. and Nancy had. Before you listen, try to remember what their problem was. Then listen and say who the people in the song are.*

◆◆ **b** *Listen to the song again. Take notes only on what Sylvia's mother says. Compare notes with your partner and add what is missing.*

c *The song doesn't tell the whole story of Sylvia, her mother and the singer. Imagine the rest of it. How did Sylvia and the singer become friends? What happened then? Why doesn't Mrs Avery want them to be together?*

d *Read the information about Country & Western music on the right. (You will find the new words in the dictionary, pp. 166–192.) Does 'Sylvia's Mother' seem to be a typical C&W song? Why?/Why not?*

Country & Western, also C&W

C&W is the music of America's heartland. In an early form it was probably brought to America by British immigrants. C&W songs often tell a simple story, and the texts are usually more important than the music. Typical instruments are the guitar, banjo or mandolin – all in the style of the fiddle (→ violin). In this it shows its beginnings in Scottish and Irish folk music. Today C&W is often mixed with elements of rock music (→ rock).

WORD WATCH

❖ 10 WORD BUILDING Nouns and verbs with the same form

All the words in the box can be used as nouns or verbs. Make two teams. When it's your team's turn, make one sentence with your word as a noun and another sentence with the same word as a verb. You'll get one point for every correct sentence and an extra point if you can think of a word that is not in the box.

book • call • change
copy • drink • drive
end • form • guess
guide • joke • launch
lie • murder • plant
smile • visit • walk • ...

TEAM A We're going to use the word *lie*.
Our first sentence is: Nancy told a *lie* but her parents found out.
Our second sentence is: Can you ever believe somebody who has *lied* to you?

TEACHER OK, that's fine. Two points to you. Now, Team B?

TEAM B We've chosen ...

11 ▶ Synonyms

a *Find pairs of words or phrases that mean the same or almost the same.*
Example: begin ≈ start

also • at the moment • begin
child • correct • difficult • discuss
easy • fantastic • friendly • great
hard • kid • kind • now • right
sad • simple • speak • start • talk
talk about • too • unhappy

◆◆ **b** *Choose one of the words or phrases and use it in a sentence. Now your partner must change your sentence by using the synonym. (Take it in turns.)*

12 TROUBLE SPOT Which word is right?

1 Nancy had to (practise/practice) hard to get in the school band. And when she was in it, she usually had to go to (practise/practice) several times every week.
2 J.D. is (kind of/the kind of) guy everyone likes. Nancy was (kind of/the kind of) sad when her parents said she shouldn't see him any more.
3 After looking at the school (notes/notices), J. D. found a (note/notice) from Nancy.
4 A week after the MADD group had been (found/founded), things began to look better for J.D. and Nancy. Before that, J.D. had (found/founded) life miserable.

13 ▶ Country and city

Look at these two photos. Describe them and say what impression they give of life in the country and life in a big city. What aspects are missing in the photos? Where would you prefer to live when you are 20, 40, 60? Why?

How do students become popular? Why are some students more popular than others? Do you think it's important to be popular? Why? / Why not?

→ How to use a dictionary, p. 63

I Heard the Weirdest Rumor

The following scene is adapted from *Class Action,* a play by Brad Slaight. The author writes: "Events outside the classroom are sometimes the most important things that young people experience at high school."

Laura is sitting at a table in the school library. Melanie and Janine enter and sit next to her. There are other students in the library who "shush" when the conversations get too loud. On entering the library, Mike notices Laura with her friends and decides to sit with Scooter at a table near Laura.

MELANIE I can't believe the cafeteria served mystery meat again. I wonder what we ate today.

LAURA I think it was beef.

JANINE It might have just been bad chicken.

MELANIE Yuck. *(She looks at Janine.)*

JANINE You know, I heard the weirdest rumor about you, Laura.

MELANIE I heard it, too.

LAURA Really?

JANINE Somebody said they saw you out on a date last night with that fat kid, Mike Howard. *(Janine notices Mike.)* Oh God, he's sitting over there. *(Laura reacts.)*

MELANIE We told them that you were both in the school play and were probably just practicing your lines.

JANINE That had to be it, right? *(They wait for Laura to react.)*

LAURA We are both in the school play.

MELANIE *(happy now)* See, I knew there was a good reason.

LAURA And we also went out on a date.

We move to Mike and Scooter. They are whispering to each other.

SCOOTER I tell you you're the King of the Misfits. You've given every nerd in this school a reason to live.

MIKE Thanks a lot!

SCOOTER Laura Rivers … you got the crown jewels, baby!

STUDENT Ssshhhh!

MIKE You make it sound like a sport.

SCOOTER Of course dating is a sport. And you just won the championships.

MIKE You make Laura sound like some kind of trophy. She isn't.

SCOOTER That's good. Defending your woman is what you should do.

MIKE She's not my woman.

SCOOTER You went out with her, didn't you?

MIKE We went to a movie together. That's all.

SCOOTER That's all? You make it sound like she'd go to a movie with just anybody.

Back to Laura, Melanie and Janine.

JANINE The two of you have nothing in common. You're a Senior, he's a Junior; you're popular, he's a nerd; you're pretty, he's fat.

MELANIE People are talking. They're calling you two "Beauty and the Beef".

LAURA And of course you defended me because I'm your friend?

JANINE Yes, we told them that you just feel sorry for him.

MELANIE Because that is why you went out with him, isn't it?

LAURA I went out with Mike Howard because he's talented, sincere and has a great sense of humor.

JANINE You could have any guy in this school.

LAURA He's really sweet. You don't know him …

MELANIE We don't want to know him.

JANINE Right.

LAURA He's very special to me.

JANINE Special enough to ruin your whole life? Because that's what's going to happen if you date him again.

LAURA Ruin my life?

MELANIE He's just using you, Laura. To make himself look good.

Back to Mike and Scooter.

MIKE Laura is very sweet.

SCOOTER She's been in a magazine ... she's a model. Models aren't sweet ... they're exciting, they're dangerous, they're sexy.

MIKE It's not like that with us.

SCOOTER Ah-hah, you used the "us" word. This is serious.

MIKE We're just friends.

SCOOTER No, you and I are friends. You and Laura are lovers.

MIKE Yeah, right.

SCOOTER The whole school is talking about it.

MIKE Yeah, I heard ... "Beauty and the Beef".

Back to Laura, Melanie and Janine.

LAURA It's bad enough that my parents want to make decisions about who I can date. I shouldn't have to ask my friends if it's OK ...

JANINE It's because we're your friends that we're telling you this.

MELANIE We don't want to see you get hurt.

LAURA Jeff hurt me, Rick hurt me ... Mike Howard is the first guy I've ever gone out with who actually cares how *I* feel.

MELANIE If he really cares about you, he'll realize that he's wrong for you.

JANINE Dating a guy like that can give you a bad reputation. People judge you by who you're with.

LAURA Like when I hang out with you two?

JANINE You know what I mean.

LAURA So I go out on a date with someone and if other people don't like him, I'm going to lose my "position" here at school?

MELANIE You say it like you don't think it matters, but you know it does.

JANINE This is the most important time of your life. Don't make any mistakes.

MELANIE We're only trying to help you.

Back to Mike and Scooter.

SCOOTER They wouldn't talk if nothing was going on. And something is going on, isn't it?

MIKE Why are you going on about this? Look, she's the first girl who ever paid any attention to me ... and I like that.

SCOOTER I think you can get more than attention from her.

MIKE Right now, I enjoy being with her. If I ask for more, I may ruin it. I may not have her love, but I have *her*. And I don't want to lose that.

SCOOTER That's poetic, but life doesn't work that way.

Back to Laura, Melanie and Janine.

JANINE Look, there's a party over at Kelly's house this weekend. And I know that Martin Dole has been asking about you ever since you broke up with Rick. This would be the perfect time for you and Martin to talk ...

MELANIE It's going to be the party of the year. Everybody will be there. It'll be the perfect time to let people know that you're ... you know ... *(Janine and Melanie both look at Laura. They are waiting for an answer.)*

LAURA All right. I'll go to the party. *(They are both happy now.)*

MELANIE You've made the right decision.

JANINE We were really worried.

LAURA What time should Mike and I be there? *(Laura and Mike both get up and leave the library together.)*

WORKING WITH THE TEXT

1 ▶ Relationships

a *Copy this diagram into your exercise book.*

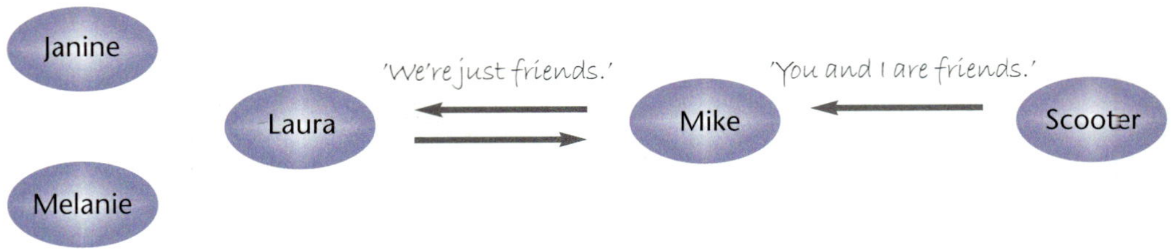

Now add more arrows to show the relationships between the students. Write a short sentence or phrase from the scene that describes each relationship.

b *Collect the main information from the scene on these points:*
- Laura's feelings towards Mike and Mike's feelings towards Laura
- Melanie and Janine's opinion of Laura's date with Mike
- Laura's reaction to her friends' opinions of Mike
- Scooter's behaviour towards Mike

2 ▶ What they say and what they really mean

Explain what the speakers are probably thinking when they make these statements.
1 Melanie: 'We told them that you were both in the school play.' (p. 74, ll. 17/18)
2 Scooter: 'Laura Rivers … you got the crown jewels, baby!' (p. 74, ll. 32/33)
3 Laura: 'He's very special to me.' (p. 74, l. 71)

3 ▶ Beyond the text

a *Explain why you agree or disagree with these ideas from the scene:*
- Dating is a sport. (p. 74, l. 36)
- You need a boyfriend or girlfriend who helps you to look good. (p. 74, ll. 76/77)
- You get a bad reputation if you date the wrong person. (p. 75, ll. 31/32)

b *What do you know from TV or films about dating among American teenagers? What do teenagers do on dates? Where do they go? Who pays? How important are cars? How is America different from or similar to Germany?*

c *Choose one of the characters from the scene and write his or her diary entry for that evening (not more than ten lines).*

d *What might happen at the party at Kelly's house? Write about it as the next scene of the play.*

❖ 4 ▶ Putting the scene on stage

Try and put 'I Heard the Weirdest Rumor' on stage. Think about these questions:
- *How many people will you need?*
- *What are the people like? How do they speak and act?*
- *What things will you need on stage?*
- *How will the actors have to sit so that the dialogues will work?*
- *How can you change from one dialogue to another?*

→ Revision p. 119

HOW TO ... brainstorm

1 ▶ **Finding answers in a group**

When you are working in a group, you often have to get a lot of good ideas together. One useful technique that will help is brainstorming. It's easy and also fun – and it helps you to be creative. You just have to follow four steps.

Let's say you want to collect ideas for your school's web site. How can you best present your school to 'virtual visitors' from other countries?

2 ▶ **The steps**

1 COLLECTING
In a specific time (e.g. five minutes) everyone in the group writes down, quietly, on a piece of paper all the ideas they have. There is no 'right' or 'wrong' idea. Every idea is welcome, even the weird ones. Just try to find as many ideas as you can, but don't try to order them yet.

2 POOLING
Everyone puts their piece of paper in a 'pool' on the table.

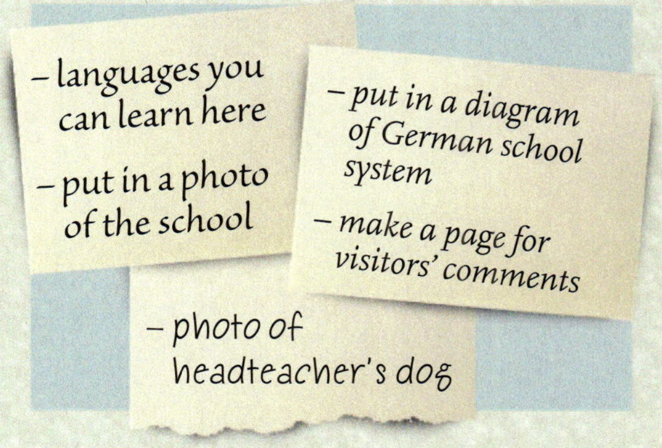

3 SHARING
Everyone takes someone else's piece of paper from the pool and reads it on their own. You must not give your opinion on any of the ideas yet. If you suddenly think of new ideas, add them on the piece of paper in front of you.

4 STRUCTURING
Now discuss all the ideas and order them. Try to find headings for groups of ideas and decide where each idea can go.
Finally, discuss which of the ideas are best for your project or task, which are really the same as others and which are not so useful. One of you writes down those ideas you have decided on. And don't forget: it's important to find the best ideas for the work of the whole group (even if they are not yours).

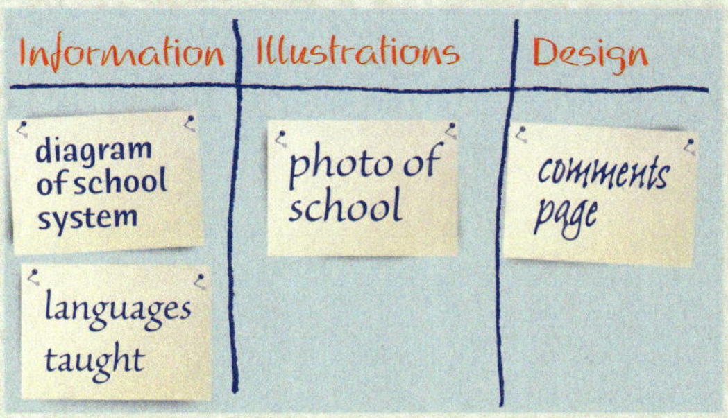

REMEMBER

1 In five minutes write down all the ideas you have on a topic.
2 Don't worry about 'right' or 'wrong' or 'weird' ideas. More ideas are better!
3 Read the others' ideas.
4 Decide on headings for groups of ideas and then order what you have collected.
5 Write down the best ideas.

6

UNIT 6 Dreamland California

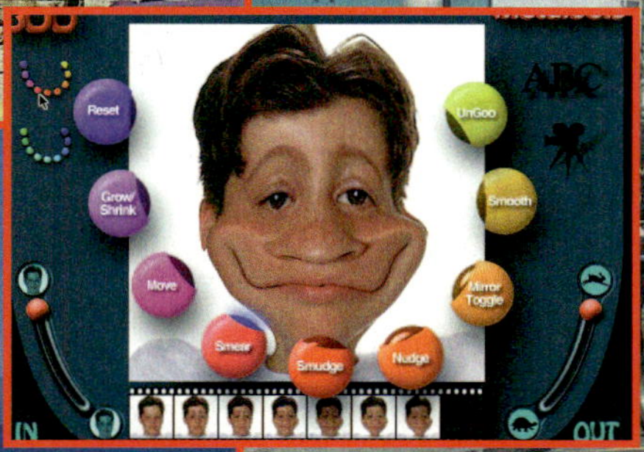

1 *Look at the California collage for two minutes. Then shut your book and try to remember as many pictures as you can. Make a list. Use a dictionary if you need to find out an English word.*

◆◆ 2 *Compare your list with your partner's and add to it.*

3 *Now look at the collage again. What do you know about the places, buildings, etc. in the pictures? Swap information and ideas with other students in the class.*

California places

▶ 1

DEATH VALLEY

"Tomesha", the Native Americans' name for Death Valley, means "land where the ground is on fire". That's a good name for this desert where temperatures can reach 130° F (54° C) in the summer! If you want to find out more about the hottest place on earth but stay cool, there is a video twice an hour at the visitor center.

Get ready for the most fantastic adventure in 65 million years on JURASSIC PARK – THE RIDE. Deep in the forest, on the most awesome water ride of all time, T-Rex is waiting for you!

Feel a huge EARTHQUAKE.

Fly with E.T.

Take the greatest rides through the biggest movies. **See** how a real movie studio works. And **enjoy** many more rides and adventures – only at Universal Studios Hollywood!

Sequoia has been a national park since 1890. It is famous for the largest trees on earth: the giant sequoias or redwoods. The biggest is the 3,000-year-old General Sherman tree. It is 275 ft (84 m) tall and still grows about half an inch (1 cm) every ten years.

The Golden Gate Bridge

- Joseph Strauss from Chicago designed the bridge. Work started on it in 1933 and finished in 1937.
- The bridge is 1.7 miles (2.7 km) long, and the road on it is 220 ft. (67 m) above the water.
- 120,000 vehicles a day cross the bridge.
- The speed limit on the bridge is 45 miles (72 km) an hour.

? *Match pictures from pages 78/79 to the four texts. Put the four places in order from 'most interesting' to 'least interesting' (in your opinion).*

◆◆ ACTIVITY

Partner B: Look at page 115.
Partner A: You and your partner have got different information about Bodie State Historic Park. Ask your partner these questions and take notes on the answers. (Then your partner will ask you.)

1 Who first found gold in California?
2 When did people first find gold in Bodie?
3 Why can't you see all of the town's old buildings any more?
4 How long has Bodie been a state park?

Now write a new text with all the information you have.

Bodie State Historic Park

The discovery of gold in California on January 24, 1848, started the Gold Rush that brought hundreds of thousands of people to California. Most came in 1849 and people called them Forty-Niners. Bodie became a busy gold-mining town of 8,000 people. In 1882 there was no more gold and everybody left. Bodie is now California's largest ghost town and still has 170 of the old buildings.

→ P 1, 2 → How to give a presentation, p. 91 → U.S. Mag, p. 108

California people

▶ 2

Kai Krause is a software developer with a difference. Programs like Kai's Power Tools and Kai's Photo Soap that let people play with pictures and photos have made him an international star in the computer world. He also designed special effects for Star Trek, The Movie. Krause was born and grew up in Germany, but he now works and lives at the top of a mountain near Santa Barbara, California.

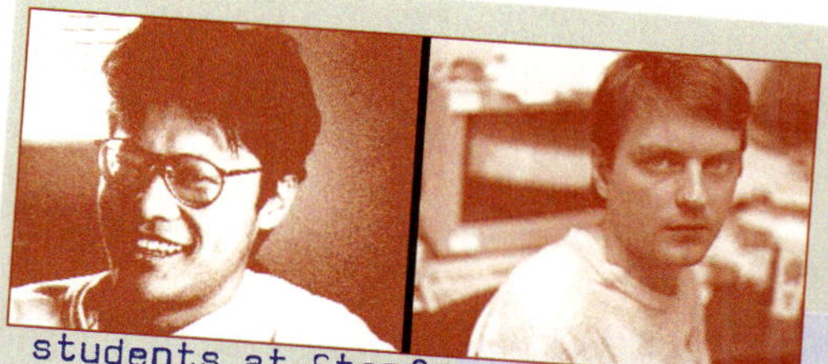

When Jerry Yang and David Filo were students at Stanford in California, they preferred surfing the World Wide Web to studying. In 1994 the two of them started making lists of the web sites they had visited. Then they put their lists on the Internet as "Jerry and David's Guide to the World Wide Web". It became wildly popular. They changed its name to "Yahoo!" and it has since become the Internet's favorite search engine. Jerry and David's Silicon Valley company is now worth a cool $18 billion.

Dina Mohajer was just another cool, young student in Southern California when she decided she needed blue nail polish that would go with her blue shoes. So she made her own. Her friends were crazy about it, so she borrowed $50,000 from her parents to start her own company, "Hard Candy". Soon Hollywood stars like Drew Barrymore, Cher and Antonio Banderas (yes, boys wear it, too!) were buying her nail polish.

FOCUS ON GRAMMAR

Look at A1 again and find the English expressions for these German phrases: 120 000 Fahrzeuge am Tag, 45 Meilen pro Stunde, zweimal in der Stunde. *What do the English phrases have in common?*

→ S 6: 1 (p. 138)
→ P 3, 4, 5

FOCUS ON WORDS Famous sights, famous people

1 *Collect words and phrases for what you can do or see at tourist sights. First look at A1.*

Universal Studios
– feel an earthquake
– fly ...
– ...

2 *Collect words and phrases for what people have done to become successful or famous. First look at A2.*

Kai Krause
– write computer programs
– ...

ACTIVITY Dreamland California

A magazine has asked readers to send in stories, poems, posters, etc. that show California as a place where people can make their dreams come true. Make up an entry for this 'Dreamland California' competition. The photos and information on pages 78–81 could give you some ideas. You can put your entry in your American album.

→ P 9
→ U.S. Mag, p. 109

▶ 3

San Francisco Vietnamese Community News

Meet the Family: This Week – the Truongs

"I loved Vietnam, so leaving made me very sad," says Nguyen Duc Truong quietly. "But I have never regretted it. After the war, life in Vietnam was very difficult. I tried really hard to help my family. But then in 1976 they put me in a work camp. That was the most terrible time of my life. So I am glad I came here to the U.S."

Truong met his wife, Hoa, on the boat to America in 1981. First he worked on a farm in the Central Valley. Then the family moved to the city and he got a job in a laundry. But he lost that job last year.

"I haven't been able to find another job yet because I don't speak English very well. All my friends are Vietnamese, so I don't often talk to Americans."

Hoa Truong works full-time as an office cleaner and sometimes in the evenings in the kitchen of a Vietnamese restaurant.

Their son, Scott, 14, is in high school and would like to study math and computer science in college. This year Scott won a trip to Space Camp Florida. "I had a great time. I met people from all over the U.S. and even from Europe," he says. "It was fantastic!"

→ S 6: 2 (p. 138)
→ F 7

◆◆ **ROLE-PLAY** 'Can you tell me ...?'

Imagine you have the chance to interview one of the Californians from pages 81–83 for your school magazine. Decide which Californian you want to interview, then record the interview or act it out for the class. Write your own role cards, or use the ones your teacher has.

▶ 4

Scott loves visiting his Aunt Phuong and his cousin Jennifer at their modern West Hollywood apartment in Los Angeles. It is so different from his home in San Francisco. And last time something really exciting happened. He wrote to Conchita, his friend from Space Camp, about it.

Hi Conchita,

Just back from Venice Beach with an L.A. story for you. I went there with my cousin this morning. We were about three blocks from the beach when we heard police sirens. The sirens got louder and then two police cars drove past us and round a corner. Seconds later we heard an explosion. We started running and saw the police cars in front of a store. There was a big crowd outside and a police officer shouted, "This is the police. Come out with your hands in the air – real slow."

LISTENING

◆◆ **a** *What do you think happened next? Discuss with your partner.*

b *Now listen to the cassette/CD and find out what happened next.*

→ P 6, 10

▶ 5

'This is your last chance. Throw down your gun and come out with your hands up,' the police officer on TV shouted. Scott laughed as he remembered the scene he had seen months ago in L.A.
Then his father came into the room and told him to go to the bus stop and meet his mother. She was scared of walking home alone because of the gangs in the area.
Scott's father went on, 'It isn't fair that your mother has to work on Tet. Why isn't our New Year a holiday here – like Christmas?'

On the way home from the bus stop fifteen minutes later, Mrs Truong said with a smile: 'I'm so much looking forward to Tet.'
Scott asked his mother why they couldn't just celebrate Christmas, like other Americans. Her smile disappeared. 'We don't celebrate Christmas,' she replied. 'We're Buddhists.'
She told Scott that he visited his aunt and cousin in L.A. too often and was learning too much of their western ways. Mrs Truong loved all 'that old Vietnamese stuff', as Phuong and her daughter rudely called their traditions. She enjoyed making the banh chung for the Vietnamese 'spring festival' Tet. And she was so excited when the children got money in red envelopes for good luck. She even liked the noise of the firecrackers that protected them from evil spirits.
'But this is America, Mom,' Scott said. 'We're not in Vietnam now.'
'That's right, Scott,' his mother answered. 'And you should work hard at being American. But always remember where you come from.'

? *Mr and Mrs Truong are first-generation immigrants. What is life like for them in the USA?*
Scott is a second-generation immigrant. How is he different from his parents?
How is the situation of immigrants in Germany similar or different?

→ P 8, 11
→ U.S. Mag, pp. 110/111

ACTIVITY The American in me

You like watching Hollywood movies, don't you? But there are probably lots of other things from California and the USA that play a role in your life. Think of:
- *what you wear,*
- *what you eat and drink,*
- *what sports you like,*
- *what music you listen to.*

Make a collage in your American album. You can use pictures from adverts.

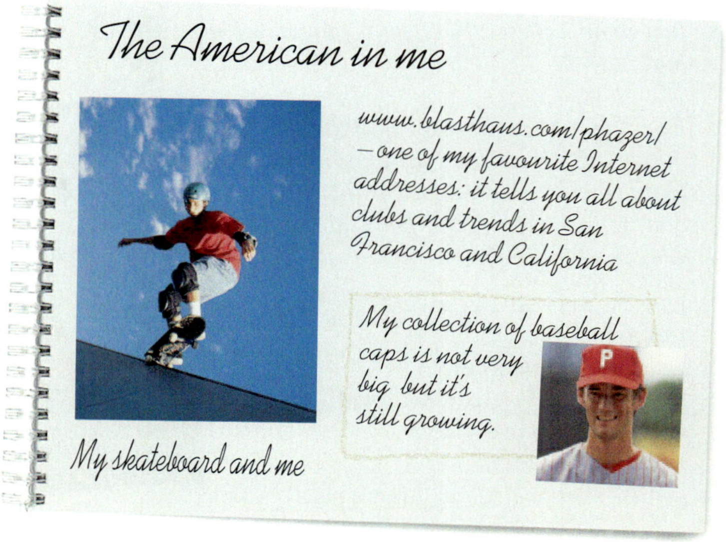

1 **California or Germany – which is bigger?**

a *Compare California to Germany and write down what you think.*

1 Which is bigger?
I think ... is bigger than ...
2 Which is farther north?
3 Which has more people?
4 Which has more kilometres of coast?
5 Which has higher mountains?
6 Which has fewer murders?

◆◆ b *Swap your answers with your partner. Then look at the statistics on page 115 and check your partner's answers. There is one point for each correct answer. Who is the winner?*

Tomales Point, Point Reyes National Seashore

2 **LISTENING** Tourist information

a *Imagine you're travelling in California and see these two photos in a brochure. What do you think you can do or see at Point Reyes?*

b *In your car you hear some tourist information on the radio. Listen to the cassette/CD. Which of your ideas were correct?*

Point Reyes Lighthouse

c *Listen again for the answers to these questions. Take notes on what you find out.*
1 Where is the main entrance?
2 When is the visitor centre open?
3 Who were the Miwok Indians?
4 What happened in 1906?
5 When are the lighthouse steps open?
6 In what weather are they closed?
7 When can you see whales?

d *Use your notes and write some short information for a Point Reyes brochure on the visitor centre, the lighthouse or some other interesting feature of the park.*

❖ 3 **GAME** What's my job?

a *In a group, collect all the words you know for jobs.*

b *Now one student chooses one of the jobs but doesn't tell the others. They must ask questions to find out which job it is. The first student may only answer 'yes' or 'no'. The student who guesses correctly chooses another job.*

Do you work in an office/in a school/indoors/...?
Do you help people?
Do you need English/wear a uniform/...?
Can you help me if I ...?
Would I see you if I ...?
I think you're a(n) ... / Are you a(n) ...?

4 ▶ Half a mile

a *What are the people saying? Complete the sentences and add a phrase from the box.*

> half a bottle • half a mile
> miles an hour • once a day
> vehicles a day • visitors a year

1 'traffic – terrible / only move … last hour'
'The traffic is terrible. We've only moved half a mile in the last hour.'
2 'road signs say – speed limit of 65 …, ha-ha!'
3 'you think – we – enough to drink? / only … of water'
4 'traffic – not always like this / only …, from morning till night'
5 'guidebook says – 520,000 … use this road'
6 'you know – California – 250 million …?'

◆◆ **b** *Choose a phrase from the box below and write three sentences with it. Two sentences should be true and one false. Can your partner guess which is false?*

> half a(n) … • … an hour • once a …
> twice a … • three times a …

1 I've got half an apple in my bag.
2 I can run 200 metres in half a minute.
3 I know someone who has won half a million euros.

5 REVISION As a tourist in L.A. → S 6: 3 (p. 139)

What questions might you need to ask in these situations?

1 You've just bought some postcards in a shop.
Do you sell stamps, too?
2 You've just decided to go on a tour by coach.
3 You would like to go to a show but it's 7 pm already.
4 You'd like to buy a map to the stars' homes.

5 You want to find Schwarzenegger's house but you don't know the way.
6 You want to see Madonna's old house, too, but you can't walk much farther.
7 You don't know the price of the cassette tour to the stars' homes.
8 You need 75 cents for a cold drink from the machine.

❖ 6 GAME On TV or at the movies

Write a description of your favourite film or TV show. Give the same sort of information as in the TV magazine below, but don't give the name of the film or show. Read your description to the class. Can anybody guess the name of the film or the show?

This week's movies on TV

Hostages[1] in L.A. ★★★ (drama) Cheryl Mann, Rod Silver. Cheryl Mann is great as a police officer from the country in this action drama. Gangster Silver has 20 hostages in an L.A. store. When some of the hostages escape, the showdown[2] begins.

[1] hostage ['hɒstɪdʒ] *Geisel*
[2] showdown ['ʃəʊdaʊn] *Entscheidungskampf, Kraftprobe*

7 REVISION California immigrants → S 6: 2 (p. 138)

a *The adverbs and adverbial phrases on the right are all from A3, p. 82. Put them under the right headings. Then try and add more adverbs to each list.*

after the war • full-time • hard • here • in 1976 • in a work camp • in college • in the evenings • in Vietnam • last year • never • often • on the boat • quietly • really (hard) • sometimes • then • this year • to the U.S. • to the city • very • well

Frequency (how often?)	Time (when?)	Place (where?)	Manner (how?)	Degree (how big/hard/...?)
never	*after the war*	*here*	*full-time*	*really (hard)*

b *Read what a student from Scott's class has written about California immigrants. Add the adverbs and adverbial phrases in brackets to the sentences. Be careful with the word order.*

1 For over 150 years, California has welcomed immigrants. (from all over the world)
2 More immigrants live in California than in any other state. (here)
3 Asian immigrants have been coming to this state. (since 1849)
4 They have worked in their new home country. (always – hard – very)
5 They come from many different Asian countries. (today)
6 California's culture is becoming more and more Asian. (slowly)
7 In parts of San Francisco, it's easy to think that you are in an Asian city. (often – really)
8 Some Chinese who have lived there all their lives don't speak English. (still – very – well)

8 ▶ The USA: a quiz on the whole book

a *You've learned a lot about the USA in this English book. But what can you remember? Answer these questions as quickly as you can. All the answers are somewhere in this book.*

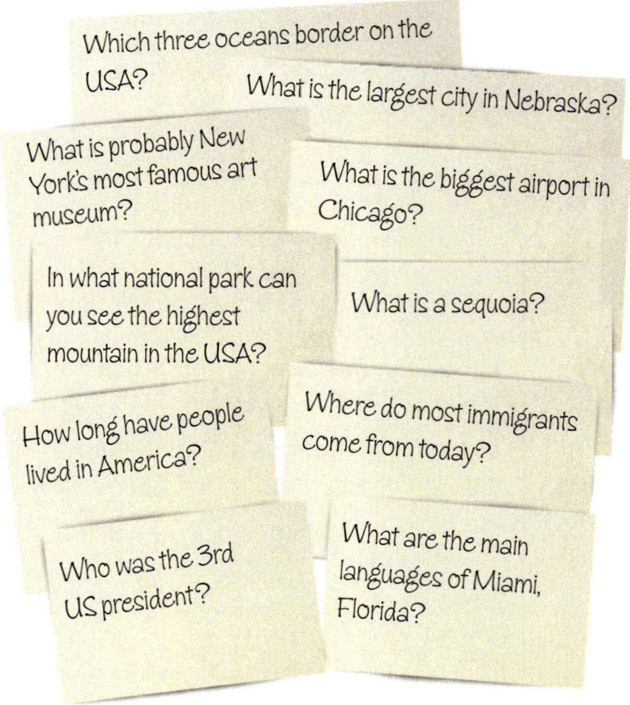

❖ **b** *Make your own USA quiz in a group. On each of 24 cards, write down a question about the USA on one side and the answer on the other. Make four cards for each of these topics:*

- history
- geography
- cities
- nature
- immigrants
- 'mixed bag'

Now swap your cards with another group and play their quiz. You need a dice. Player A throws the dice for a topic. Player B takes a card and asks A the question. A tries to answer it:
- *correct answer = 1 point for A, and A may throw the dice again*
- *wrong answer = B may now throw the dice, player C takes a card, etc.*

Use up all the cards. Who has got the most points at the end?

WORD WATCH

9 WORD LINK

a *Choose a verb from the box for each group of words below.*

dream • have • make • start
visit • win • write

... a book, a program, software, a story
... your aunt, California, a museum, a web site
... a prize, a race, a scholarship, someone's heart
... a company, crying, a family, a race
... a decision, a dream come true, money, someone cry, a speech
... a break, dinner, a dream, a look, something in common
... of being rich, a lot, about your best friend, that you can fly

b *Write seven sentences that include the people or things below.*
For each sentence use a different verb (and phrase) from **a.** *Also use as many different tenses for your sentences as you can.*

1 Kai Krause
2 Hollywood star
3 my mother/father
4 Space Camp
5 high school yearbook
6 film
7 the Internet

Examples:
1 *Kai Krause has written a lot of software.*
2 *I dream a lot about being a Hollywood star.*

10 WORD BUILDING Compound nouns

a *Match the words from the two clouds and make nine compound nouns. Be careful whether you spell the new words as one word, with a hyphen (-) or as two words. Check in a dictionary.*

ghost	+	bag
high		ball
oil		call
phone		kilometre
side		owner
slave		school
sleeping		*town*
square		walk
street		well

ghost town, ...

b *You know two or more combinations for each of the following words. See who can find the most:*

phone + ... • post + ...
school + ...

phone number, ...

... + ball • ... + board • ... + room

football, ...

11 LISTENING Weak forms

a *Some English words don't always have the same pronunciation. Listen to the cassette/CD. How is* from *pronounced in these three sentences –* [frəm] *or* [frɒm]*?*
This letter is from Megan, not for Megan.
This letter is from Scott.
Who is this letter from?

The strong form [frɒm] *is only used when* from *is stressed or comes at the end of a sentence. Usually the weak form* [frəm] *is used.*

b *Decide which of the underlined words use the weak* [ə]*-sound. Then listen to the cassette/CD and check if you were right.*

1 I'll tell you what I'm thinking of. A lovely cup of tea.
2 Can I have an English breakfast? – Yes, you can.
3 Bacon and eggs, please. Oh, and coffee.
4 There's some cola in the fridge. Do you want some?
5 Where's your dad from? – My dad? From Canada.

c *Listen again and practise saying the sentences with the right pronunciation.*

Next Month ... Hollywood

Look at the title of the story and the picture. In your opinion:
- what is the text about?
- what is a 'high school talent night'?
- what are the relationships between the three people in the background of the picture?

→ How to use a dictionary, p. 63

"This is your last chance, Rodney," I said to myself as I looked at the poster on the wall. Today was May 19 and the activity office closed in two minutes. I went into the office and signed my name ... Rodney Suyama.
I want to be the first great Asian rapper – totally new, full of hope, maybe a few lines about the earth, stuff like that. I've written a lot of raps but I just haven't known what to call myself. A rapper needs to have the right name. The name *Rodney Suyama* just doesn't work as a rap name.
Actually, I should mention that I'm not all Asian. I'm half Asian and half Polish. But like a lot of kids who are half white, I don't think of myself as white. Anyway, most people think that my sister Suzanne and I are totally Asian. But Suzanne says an Asian guy can't be a rapper.
"Why the hell not?"
"You have to be black; they're the only guys that are cool rappers."
But my girlfriend wants to help me. Well, she's not exactly my girlfriend. I've been sitting next to Ivy Ramos all year in language class. She always talks to me and we've become good friends. Ivy's dad is Filipino and her mom is black and Ivy is beautiful. And nice, too.
Ivy was the girlfriend of the famous Lavell Tyler, the greatest footballer to play at Franklin High. Guys like Lavell Tyler don't breathe the same air as guys like me. All year Ivy told me about her and Lavell Tyler. Then last month it all changed.

When Ivy came into class, she looked like someone had died and she was crying.
"Ivy ... what's wrong?" I whispered.
"That bitch!" she said.

After class she sat there while everyone else left. "Rodney, will you take me to the pizza place?"

Music, that was what those words were. As we walked out of the building, I put my arm around her.

At the pizza place the whole story came out. She had seen Lavell Tyler in Deleisha Johnson's car. He was kissing Deleisha Johnson.

"I felt like a total idiot! He was kissing that girl in front of everyone. That bitch!"

"That's terrible," I said.

"Then when I saw him before class and told him I'd seen them, he said I should try to understand him and that he just wanted to see us *both*! I told him what he could do with that idea!"

"So you finished it?" I tried not to sound too happy.

"Of course! I want a guy who'll be reliable – you hear what I'm saying, Rodney?"

Reliable Rodney, that's what they call me.

From then on, Ivy and I were together all the time. We were more than friends, although I don't think she thought of me exactly as her boyfriend. She got closest to me when Lavell was in sight. When she saw him, she took my hand and looked into my eyes and smiled as if we were the only two people in the world. The one time she kissed me was when we were walking past him. Ivy stopped, put her lovely brown arms around my neck, lifted her face, and kissed me. Did I worry that this was all a show for Lavell Tyler? No, I did not. I'm not a proud person and I wanted Ivy.

Ivy wanted to help me to find a good rapper name. "What about Havana Banana?" she asked.

"I don't know – sounds like I'm Hispanic. Anyway, banana means you aren't really Asian. Remember?"

"Yeah ... Asian on the outside but white on the inside," Ivy said. "I'm telling you, Rodney, if I was worried about stuff like that, it would make me crazy."

I thought about this for a minute. "Being Hispanic would be cooler than being half Japanese and half Polish." But then I had an idea. "Ivy, why not something with *happa*?"

"*Happa?* Like people who are half Asian?"

"Sure. I think it came from Hawaii, from *happa haole*."

"*Happa haole* means half white, right?"

"Yeah, what do you think? MC Happa? Or DJ Happa? I know – I've got it! Ice Happa."

"That's not bad, Rodney. In fact, it's cool."

"OK, Ice Happa it is."

Back at my house, Ivy and I were in the kitchen with Mom when I had another idea.

"Ivy, why can't you be in the act with me?"

"I thought you had a drum machine."

"I do, I do." I was getting excited. "I'll do the rap and you'll walk up and down with a big drum –"

Ivy was getting interested.

"Yeah, and you'll walk up and down, and there'll be the Japanese flag on one side of the drum and a picture of the earth on the other side."

Ivy got excited. "I'll be like the model in the TV ad! The one in that cute outfit who beats the drum for those veggie burgers! You'll do the rap and I'll carry the drum! We have to do it in front of people before Talent Night," Ivy said, "because we *have* to be good."

"You can." Mom jumped up and looked for something by the kitchen phone. "Look, this came yesterday." AN EVENING OF MUSIC AT THE ASIAN AMERICAN THEATER it said on the front.

"It's a talent show and it's open to everyone," Mom said.

Ivy and I practiced every night for the next two weeks in my garage until we were perfect. And she looked sexy. Very sexy.

"This week the AAT, next week FRANKLIN, next month HOLLYWOOD ... then LONDON! ... TOKYO ... THE WORLD!" Ivy had big plans for us.

The night of the AAT show, we were the fourth act. The presenter was Philip Omori, a local weather guy on TV. He introduced the first act.

"We are proud to present Eric Lew. He will play Max Reger's Cello Suite Number One."

His parents probably gave him a cello when he was a baby – the guy was fantastic. The audience clapped for five minutes. Next Julie Muramoto played Paganini. She was awesome on the violin. The audience went crazy. I turned to Ivy.

"They're all playing classical stuff."

"Be cool, Rodney," whispered Ivy.
After that Martin Wong played a Chopin piece on the piano and everyone clapped for a million years. Then the weather guy said, "Ladies and gentlemen, we are happy to present Ice Happa."
I went up on to the stage, turned on the drum machine and started to rap. Then Ivy came out with the drum with the Japanese flag and the earth. There was a lot of noise from the audience when they saw her. As Ivy walked up and down, she held her head high. I went on rapping:

Don't hurt the earth / you gotta love this planet / don't break it, we can make it.

Then Ivy fell over a cable. *Splat!* Her drum flew through the air and hit me in the stomach. *Bam!* Ice Happa and the veggie queen are on the floor. The audience goes wild, everyone is laughing.
Later, on the way to the car, the Franklin kids say we should do the act for Talent Night.
"That was the funniest thing I've ever seen," says Julie Muramoto. "Great act, you two."

Ivy and I sat in the car after the show.
"Damn."
"What's the matter, Rodney?"
"I wanted to be cool."
"So? No one has to know that."
"Damn, I really wanted to be cool."
Then Ivy came close to me. "Making people laugh is good, Rodney. I like going out with someone who can do that."
Then she started kissing me but stopped suddenly. "You stay reliable, you hear what I'm saying, Rodney?"
Then I kissed her and we stayed in the car in the dark for a long time.
Lavell Tyler was nowhere in sight.

Adapted from:
Jean Davies Okimoto, *Next Month ... Hollywood*

WORKING WITH THE TEXT

1 ▶ What is the story about?

a *Finish these sentence beginnings.*
1 Rodney Suyama went into the school activity office because he ...
2 Rodney wanted to be a great rapper but he couldn't find a ...
3 A month before, Ivy Ramos had been very sad because ...

◆◆ **b** *Write three or four more sentence beginnings (like the ones in* **a***) about the end of the story. Can your partner finish them?*

c *In no more than three sentences, explain what the story is about.*

2 ▶ Who are Rodney and Ivy?

1 "But like a lot of kids who are half white, I don't think of myself as white." (p. 88, ll. 14–16)
Why do you think Rodney calls himself Asian, although he is half white?
2 *What do Rodney and Ivy have in common?*
3 *Explain why Rodney doesn't like the name* Havana Banana.
4 "Being Hispanic would be cooler than being half Japanese and half Polish." (p. 89, ll. 48–50)
Why does Rodney say this? Can you give any reasons?
5 *Explain why Rodney and Ivy think that* Ice Happa *is a good name for him.*

3 ▶ Beyond the text

1 *Why do you think American high schools have talent nights? How might they help students? If your school had a talent night, what act could you do for it?*
2 *Rodney says,* "I wanted to be cool" (p. 90, l. 31). *Ivy says,* "Making people laugh is good" (p. 90, ll. 32/33).
And you? Do you like 'cool people' or 'people who make other people laugh'? Say why.
3 *Find Rodney's rap in the text. Can you write a few more lines? What does your rap sound like?*
4 *Imagine what will happen when Rodney and Ivy do their act at their school's talent night. Write a report about the act for the Franklin High School newspaper.*

→ Translation, p. 121

HOW TO ... give a presentation

1 ▶ A good presentation?

a *Katrin and Sven are giving their class a presentation on an important date in American history. Listen to them on the cassette/CD. How do you like their presentation? Why?*

b *Here are some tips on making presentations interesting and easy to follow. Did Katrin and Sven do these things? Listen again.*

1 Tell the listeners about your topic before you begin.
2 Make sure each of you presents a part.
3 Write difficult and important words on the board and explain them.
4 Tell the listeners that they can ask questions.
5 Speak clearly and loudly, as freely as possible, and not too fast.
6 Use things like pictures, objects, OHP transparencies and maps.
7 Prepare a handout.
8 Read out interesting quotations.

Which four of these tips do you find most important? Why?

2 ▶ Preparing your presentation

Everybody gets nervous when they speak in front of a group. So it is important to prepare your presentation well:

1 Make notes in English, perhaps on cards.
2 Check your English. Or ask a partner to check it for you.
3 Check the pronunciation of difficult words in a dictionary.
4 Practise your presentation alone, perhaps in front of a mirror or with a cassette recorder. Then try it in front of your family or friends.

1 (Sven)
– '49ers'
– Jan. 1848: John Marshall discovered gold nugget at Sutter's Mill, Am. River (map – State Hist. Park)

2 (Katrin)
– JM + John Sutter kept quiet
– news spread fast: SF (small); headline in Cal. Star: 'Gold'
– quotation from museum brochure: 'I found California in another revolution ...'

3 ▶ Body language

What you say in your presentation and how you say it is important. But good speakers know that you also talk with your body. Here is what you should pay attention to:

1 Stand straight and don't move around.
2 Breathe slowly and deeply.
3 Look at the listeners to make sure they understand what you are saying.

REMEMBER

1 Be prepared! Have everything ready before your presentation.
2 Make your presentation clear and interesting.
3 Use your notes but speak freely.
4 It's best if your listeners have to look *and* listen.
5 Pay attention to your body language.

U.S. MAG

Welcome to the U.S. Mag. It's full of articles, stories and photos about life in the U.S.A. You can read it on your own or with your class. You might not know every word in the magazine, but we're sure you'll understand most of it. The most important new words are in the dictionary on pages 166–192.
Have fun with the U.S. Mag!

Includes a CD

inside

AMERICAN

People from Britain and the U.S.A. both speak the same language – English – so they understand each other. But Americans sound different, they spell some words differently, they even use some different words.

DIFFERENT SOUNDS

Back in 1937, the American songwriters George and Ira Gershwin wrote their famous song "Let's call the whole thing off!". Fred Astaire and Ginger Rogers sang it in the movie "Shall we dance?" Listen to the song on the U.S. Mag CD.

You say a-fter and I say ah-fter,
You say la-fter and I say lah-fter.
A-fter – ah-fter,
La-fter – lah-fter,
Let's call the whole thing off.

Now check out the conversations between an American man and a British woman and you'll hear that they say words like last, Tuesday, hot, car or city differently!

ENGLISH IS DIFFERENT!

DIFFERENT SPELLING

The Lyceum Theater is just a few blocks from the Rockefeller Center.

WE TAKE TRAVELER'S CHECKS!

ALL YOUR FAVORITE TV PROGRAMS

Fantastic new color printers!

JUST ORDER FROM OUR EASY-TO-USE CATALOG.

DIFFERENT WORDS

Listen to the U.S. Mag CD and you'll be able to match the British and American words.

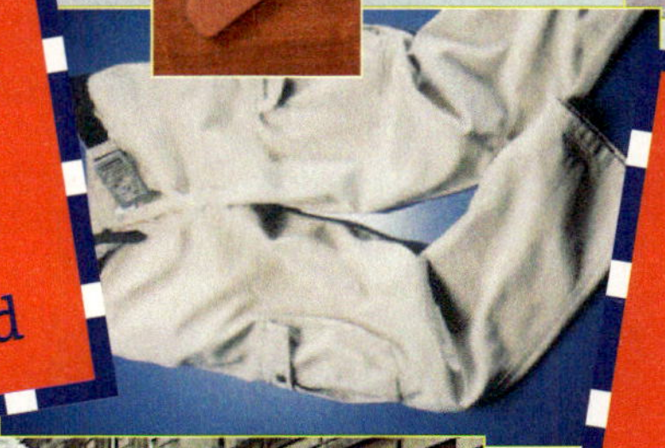

WHAT THE BRITISH SAY

chips * crisps
notice board * pavement
phone box * postbox
rubber * rubbish
timetable * tram
trousers * underground

WHAT THE AMERICANS SAY:

bulletin board * eraser
French fries * garbage
mailbox * pants
phone booth * potato chips
schedule * sidewalk
streetcar * subway

	Monday	Tuesday			
	Maths	French			
	Science	Design &			
5	Science	Technoloc			
ak 11.20 – 11.40					
11.40	Art	Geography			
12.20	Art	English	French	Spanish	English
Lunch 13.05 – 14.05 and Assembly 14.05 – 14.15					
14.15	History	PE	Science	Design &	Maths
14.55	English	Drama	Dance	Technology	Music

space camp

U.S. Mag sent youth reporter Marcie Wayne to Space Camp Florida to find out what it's like to be an astronaut.

The days at Space Camp were all real long. Here's a typical one.

0700	Wake up
0800	Breakfast in the Milky Way Café
0900	Space Walk simulator and Apollo history
1000	Mission training
1300	Lunch in the Milky Way Café
1400	Grow food in space
1500	Build a rocket
1600	Astronaut Hall of Fame
1800	Dinner in the Milky Way Café
1900	IMAX movie on living on Neptune in the future
2000	Return to Habitat
2200	Lights out

The Habitat

The building I ate and slept in for my five days as a Space Camper is huge and made of metal. It looks a bit like a space station. They call it the Habitat.

Weightless in space

The simulators are great. They let you practice walking on the moon, being weightless in space or going out of control in a spaceship.

Mission Control

We did a real space shuttle mission in a simulator. The shuttle took off and went into space. There were lots of experiments to do. Then the shuttle landed again at the end. I was in Mission Control. It was great.

You can walk on the moon!

Building a rocket

We built a rocket and launched it. It went up and up till I couldn't see it anymore. Then the parachute opened and it came back down again.

Yes, Space Camp was just out of this world!

American Poems

GOING INTO SPACE

So I guess they are going into damn
space again soon.
A two and a half billion dollar
camping trip.
Oh sure these three have accomplished
much in their lives.
Their boy scouting will finally
come into a real test.
Why don't they hover their spacecraft
over the reservations
or hover their screaming steel over
the ghettos and see?
But I guess you cannot see poverty
from 28 miles above the earth.

Francis Becenti, 1971

SCIENCE

Science
tells you
Black is the
absence of light
but
your soul
tells you Black
is the light of the
world

Gordon Nelson, 1972

INCIDENT

Once riding in old Baltimore,
Heart-filled, head-filled with glee,
I saw a Baltimorean
Keep looking straight at me.

Now I was eight and very small,
And he was no whit bigger,
And so I smiled, but he poked out
His tongue and called me "Nigger".

I saw the whole of Baltimore
From May until December;
Of all the things that happened there
That's all that I remember.

Countee Cullen, 1925

SAYING YES

"Are you Chinese?"
"Yes."

"American?"
"Yes."

"*Really* Chinese?"
"No … not quite."

"*Really* American?"
"Well, actually, you see …"

But I would rather say
yes

Not neither-nor,
not maybe,
but both, and not only

The homes I've had,
the ways I am

I'd rather say it
twice,
yes.

Diana Chang, 1985

Alaska

In Alaska, there are lots of places you can't get to by road – the capital, Juneau, for example. So you often have to fly. That's why one of every 60 Alaskans has a plane. That's more planes per person than in any other U.S. state. Most of the 560 "airports" in Alaska are small airstrips. Of course, you don't always need an airport – with the right plane you can just land on the nearest lake!

U.S. Mag's quiz

See the State
looks at Alaska

Everybody knows that Alaska is really cool, right? Well, not just cool, it's freezing! Back in 1867, U.S. politician William Seward paid Russia $7.2 million for 586,000 square miles (1.7 million square km). That's only $12 per square mile or $4 per square km! But a lot of people laughed at "Seward's ice-box" and wondered what could be done with this huge, cold place in the middle of nowhere.

Today Alaska is one of the richest states in the U.S.A. But what do you know about it? If you get all the answers to our quiz right and find the magic word, you could win a U.S. Mag T-shirt.

The numbers in brackets tell you which letter of your answers you should use. The magic word is the town near Anchorage where the dog sled race starts.

1 the northernmost town in the state (6)
2 the capital of Alaska (5)
3 the old Russian capital of Alaska (1)
4 the language most Europeans in Alaska spoke at the beginning of the 19th century (5)
5 where a tanker lost millions of liters of oil in 1989 (9)
6 Indian name for the "High One" (5)
7 the most famous dog sled race in the world (5)

How about a short walk with your dog? The Iditarod Dog Sled Race is 1,049 miles (1,688 km) long through some of the coldest and unfriendliest country in the world. But if that's too much for you, there is a junior race for kids, and it's only 130 miles (210 km) long.

Only stuff for tough guys? Not true! Susan Butcher has been the champion of the race four times.

Oil's good side: Oil and gas have brought a lot of money into the state. Oil is carried through the Trans-Alaska pipeline from the oil-fields in Prudhoe Bay to the harbor at Valdez. Over half of the 800 miles (1,300 km) of pipeline was built above ground so that the heat from the pipeline does not hurt the environment.

What!? There are Indians in Alaska? Not just Inuit? That's right. And it's only the Natives of the northwest coast of North America that make totem-poles. If you know how to read these poles, they will tell you stories of a family's history.

Russia, Alaska's neighbor in the west, is only 51 miles (82 km) away – much nearer than any U.S. state. The Russians were the first Europeans in Alaska. St. Michael's Cathedral is in Sitka, the old Russian capital of Alaska.

Oil's bad side: After an accident in March, 1989, over 40 million liters of oil from the Supertanker Exxon Valdez covered hundreds of kilometers of the Alaskan coast. It was a tragedy for the wildlife of Prince William Sound.

On the History Trail with U.S. Mag

Benjamin Franklin's political cartoon showed why the colonies had to come together.

This month:
Where a nation was born

It's time to pack your bags, put on your walking shoes and start on the history trail again. This time we're going to find out how the United States began.

The founders: You've probably heard of the most famous settlers in the U.S.A. – the Pilgrims. They landed their

ship, the Mayflower, on Plymouth Rock (Massachusetts) in 1620 and, one year later, started the Thanksgiving tradition. You might think that these Pilgrims were the first British settlers in North America. Many people think so. But no, they weren't the real founders of the United States – the first had arrived 13 years earlier.

History made in Virginia: The lucky thing is that just a short drive in Virginia will take you on a journey through the history of the British colonies from their beginnings in 1607 until the birth of the United States in 1776. So, let's start …

Next stop:
Williamsburg

It's just a short drive from the first capital of Virginia to the second. Take the bus from the Visitor Center to Colonial Williamsburg and you move back in time. The place still functions as an 18th-century town. Everyone acts as if it's still a day back in the 1770s.

By the time Williamsburg became capital in 1699 the Indians had all gone – pushed to the west or killed by war and disease. Tobacco had made Virginia the richest colony in North America. At first, the owners of the large plantations thought of themselves as British gentlemen. But as time went on, they no longer wanted to be ruled by London and pay British taxes. More and more, they began to think of themselves as Americans. They wanted liberty.

First stop:
Jamestown

In 1607, 104 settlers from Britain – all men – arrived here and named their fort in honor of the English King James I. It was the capital of the colony of Virginia for over 90 years.

Check out the living-history museum at Jamestown. The guides – all in 17th-century costume – will help you experience how difficult life was in early Jamestown. By the spring of 1608, half the settlers were dead. Not a good start!

But more ships arrived with new settlers. They came for gold but found hunger, disease, fire, and war with the Powhatan Indians instead. What kept the new colony alive through these terrible times? Tobacco. Of course, you can't eat tobacco – but you could sell it in Britain and make a lot of money. The first planter to grow tobacco was John Rolfe. He later married the Powhatan princess Pocahontas.

SEVERAL VIRGINIAN PLANTERS PLAYED AN IMPORTANT PART IN THE REVOLUTION AGAINST BRITAIN: HERE ARE THE TWO MOST FAMOUS ONES.

George Washington, commander of the American army, was later the first president of the U.S.A. (1789 – 1797).

Thomas Jefferson wrote the Declaration of Independence in 1776 and was the third U.S. president (1801 – 1809).

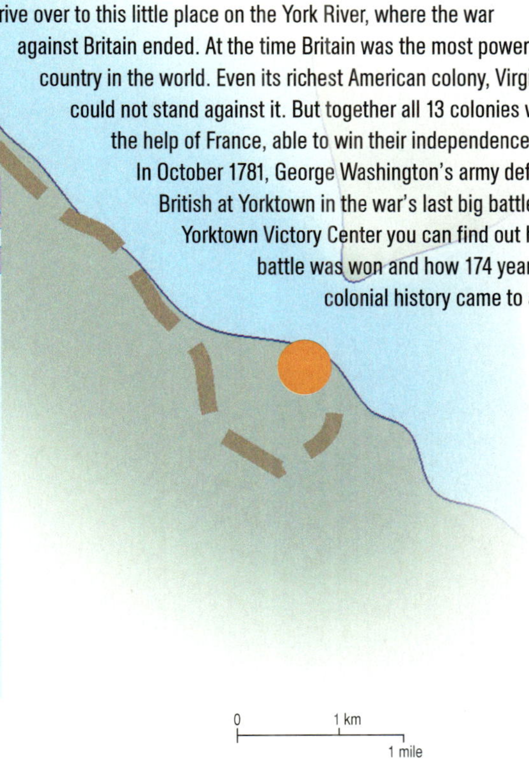

LAST STOP: YORKTOWN

Drive over to this little place on the York River, where the war against Britain ended. At the time Britain was the most powerful country in the world. Even its richest American colony, Virginia, could not stand against it. But together all 13 colonies were, with the help of France, able to win their independence.

In October 1781, George Washington's army defeated the British at Yorktown in the war's last big battle. At the Yorktown Victory Center you can find out how the battle was won and how 174 years of colonial history came to an end.

THE FIRST AMERICAN COLONIES

1 New Hampshire
2 Massachusetts
3 Rhode Island
4 Connecticut
5 New York
6 New Jersey
7 Delaware
8 Pennsylvania
9 Maryland
10 Virginia
11 North Carolina
12 South Carolina
13 Georgia

Many of the settlers hated him, but Captain John Smith did more for the Jamestown colony than anyone else. He was captured by the Powhatan Indians but was saved from death by the chief's daughter, Pocahontas. Smith later became the chief's friend. He made the British "gentlemen colonists" work for food – that's why they hated him!

When Smith returned to England in 1609, he thought the colony was doing well. But without him chaos returned, and in the next winter 440 of the 500 colonists died.

WHO WERE Lewis AND Clark?

You probably know their names, but do you know what they did? U.S. Mag has been finding out about a different kind of trail.

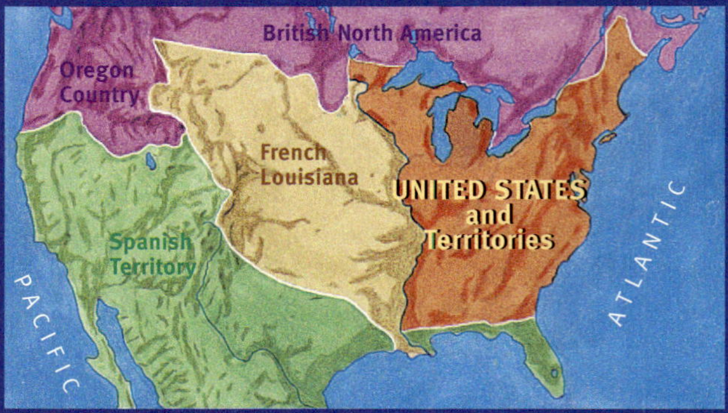

Imagine the U.S.A. without California and Texas, San Francisco and L.A., Dallas and Houston. Two centuries ago these areas were not part of the U.S.A. but belonged to Spain.

And imagine the U.S.A. without Nebraska, New Orleans, and the Missouri River. These were all in a French territory called "Louisiana".

The French leader Napoleon was too busy in Europe to think about the other side of the Atlantic and sold his territory for just over $80 per square km. So, in 1803, the size of the U.S. was more than doubled.

President Jefferson sent his private secretary Meriwether Lewis and Lewis's friend William Clark to explore this new territory and to answer these questions: What is there between the U.S. and the Pacific? Who and what lives there? Does the future of America lie out there?

From 1804 to 1806, the expedition team of fifty traveled for over two years. They labeled, mapped and recorded everything they saw. They met Native Americans, had hard times and happy times. There was only one death, and there was one birth, too.

Listen to the U.S. Mag CD and hear William Clark – as an old man – remembering the expedition.

Follow the red line on the map and you're following one of the greatest adventures in history – a 4,000-mile expedition through the wilderness.
On page 102 is a scene from the team's winter camp for you to record. Or maybe you would like to write and record your own version of "The strangest day of our trip", up in the Rocky Mountains ...

The strangest day of our trip:

Looking for the Shoshoni – no luck!
Must find them (need food and horses!).
Sacajawea says she was kidnapped from here.
Saw Indians, but they ran away (frightened).
Stopped 2 Shoshoni women & gave presents.
Chief Cameahwait came with 60 men – angry!
Women showed presents we'd given them.
Shoshonis followed us to our camp.
We saw their horses – 700 wonderful animals!
Called Sacajawea to translate.
Surprise – Chief Cameahwait is her brother!
Sacajawea laughed and cried
Peace & good talk with Indians ...
Sacajawea wants to stay on expedition – good for us.

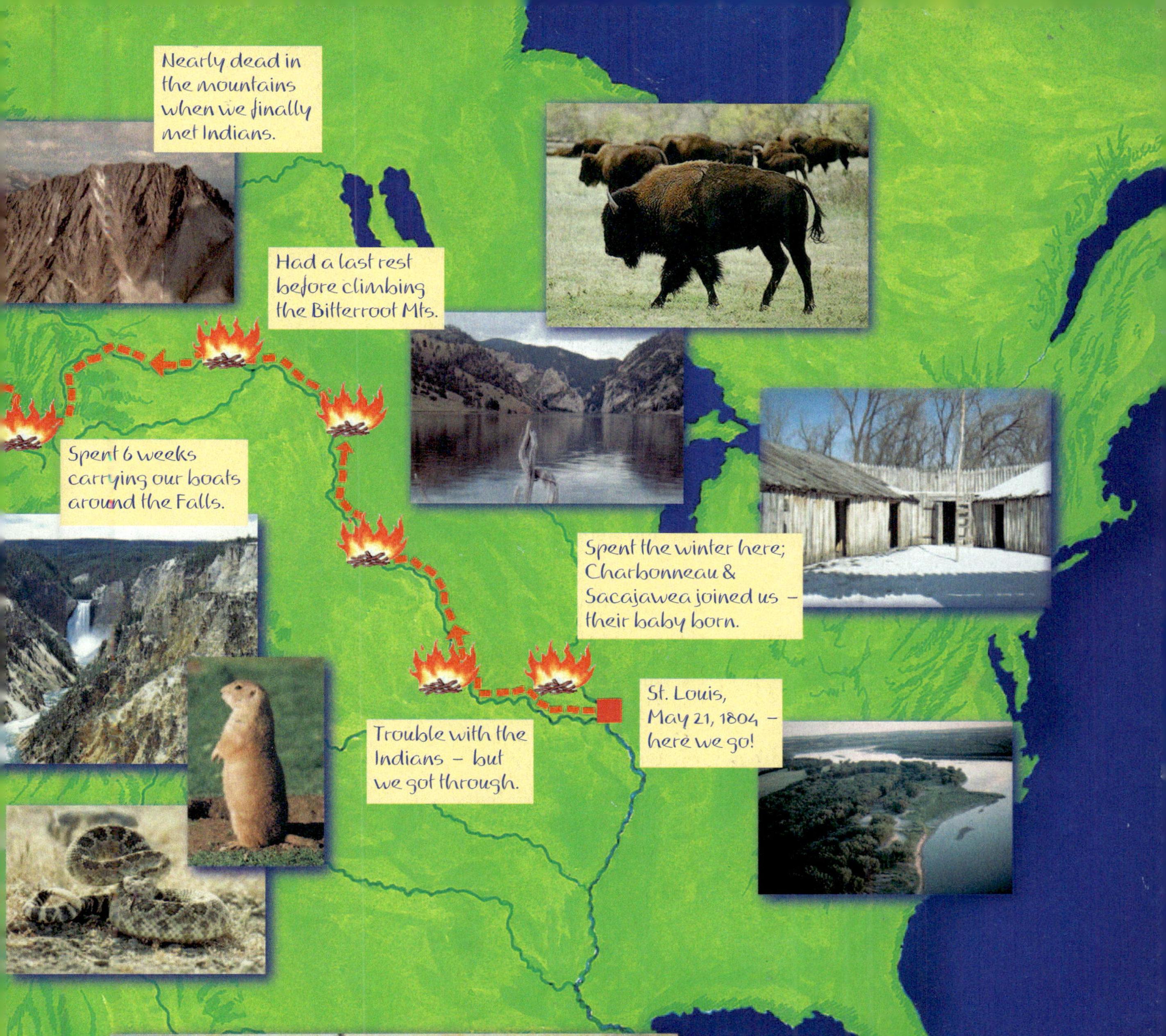

MEMBERS
OF THE EXPEDITION TEAM
Front:
Captain Meriwether Lewis and
Captain William Clark
Back:
Sacajawea, a Native American
interpreter, and
her husband Charbonneau,
a French interpreter

Painting by Frederic Remington
(1861–1909)

Lewis and Clark's winter camp

A RADIO PLAY

Characters: • William Clark • Meriwether Lewis • Charbonneau • Smith, another guide and interpreter • Chief One Eye

• **Clark** Right, have we got everything in the box? One pair of elk's horns, two skeletons of the prairie wolf, a painted buffalo robe from Chief Sucadoha …

• **Lewis** Have you put in the corn too? We must send Mr. Jefferson some corn.

• **Clark** Right, the Indian corn. That should keep him busy. I've told him to plant it in the White House garden.

• **Lewis** He'll do it too, you'll see! So, in the next box, we'll send him … Oh, Mr. Charbonneau, please sit down somewhere! You make us nervous when you walk around all the time. What is the matter?

• **Charbonneau** C'est ma femme, c'est le bébé! C'est trop …

• **Lewis** What's his problem?

• **Clark** It's his wife, remember? She's having her baby today.

• **Lewis** She's been having it all week!

• **Clark** Yes, it's taking a long time. That's what he's so nervous about.

• **Lewis** I think I've got something in my medicine box to help the girl. An old medicine man down the river gave me a powder made from dried snake. He said it helped babies come into the world quicker. I don't believe it myself but she can try it. Here, explain it to him. *Mumbles* I don't know if a woman should be on our expedition.

• **Clark** Oh, but she isn't just any woman, Lewis. Sacajawea is a Shoshoni, you know, from the Snake tribe up in the Rocky Mountains. Charbonneau said she was kidnapped from her people three years ago. She was 13 then.

• **Lewis** Yes, but do you think she will be useful to the expedition?

• **Clark** Of course. Look, when we're up in the mountains after the winter, we'll need horses. And the Snake people have the best horses anywhere in the West. And Sacajawea belongs to that tribe!

• **Lewis** *Sighs* If you say so, she can come along with us. And her baby too! Now then, just put that corn in the box, and we'll put the rest in …

Fade out to packing noises.

Fade in to same.

• **Lewis** Right, that's finished. *Door opens, storm outside.* Hey, close that door, will you, there's a blizzard outside!

• **Smith** Sir! It's Chief One Eye from the village. Says he wants to talk with you.

• **Clark** Chief One Eye? Let him in! We must speak to him. Smith, can you interpret for us? He must tell us more about the route ahead. Bring some brandy and some corncakes. *Now very polite* Chief One Eye, in the name of the Great White Father of the Seventeen States, welcome!

Smith interprets quietly, Chief One Eye answers.

• **Smith** He says he wants to talk about guns. His tribe needs more.

• **Lewis** Clark, we must not give them any more guns. It will make the area unsafe.

• **Clark** Leave it to me. Chief, let us speak about your homeland. It is the Great Falls where you live, isn't it? We will soon be traveling up that water – but can our boats pass the Great Falls?

Smith interprets quietly. The chief laughs and answers.

• **Smith** Sorry, he wants to have some guns before he says any more.

• **Clark** Tell him this: The Great White Father does not want his children to fight. He wants them to live in peace together. They can hunt and they can trade; he likes this. The Great White Father will protect his children.

• **Lewis** *While Smith interprets* Boy, go and fetch that knife with the bone handle from my bags. We don't want Chief One Eye to be angry when he leaves.

• **Smith** He says that if you don't give him guns, he will get them from the French trappers. He wants to know if we are friends.

• **Clark** We are friends, and here is a present to prove it. We want to give him this beautiful knife if he …

He is interrupted by shouts and laughter.

• **Lewis** Order, keep order, men! In the name of God, what is this noise?

• **Charbonneau** Le bébé, monsieur le capitaine. Mon fils est né!

• **Clark** So the powder worked, Lewis! Excuse us, Chief One Eye, but our expedition now has a new member! I think we might have some brandy to celebrate. Chief, may we invite you to our feast? *Smith interprets.* So what's the little one's name, Charbonneau?

• **Charbonneau** Il s'appelle Jean Baptiste.

• **Clark** Don't be silly, man – Jean Baptiste! That's much too long a name for a baby. I'm going to call him, er, something short … Pompy!

• **Charbonneau** Excusez-moi – "Pompé"?

• **Clark** Yes, that's it! Brandy for Pompy!

Everybody laughs, and a fiddle plays up. Fade.

Portrait of Sacajawea on the one-dollar coin

Big City Impressions

U.S. Mag checked out the subway mosaic for you. It really is "out of this world".

★ In the last issue of U.S. Mag, we asked readers to send in pictures and poems that best describe the city they live in.

★ The most unusual entry came from Jenny Jones in Brooklyn: Richard Estes's 1978 painting "Downtown" and Grace Paley's 1985 poem "On the Subway Station".

★ What do you think of Jenny's choice? Write us a letter and say whether you think the painting and the poem go together well or not.

★ Or write your own city poem for us. You could also send a picture of your favorite city, or even draw your own.

★ If we publish what you send, you'll win a U.S. Mag T-shirt.

Grace Paley

On the Subway Station

The child is speaking to the father
he is looking into the father's eyes
father doesn't answer
child is speaking Vietnamese
father doesn't answer
child is speaking English
father doesn't answer
The father is staring at a mosaic in blue and green
and lavender   three small ships in harbor
set again and again in the white tiled
beautiful   old   unrenovated subway
station   Clark Street   Brooklyn

Celebrate!

Like most people, Americans love to celebrate – and in the multicultural U.S.A. there is always a reason for a parade or a party! The Chinese and other Asians celebrate the lunar new year, Mexicans their Day of the Dead, Jewish Americans Hanukkah – and there are lots more. So, how do you make the many different ethnic groups all feel American? Well, public holidays in the U.S. (except for Christmas and New Year's Day) all celebrate important events in American history.

On these days, Americans remember ...

... the black leader who was murdered in 1968	**Martin Luther King, Jr. Day** (3rd Monday in January)
... the birthdays of Presidents Washington and Lincoln	**Presidents' Day** (3rd Monday in February)
... all who have died in wars	**Memorial Day** (last Monday in May)
... independence from Great Britain in 1776	**Independence Day** (July 4)
... the working class, since 1894	**Labor Day** (1st Monday in September)
... Columbus's landing in America in 1492	**Columbus Day** (2nd Monday in October)
... 1620 and how the Pilgrims survived their first winter	**Thanksgiving** (4th Thursday in November)
... all U.S. soldiers who have fought for their country	**Veterans' Day** (November 11)

U.S. Mag asked some New York kids which special days and holidays they liked best.

The holiday I like the most here in NYC is **New Year's**. It's really great because there's a big silver ball on a building on Times Square. During the last minute of the old year, it slowly drops down until it is exactly midnight, then everyone screams and goes crazy. People throw confetti and balloons from all the buildings, and there are fireworks, too. I don't like crowds so I don't go there, but we always watch it on TV. When the ball drops, we scream and go crazy – just like the people on the street. It's fun and it brings everyone together.
Anna (14)

I enjoy **St. Patrick's Day** on March 17th. I'm not really Irish, but everyone's Irish on St. Patrick's Day. Lots of people put on green clothes. Why green? Because it's the color of Ireland, the Emerald Isle. In fact, everything's green on this day: even bagels and beer! And the parade is great, of course. Last year my sister was in the parade with her school band.
Tom (13)

I like fireworks, so I like the Fourth of July – **Independence Day**. In New York City they launch some fantastic fireworks from boats in the East River. I also like the Fourth of July because we always have a big family picnic where I play volleyball with all my cousins and eat tons of hamburgers and watermelon.
Chris (14)

My favorite holiday is **Halloween**. It's the only night of the year when young kids are allowed to go out at night. When I was younger, I loved to dress up in a scary costume and go trick-or-treating – that means going from door to door with my friends and getting candy from everyone. I'm too old for that now, but this year we were allowed to wear costumes to school on Halloween – I was a belly-dancer! We had a party at the end of the day. Oh, and lots of people have shaving-cream fights on Halloween, too.
Emily (14)

I think **Christmas** is my favorite holiday. At my school, most of the kids – including those who are Jewish, atheist or Muslim – get into the "holiday spirit". My favorite thing in New York City at Christmas is the giant Christmas tree (it's really GIGANTIC!) at Rockefeller Center with lights and beautiful decorations. People from all over the world come and visit this tree. There are other reasons why I like Christmas: I get presents and new clothes and the next holiday, New Year's, is only a week away.
Erwin (14)

Before they sit down to eat their turkey and pumpkin pie, millions of people all over America watch the Macy's Thanksgiving Parade on TV, with all the huge balloons of characters like Snoopy and Kermit. It's this parade that makes **Thanksgiving** my favorite holiday, because I live right on the street where they blow up those balloons. This happens on the Wednesday before Thanksgiving, and hundreds of people come to watch. But everyone has to stay behind a police barricade. I can cross the barricade because I live there! I love "my" balloons and the special feeling I get when I think that so many people are looking at them in the parade on Thanksgiving.
Rebecca (15)

Since the early days of the U.S.A., people have gone West for different reasons. And – luckily for us – lots of them have written about their journey.
Travel across the continent with U.S. Mag.

Just six weeks after their marriage, Mary Richardson and Elkanah Walker traveled 2,000 miles through territory that had not been known to whites until Lewis and Clark's expedition (see page 100). 129 days later, they arrived in the Oregon Country to work as missionaries. This is Mary's story of their journey.

Going West, 1838 – a Diary

APRIL 23 Left the States about midday. Baggage on wagons, we on horses, close behind our guide. The prairie is in front of us as far as we can see.

APRIL 24 Rested well on my ground bed in tent. Would feel better if Mr. W. was more polite. God help me to make him happy.

APRIL 25 Cold but not rainy. Rode 21 miles without a break. Argued with Mr. W. He spoke so angrily but became friendly when he saw how bad I felt.

APRIL 27 Some horses have run away. I feel anxious, think that dangers are waiting for us. Every day could be our last. The other travelers do nothing but argue.

MAY 6 Traveled 24 miles: on a Sunday! Very cold, almost like winter. Had no idea that we would have so much wind & cold.

MAY 7 13 miles before lunch, 10 after. Mr. W. sick. My health good. Wish Mr. W. was as well as I am. Real worried that he thinks I cannot be a good wife.

MAY 16 Got up early, made fire, washed clothes all morning. Rode in the wagon. We met Mr. Clark, son of the Clark who went with Lewis, at dinner.

JUNE 10 So much danger. A long journey before me, and where to? Miss my mother & sister. Will I survive?

JUNE 11 Rainy. Water comes into the tent. In morning I thought of my father's farm and cried. We crossed the Platte River in boats made of buffalo skins and the bottom of two wagons. Snow-covered mountains appear.

JUNE 18 Rode with Mr. W. – had not done this for a long time. Camped in a beautiful place.

JUNE 24 Mr. W. preached in morning. 18 listened. We wore Sunday dresses and acted like at home. I think I am quite happy.

JULY 6 Met group of travelers. Their faces were painted: it is said that many white men in the mountains would like to be Indians. Noise in camp all night.

JULY 13 Felt my baby inside me for the first time. Last night a large group of buffalo passed so near we heard them breathe. Rode 16 miles over red rocks and earth. I think I have not felt so weak since I left the States. Passed some snow, ate some of it. Camped with Snake Indians and traded with them.

JULY 16 On reaching the foot of the mountains, we came to an open prairie with tall grass and many flowers. Picked flowers until my tent was up. Find I am slowly falling in love with Mr. W. Each day he seems more kind and I am more & more confident that I will be able to make him happy.

AUGUST 25 Crossed top of the mountains & went down the longest hill I had ever seen. Mrs. Connor had a baby in the evening.

AUGUST 29 Left wagons behind and rode my pony through woods. Arrived at Waiilatpu about 2 p.m. Just as we were sitting down for lunch, the house became full of Indians and we had to stop eating & shake hands with 30, 40 or 50 of them. In the evening we ate a fine dinner of vegetables, fish, bread, butter, cream, etc. Our long journey is over.

Based on: Cathy Luchetti and Carol Olwell, *Women of the West*

Going West, 2000 – a Story in Postcards

June 3

Dear Marcia,
I know we just said goodbye yesterday, but it seems like such a long time. We spent 12 hours on the road today, and now we're in this horrible little place in Ohio called Mitiwanga (can you believe it?) – the motel doesn't even have cable!
I miss Boston – and you!!! – already.
All my love, Gary

June 4

Dear Marcia,
I hate my dad. First he gets a job in L.A., makes me leave my school and the only girl I will ever love, and now he decides not to drive on the Interstate! Says he wants to see more of "our great country", and just takes the next exit. Now we'll be on the road forever. I miss you!
XXXOOOXXX, Gary

Post Card

Marcia Donnelly
1211 Commonwealth Avenue
BOSTON, MA 02167

June 5

Dear Marcia,
We go from stupid little town to stupid little town. Cornfields everywhere. Sometimes we stop at the next best drugstore and eat at the counter! My dad says it's the only way to meet people. But who wants to meet anybody in Iowa??!! I think I'm going to die. But my love for you will never die, my Juliet!
Your Romeo

June 6

My dearest Marcia,
This trip is getting real scary. My dad talks about "where America is still America" all the time. And now my mom is starting to act crazy, too. She wanted to go to Kinderhook – because she liked the name! We'll never get to California this way!!! At the end of our 4th day on the road, we're only in Missouri (I think).
Lots of love, Gary

June 7

Marcia, my love,
Today we saw lots of neat things from the days of the Old West. We even got out of the car and walked along a mile of the old Oregon Trail. It was real hot, so we couldn't go farther than that. We were all happy to get back in the air-conditioned car! But there's a lot of interesting history in "these parts".
Love, Gary

June 8

My dear, dear Marcia,
Our "vacation" is coming to an end. Mom finally told Dad to get back on the Interstate. California, here we come. I know I'm going to hate all the crazy people there! When I'm 18, I'm going to come back to you, my love. Will you wait for me?
Forever yours, Gary

June 10

Dear Marcia,
Sorry I didn't write yesterday – we were kind of busy. We moved everything into the new house. The place is huge, and from my room I can see the Pacific!
I met some other kids from the neighborhood – we're going to have a beach party tonight. Maybe this place won't be so bad. Of course it would be better if you were here …
Much love, Gary

June 17

Hi Marcia,
I'm starting to like the California life-style: get up late, eat an orange off the tree for breakfast, go for a quick swim in our pool, meet friends and cruise up and down Rodeo Drive in our cars. Of course it won't be like this when school starts, but we can still go surfing after school, Chloe says. Chloe is teaching me how to surf. She's real nice and – but this card just isn't big enough to tell you everything!
Your friend, Gary

California

– Where the Earth Never Stops Moving

This January, as every year, Brian Watson remembers January 17, 1994, when the earth below Northridge in Los Angeles moved. "It felt like Godzilla picked our building up, shook it, didn't like his new toy and threw it back down on the ground," he told U.S. Mag. The 6.7-magnitude earthquake killed 60 people and caused damage of more than $20 billion.

An even bigger earthquake hit the San Francisco Bay area in October, 1989, and 62 people died. These were just two of the thousands of earthquakes in California every year. Most are small and nobody notices them. All over the state people are waiting for the "Big One", like the earthquake that destroyed San Francisco and killed 3,000 in April 1906. So if you're going to California this year, here's what you can do to protect yourself in an earthquake:

San Francisco after the earthquake in 1906

DUCK

DUCK down to the floor.

COVER

Take COVER under a desk or table. If you can't do that, take COVER by an inside wall and protect your head with your arms.

HOLD

If you take cover under a desk or table, HOLD on to it and move with it until the earthquake stops.

Only in L.A.

A True Story

Does something about this L.A. school bus tell you the school can't be very good?

Since he was a boy, Larry Waters had always wanted to fly a plane, but he couldn't because his eyes were too bad. Then he had an idea:

"I bought 45 weather balloons. I tied the balloons to a chair and the chair to my jeep. Then I put helium into the balloons and got some sandwiches, beer and my gun. I thought I'd float up fifty feet or so, look around for an hour, and then shoot a few balloons and come slowly back to earth.

Things happened a little differently. When I cut the rope to the jeep, the chair went straight up very fast to 11,000 feet. It was cold and I was scared of shooting the balloons. Then after 14 hours things got worse because I moved close to Los Angeles International Airport. They saw me on their radar and sent a helicopter up. They rescued me. When they pulled me out, the chair went up higher and I never saw it again.

Then, would you believe it, when I got back to earth, the police arrested me and asked me why I'd done it. Well, it's a hobby, isn't it?"

Dream of Being Stars

Since the 1920s **Hollywood** has been a magnet for people with one thought in their heads: *I want to be a star!* A few made it, most didn't. Of course, Dionne Warwick's sixties hit and Neil Young's seventies song – both on U.S. Mag's CD – might not be your style. Write and tell us about any new songs you know about people who went to Hollywood because they dreamed of being a star.

Do you know the way to San Jose?

…
L.A. is a great big freeway.
Put a hundred down and buy a car.
In a week, maybe two, they'll make
you a star.
Weeks turn into years. How quick
they pass!
And all the stars that never were
Are parking cars and pumping
gas.
…
Fame and fortune is a magnet.
It can pull you far away from home.
With a dream in your heart,
you're never alone.
Dreams turn into dust and blow away,
And there you are without a friend.
You pack your car and ride away.
I've got lots of friends in San Jose.
Do you know the way to San Jose?
Can't wait to get back to San Jose.

Dionne Warwick

Don't be denied

…
Well, pretty soon I
met a friend,
He played guitar.
We used to sit on
the steps at
school
And dream of being stars.
We started a band,
We played all night.

Don't be denied, don't be denied
…
The businessmen crowded around.
They came to hear the golden sound.
There we were on the Sunset Strip,
Playing our songs for the highest bid.
We played all night,
The price was right.
…

Neil Young

Across the Wire

Life and Hard Times on the Mexican Border

Every year, hundreds of thousands of immigrants come to live in the United States. Hundreds of thousands more, mainly from Mexico and other Latin American countries, try to enter the country illegally. Luis Alberto Urrea, born of a Mexican father and an American mother, describes his years of work on the Mexican border in his book "Across the Wire". This part (adapted by U.S. Mag) shows what life on the border is like for those Latin Americans who come in search of the American Dream.

At night the Border Patrol helicopters are in the air all along the wire. You can sit in the Mexican hills and watch them herd people across the valley. Take a stranger to the border, and he or she will *see* the show: huge trucks, lights, guns, dogs, people running, Border Patrol officers putting people on buses, and the endless noise of the helicopters. A Dutch woman once told me it all seemed "un-American".

But the Mexicans keep on coming – and the Guatemalans, the Salvadorans, the Panamanians, the Colombians.

The seven miles of freeway nearest the Mexican border is, at times, so full of Latin Americans that it looks like a town square. They walk along next to the wall on the center island of the freeway. If the "illegals" are walking north and a Border Patrol vehicle comes along, they climb over the wall and walk south. The American police officer will have to drive maybe ten miles to get to them. When he does, they go back over the wall and walk north.

It might seem fun when you read about it. But imagine that poverty, violence, natural disasters, or political fear are driving you away from everything you know. Imagine how bad things must be to make you leave your family, your friends, your lovers, your home, your church, the dog, the mountains, your favorite place on the river where you fished and took time to think.

Then you come hundreds – or thousands – of miles across country to Tijuana. You might be lonely, scared, tired, cold, hot, ill, thirsty, hungry. With the other immigrants you go to the bad parts of town. You stay in a little hotel. Or you find your way to the garbage dumps, where you build a little cardboard nest for yourself.

In town the police come after you, street gangs come after you. If you are a woman, the men come after you. They call you "good-looking" and "bitch" and "*mamacita*", and they make kissing sounds at you when you pass.

If you have enough money, you go to one of the *coyotes*. They guide people through the canyons north of the border. You pay them all your money – sometimes it's all your family has saved – and join a group of *pollos* (chickens) behind the *coyote*. A mile east, the famous American Border Fence just stops. To enter the United States you step around the end of it. And you follow your guide into the canyons. If you have your daughters or mothers or wives with you – or if you are a woman – you become scared, because there is so much rape in this darkness. If you have any money left, you try to hide it because you might meet gangs or thieves.

If the *coyote* does not suddenly turn on you with a gun and take everything from you himself, the gangs might. Often the *coyote* will turn and run at the first sight of a gang. What's a group of chickens to him? He's just taking care of business. If the *coyote* doesn't run, the gang will beat him, or they might kill him in front of the *pollos* if they think the immigrants need a lesson.

Now, say you are lucky enough and get past all these dangers, others are still waiting. White racists patrol the border like

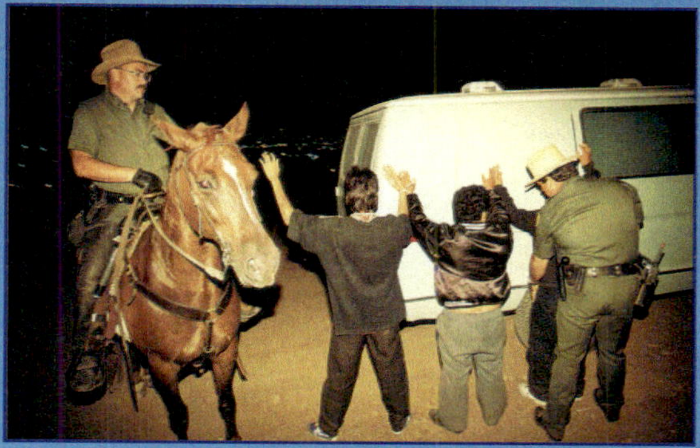

soldiers with radios, flashlights and guns. Rattlesnakes hide under rocks. And, of course, there is the Border Patrol.

They come over the hills on motorcycles, on horses, in huge jeeps. They shout, wear frightening goggles, have guns. They collect you and put you into trucks that take you to compounds, where they load you on buses that take you back to Tijuana. Your *coyote* doesn't care. But for you, things are different. You have been brought back with no place to sleep. You have spent all your money. Perhaps you have been robbed, or beaten by gangs, or separated from your family. You can't eat. As you walk back into Tijuana, the locals laugh at you.

If you were killed, you have nothing to worry about.

1 B

Unit 1

5 ▶ Florida and the USA

a *Look at the table below. The USA information is missing, but your partner has it. Answer your partner's questions about Florida and ask him/her questions about the USA.*

	Florida	USA
capital	Tallahassee	?
size	140,000 square km	?
population	12.9 million	?
Hispanics	c. 2 million (= 15.5%)	?
state bird	mockingbird 	?

A What's the capital of Florida?
B It's …
What's the capital of the USA?
A It's …
How big is …?
B It's …
How big is …?

b *Write down what you have found out about the USA. You can put the information about the USA and Florida in your American album.*

c *Make a similar table for Germany or your home state in Germany. Compare the facts for Germany with the facts you have for the USA and Florida.*

2 B

Unit 2

6 ▶ They want her to listen to them all!

Look at the picture. Everybody wants the girl to do something. Answer your partner's questions.

A What does her friend want her to do?
B She'd like her to go to the cinema with her.
What is her mother asking her to do?
A She's asking her to …

Now ask your partner what the people in the box want/would like/ are asking the girl to do.

mother • father • dog • boyfriend

Unit 2

B 2

ACTIVITY (p. 25)

You and your partner have different information about four of the animals in Denali. Listen to what your partner tells you about them and take notes. Then read your information, shut your book and tell your partner what you know about the animals.
Use your information and notes and write in your American album about one of the animals.

Some animals of Denali

◀ Moose
Moose are not herd animals. Bulls may live alone or in groups of three or four. The young are born in spring. At this time of year, be careful. A moose that is protecting its young can be very dangerous.

Caribou ▶
Caribou travel in groups but the numbers of the Denali herd have changed a lot in the last 30 years. Today groups of 20 or more may be seen from the park road. Years ago it was thousands.

◀ Wolf
Wolves are not seen often. In winter, they usually hunt in packs but they can be seen alone, too. If you see a wolf, you're a very lucky person.

Grizzly bear ▶
Grizzly bears are seen all over the park. Mothers usually have two young, sometimes one or three. They are very dangerous when they are protecting their young.

Unit 3

B 3

10 ▶ Make a crossword

a *Partner A will read you four clues. Listen to them and choose the right words from this list. Write them down.*

colony • honour • independence
plantation • planter • printout • Virginia

Now read clues 5–8 to your partner.

Clues for partner A
5 a plant which is smoked in cigarettes
6 a person who lives in a colony
7 the top person in a British colony
8 the blacks who had to work on 'King' Carter's plantations

Answers: 5 *tobacco* 6 *colonist* 7 *governor* 8 *slaves*

b *With your partner try to make a crossword with the eight correct words. (Letters next to or above each other must all be part of a word.)*
Which team can make the crossword first?

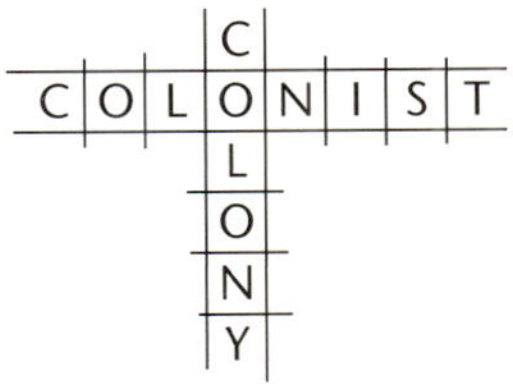

ACTIVITY (p. 53)

Here is some information about New York City. Look at the map and read the text below. Find out:
- *What are the names of the five boroughs and where are they?*
- *How many people live in each borough?*
- *What special things can you see there?*

For the things you can't find out, ask your partner.

New York City is made up of five boroughs. The Bronx is north of Manhattan, Staten Island is south. 1.2 million people live in the Bronx. There's a lot to do there at the weekend. You can go to the zoo or watch a baseball game at Yankee Stadium. Less than half a million people live on Staten Island and there's still a lot of countryside there. The most famous thing about this borough is the ferry that takes you to it, because it goes past the Statue of Liberty and you have a fantastic view of Manhattan and sights like the Empire State Building.

3 ▶ A tour of New York

When Daniel or Josh have visitors from out of town, they usually show them the sights. Look at the list on the right and answer your partner's questions about Daniel's tour of New York. Be careful – some place names need the definite article, some don't.

Where Daniel takes his visitors
1 Empire State Building
2 Statue of Liberty
3 Chinatown
4 Lincoln Center
5 Central Park
6 Broadway

Now complete sentences 1–6 about Josh's tour of New York. Ask your partner.

1 First Josh goes to …
2 Next he shows his visitor …
3 They always have lunch in …
4 They sometimes sit in …
5 They usually walk down …
6 In the evening they go to …

B Where does Josh go first?
A …
B What does he show his visitor next?
A …

Finally, find all the places on the Manhattan street map at the back of the book.

Unit 5

B 5

1 **GAME** A quiz on Nebraska

a *Your partner will ask you questions about Nebraska. Give him/her answers 1–4 on the right to choose from. (The correct answers are underlined.)*

A What's the population of Nebraska?
B It's 1.66 million or 2.66 million or 3.66 million. Which is correct?
A I think it's …
B No, try again./Yes, that's right.

1 a) 1.66 million b) 2.66 million c) 3.66 million
2 a) Bismarck b) Omaha c) Lincoln
3 a) Marlon Brando b) Madonna c) Fred Astaire d) Henry Fonda
4 a) farming b) making films c) making machines

Now it's your turn to ask your partner questions 5–8. Guess which of his/her answers is correct.

5 How many Nebraskans – in towns?
6 population – biggest town – Nebraska?
7 US president – born – Omaha?
8 famous black American – born – Omaha?

b *Write all the correct answers into your American album.*

Unit 6

B 6

ACTIVITY (p. 80)

You and your partner have got different information about Bodie State Historic Park. Answer your partner's questions. Then ask him/her these questions and take notes on the answers.

1 What was the exact date of the discovery of gold in California?
2 What was the special name for the people who came to California in 1849?
3 How many people lived in Bodie?
4 How many of the town's old buildings are still there?

Bodie State Historic Park

When James Marshall found gold in California in 1848, he started the Gold Rush. The greatest numbers of people came in 1849. It was ten years later that somebody found gold in Bodie, and it soon became a busy gold-mining town. In 1882, when there was no more gold, everybody left. Fires destroyed a lot of the town. Then everyone forgot Bodie until it became a State Historic Park in 1962.

Now write a new text with all the information you have.

1 ▶ **California or Germany – which is bigger?**

	California	Germany
size	411,060 square km	356,733 square km
position[1]	c. 32°–42° N[2]	c. 47°–55° N
population	c. 32 million	c. 82 million
kilometres of coast	2222 km	1975 km
highest mountain	Mount Whitney (4418 m)	Zugspitze (2962 m)
murders in 1997	8.0 per 100,000 people	1.4 per 100,000 people

[1] position [pəˈzɪʃn] *Lage* [2] 32°–42° N = 32 to 42 degrees north *32 bis 42 Grad nördlicher Breite*

REVISION

You don't know all the words on these four pages. But you'll find them in the dictionary on pages 166–192.

AFTER UNIT 2

1 ▶ Glen's photos → S 3: 1 (p. 129)

Glen is showing a new friend some photos. Complete his sentences with the simple present or present perfect of the verbs in brackets.

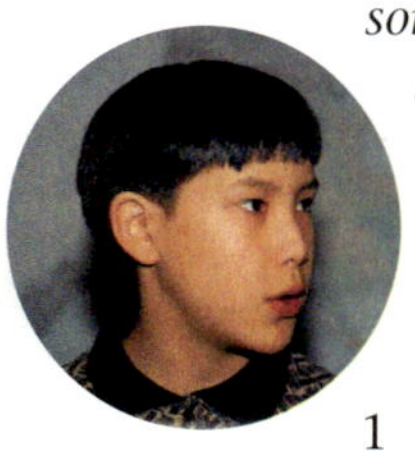

1 That's my dad. He (work) as an engineer on the oil pipeline. My parents (be) divorced for more than five years now.
2 Here's my mom. She (live) in Anchorage, too.
3 Here's a picture of my aunt in Barrow. I (not see) her since last summer.
4 That's my sister Amy with my aunt. She (go) to Barrow every year. She went whaling there last spring. The Inuit still (hunt) whales but I (always hate) whaling.
5 That's me and some friends at Space Camp. I (write) to them all since our time in Florida. They all (live) in different parts of the USA. Or abroad.

2 ▶ Remembering the *Exxon Valdez*

Complete the text. Put in who, which *or* whose, *but leave them out if you can.*

Everybody in Alaska remembers the name of the oil tanker ... caused the biggest oil disaster in U.S. history: Exxon Valdez. But few still know the name of the captain ... ship hit the rocks that March night in 1989: Joseph Hazlewood. In Prince William Sound there is a red buoy ... shows where the tragedy began. The fishermen ... work in the area call it *Hazlewood's Stick*. "It's not something ... people here can easily forget," said one of them.

Visitors ... come to the area now, more than ten years after the accident, cannot imagine what a disaster it was. The water ... they travel through now looks so wonderfully clean. But, as scientist Stan Senner says: "The ecosystem ... is there today is not the ecosystem ... we had before the disaster."

CHECK YOUR ENGLISH Prepositions

English prepositions are often different from the German ones. That's why it is better to learn them as part of a whole phrase.
In a copy of the text on the right, find and correct the nine mistakes. The first one is shown.

TIP!
What sort of mistakes do you often make? Make a list and read through your text for every sort of mistake you make. The first time only check the spelling. Then read it again and check the verb forms. Then read it again and check the prepositions, etc., etc.

I'm an astronaut by NASA and since six months I've been living on the new space station in the near of the moon. I've just returned from my most exciting trip. We went to Jupiter with space shuttle. Of course spaceships can't land on Jupiter, so we just flew around it. But we landed on one of the planet's moons, Io. It's a fantastic place. I'm waiting on my parents in the moment. They're coming to a visit. They've been a bit lonely since I don't live by them any more. They'll love the photos I took from my trip.

AFTER UNIT 3

1 ▶ Virginian plantations

Use the notes and write about plantations in Virginia. Use passive forms where you need to.

1 colony of Viginia – keep alive – tobacco plantations
The colony of Virginia was kept alive by its tobacco plantations.
2 black slaves – bring from Africa + sell to planters in Virginia
3 on Virginian plantations – slaves – do all the work
4 tobacco – grow for sale / pick – slaves – then load onto ships
5 tobacco – take to Britain – where sell
6 goods – plantations need – bring from Britain or make – slaves
7 three of first four US presidents – have plantations in Virginia
8 some of their plantation houses – can still visit today
9 Monticello – be Thomas Jefferson's home for almost 60 years
10 slave quarter there – call Mulberry Row

2 ▶ The life of a slave → S 3: 1, 2b (pp. 129–131)

Complete the sentences with the correct forms of the words in brackets.

1 Eve (belong) to the Randolph family in Colonial Williamsburg.
2 She (be) one of their most valuable slaves because (work – quick).
3 The material she (make) (use) for clothes for the Randolphs' slaves.
4 Eve (hate – work) 14 hours every day, so she (take) the chance of (win) her liberty.
5 During the War of Independence, 1775–83, the British governor (promise) he (give) slaves their liberty if they (fight) for the British. Eve was one of these slaves.
6 By 1780, Eve (return) to Williamsburg and (live) with the Randolphs again.
7 Later, Mrs Randolph (write) that she (sell) Eve and (use) the money she (get) in order (buy) two new slaves.

CHECK YOUR ENGLISH Verb forms

Read the text on the right twice. First just find out what it's about. Then, on a copy of the text, find and correct the 11 mistakes in verb forms.

Choose the correct form of the cartoon caption:
'(We're/We'll be) glad when he (starts/will start) walking.'

My most interesting relative is my Aunt Beate. She lives in the U.S.A for nearly ten years and work there as a reporter.
After university she leaved on a world trip. On that trip, she has found a job in Australia, where she stayed for three years. She was working as a teacher there when she was meeting Uncle Ron. After Uncle Ron was kill in an accident, Aunt Beate returned to Germany but she didn't came back to our town. She was always wanting to work in radio, so she got a job at a radio station in Hamburg. Three years later, she has moved to San Francisco.
Now she says she can't imagine to live in Germany. That's why I visit her in San Francisco next week!

1 ▶ She said, he said → S 3: 2a, b, e (pp. 130–132)

Imagine you met these two kids at a party. Tell a friend about them.

I've never been to New York City but I'm going next week. I'm staying with my pen-friend in Manhattan. He visited me in London last year. I'll spend two weeks with his family in their apartment near Central Park. I can't wait to see all New York City's sights and lights.

I've always lived in New York. My parents came to the Barrio in Harlem 20 years ago. They grew up in Puerto Rico. I visited my family there last winter. You won't find better beaches anywhere! It was fantastic to get away from the snow in the city. I want to buy a house and live in Puerto Rico.

I met this girl from London. She told me/said that she had never … She added that … / She explained …

2 ▶ Famous New Yorkers

Use the words in brackets to complete the texts correctly.

Some of the famous people (which/who) (make) New York such a colourful place were first-generation immigrants or visitors.

Irving Berlin (1888–1989), born Israel Baline in Siberia, (grow up) in Manhattan and later (write) *White Christmas*, one of the (popular) songs of all time.

Andrew Carnegie (1835–1918) (be born) in Scotland but (become) one of America's (famous) industrialists. His home (now use) as a museum.

John Lennon (1940–1980), of the *Beatles*, (murder) outside his home (in the Dakota Building – in 1980 – near Central Park).

Dylan Thomas (1914–1953), the Welsh poet who (drink) himself to death, (spend) his last years at the Chelsea Hotel. He died (in 1953 – in New York).

CHECK YOUR ENGLISH

Adjectives and adverbs

Before you check the text on the right, think about these questions.

- *What sort of words do adjectives and adverbs describe?*
- *How do you make adverbs from adjectives? What are the exceptions?*
- *Do you use an adverb or adjective after verbs like* look, feel*?*

Now correct the six mistakes in a copy of the text on the right.

I met a boy at a party last night. He looked really coolly with his beautiful brown eyes and long dark hair. Even his clothes looked well on him. You can't say that about many boys! Anyway, when we talked, I found out how arrogant he was. He spoke in a loudly voice so that everyone would hear. His parents own a city boutique. That's why he's able to dress so fashionable. He told me about his expensive holidays and how good he plays tennis. He didn't stop talking and didn't let me say a word. In the end I felt so tiredly, I just left him there. I'm not usually unfriendly like that.

TIP!

Swap what you have written with a partner. You see mistakes more quickly in somebody else's texts. Correct the mistakes and explain to your partner what was wrong.

AFTER UNIT 5

1 ▶ What did they want to know?
→ S 3: 2b, c, e (pp. 130–132)

How did Nancy and J.D. report their parents' questions to each other?

1 'Was there really band practice after school, Nancy?'
2 'Did you lie to us?'
3 'What were you really doing?'
4 'How did you get there?'
5 'Who went with you?'

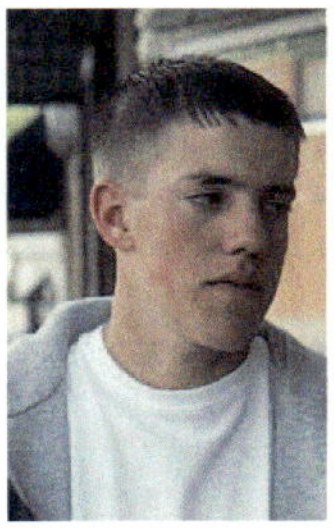

1 'Why have you been so quiet, Jimmy?'
2 'Is anything worrying you?'
3 'What do you think of this "Contract for Life"?'
4 'Can we discuss it with you?'
5 'Will you sign the contract now?'

1 My parents asked me if there had really ... *2 Then they wanted to know ...*

2 ▶ Country boy
→ S 3: 1 (p. 129), S 4: 2 (pp. 134/135)

a *Complete this paragraph about life in Nebraska. Use the present perfect or simple past of the verbs in brackets.*

Trevor Wills, 35, (live) all his life on a farm. He (never want) to live in the city. Last weekend, he (go) to Broken Bow, a town of only 4000: 'I (hate) it,' he (say). All Trevor's friends from school (leave) the small town they (grow up) in. 'My sister Nicola (move) to Lincoln a year ago. She (be) the last'. A company in North Platte (offer) Trevor a job a few weeks ago. But he (not take) it, even though the farm (lose) money in the last few years. But that (happen) several times before. Then it always (get) better afterwards.

b *Complete Trevor's sentences. Use* if*-clauses.*

1 get good rain – make money next year
If we get good rain, we'll make ...
2 but beef prices stay low – life be hard
3 son come home for Christmas – it make his mother happy
4 move to the city – die
If I moved to the city, ...
5 not so cold in winter – more people stay
6 sell the farm – not have to work again
7 take that job in North Platte – make a lot of money
If I'd taken that job ...
8 leave the farm – never meet my wife
9 be born in New York – never know this paradise called Nebraska

CHECK YOUR ENGLISH Word order

Word order in English sentences is often different from German. In the story on the right there are five mistakes in word order. Correct them and say why the word order is wrong.

TIP!
You can practise grammar and vocabulary like this:
Find a text in English. Copy it but leave a gap for every 5th or every 7th word. (Your partner should do the same.) Now swap your texts and try to fill in the gaps.

We had to interview some English-speaking people on video for a project. So we took the bus one afternoon after school to Tegel Airport. While we were waiting for passengers who looked English, I turned and the video camera hit the woman who next to me was standing. I do often this sort of thing. The woman was very polite about it. Later, my friend Lisa said, 'Nina Hagen you don't like, I know – but you didn't have to beat up her like that!' I hadn't recognized Nina Hagen without her make-up!

◦ TRANSLATION English-German

When you are translating from English, it is important to be as exact as you can – but you must be careful to write good, correct German, too.
These four steps can help:

1 *First, read the whole text and find out what it is about.*

2 *Then do a rough*[1] *translation. (Use a dictionary if you don't know a word.) Only write on every second line so you can correct your work later. Don't translate word for word – always look at whole phrases or sentences.*
Highlight[2] *the problems or leave gaps*[3].

3 *Now look at the problems again. Remember:*
- *Some English words have more than one German meaning.*
  pass vorbeifahren; herüberreichen; *Prüfung* bestehen
- *Watch out for 'false friends'.*
  brave tapfer (*not:* ~~brav~~)
  map Landkarte (*not:* ~~Mappe~~)
- *You sometimes have to use a different type of word.*
  I'm hungry. (*adjective*) Ich habe Hunger. (*noun*)
  I prefer dancing. (*verb*) Ich tanze lieber. (*adverb*)
- *German phrases often have different collocations*[4].
  Take a break. Mach mal Pause.
  Welcome to … Willkommen in/bei …
- *English and German word order is often different.*
  Go home now. Geh jetzt heim.
- *You sometimes have to use a different tense or grammatical structure*[5].
  I'll do it later. Ich mache es später.
  I want you to go. …, dass du gehst.
- *Decide whether you translate proper names*[6] *(like buildings, e.g.* **World Trade Center***) or leave them as they are.*

4 *Work on your translation until the German really sounds good. It helps if you read it out loud (or if someone reads it to you).*

→ How to use a dictionary – Part 2: English-German, p. 63

AFTER UNIT 2

1 ▶ Inupiat basketball

An extract from the book The Last Light Breaking: Living among Alaska's Inupiat Eskimos *is going to appear in a German magazine. Can you translate the following passage?*

In just a few years the new gym with its basketball court has become the center for the young of the village, just as the church is for elders. Many students arrive at school a half hour early so that they can shoot baskets. After school there is an hour and a half of basketball practice. After practice the kids walk home, eat supper, do a little homework, and head back for their scheduled hour in the gym. At precisely 8:00 p.m. they're on the floor. At 7:30 the next morning, a handful of the faithful are out there again.

Hat just hier beide Male die gleiche Bedeutung?

Fällt dir etwas Besseres als „es gibt" ein?

Handelt es sich hier um Studenten/-innen?

Gebrauch des Artikels im Englischen und im Deutschen?

„Schießt" man im Deutschen Körbe?

„Basketballübung"?

Schedule *heißt „Zeit-, Stundenplan". Und* scheduled?

Hat dies etwas mit Köpfen zu tun?

Was kann man statt „die Treuen" sagen?

„Fußboden"?

[1] rough [rʌf] *roh, grob* [2] (to) highlight ['haɪlaɪt] *markieren, hervorheben* [3] gap [gæp] *Lücke* [4] collocation [ˌkɒlə'keɪʃn] *Kollokation (Verbindung, die ein Wort mit anderen Wörtern eingeht)* [5] structure ['strʌktʃə] *Struktur, Konstruktion* [6] proper name [ˌprɒpə 'neɪm] *Eigenname*

AFTER UNIT 4

2 ▶ The Empire State Building

The following excerpts are from the Dorling Kindersley Travel Guide to New York. Can you translate them for German tourists who don't speak English?

Although it lost its title as the world's tallest building to the World Trade Center in the 1970s, the Empire State is still New York's most famous skyscraper, a symbol of the city all over the world. Construction began only weeks before the Wall Street Crash of 1929, and by the time it opened in 1931, space was so difficult to rent that it was nicknamed "the Empty State Building".

Sollte man diesen Gebäudenamen übersetzen?

Die Wall Street ist das Finanzzentrum New Yorks. Der „Börsenkrach" führte zur Weltwirtschaftskrise.

Als ein Wort übersetzen.

„Mieten" oder „vermieten"?

Verwende eine Satzkonstruktion mit „es".

Verstehst du das Wortspiel? Kann man es auf Deutsch wiedergeben?

Lightning strikes

The Empire State is a natural lightning conductor and is struck up to 500 times a year. The outside deck is shut during storms, but it is safe to view from inside.

Wie übersetzt man die Wendung a year *hier?*

Was heißt storm *außer „Sturm"?*

„Deck" sagt man nur bei Schiffen. Welche Übersetzung passt hier?

Hier solltest du freier übersetzen.

AFTER UNIT 6

3 ▶ The Bold and the Beautiful – an American TV series

The police are asking Sally Spectra, her daughter Macy Forrester and Macy's friend Dylan about some stolen designs. Translate the script[1] for German television („Reich und schön").

MACY Mother, this is harassment. They can't prove that we stole any designs. My God, I am a Forrester. Why would I steal from my husband's company?

COP 1 We didn't say you were involved.

MACY No, just my mother. Now you listen to me: we are trying to run a business here, we don't have time … for this foolishness. So unless you can show me some proof that we did this, I'm asking you to leave!

COP 1 Look … we're only …

MACY Proof … gentlemen … where is it? You don't have any. I suggest you inform your superior that if this continues they can expect a lawsuit from Spectra … and from Forrester. Now good day, gentlemen.

COP 1 Let's go. We may be back.

MACY Bring a warrant or you're not going to be let in the gate. – Do we still have those Forrester designs?

DYLAN They're in the safe.

MACY Burn them.

Wer ist hier mit they *gemeint?*

„Erwarten" passt nicht so recht.

Was braucht die Polizei, um jemand verhaften zu können?

Das ist eine Aufforderung zuzuhören.

„Stehlen von"? Oder geht es auch ohne Präposition?

Welche Bedeutung von run *passt hier?*

You + Imperativ drückt einen barschen Befehl aus.

[1] script *Drehbuch*

INTERPRETING[1]

When you interpret, you help people who don't speak the same language to talk to each other. Or you explain something you hear or read to someone who doesn't understand it. You don't have to know all the words or interpret everything – you just need to give people the most important information.

If you don't know how to say a German word in English, try to get around the problem.
Example: Verbundfahrschein – *a ticket that you can use on trains and buses in and near a big city*

1 ▶ Manatees[2]

You are on holiday in Florida with your parents. Today you are all in a boat at the start of a snorkelling[3] tour to see manatees. Your parents haven't used their English for a long time, so they find it hard to understand the tour guide. Tell your parents what the tour guide says and answer their questions.
Then listen to the cassette/CD and compare what the girl says with what you said.

GUIDE OK, everybody, I'm going to tell you a little bit about the do's and don'ts of manatee watching. So if you could all come over here, please.
MOTHER Was sollen wir machen?
YOU Zu ihr hingehen. Sie will uns sagen …
GUIDE Now, this tour is about manatee watching. Watching is the important word. And the first rule is 'look, don't touch'.
FATHER Was sagt sie?
YOU Wir sollen …
GUIDE This is a snorkelling tour. And the best way to see manatees is to stay on the surface[4] of the water and watch them from a distance.
FATHER Wie, sagt sie, kann man die *Manatees* am besten sehen?
YOU …
GUIDE We'll all see more if you enter the water quietly and make as little noise as possible.
YOU …
GUIDE A lot of noise will make the manatees leave.
YOU …
MOTHER Ach so.
GUIDE And please don't feed the manatees. Human[5] food is bad for manatees And it is dangerous for them if they always associate[6] people with food.
MOTHER Was sollen wir nicht machen?
YOU …
FATHER Und wieso nicht?
YOU …

2 ▶ In Wuppertal

You are a visitor on a guided tour of Wuppertal. There is an American in the group who asks you for help, because he cannot understand the tour guide.

Listen to the cassette/CD. When the teacher stops it, try to interpret for the American visitor. When it starts again, compare what you said with the version on the cassette/CD.

[1] interpreting [ɪn'tɜːprɪtɪŋ] *(das) Dolmetschen* [2] manatee [BE: ˌmænə'tiː; AE: 'mænətiː] *Seekuh* [3] snorkelling *Schnorcheln*
[4] surface ['sɜːfɪs] *Oberfläche* [5] human ['hjuːmən] *menschlich, für Menschen* [6] (to) associate [ə'səʊʃieɪt] *(gedanklich) verbinden*

3 ▶ On the train

You are on an ICE train from Bochum to Düsseldorf. Try to interpret for the ticket inspector[1] and a foreign passenger. Complete this dialogue.

TICKET INSP. Die Fahrausweise, bitte. – Nein, das ist keine ICE-Fahrkarte. Die hier gilt nur für den Verbund.
WOMAN Sorry – no Deutsch.
TICKET INSP. Er, the ticket, er … she …
YOU Kann ich vielleicht helfen?
TICKET INSP. Ja, bitte. Kannst du der Dame sagen, dass dieser Fahrschein nicht im ICE gilt?
YOU Er, I'm sorry, but …
WOMAN Oh – but I bought it from a ticket machine. It said *Düsseldorf* – so I pressed the button and paid for the ticket. I don't understand what's wrong.
YOU Sie sagt …
TICKET INSP. Ja, das tut mir Leid, aber sie hat einen Verbundfahrschein. Sie muss eine ICE-Fahrkarte kaufen. Macht – Moment mal – 16 Euro.
YOU …
WOMAN Well, why don't I pay the difference between my ticket and the ICE ticket?
YOU …
TICKET INSP. Nein, das geht nicht. Entweder zahlt sie 16 Euro oder sie steigt in Duisburg aus.
YOU …
WOMAN Welcome to Germany! Thank you, I'll get off at the next stop.

4 ▶ Star Trek

Your pen-friend[2], Marita, is visiting from Sweden. One afternoon you are watching TV with her.

YOU Let's see what's on TV. Oh, *Raumschiff Enterprise*!
MARITA What?
YOU *Raumschiff Enterprise*.
MARITA You mean *Star Trek*. Ssshh. Let's see if I can understand any German …

Listen to the cassette/CD. (Captain Picard has just come to the room of Deanna Troi, the spaceship's counsellor.)
Now answer Marita's questions.

MARITA Oh, you have adverts in the middle. I didn't understand much of the programme. Why did the Captain come to Deanna Troi's room?
YOU …
MARITA I see. What has she been doing with her mother's things?
YOU …
MARITA Who was the man in the photo?
YOU …
MARITA What did she say about him?
YOU …
MARITA What did she say at the end?
YOU …

[1] ticket inspector *Fahrkartenkontrolleur/in, Zugbegleiter/in*
[2] pen-friend *Brieffreund/in*

LANGUAGE SUMMARY

Die folgenden Seiten fassen – Unit für Unit – den Grammatikstoff dieses Buches zusammen. Grammatische Begriffe kannst du auf den Seiten 196/197 nachschlagen.

Links
stehen grammatische **Regeln** und Hinweise sowie

Lerntipps und Merkkästen.

Eine Zusammenschau verschiedener bekannter Strukturen findest du bei dem Hinweis

IM ÜBERBLICK ▶

Rechts
stehen **Beispiele** und Übersichten sowie weitere wichtige Hinweise:

⚠ = Achtung! Fehlerquelle oder wichtige Regel!

REMEMBER = Das kennst du bereits – versuche dich zu erinnern.

→ P 2 (p. 13) = Hierzu gehört die Übung 2 von Seite 13.

In English:
Hier stehen kurze englische Zusammenfassungen der neuen Regeln, damit du auch auf Englisch über die Grammatik sprechen kannst.

Am Ende jeder Unit ...
– zeigt eine Übersicht, was du jetzt auf Englisch ausdrücken kannst. ▶ I've learned to say ...

Unit 1

1 Wiederholung: *let/make* + Objekt + Infinitiv ohne *to*

Ein Verb, das auf *let* + Objekt oder *make* + Objekt folgt, steht im Infinitiv (ohne *to*).
Let + Objekt + Infinitiv bedeutet **„(zu)lassen, erlauben"**.
Make + Objekt + Infinitiv bedeutet **„(veran)lassen, dazu bringen, zwingen"**.

Revision: *let/make* + object + infinitive without *to*

Mum often **lets us stay up** later at the weekend.
Mama lässt uns am Wochenende oft länger aufbleiben.
That teacher can't **make the kids sit** still.
Dieser Lehrer kann die Kinder nicht dazu bringen, still zu sitzen.

He **is letting him drive**.

He **is making him drive** to the airport.

→ P 2 (p. 13)

2 **Wiederholung:**
Das *present progressive* mit futurischer Bedeutung

Wenn man ausdrücken will, dass etwas für die Zukunft fest **geplant** oder **vereinbart** ist, verwendet man das *present progressive.*

Revision:
The present progressive with future meaning

I'**m meeting** Greg **tomorrow afternoon**. We'**re going** shopping.
Ich treffe Greg morgen Nachmittag. Wir gehen einkaufen.
(Das haben wir vereinbart.)

→ P 3 (p. 13)

3 **Verben der Wahrnehmung + Objekt + Infinitiv ohne *to***

Nach Verben der Wahrnehmung wie *see, watch, notice, hear, listen to, feel* kann ein **Objekt** + **Infinitiv** (ohne *to*) stehen.

Verbs of perception + object + infinitive without *to*

I didn't **see anyone leave** the house.
Ich habe nicht gesehen, ob/dass jemand das Haus verlassen hat.
I woke up because I **heard the phone ring**.
Ich bin aufgewacht, weil ich das Telefon klingeln hörte.
Sue **felt something wet touch** her feet in the dark.
Sue fühlte, dass etwas Nasses ihre Füße in der Dunkelheit berührte.

In English: Verbs of perception + object + infinitive
After verbs of perception *(see, watch, notice, hear, listen to, feel)* we can use an object + infinitive without *to*.

→ P 4 (p. 14)

In Unit 1 hast du gelernt ...
– zu sagen, was jemand hört, sieht oder fühlt.

▶ I saw a space shuttle take off from Cape Canaveral.
I heard Conchita talk to her parents in Spanish.

Unit 2

1
a **Das *past perfect***
Gebrauch

Wie du weißt, drückt das *simple past* aus, dass Handlungen oder Ereignisse zu einem bestimmten Zeitpunkt in der Vergangenheit stattfanden.

Wenn man über zwei vergangene Ereignisse redet, kann man das *past perfect* verwenden, um zu sagen, welches Ereignis **zuerst** geschah.

The past perfect
Use

REMEMBER

Amy **phoned** her grandmother in the afternoon.
Glen **was** late yesterday.

When she **had finished** her meal, Amy **phoned** her grandmother.
Als Amy aufgegessen hatte, rief sie ihre Großmutter an.
Glen **was** late because he'**d missed** the bus.
Glen kam zu spät, weil er den Bus verpasst hatte.

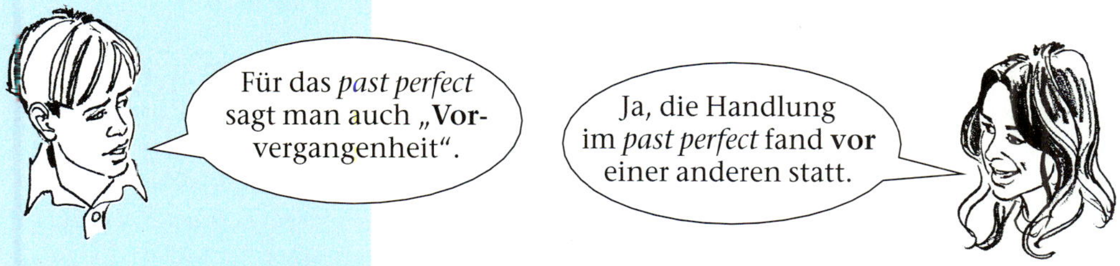

Auch für Zustände (vor einem vergangenen Ereignis) wird das *past perfect* verwendet.

When Glen came back home, one of his friends **had been** in hospital for ten days.
Als Glen wieder nach Hause kam, lag einer seiner Freunde schon seit zehn Tagen im Krankenhaus.

⚠ Je nachdem ob man das *past perfect* oder das *simple past* verwendet, verändert sich die Bedeutung.

The lesson **had started** when Glen arrived.
Der Unterricht **hatte** (schon) **begonnen**, als Glen kam.
The lesson **started** when Glen arrived.
Der Unterricht **begann** (erst), als Glen kam.

Wenn die Reihenfolge der Ereignisse klar ist, steht oft das *simple past* anstelle des *past perfect*, z.B. nach *after* (= „nachdem").

After I **had left** school, I went to America.
oder: After I **left** school, I went to America.

b Form

Das *past perfect* wird mit ***had*** (Kurzform *'d*) + **Partizip Perfekt** gebildet.
⚠ Im Deutschen wird für das Plusquamperfekt „hatte" oder „war" verwendet. Im Englischen steht immer *had* (oder *'d*).

Form

When Amy **had saved** enough money, she bought a CD player. Als Amy genug Geld **gespart hatte**, …
Tom was sad because the letter from Sue **hadn't arrived**.
…, weil der Brief von Sue **nicht angekommen war**.
Had they **known** each other for a long time before they got married?

When Mary got to the platform, the train **had** just **left**.

Auch das *past perfect* hat eine *progressive form*.

The letter came on Friday. Amy **had been waiting** for it since Monday.
… Amy hatte schon seit Montag darauf gewartet.

In English: The past perfect

1 We use the past perfect to show that one thing in the past happened before another thing in the past.
2 We form the past perfect with *had* + past participle.

→ P 1, 2 (p. 26)

2 Der Infinitiv mit *to*

a Verben + *to*-Infinitiv

Der *to*-Infinitiv kann nach bestimmten Verben (z.B. *decide, forget, learn, plan, promise, start*) stehen. Er entspricht einem deutschen Infinitiv mit „zu". Beachte aber die deutschen Entsprechungen für:

want to do	„tun wollen"
would like to do	„tun mögen"
be able to do	„tun können"
be allowed to do	„tun dürfen"
have to do	„tun müssen"

The *to*-infinitive

Verbs + *to*-infinitive

REMEMBER

Joshua **forgot to do** his homework last night.
Joshua **vergaß** gestern Abend seine Hausaufgaben **zu machen**.
You **promised to help** me.
Du **hast versprochen** mir **zu helfen**.

He **wants to go** home now. Er **will** jetzt nach Hause **gehen**.
She **would like to stay**.
Fiona **wasn't able to answer** the questions.
You **aren't allowed to leave** your car here.
When do you **have to get up** on a school day?

→ F 3 (p. 26)

b **Adjektive und Nomen + *to*-Infinitiv**

Der *to*-Infinitiv kann auch nach bestimmten Adjektiven (z.B. *good, easy, nice*) und nach bestimmten Nomen (z.B. *decision, plan, wish*) stehen.

Adjectives and nouns + *to*-infinitive

REMEMBER

It was **nice** to meet you.
Es war **schön**, Sie kennen zu lernen.
Our **decision** to help him was right.
Unsere **Entscheidung**, ihm zu helfen, war richtig.

c **Fragewörter + *to*-Infinitiv**

Der *to*-Infinitiv kann nach Fragewörtern (z.B. *how, what, where, when*) stehen. Er entspricht einem Nebensatz mit modalem Hilfsverb („sollen", „können" usw.).

Question words + *to*-infinitive

REMEMBER

Can you tell me **how** to get to the library?
Können Sie mir sagen, wie ich zur Bücherei komme(n kann)?
Rob didn't know **what** to say.
Rob wusste nicht, was er sagen sollte.

→ P 4 (p. 27)

d ***a place to visit***

Nach bestimmten Nomen oder *something, anybody* usw. entspricht der *to*-Infinitiv einem Relativsatz mit modalem Hilfsverb.

a place to visit

Barrow is **a place** | to visit in the summer. / that you must/should visit …
…, den man im Sommer besuchen sollte.

Mr Oktollik is **the man** | to help us. / who can/could/will help us.
…, der uns helfen kann/könnte/wird.

I don't know **anybody** | to talk to. / who I could/might talk to.
…, mit dem ich sprechen kann/könnte.

→ P 5 (p. 27)

e ***the first / the last / the next / the only* + *to*-infinitive**

Der *to*-Infinitiv kann nach *the first, the last, the next, the only* sowie nach Superlativen verwendet werden. Er entspricht einem Relativsatz.

⚠ Nach *the only* **muss** immer ein Nomen oder *one/ones* stehen.

***the first / the last / the next / the only* + *to*-infinitive**

Armstrong was **the first (person)** | to walk on the moon. / who walked …
Armstrong war der erste Mensch/der Erste, der den Mond betrat.

The captain is **the last (one)** | to leave the ship. / who leaves the ship.
Der Kapitän verlässt als Letzter das Schiff.

Glen was **the youngest kid** | to go to Space Camp. / who went to Space Camp.
Glen war der jüngste Teilnehmer am Space Camp.

Sally was **the only person/one** to say what she thought.
Sally war die Einzige, die gesagt hat, was sie dachte.

f **Der *to*-Infinitiv zum Ausdruck eines Zweckes**

Der *to*-Infinitiv kann zum Ausdruck eines **Zwecks** oder einer **Absicht** verwendet werden. Die Form *in order to* ist etwas förmlicher als *to*, bedeutet aber dasselbe.
Im Deutschen steht meist „um zu".

The *to*-infinitive to express purpose

Amy visited her grandmother to find out more about Inuit traditions.
…, um mehr über die Traditionen der Inuit herauszufinden.
Chloe went to Paris in order to learn French .
…, um Französisch zu lernen.

g Verb + Objekt + *to*-Infinitiv

Nach bestimmten Verben (z.B. *ask, help, invite, teach*) kann ein **Objekt** + *to*-**Infinitiv** stehen. Im Deutschen steht meist ein Infinitiv mit „zu".

Auch nach *cause, expect, tell, want, would like, would love* kann ein **Objekt** + **to-Infinitiv** stehen. Nach den entsprechenden deutschen Verben steht jedoch ein Nebensatz mit „**dass**".

⚠ Beachte die unterschiedliche Bedeutung der zwei *want*-Sätze.

Nach 'want' / 'would like' (und das ist wichtig) steht niemals 'that' – mach das bloß richtig!

Verb + object + *to*-infinitive

REMEMBER

My dad **asked** me to help him.
Mein Vater bat mich, ihm zu helfen.
Who **taught** you to play the guitar?
Wer hat dir beigebracht, Gitarre zu spielen?

I **expect** you to be home by ten.
Ich erwarte, **dass du** bis 10 Uhr zu Hause **bist**.
Would you **like** me to clean the board?
Möchten Sie, **dass ich** die Tafel **abwische**?
I **told** him not to worry.
Ich sagte ihm, **dass er** sich keine Sorgen **machen sollte**.

Sue **wants** to help John.	Sue **will** John helfen.
Sue **wants** me to help John.	Sue **will**, dass ich John helfe.

'Because I want to find out if you've been a good boy, Tommy. That's why I **want** you to take this lie detector test ...'

lie detector [dɪ'tektə] *Lügendetektor*

→ P 6, 7 (pp. 27/28)

In English: The *to*-infinitive

We can use the *to*-infinitive

- after nouns instead of[1] a relative clause *(a book to read = a book that I can read/that you should read)*,
- after *the first/last/next/only* and superlatives *(the oldest)* instead of a relative clause *(the first to arrive = the first who arrived)*,
- to express purpose[2] (German 'um zu'),
- in the structure[3] *ask/expect/tell/want/would like sb. to do.*

[1]instead of *statt, anstelle* [2]purpose ['pɜːpəs] *Zweck* [3]structure ['strʌktʃə] *Struktur, Konstruktion*

In Unit 2 hast du gelernt ...

- zu sagen, dass etwas vor etwas anderem passiert ist. ▶ I arrived at the station after the train had left.
- anderen zu raten, wohin sie fahren sollten, wen sie fragen können usw. ▶ Alaska is a great state to visit. Amy is the person to talk to.
- über Absichten zu sprechen. ▶ Glen went to Space Camp to learn about space travel.
- Wünsche und Erwartungen an andere auszudrücken. ▶ I want you to come home at once.

Unit 3

1 Wiederholung: Die Zeitformen

Revision: The tenses

IM ÜBERBLICK ▶

	Active	Passive
• ***Simple present*** → P 7 (p. 72) regelmäßige Vorgänge, Gewohnheiten und Dauerzustände	I **read** a lot, and I **love** books by Joanne Rowling.	Puddlebottom Castle **is visited** by over 200,000 tourists every year.
• ***Present progressive*** – gerade ablaufende Vorgänge – etwas für die Zukunft fest Geplantes; Vereinbarungen	At the moment, I**'m reading** her new book. I**'m getting** the cassette of the book for my birthday next month.	
• ***Simple past*** → P 1 (p. 42), P 7 (p. 72) Ereignisse, die zu einem bestimmten Zeitpunkt der Vergangenheit stattfanden	I **was** very happy when I **found** her new book last week when I **was** in London.	It **was built** in 1077 and **was used** for over 700 years as the home of the Puddlebottom family.
• ***Past progressive*** → P 1 (p. 42) zu einem bestimmten Zeitpunkt der Vergangenheit ablaufende Vorgänge	I **was visiting** my aunt when I bought it.	
• ***Present perfect (simple)*** – Was (irgendwann) passiert ist – Zustände, die von der Vergangenheit bis jetzt andauern	I**'ve** already **read** over 100 pages. The book **has been** in the shops for two weeks.	A lot of work **has been done** during the last few years to make the castle beautiful again.
• ***Present perfect progressive*** Vorgänge, die von der Vergangenheit bis jetzt andauern	I**'ve been enjoying** the story very much.	
• ***Past perfect (simple)*** → P 1 (p. 42) Ereignisse und Zustände vor einem anderen Ereignis in der Vergangenheit	Before this one, I **had** already **read** four others by Joanne Rowling.	When the work started, the castle **had** almost **been forgotten** for over 100 years.
• ***Past perfect progressive*** Vorgänge, die bis zu einem Zeitpunkt in der Vergangenheit andauerten	I **had been waiting** for the new one until last Monday.	
• ***will-future*** – Vorhersagen, Vermutungen – spontane Entschlüsse, Angebote	I**'ll** probably **finish** it tomorrow. If you want, I**'ll let** you read it, too.	We expect that the millionth visitor **will be welcomed** next year.
• ***going to-future*** – Absichten – Vorhersagen aufgrund von äußeren Anzeichen	I**'m going to buy** the next one when it appears. After the first five, I just know that it**'s going to be** good.	A video of the castle **is going to be made** soon.

Suche bei den Formen nach Gemeinsamkeiten, z.B.:
*Alle **progressive forms** bildet man mit **be** + **-ing-form**.*

→ Fragebildung im Englischen → S 6: 3 (p. 139)

2 Die indirekte Rede — Indirect speech

a Direkte und indirekte Rede — Direct and indirect speech

Man kann das, was jemand sagt oder gesagt hat, auf zweifache Art und Weise wiedergeben:

- In der **direkten Rede** *(direct speech)* wird **wörtlich wiedergegeben**, was jemand sagt, schreibt oder denkt.
- In der **indirekten Rede** *(indirect speech)* wird **berichtet**, was jemand sagt, schreibt oder denkt. Häufige Verben, die die indirekte Rede einleiten, sind: *say, tell sb., answer, explain, mention, write, believe, know, think, ask, want to know.*

Mr Haynes: 'Williamsburg is a place for white people.'
Kimberley said, 'I would like to find out for myself.'

Mr Haynes **says (that) Williamsburg is a place for white people**.
Kimberley **said (that) she would like to find out for herself**.

b Veränderungen der Zeitform — Tense change

Wenn das **einleitende Verb im *simple past*** steht (*said, told* usw.), werden die Zeitformen der direkten Rede meist verändert. Sie werden um eine Zeitstufe in die Vergangenheit **„zurückverschoben"** *(backshift of tenses)*:

		Direct speech	Indirect speech
present	▶ past	'I **play** hockey every Saturday.'	▶ Liz **said** she **played** hockey every Saturday.
		'I'**m enjoying** my holiday in France.'	▶ Pete **wrote** that he **was enjoying** his holiday in France.
past	▶ past perfect[1]	'I **met** the others at the club.'	▶ Lucy **mentioned** that she **had met** the others at the club.
		'We **were watching** a football match on TV.'	▶ Bob **said** they **had been watching** a football match on TV.
present perfect	▶ past perfect	'My parents **have been** to the USA once.'	▶ Colin **explained** that his parents **had been** to the USA once.
will-future	▶ *would* + Infinitiv	'I'm sure Tom **will arrive** in time.'	▶ Sue **was** sure that Tom **would arrive** in time.
going to-future	▶ *was/were going to* + Infinitiv	'I think Sally **is going to work** hard.'	▶ David **thought** Sally **was going to work** hard.
can	▶ *could*	'I'm sorry we **can't come**.'	▶ Eric **was** sorry that they **couldn't come**.
may	▶ *might*	'Dad and Mum **may be** late.'	▶ Jean **told** us that her parents **might be** late.

[1] In der Umgangssprache werden *past tense*-Formen der direkten Rede manchmal beibehalten, d.h. nicht ins *past perfect* verändert.

⚠ 1 Ein Verb im *past perfect* sowie *would, could, should, might, must, needn't* bleiben unverändert.

'The bus **had** already **left**.' ▶ John **said** the bus **had** already **left**.'

'I **would** like to go to Space Camp.' ▶ Mary **said** that she **would** like to go to Space Camp.

2 Anders als im Deutschen gibt es in der indirekten Rede im Englischen **keinen Konjunktiv** *(sei, habe)*.

She **told us** that her husband **had** a job at Chester Zoo.
Sie sagte uns, dass ihr Mann eine Stelle im Zoo von Chester **habe**.

Wenn das einleitende Verb im ***simple present*** steht, bleibt die Zeitform der direkten Rede **unverändert**.

'I**'ve lived** in Florida since 1983.' ▶ Julie **says** that she **has lived** in Florida since 1983.

→ P 3, 4, 5, 6 (pp. 42/43)

c Fragen in der indirekten Rede

Questions in indirect speech

Die Regeln für die Veränderung der Zeitformen gelten auch für Fragen in der indirekten Rede.

'How **do** you **like** Space Camp, Glen? ▶ The counsellor **asked** Glen how he **liked** Space Camp.

Wenn die direkte Frage mit einem **Fragewort** *(how, what, when, where* usw.*)* beginnt, wird das Fragewort in der indirekten Rede beibehalten.

'**When did** you **leave** home, Jake?' ▶ Margo **asked** Jake **when** he **had left** home.

Ist in der direkten Rede **kein Fragewort** vorhanden (Entscheidungsfrage), wird die indirekte Frage mit ***if*** oder ***whether*** (= „ob") eingeleitet.

'**Are** you **coming** to the party on Saturday, Brian?' ▶ Anne **wanted to know if/ whether** Brian **was coming** to the party on Saturday.

⚠ Die Wortstellung in indirekten Fragen ist wie in Aussagesätzen, nämlich **Subject – Verb**. Es gibt keine Umschreibung mit *do*.

		Subject	Verb
Statement:		Fiona	smokes.
Indirect question:			
I wondered	if whether why	**Fiona**	**smoked.**

'It's your boss. He wants to know why you're not at work.'

→ P 7, 8 (p. 44)

d Aufforderungssätze und Bitten in der indirekten Rede

Commands and requests in indirect speech

Aufforderungen und Bitten werden in der indirekten Rede meist mit ***tell sb. to do*** bzw. ***ask sb. to do*** wiedergegeben.

'Make notes on the text.' ▶ Mr Clark **told the students to make** notes on the text.

'You shouldn't work at night.' ▶ The doctor **told me not to work** at night.

'Dad, could you call a taxi, please?' ▶ Jane **asked her dad to call** a taxi.

→ P 9 (p. 44)

e Veränderung der Pronomen, der Orts- und Zeitangaben

Changes of pronouns, place and time

Wie im Deutschen werden im Englischen in der indirekten Rede Pronomen, Orts- und Zeitangaben **aus der Sicht des Berichtenden** gewählt. Sie werden, je nach der Situation, in der indirekten Rede verändert:

– **Pronomen**

Direct speech	Indirect speech
Paula: 'Can **I** use **your** bike, Scott?'	▶ Scott (to his parents): 'Paula asked me if **she** could use **my** bike.' ▶ Paula (to her brother): '**I** asked Scott yesterday if **I** could use **his** bike.'

– **Ortsangaben**

▶

– **Zeitangaben**

now	▶ *then, at that time*
today	▶ *(on) that day, yesterday, on Monday, …*
yesterday	▶ *the day before, on Monday, last Monday, …*
last night	▶ *the night before, on Monday night, …*
three days ago	▶ *three days before, three days earlier*
tomorrow	▶ *the next/following day, today, …*

▶

→ P 2 (p. 42)

In English: Indirect speech

1 If the reporting verb (*say, tell, answer,* etc.) is in the past tense, there is usually a change of tenses ('backshift').

present	▶ past	*will*-future	▶ *would* + infinitive
present perfect / past	▶ past perfect	*going to*-future	▶ *was/were going to* + infinitive
		can, may	▶ *could, might*

2 The word order in indirect questions is subject – verb.

3 The *to*-infinitive after verbs like *tell sb.* or *ask sb.* is used to report commands[1] and requests.

[1]command [kə'mɑːnd] *Befehl(ssatz)*

In Unit 3 hast du gelernt …

… wiederzugeben,

– was jemand berichtet hat. ▶ The guide said that Carter had been very rich.
– was jemand gedacht hat. ▶ Kimberley thought their project would win first prize.
– was jemand gefragt hat. ▶ The girls wanted to know who Carter was.
– worum jemand gebeten hat. ▶ We asked Grandpa to help us.
– wozu jemand aufgefordert hat. ▶ The teacher told me to wait outside.

Unit 4

1 Der bestimmte Artikel *the*

The definite article *the*

a Abstrakte Nomen, Stoffbezeichnungen und Nomen im Plural

Abstract nouns, material nouns and plural nouns

Nomen stehen **ohne** den bestimmten Artikel, wenn sie **ganz allgemein** gebraucht werden – auch wenn ein Adjektiv davor steht. Dies gilt insbesondere für

- abstrakte Nomen (*life, history, …*),
- Stoffbezeichnungen (*oil, penicillin, …*),
- Nomen im Plural (*people, cars, …*).

Life is too short – enjoy it. — **Das Leben** …
I know a lot about Irish history. — … **die** irische **Geschichte**.

Oil is quite cheap this year. — **(Das) Öl** …
Who discovered penicillin? — … **(das) Penizillin** …?

Most people like music. — **Die** meisten **Leute** …

Folgt auf solche Nomen jedoch eine **nähere Bestimmung**, z.B. eine *of*-Fügung *(of Gandhi)* oder ein Relativsatz *(we bought last year)*, dann stehen die Nomen wie im Deutschen **mit** dem bestimmten Artikel.

⚠ Aber: *life in America* = das Leben in Amerika
poverty in Germany = die Armut in Deutschland

The life **of Gandhi** is very interesting.
Das Leben Gandhis …
I know a lot about the history **of Ireland**.
… **die Geschichte** Irlands.
The oil **we bought last year** was expensive.
Das Öl, das wir letztes Jahr gekauft haben, …
Someone took the penicillin **from the top shelf**.
… **das Penizillin** vom obersten Regal.
The people **in our street** are really nice.
Die Leute in unserer Straße …

→ P 1, 2 (p. 56)

b *Church, hospital, school* usw.

Church, hospital, school, etc.

Einige Gebäudenamen werden **ohne** Artikel verwendet, wenn man an den **Verwendungszweck** denkt:

- *church* (Ort des Gottesdienstes)
- *school* (Ort des Unterrichts)
- im britischen Englisch auch *hospital* (Ort der Krankenbehandlung).

Do you go to church on Sundays?
Gehst du sonntags in **die Kirche** (= zum Gottesdienst)?
When does school finish?
Wann ist **die Schule** (= der Unterricht) aus?
Ed is in hospital (*AE:* in the hospital) with a broken leg.
Ed liegt mit einem gebrochenen Bein im (= in **dem**) **Krankenhaus**.

c Namen von Straßen, Plätzen und Parks

Names of streets, squares and parks

Straßen, Plätze und Parks stehen im Englischen gewöhnlich **ohne** den bestimmten Artikel.

Take a taxi to Fifth Avenue.
… zur (= zu **der**) **Fifth Avenue**.
Or take a walk in Central Park and check out Times Square later.
… im (= in **dem**) **Central Park** … **den Times Square** …

→ P 3 (p. 56)

In English: The definite article

1 We do not use *the* with abstract nouns (e.g. *time, love*), material nouns (e.g. *water, bread*) and plural nouns (e.g. *students, children*) when they are used in a general sense[1]. But we use *the* with these nouns when they are used in a specific sense, e.g. when an *of*-phrase or a relative clause follows.
2 We do not use *the* with *church, school, hospital* when we are thinking about their function[2].
3 We do not use *the* with the names of streets, squares and parks.

[1]sense *Sinn* [2]function [ˈfʌŋkʃn] *Funktion*

2 Bedingungssätze

Wie du weißt, beziehen sich Bedingungssätze der Typen I und II auf die Gegenwart oder auf die Zukunft.

Conditional sentences

REMEMBER

Typ I – Der Sprecher meint, etwas wird auf jeden Fall passieren, wenn eine Bedingung erfüllt wird:
If you **turn** right at the corner, you**'ll see** Lincoln Center.
(In allgemein gültigen Aussagen steht auch im Hauptsatz das *simple present*: If you **add** blue to yellow, you **get** green.)
Typ II – Der Sprecher hält es für unwahrscheinlich, dass die Bedingung erfüllt wird, stellt sich aber vor, was dann passieren würde: If we **spent** a year in Turkey, we**'d learn** the language.

→ P 4 (p. 57)

a Bedingungssätze III – Gebrauch

Bedingungssätze des Typs III beziehen sich auf die **Vergangenheit**. Sie drücken aus, was passiert wäre, wenn eine Bedingung erfüllt worden wäre („Was wäre gewesen, wenn ...?"). Die Bedingung wurde aber **nicht erfüllt** und man kann daran auch nichts mehr ändern.

Conditional sentences, type III – Use

If Sam **had phoned** his mum, she **wouldn't have been** so angry when he got home.
Wenn Sam ... angerufen hätte, wäre sie nicht so wütend gewesen ...
(Sam hat also nicht angerufen; deshalb war seine Mutter wütend.)

If you **had asked** me, I **would have helped** you.
Wenn du mich gefragt hättest, hätte ich dir geholfen.
(Der Mann hat seine Frau aber nicht gefragt; deshalb konnte sie ihm auch nicht helfen.)

b Bedingungssätze III – Form

Im *if*-Satz steht das *past perfect*; im Hauptsatz steht ***would/could/might*** + ***have*** + **Partizip Perfekt**.

Conditional sentences, type III – Form

If you **had gone** to the museum, you**'d have seen** / you **would have seen** some great pictures.
Wenn du ins Museum gegangen wärst, hättest du einige großartige Bilder gesehen.
If Jenny **had run**, she **could have won** the race.
Wenn Jenny mitgelaufen wäre, hätte sie das Rennen gewinnen können.
If we **hadn't missed** the last lesson, we **might have got** better marks in the test.
Wenn wir die letzte Stunde nicht versäumt hätten, hätten wir vielleicht bessere Noten bei der Klassenarbeit bekommen.

Im Hauptsatz kann ausnahmsweise auch *would* + Infinitiv stehen, wenn man sagen will, was jetzt (in der Gegenwart) der Fall wäre.

If Ann had stayed, we**'d have** enough players.
Wenn Ann geblieben wäre, hätten wir (jetzt) genug Spieler/innen.

In English: Conditional sentences III

1 *If*-clause: past perfect; main clause: *would/could/might* + *have* + past participle.
2 We use this structure[1] (type III) to talk about something that did **not** happen in the past.

[1]structure ['strʌktʃə] *Struktur, Konstruktion*

→ P 5, 6 (p. 57)

IM ÜBERBLICK ▶

Typ I: reale, erfüllbare Bedingung: **„Was ist, wenn …?"** (*simple present – will/can/may* + Infinitiv)

Typ II: Bedingung, die wahrscheinlich nicht erfüllt wird: **„Was wäre, wenn …?"** (*simple past – would/could/might* + Infinitiv)

Typ III: irreale, nicht mehr erfüllbare Bedingung: **„Was wäre gewesen, wenn …?"** (*past perfect – would/could/might* + *have* + Partizip Perfekt)

Type I: If I **get** a computer for my birthday, I**'ll help** you with your report.
Die Sprecherin sagt, was sie tun wird, wenn sie einen Computer zum Geburtstag bekommt.

Type II: If I **got** a computer for my birthday, I**'d help** you with your report.
Die Sprecherin hält es nicht für wahrscheinlich, dass sie einen Computer zum Geburtstag bekommt. Sie sagt aber, was sie tun würde, wenn sie doch einen bekäme.

Type III: If I **had got** a computer for my birthday, I**'d have helped** you with your report.
Der Geburtstag ist vorbei und die Sprecherin hat keinen Computer bekommen. Sie sagt aber, was sie getan hätte, wenn sie einen bekommen hätte.

3 Modale Hilfsverben + *have* + Partizip Perfekt

Modale Hilfsverben (z.B. *can, may, might, should*), auf die ***have*** + **Partizip Perfekt** folgt, beziehen sich auf die Vergangenheit. Sie drücken aus, was möglicherweise geschehen ist oder was hätte geschehen können, sollen, müssen usw.

Modal auxiliaries + *have* + past participle

What **can have happened** to Susan?
Was kann nur mit Susan passiert sein?
She **may/might have missed** the bus.
Sie hat vielleicht den Bus verpasst./Sie könnte den Bus verpasst haben.
She **must have forgotten** the meeting.
Sie muss das Treffen vergessen haben.
I **needn't have run**. There was lots of time.
Ich hätte nicht rennen müssen./Ich hätte nicht zu rennen brauchen.
You **should have been** more careful.
Du hättest vorsichtiger sein sollen.

In English: Modal auxiliaries + *have* + past participle
We can use modal auxiliaries with *have* + past participle to say what possibly[1] happened in the past or to imagine how things could have been different.

[1] possibly ['pɒsəbli] *möglicherweise*

→ P 7 (p. 58)

In Unit 4 hast du gelernt …

- allgemeine Themen wie Technik, Geschichte, Liebe usw. anzusprechen.
  ▶ I'm not really interested in history, but I like learning about the history of the USA.
- über Nahrungsmittel und verschiedene Materialien zu sprechen.
  ▶ Coffee is more expensive than tea.
- zu sagen, was geschehen wäre, wenn bestimmte Dinge in der Vergangenheit anders gewesen wären.
  ▶ If I had known about Josh's accident, I would have visited him.
- zu sagen, was möglicherweise geschehen ist oder was hätte geschehen können, sollen, müssen.
  ▶ He must have had an accident.
  She could have talked/should have talked to a friend about her problems.

Unit 5

1 Das Gerundium

Nach folgenden Verben steht ein zweites Verb in der *-ing*-Form (Gerundium): *avoid, consider, enjoy, finish, give up, go on, imagine, mention, miss, practise, risk, stop, suggest.*

The gerund

REMEMBER

You should **stop** smoking.
Du solltest mit dem Rauchen aufhören.
Debbie **suggested** watching the match on TV.
Debbie schlug vor, das Spiel im Fernsehen anzuschauen.

Nach *begin, continue, hate, like, love, prefer, start* kann entweder ein Gerundium oder ein Infinitiv mit *to* stehen.

It **started** raining. / to rain. — Es fing an zu regnen.

I **love** meeting / to meet new people. — Ich treffe sehr gern neue Leute.

Nach *would like, would love, would hate, would prefer* steht aber nur der *to*-Infinitiv.

I'**d love** to meet your brother. — Ich würde gern deinen Bruder kennen lernen.

Nach Präpositionen, die mit einem Adjektiv, Nomen oder Verb verbunden sind, muss die *-ing*-Form (Gerundium) des Verbs verwendet werden.

REMEMBER

Are you **interested in** learning German?
Bist du interessiert daran, Deutsch zu lernen?
I like the **idea of** staying in a youth hostel.
Mir gefällt die Idee, in einer Jugendherberge zu übernachten.
My little sister **dreams of** becoming a pilot.
Meine kleine Schwester träumt davon, Pilotin zu werden.

→ P 2, 3, 4 (pp. 70/71)

Das **Gerundium** folgt auch auf allein stehende **Präpositionen**, z.B. *after, before, by, for, instead of, on, without.* Im Deutschen werden meist Nebensätze mit *nachdem, (an)statt zu, indem, ohne zu* usw. verwendet, gelegentlich auch eine Verbindung aus Präposition + Nomen.

After dancing for three hours, the kids were very tired.
(= After they had danced for three hours, ...)
Nachdem die jungen Leute drei Stunden lang getanzt hatten, ...

Nach einer Präposition steht das Verb in der -ing-Form.

You can put people's lives in danger by driving too fast.
..., indem du zu schnell fährst. / ... durch zu schnelles Fahren.

This knife is only for cutting bread.
Dieses Messer ist nur zum Brotschneiden da.

Jimmy started to cry on hearing the news.
(= Jimmy started to cry when he heard the news.)
Jimmy fing an zu weinen, als/sobald er die Nachricht hörte.

We decided to walk instead of waiting for the bus.
... statt auf den Bus zu warten.

He just took my pen without asking.
... ohne zu fragen.

In English: Preposition + gerund
The gerund is used after prepositions, e.g. *after, before, by, for, instead of, on, without.*

→ P 5, 6 (p. 71)

2 ***a friend of Mrs Cook's / of mine***

Mit Wendungen wie *a friend of Mrs Cook's, a friend of Sue's, a friend of my sister's, a friend of the Domeiers'* drückt man aus, dass es sich um **einen/eine von mehreren** Freunden/Freundinnen handelt.

a friend of Mrs Cook's / of mine

Mrs Walker is **a friend of Mrs Cook's.**
(= Mrs Walker is one of Mrs Cook's friends.)
Frau Walker ist eine Freundin von Frau Cook. (D.h., Frau Cook hat mehrere Freundinnen – Frau Walker ist eine von ihnen.)

Vergleiche:
Mr Brown is Mr Cook's friend.
Herr Brown ist der (beste) Freund von Herrn Cook.

I met **some friends of my sister's.**
(= I met some of my sister's friends.)
Ich traf einige Freunde (von) meiner Schwester.

Statt des *s*-Genitivs kann man in solchen Wendungen auch ein Possessivpronomen *(mine, yours, his, ...)* verwenden:
a friend of mine, a cousin of hers, neighbours of ours.

I was talking to **a friend of mine.** ⚠ *Nicht:* ~~a friend of me~~
(= I was talking to one of my friends.)
Ich sprach mit einem meiner Freunde.
The Domeiers are **neighbours of ours.**
(= The Domeiers are some of our neighbours.)
Die Domeiers sind Nachbarn von uns.

In English: *a friend of Mrs Cook's / of mine / of yours / ...*
We use the structure[1] *a friend of Mrs Cook's, a friend of mine*, etc. to mean one of a number of friends.

[1]structure ['strʌktʃə] *Struktur, Konstruktion*

→ P 8 (p. 72)

In Unit 5 hast du gelernt ...

- zu sagen, dass eine Handlung vor/nach/anstelle usw. einer anderen geschieht.
  ▶ Before leaving, I closed all the windows.
  After comparing prices, I decided to buy on the Internet.
  He watched TV instead of doing his homework.
- zu sagen, wie jemand etwas erreicht oder tut.
  ▶ I got some help by asking my friends.
  We cycled up the hill without stopping once.
- auszudrücken, dass eine von mehreren Personen oder Sachen gemeint ist.
  ▶ Don is a friend of mine.
  This is a favourite restaurant of ours.

Unit 6

1 Der unbestimmte Artikel

Vor **Berufsbezeichnungen** steht im Englischen der Artikel *a/an*.
Bei ***half*** und ***quite*** wird der Artikel nachgestellt.

The indefinite article

REMEMBER

My mum is **a taxi driver**. My dad is **an engineer**.
Meine Mutter ist **Taxifahrerin**. Mein Vater ist **Ingenieur**.
Could I have **half a** kilo of tomatoes, please?
Könnte ich bitte **ein halbes** Kilo Tomaten haben?
We saw **quite an** interesting film yesterday.
Wir sahen gestern **einen recht** interessanten Film. → P 3 (p. 84)

Der unbestimmte Artikel steht in der Bedeutung **„pro/je"** vor **Zeitangaben** *(a week, a day, a year, an hour)* sowie vor **Maß- und Mengenangaben** *(a square metre, a pound, a kilo).*

I get ten euros pocket money **a week**.
… pro Woche/in der Woche.
My friends in California phone four times **a year**.
… pro/im Jahr
That material costs ten dollars **a square metre**.
… pro/je Quadratmeter.
Potatoes are very cheap – only 60 cents **a kilo**.
… pro/das Kilo.

In English: The indefinite article

The indefinite article *a/an* is used in phrases of time, price, measurement[1], etc. In these phrases *a/an* means *per*.

[1]measurement ['meʒəmənt] *Maß*

→ P 4 (p. 85)

2 Wiederholung: Stellung der Adverbien

Es gibt drei mögliche Stellungen für Adverbien:
- **vor dem Subjekt** *(front-position)*: Hier stehen gewöhnlich **Satzadverbien** wie *maybe, suddenly, of course, in fact, finally, at first, then.*
- **zwischen Subjekt und Vollverb** bzw. **nach dem (ersten) Hilfsverb** *(mid-position)*: Hier stehen gewöhnlich Adverbien der **unbestimmten Zeit oder Häufigkeit** wie *ever, always, often, never.*
- **nach dem Vollverb** bzw. **nach dem Objekt** *(end-position)*: Hier stehen gewöhnlich Adverbien der **Art und Weise** *(carefully, hard, well)*, Adverbien des **Ortes** *(here, everywhere, in/to London)* und Adverbien der **Zeit** *(yesterday, next week, in 1998)*. Treten mehrere dieser Adverbien in einem Satz auf, gilt die Reihenfolge **Art und Weise – Ort – Zeit**.

Gradadverbien – z.B. *very, quite, really, too* (= „zu") – stehen meist direkt vor dem Wort, das sie verstärken oder abschwächen.

Revision: Position of adverbs

Suddenly **the lights** went out.

My sister **always** **walks** to school.
This story **will** **never** be forgotten.

You should always **drive** **carefully**.
My parents **are visiting friends** **in London**.
We're going to **buy a new car** **next week**.

	manner	place	time
I hope I'll do	well	in the test	tomorrow.
Mike can't go		to school	today.

Our new French teacher is **quite/really/too/very** **strict**.
Do you **really** **believe** that?
Daniel ran **really/very** **slowly**.

→ P 7 (p. 86)

3 Wiederholung: Fragen im Englischen

Revision: Questions in English

*Hast du Probleme mit der Bildung englischer Zeitformen? Dann schreib ein paar Sätze in deiner Problem-Zeitform **mit albernen Reimen** (wie in den Beispielen unten) auf. Lass sie von deiner Lehrerin/deinem Lehrer durchsehen und lerne sie dann auswendig. (Das Auswendiglernen geht wegen der Reime ganz leicht!) Immer wenn du unsicher bist, rufst du deine Sätze im Gedächtnis auf – und machst keine Fehler mehr!*

IM ÜBERBLICK ▶

	Auxiliary (in questions)	Subject	Auxiliary (in statements)	Main verb	
Modal auxiliaries		Pete	can	eat	meat.
	Can	Pete		eat	meat?
Present/Past progressive		Steve	is/was	leaving	Eve.
	Is/Was	Steve		leaving	Eve?
Simple present		Trish		likes	fish.
	Does	Trish		like	fish?
Simple past		Kate		came	late.
	Did	Kate		come	late?
Present/Past perfect		Kurt	has/had	hurt	Bert.
	Has/Had	Kurt		hurt	Bert?
Present/Past perfect progressive		Rory	has/had been	reading	stories.
	Has/Had	Rory	been	reading	stories?
will-future		Keith	will	brush	his teeth.
	Will	Keith		brush	his teeth?

⚠ Vorsicht bei **Fragen nach dem Subjekt** („Wer oder was tut etwas bzw. hat etwas getan?"): Sie werden **ohne *do/does/did*** gebildet.

Who **likes** fish? – Trish (likes fish). Wer mag Fisch?
Who **came** late? – Kate (came late). Wer kam zu spät?
What **happened**? – Nothing (happened). Was ist passiert?

⚠ **Subject question:** Who **asked** you? **Wer** hat dich gefragt?
Object question: Who **did** you **ask**? **Wen** hast du gefragt?

→ P 5 (p. 85)

In Unit 6 hast du gelernt ...

- zu sagen, wie oft in der Woche, im Jahr usw. etwas geschieht.
  ▶ We have English four times a week. We go to church twice a month.
- über Maße und Mengenangaben zu reden.
  ▶ I drank half a litre of water after the race. That cheese costs £8 a kilo.

VOCABULARY

Das *VOCABULARY* (Vokabelverzeichnis) enthält die neuen Wörter dieses Buches in der Reihenfolge, in der sie in den Units vorkommen.

- Fett gedruckte Wörter musst du verstehen und benutzen können.
  ➨ **state** [steɪt] Staat; (Bundes-)Land
- Normal gedruckte Wörter sollst du verstehen können, wenn du sie hörst oder liest.
  ➨ caption ['kæpʃn] Bildunterschrift

Symbole

° Wörter und Ausdrücke mit einem **Kringel** sind nur in der Unit wichtig, in der sie vorkommen. Sie werden in späteren Units nicht vorausgesetzt. *Beispiel:* °orbit ['ɔːbɪt] Umlaufbahn

[P 6] **Eckige Klammern** bedeuten, dass diese Übung nicht Pflicht ist. Dein Lehrer/Deine Lehrerin wird dir sagen, ob du die (*kursiv* gedruckten) Wörter lernen sollst.

~ Die **Tilde** in der dritten Spalte steht für das neue Wort. *Beispiel:* **course** – My mum is doing an English ~.

▸◂ Dies ist das „**Gegenteil**"-Zeichen. *Beispiel:* (to) **freeze** ▸◂ (to) **melt**
(to) freeze („frieren; gefrieren; einfrieren") ist das Gegenteil von *(to) melt („schmelzen")*.

⚠ Achtung, aufpassen – hier macht man leicht Fehler.

Betonung

['] und [ˌ] sind Betonungszeichen. Sie stehen vor der betonten Silbe.
['] zeigt die Hauptbetonung, [ˌ] die Nebenbetonung. *Beispiel:* exploration [ˌekspləˈreɪʃn]

Abkürzungen

p.	=	page	pp.	=	pages
pl	=	*plural*	*no pl*	=	*no plural*
adj	=	*adjective*	*adv*	=	*adverb*
conj	=	*conjunction*	*n*	=	*noun*
prep	=	*preposition*	*v*	=	*verb*
sb.	=	somebody/ someone	jd.	=	jemand
			jm.	=	jemandem
sth.	=	something	jn.	=	jemanden
AE	=	*American English*	*BE*	=	*British English*
infml	=	*informal* (umgangssprachlich, informell)			
fml	=	*formal* (förmlich, formell)			

Ländernamen (und davon abgeleitete Adjektive) findest du auf Seite 193; **Personen- und Ortsnamen** findest du auf den Seiten 194/195.

Grammatische Fachbegriffe stehen gesammelt auf den Seiten 196/197, und auf Seite 200 findest du eine Liste von ***Useful classroom phrases***.

Englische Wörter wie *skateboard, thriller* oder *software*, die du ohne weiteres verstehst, werden nicht im *VOCABULARY* erklärt – du findest sie mit Angabe ihrer Aussprache im *DICTIONARY* (Seiten 166–192).

▸▸▸ Welcome to the United States of America

pp.6/7	**state** [steɪt]	Staat; (Bundes-)Land	⚠ The USA (United *States* of America) is very big. It has got an interesting history. *(singular!)*
	crime [kraɪm]	Verbrechen; Kriminalität	⚠ *crime, pl crimes* = Verbrechen: It's a ~ to kill someone. When did you hear about the ~ / the ~*s*? *crime (no pl)* = Kriminalität: There's a lot of ~ in this area.
	caption ['kæpʃn]	Bildunterschrift	
	streetball ['striːtbɔːl]	*eine Art Basketball (wird auf der Straße mit nur einem Korb gespielt)*	
	high school ['haɪ skuːl]	(US) *Gesamtschule mit den Klassen 7–12 für 13- bis 18-Jährige*	⚠ 'False friends': *high school* = *amerik. Gesamtschule*; *university* = Hochschule, Universität
	(to) **prefer** sth. **(to)** (**-rr-**) [prɪ'fɜː]	etwas lieber haben/tun (als), etwas *(einer anderen Sache)* vorziehen	What do you like better, milk or cola? – I ~ milk. *Do* you really ~ milk *to* cola? I ~ drinking milk. (= I ~ to drink milk.)

German 'gern', 'lieber'

Ich lese **gern** im Bett.	I **like** reading in bed.
Ich würde/möchte **gern** ihren Namen wissen.	I'd **like to** know her name (= I would **like to** ...).
Willst du meinen neuen Computer sehen?	Do you want to see my new computer?
– Oh ja, sehr **gern**.	– Oh yes, I'd **love to** (= I would **love to**).
Was magst du **lieber** – Cola oder Orangensaft?	What do you like **better** – cola or orange juice?
Ich würde **lieber** zu Hause bleiben.	I'd **prefer to** stay at home (= I would **prefer to** ...).

TIPP **Wiederholung ist die Mutter der Weisheit**

Du hast inzwischen schon eine ganze Menge englische Wörter und Ausdrücke gelernt. Damit du sie nicht wieder vergisst, solltest du sie regelmäßig und in bestimmten „Portionen“ wiederholen.

Wie beim Essen musst du aber darauf achten, dass du die „Portionen“ nicht zu groß wählst und dass die Abstände nicht zu groß werden. Es ist besser, 10–15 Vokabeln mehrfach zu wiederholen als 30 oder mehr Wörter auf einmal zu üben.

▶▶▶ Unit 1: Space Camp Florida

p.8	**detail** [⚠ *stress:* 'di:teɪl]	Detail, Einzelheit	I read that story years ago, so I've forgotten most of the ~*s*.
	payment ['peɪmənt]	(Be-)Zahlung	verb: (to) pay – noun: *payment*
	program ['prəʊgræm] *(AE)*	Programm	= *BE* programme
	during *(prep)* ['djʊərɪŋ]	während	We met for a day ~ the summer holidays.

German ‘während’

Ann phoned **during** lunch.
*Ann rief **während** des Mittagessens an.*
Ann phoned **while** we were eating.
*Ann rief an, **während** wir aßen.*

before a noun: **during** *(preposition)*
before a clause: **while** *(conjunction)*

	stay (with) [steɪ]	Aufenthalt, Besuch (bei)	verb: (to) stay – noun: *stay*
	desire [dɪ'zaɪə]	Wunsch, Verlangen	My biggest ~ is to travel in a spaceship.
	exploration [ˌeksplə'reɪʃn]	Erforschung, Erkundung	
	(to) **explore** [ɪk'splɔ:]	erforschen, erkunden	
	course [kɔ:s]	Kurs, Lehrgang	My mum is doing an English ~ on Monday evenings.
	(to) **offer** ['ɒfə]	bieten, anbieten	The language school ~*s* French and Spanish courses. She ~*ed* me $150 for my guitar, but I wanted more.
	scholarship ['skɒləʃɪp]	Stipendium	(to) win a ~ (= ein Stipendium bekommen)
	student [⚠ *stress:* 'stju:dənt]	Student/in, Schüler/in	How many ~*s* are there at this university?
	grade [greɪd] *(AE)*	(Schul-)Klasse, Jahrgangsstufe	Mark has just finished ninth ~. Next year he'll be in tenth ~. (= *BE* form, class)
	from … through [θru:] *(AE)*	von … bis (einschließlich)	The museum is open ~ Tuesday ~ Sunday. = *BE* from … to

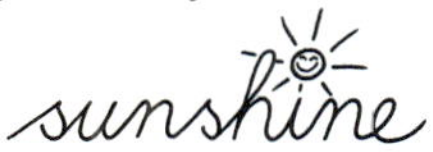

p.9	**sunshine** ['sʌnʃaɪn]	Sonnenschein	
	(to) fall in love (with sb./sth.)	sich verlieben (in jn./etwas)	My best friend *has fallen in* ~ with my brother.
	alligator [⚠ *stress:* 'ælɪgeɪtə]	Alligator	
	(to) **produce** [prə'dju:s]	produzieren, erzeugen, herstellen	Charles Rolls and Henry Royce ~*d* their first car in 1904.
	grapefruit, *pl* grapefruit ['greɪpfru:t]	Grapefruit	
	°theme park ['θi:m pɑ:k]	*Freizeitpark mit Attraktionen zu einem bestimmten Thema*	
	Hispanic *(n; adj)* [hɪ'spænɪk]	Hispano-Amerikaner/in *(Einwanderer aus Lateinamerika und dessen/deren Nachkommen)*; hispanisch	
	attraction [⚠ *stress:* ə'trækʃn]	Attraktion, Anziehungspunkt	

AE spelling – BE spelling

American English: *'-ter'*	British English: *'-tre'*	American English: *'-or'*	British English: *'-our'*
cen**ter**	cen**tre**	col**or**	col**our**
me**ter**, kilome**ter**	me**tre**, kilome**tre**	favor**ite**	fav**our**ite
thea**ter**	thea**tre**	harb**or**	harb**our**

AE: program – **BE:** progra**mme**
AE: traveled, traveling – **BE:** trave**ll**ed, trave**ll**ing

p.10/A1	briefing ['bri:fɪŋ]	Einsatzbesprechung	
	counsellor ['kaʊnsələ] (*AE auch:* counselor)	Berater/in	John's parents are having problems with each other. They are going to see a ~.
	mission ['mɪʃn]	Einsatz, Mission; *hier:* Weltraumflug	The first US ~ to the moon was in 1964.
	(to) **need to do**	tun müssen	(to) have to do

'need' as an auxiliary – 'need' as a full verb

Auxiliary		**Full verb**
You **needn't** go now. **Need** she go now? *(fml)*	*Du brauchst jetzt (noch) nicht zu gehen. Muss sie jetzt gehen? Musste er abreisen?*	You **don't need to** go now. **Does** she **need to** go now? **Did** he **need to** leave?

⚠ • Negative statements + questions: without ***do***
• Followed by an infinitive without ***to***

Need as an auxiliary is only used in the present tense. It appears mainly in negative statements, but sometimes also in questions.

⚠ • Negative statements + questions: with a form of ***do***
• Followed by a ***to***-infinitive

The full verb *need* is also used in positive statements: He **needs to** talk to his mother.

	mom [mɒm] *(AE)*	Mutti, Mama; Mutter	= *BE* mum
	my watch is right	meine Uhr geht richtig	My watch ~*n't right*: perhaps it has stopped.
	yeah [jeə] *(infml)*	ja	= yes
	neat [ni:t] *(AE, infml)*	toll, prima, klasse	= *BE* brilliant, great
A2	**whether** ['weðə]	ob	I don't know ~ I can come to your party or not. ⚠ *whether (conj)* = ob – *weather (n)* = Wetter
	except *(prep)* [ɪk'sept]	außer	He has invited everybody ~ me. Homework is OK, ~ maths.
	(to) be serious about sth. ['sɪəriəs]	etwas ernst nehmen	She's very ~ *about* her sport. She trains every day.
	serious	ernst(haft)	Tom is in hospital with a ~ illness.
p.11	°simulator ['sɪmjuleɪtə]	Simulator *(Gerät, in dem bestimmte Bedingungen wirklichkeitsgetreu nachgestellt werden)*	
	°Eastern Time ['i:stən]	östliche Zeit *(Zeitzone an der Atlantikküste der USA)*	
	rocket ['rɒkɪt]	Rakete	*a rocket*  
	freeze-dried ['fri:zdraɪd]	gefriergetrocknet	
	awesome ['ɔ:səm] *(AE, infml)*	großartig, klasse	
A3	Gee, ... [dʒi:] *(AE, infml)*	Mensch, ...! / Mann, ...! *(Ausruf)*	At Space Camp we went on board a real rocket! – ~, that's awesome!
	hall [hɔ:l]	Halle, Saal; Flur, Diele	
	(to) **look** sth. **up** [ˌlʊk_'ʌp]	etwas nachschlagen, etwas heraussuchen	If you don't know a word, *look* it ~ in a dictionary. Can you *look* ~ John's new phone number for me?
	manual ['mænjuəl]	Handbuch	Read the ~ before you turn on your new computer.
	upside down [ˌʌpsaɪd 'daʊn]	verkehrt herum, auf dem Kopf	Can you read when the book is ~ *down*?
	real exciting *(adv)* ['ri:əl] *(AE, infml)*	wirklich aufregend, echt aufregend	= *BE* really
	I can't wait (to do sth.)	Ich kann es kaum erwarten (, etwas zu tun)	I *can't* ~ *to* see you again.
A4	launch [lɔ:ntʃ]	Start, Abschuss	
	(to) launch	*(ins All)* (ab)schießen	to send a rocket into space = to ~ a rocket
p.12/A5	vacation [*BE:* və'keɪʃn, *AE:* veɪ'keɪʃn] *(AE)*	Urlaub, Ferien	= *BE* holiday (to) be on ~; (to) go on ~; (to) take a ~
	°experimental prototype community [ɪkˌsperɪmentl ˌprəʊtətaɪp kə'mju:nəti]	*etwa:* experimentelle Mustergemeinde	

	community [kə'mju:nəti]	Gemeinde, Gemeinschaft	a group of people who live in the same place: There's a large Hispanic ~ in Florida.
	(to) **waste (on)** [weɪst]	verschwenden, vergeuden (für)	Don't spend your money on that rubbish! Don't ~ your money *on* that.
	first language	Muttersprache	German is my ~ *language.*
	in the end	schließlich, am Ende, zum Schluss	No bus came and *in the* ~ we decided to walk. ⚠ *am Ende / am Schluss* der Stunde = *at the end* of the lesson
	taco ['tɑ:kəʊ]	*eine Art Pfannkuchen, mit Fleisch oder Gemüse, Käse und Gewürzen gefüllt*	
	rice [raɪs]	Reis	In China people eat a lot of ~.
	I guess (*besonders AE*)	ich nehme an, ich denke	= *BE* I suppose, I think
	menu [⚠ *stress:* 'menju:]	Speisekarte; (Computer-)Menü	Waiter, can I see the ~ again, please? When you start the computer program, you see a ~. ⚠ Ich nehme das *Tagesmenü.* = I'll have the *dish of the day.* (*not* ~~menu~~)
P 4	**arrival** [ə'raɪvl]	Ankunft	verb: (to) arrive – noun: *arrival*
	planetary ['plænətri]	Planeten-	
	planet ['plænɪt]	Planet	
	system ['sɪstəm]	System	The British school ~ is very different from the German school ~.
	passage ['pæsɪdʒ]	Abschnitt, Passage	a short part of a text
	satellite ['sætəlaɪt]	Satellit	
	scientist ['saɪəntɪst]	(Natur-)Wissenschaftler/in	A ~ is someone who does science.
	orchestra ['ɔ:kɪstrə]	Orchester	a large group of people who play different musical instruments together

Stress on the first syllable

Careful – the following English words are **stressed on the first syllable**[1]:

[1] syllable ['sɪləbl] *Silbe*

alligator	Alligator	**in**teresting	interessant	**res**taurant	Restaurant
alphabet	Alphabet	**mo**dern	modern	**sa**tellite	Satellit
article	Artikel	**ner**vous	nervös	**stu**dent	Student/in
detail	Detail, Einzelheit	**or**chestra	Orchester	**sym**bol	Symbol
dialogue	Dialog	**per**fect	perfekt	**sys**tem	System
industry	Industrie	**pla**net	Planet	**thea**tre	Theater
instrument	Instrument	**pro**gramme	Programm	**toi**let	Toilette

P 5	**square** km (sq km) [skweə]	Quadratkilometer	square Quadrat
	°bald eagle [ˌbɔ:ld_'i:gl]	Weißkopf-Seeadler	
	°mockingbird ['mɒkɪŋbɜ:d]	Spottdrossel	
	similar (to sb./sth.**)** ['sɪmɪlə]	(jm./einer Sache) ähnlich	Joe's bike is ~ *to* mine. It's the same size and colour. ◂▸ different (from)
	home	Heimat; Heimat-	I was born and live in Hessen. Hessen is my ~ state.
	fact [fækt]	Tatsache, Fakt	It's true. It's a ~.
[P 6]	*in a minute*	*gleich, sofort*	
	You've got the wrong number.	*Sie sind falsch verbunden.*	
	beep [bi:p]	*Piepton*	
	nice and clean	*schön sauber*	
P 7	°orbit ['ɔ:bɪt]	(Erd-, Mond-) Umlaufbahn	
	seat [si:t]	Sitzplatz	There were no ~*s*, so we had to stand. Take a ~, please. (= Bitte nehmen Sie Platz.)
	file [faɪl]	(Computer-)Datei, Ordner	Open the ~ and click on the document you want.
P 8	°money matters ['mætəz]	Geldangelegenheiten *oder* Geld ist wichtig *(Wortspiel)*	

Little Miss Astronaut

p.16	(to) get time off	frei bekommen, Urlaub bekommen	Mr Jones *got time* ~ when his daughter was born.
	(to) **meet** sb. [miːt]	jn. abholen	My train arrives at 8. Can you ~ me at the station? ⚠ *(to) meet* = **1.** (sich/jn.) treffen; **2.** (jn.) abholen
	like [laɪk] *(conj, infml)*	als ob	He looked *like (= as if)* something was wrong. ⚠ *like* („als ob") is informal – most people use 'as if' instead.
	fall [fɔːl] *(AE)*	Herbst	= *BE* autumn

	guy [gaɪ] *(infml)*	Typ, Kerl	an informal word for 'man' or 'boy': Mike is a really nice ~. ⚠ Americans use the plural 'guys' *(= Leute)* for women and girls, too:

	recess ['riːses, rɪ'ses] *(AE)*	Pause *(zwischen Schulstunden)*	= *BE* break At ~ I stayed in the classroom.
	°credit ['kredɪt]	Punkt(e) *(für den High School- oder College-Abschluss)*	
p.17	**Ms** Morrison [mɪz, məz]	Frau Morrison	⚠ Some women prefer the form 'Ms' because it doesn't show if they are married or not. Others are happy with 'Mrs' (= married) or 'Miss' (= unmarried).
	not (…) any more	nicht mehr	I *don't* need this dictionary ~ ~. Do you want it?
	(to) call sb. (stupid) names	jn. verspotten, jn. beschimpfen	
	clique [⚠ kliːk]	Clique, Freundeskreis	
	jealous (of) ['dʒeləs]	neidisch (auf); eifersüchtig (auf)	John is ~ *of* his sister because she's good at school. Sue is ~ when her boyfriend goes out with other girls.
	block [blɒk]	(Häuser-, Wohn-)Block	
	college ['kɒlɪdʒ]	Hochschule, Fachschule (⚠ *nicht:* ~~Kollege~~)	(to) go to ~; (to) be in ~
	sidewalk ['saɪdwɔːk] *(AE)*	Gehweg, Bürgersteig	= *BE* pavement (⚠ *AE* pavement = Fahrbahn)
	Hang in there! [ˌhæŋ‿'ɪn] *(AE, infml)*	Halte durch!	
	glamour ['glæmə]	Glanz	
	glamorous ['glæmərəs]	glanzvoll	noun: glam<u>our</u> – adjective: *glam<u>o</u>rous*
	suit [suːt]	(Herren-)Anzug; (Damen-)Kostüm	*suits* a space*suit* ⚠ *suitcase* = Koffer

	bathroom [*BE:* 'bɑːθruːm, *AE:* 'bæθruːm] *(AE)*	Toilette *(in einem Privathaus)*	= *BE* toilet ⚠ The AE word for 'toilet' in a public place is 'restroom'.
	gang [gæŋ]	Bande, Gang, Truppe	a group of people, e.g. friends or thieves The tourists were robbed by a ~ of thieves.
	ceiling ['siːlɪŋ]	Decke *(eines Zimmers)*	▸◂ floor
	°jerk [dʒɜːk] *(infml)*	Blödmann, Trottel	
	gravity ['grævəti]	Schwerkraft	at zero *gravity* = im Zustand der Schwerelosigkeit
p.18	(to) **go with**	gehören zu, passen zu	

disappointed (with sb., **with/about** sth.) [ˌdɪsə'pɔɪntɪd]	enttäuscht (von jm./etwas)	I was very ~ when I lost the match. Your parents will be *disappointed* ~ you if they find out what you have done.
How do you feel about …?	Was denkst du über …?/ Was hältst du von …?	
(to) **act** [ækt]	handeln, sich verhalten	Tom *is ~ing* very strangely. What's wrong with him? ⚠ *(to) act* = **1.** spielen, darstellen; **2.** handeln
entry ['entri]	Eintrag, Eintragung *(in einem Tagebuch/Wörterbuch)*	There's no ~ in Jane's diary for 12th June. I've bought a new dictionary. It has 200,000 *entries*.
conversation [ˌkɒnvə'seɪʃn]	Gespräch, Unterhaltung	to have a ~ with someone = to talk to someone about something

p.19
How to present an argument

argument [⚠ *stress:* 'ɑːgjumənt]	Argument, Begründung; Streit	Prepare your *~s* before you start the discussion. Mum and Dad had an ~ last night. Dad shouted a lot.
achievement [ə'tʃiːvmənt]	Leistung, Errungenschaft	She swam 30 kilometres. It was a great ~.
talk [tɔːk]	Vortrag, Referat, Rede; Gespräch	verb: (to) talk – noun: *talk* ⚠ *einen Vortrag/eine Rede (über etwas) halten = (to) give a talk (on sth.)*
introduction (to) [ˌɪntrə'dʌkʃn]	Einführung (in), Einleitung; Vorstellung *(von Personen)*	This little book is a good ~ *to* chemistry. verb: (to) introduce – noun: *introduction*
conclusion [kən'kluːʒn]	Schluss(folgerung), Abschluss	At the end of the report they listed their main *~s*. The ~ of the book was a real surprise.
advantage (over sb./ sth.) [əd'vɑːntɪdʒ]	Vorteil (gegenüber jm./etwas)	Cats have an ~ *over* dogs. They can climb trees!
disadvantage [ˌdɪsəd'vɑːntɪdʒ]	Nachteil	Dogs are *at a ~*. (= im Nachteil)
(to) **make** sth. sth.	etwas zu etwas *(anderem)* machen	Is it true that space exploration *is ~ing* the world a safer place?
on top of that	außerdem; darüber hinaus	It's cheaper and faster by train, and *on ~ of that* I can sleep on the way.
development [dɪ'veləpmənt]	Entwicklung	The situation has changed. There have been some interesting new *~s*.
(to) **develop (from … into)** [dɪ'veləp]	entwickeln; sich entwickeln (aus … zu)	We're trying to ~ a new kind of omputer. After a boring start, our trip *~ed into* a real adventure.
medicine ['medɪsn, 'medsn]	Medizin, Arznei	People who are ill have to take ~ to get well again.
progress *(no pl)* ['prəʊgres]	Fortschritt(e)	Since my trip to the USA, I've made a lot of ~ in my English.

TIPP

Richtig lernen – leichter lernen

Du lernst Wörter leichter, wenn du **bestimmte Lern- und Merkverfahren** anwendest und dir **Gedächtnisstützen und Eselsbrücken** zunutze machst. (Eselsbrücken sind wie Haken, an denen du Informationen im Gedächtnis festmachst.) Am bekanntesten sind

- die **Reimtechnik:**

  blow – blew – blown sounds like *grow – grew – grown*
  and *sing – sang – sung* sounds like *ring – rang – rung*

- die **Ähnlichkeitstechnik:**

  ceiling – wie im Alphabet: e vor i
  lamp – Lampe
  rich – reich
  square – Quadrat
  blood – Blut
  bicycle – wie im Alphabet: i vor y

- die **Geschichtentechnik:**
  Wenn du einkaufen gehst, kannst du dir einen Einkaufszettel schreiben. Du kannst dir die einzukaufenden Dinge aber auch merken, indem du dir eine Geschichte ausdenkst, in der alle Dinge vorkommen!
  Diese Technik funktioniert auch, wenn du Wörter zu einem bestimmten Wortfeld lernen oder wiederholen willst.
  Versuch es mal mit diesen *food words*:
  bread, oranges, cheese, tomatoes, milk.

V

►►► Unit 2: Alaska – the Great Land

Unit 2

pp.20/21	imaginary [ɪ'mædʒɪnəri]	imaginär *(nur in der Vorstellung vorhanden, nicht wirklich)*	'Trogland' is not a real country, it's only ~. verb: (to) imagine – noun: imagination – adjective: *imaginary*
	range [reɪndʒ]	(Berg-, Felsen-)Kette	The Himalayas are the highest mountain ~ in the world.
p.22/A1	(to) **make friends (with** sb.**)**	Freunde finden, sich anfreunden (mit jm.)	
	supper ['sʌpə]	(warmes) Abendessen	the last meal of the day
	whale [weɪl]	Wal(fisch)	a *whale* 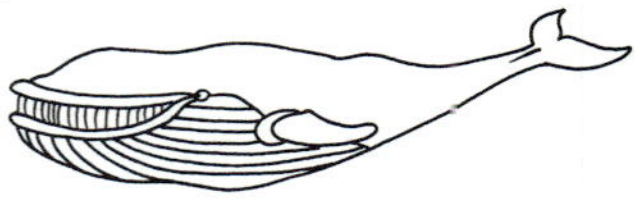
	°blubber ['blʌbə]	(Walfisch-)Speck	
	butcher ['bʊtʃə]	Fleischer/in, Metzger/in, Schlachter/in	I must go to the *butcher's* (= zum Metzger, in die Metzgerei).
	timeless ['taɪmləs]	zeitlos, ewig	
	Inuit, *pl* Inuit *or* Inuits ['ɪnuɪt, 'ɪnjuɪt]	Inuit, Eskimo	
	sled [sled] *(AE)*, sledge [sledʒ] *(BE)*	Schlitten	a *sled (AE)* / *sledge (BE)* 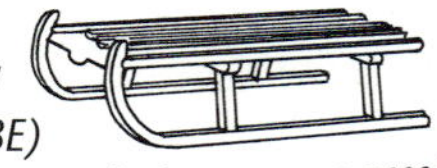
	(to) **combine** [kəm'baɪn]	kombinieren, verbinden	On our trip we tried to ~ work with fun. **combine** **kombin**ieren
	old/new ways	alte/neue Lebensweisen, Denkweisen, Bräuche	
A2	**as soon as** [əz 'su:n‿əz] *(conj)*	sobald	I'll phone you *as* ~ *as* I know the date of the meeting.
	(to) **argue (with** sb. **about** sth.) ['ɑ:gju:]	sich (mit jm. über/wegen etwas) streiten, zanken	We often ~ *about* which TV programme we should watch. Don't ~ *with* me. Just do what I say! verb: *(to) argue* – noun: argument
	(to) **make fun of** sb./sth.	sich über jn./etwas lustig machen	The children *made* ~ *of* Mr Owen's hair after he had cut it himself.
	°Inupiaq [ɪ'nu:piæk] °Inupiat [ɪ'nu:piæt]	*Sprache der Inupiat* *im Norden und Nordwesten Alaskas lebendes Inuit-Volk*	
	You can't talk to Amy any more.	Man kann mit Amy nicht mehr reden.	

German 'man'

you – **You** should brush **your** teeth three times a day.	▷	**Man (= Jeder)** sollte … **seine** Zähne putzen.
one – **One** should brush **one's** teeth three times a day.		
they – **They** say Nebraska is boring.	▷	**Man** sagt (= **Die Leute** sagen), Nebraska sei langweilig.
people – **People** say Nebraska is boring.		
(the passive) – This colour **isn't worn** any more.		Diese Farbe trägt **man** nicht mehr.

One is used mainly in formal English. In informal English ***you*** is more usual.

	at least [ət 'li:st]	wenigstens, mindestens; zumindest	You have to be *at* ~ 16 to be able to see that film. These shoes aren't cool, but *at* ~ they're warm!
	(to) **form** [fɔ:m]	(sich) bilden, formen	You ~ the simple past of regular verbs with '-ed'.
p.23/A3	whaling ['weɪlɪŋ]	Walfang	
	probably ['prɒbəbli]	wahrscheinlich	Are you going to Steve's party? – *Probably*, but I'm not sure yet.
	people ['pi:pl]	Volk	⚠ *the people* = **1.** die Leute/Menschen; **2.** das Volk *the peoples* = die Völker
	endless ['endləs]	endlos	The lesson was so boring, it seemed ~.
	culture [⚠ *stress:* 'kʌltʃə]	Kultur	
	(to) **cover** ['kʌvə]	beziehen, überziehen	That old sofa looks terrible. I *'m going to* ~ it in red. ⚠ *(to) cover* = **1.** be-, zudecken; **2.** be-, überziehen
	°umiak ['u:miæk]	*offenes, mit Robbenhaut bespanntes Boot*	
	skin [skɪn]	Haut	Put a T-shirt on so that the sun won't burn your ~.

	°snowmobile ['snəʊmə,bi:l]	Schneemobil	
	tent [tent]	Zelt	
	°harpoon [hɑ:'pu:n]	Harpune	
	°tundra ['tʌndrə]	Tundra *(baumlose Steppe)*	
	in order to do sth. ['ɔ:də]	um etwas zu tun	I went early *in ~ to* get a good seat. ⚠ No comma before *in order to.*
	(to) **celebrate** ['selɪbreɪt]	feiern	My grandma wants to ~ her 75th birthday in a restaurant. verb: *(to) celebrate* – noun: celebration
	shocked [ʃɒkt]	schockiert	When I heard she had died, I was really ~.
p.24/A4	**(to) date sb.** [deɪt] *(AE)*	mit jm. (aus)gehen	Sue is sad. She's not ~ Tom any more.
	(to) go on a date (with sb.) [deɪt] *(AE)*	mit jm. (aus)gehen	Didn't you know? Ann and Tom *have been dating* each other for two months now.
	(to) make a date (with sb.) *(AE)*	sich (mit jm.) *(zum Ausgehen)* verabreden	
	(to) **tell** sb. **(not) to do** sth.	jn. auffordern, etwas (nicht) zu tun; jm. sagen, dass er/sie etwas (nicht) tun soll	The teacher *told* the pupils *to listen* carefully. How often do I have to ~ you *not to hit* your sister?
	plenty (of) ['plenti]	eine Menge, viel(e)	lots (of); more than enough
	cute [kju:t] *(infml)*	niedlich, süß	Mum thinks Brad Pitt is horrible, but I think he's ~.
	(to) **expect** [ɪk'spekt]	erwarten, annehmen, vermuten	How many guests *are* you *~ ing*? Ann is late. I ~ she has missed the bus again.
	(to) embarrass sb. [ɪm'bærəs]	jn. in Verlegenheit bringen	
	Wow! [waʊ] *(infml)*	*(Ausruf)* Mensch! / Wahnsinn!	I've won $100! – *Wow!*
	sure *(adv)* [ʃʊə] *(infml, besonders AE)*	wirklich, echt	I ~ like that girl. (= I really like that girl.)
	fresh [freʃ]	frisch; neu	Is this milk still ~? – No, it's four days old. Let's make a ~ start.
	°all-terrain vehicle (ATV) [,ɔ:ltə,reɪn 'vi:əkl]	Geländewagen	
p.25/A5	**huge** [hju:dʒ]	sehr groß, riesig	very large
	(to) **shut (-tt-), shut, shut** [ʃʌt]	schließen, zumachen	(to) close Can I ~ the window? I'm cold. ◂▸ (to) open
	°caribou, *pl* caribou *or* caribous ['kærɪbu:]	Karibu *(nordamerikanische Rentierart)*	
	a long way	ein weiter Weg; weit (entfernt)	

fresh – frisch

German 'weit'

Questions and negative statements: *far*	Positive statements: *a long way*
Is it **far** to the town centre?	Yes, it's **a long way.**
How **far** did you walk?	We walked **a long way.**
I do**n't** live **far** from here.	My cousins live **a long way** away.
We did**n't** travel **far** on the first day.	But on the next day we went **a long way.**

	northern ['nɔ:ðən]	nördlich, Nord-	
	°moose, *pl* moose [mu:s]	*(amerikanischer)* Elch	
	deer, *pl* deer [dɪə]	Reh, Hirsch	
	member (of) ['membə]	Mitglied (in, von)	⚠ With 'a': *I'm a member of …* = *Ich bin Mitglied in …*
	herd [hɜ:d]	Herde *(z.B. Kühe)*, Herden-	Cows are ~ animals. They live in ~s.
	plant [plɑ:nt]	Pflanze	noun: *plant* = „Pflanze" – verb: (to) plant = „(ein)pflanzen"
	°grizzly bear ['grɪzli beə]	Grislibär	
	bear [beə]	Bär	

nouns:	north	south	east	west
adjectives:	northern	southern ⚠ ['sʌðən]	eastern	western

a plant

bear – Bär

	sick [sɪk]	krank	▸◂ well ⚠ – *be, feel, look* + *ill* (BE)/*sick* (AE): You look *ill* (BE). / *sick* (AE). Do you feel *ill* (BE)? / *sick* (AE)? – *sick* + noun (BE and AE): a *sick* animal, a very *sick* man
	wolf [wʊlf], *pl* wolves [wʊlvz]	Wolf	⚠ one *wolf* [wʊlf] – two *wolves* [wʊlvz] (Remember: *life, lives / shelf, shelves / thief, thieves*)
	weak [wi:k]	schwach	▸◂ strong
	(to) **support**	*(Familie usw.)* ernähren, unterhalten	
	bull [bʊl]	Bulle, Stier	
	(to) **protect** sb. **(from** sth.**)** [prə'tekt]	jn. (be)schützen (vor etwas)	Trees can ~ you *from* the sun.
	(to) hunt (for) [hʌnt]	jagen (nach); Jagd machen (auf), suchen	Do you think that people still ~ lions in Africa? I*'ve ~ed* everywhere *for* my keys, but I can't find them.
	°pack [pæk]	Rudel *(Wölfe, Hunde)*	
P 1	**situation** [ˌsɪtʃu'eɪʃn]	Situation	
P 2	**pair (of)** [peə]	Paar	a *pair of* shoes 
	(to) **connect (to/with)** [kə'nekt]	verbinden (mit)	This corridor ~s the old part of the building *to/with* the new part.
	movie ['mu:vi] *(besonders AE)*	Film	= *BE* film (to) go to the *movies* (AE) = (to) go to the cinema (BE)
	movie theater ['mu:vi ˌθɪətə] *(AE)*	Kino	= *BE* cinema
P 5	(to) **get to know**	kennen lernen	I haven't met Tom's sister, but I*'ll* ~ *to know* her at his party, I hope.
	°aviation [ˌeɪvi'eɪʃn]	Luftfahrt	
	glacier [*BE:* 'glæsiə, *AE:* 'gleɪʃə]	Gletscher	
	construction [⚠ *stress:* kən'strʌkʃn]	Konstruktion	
P 8	**e.g.** [ˌi: 'dʒi:]	z. B. (zum Beispiel)	Some English words are the same in German, *e.g.* (= for example) 'quiz' or 'computer'.

Alone on the North Slope

p.30	slope [sləʊp]	Hang	
	nice and warm/dry/...	schön warm/trocken/...	It's ~ ~ *warm* by the fire.
	(to) hurt [hɜ:t]	schaden, schädigen	Solar-powered cars *don't* ~ the environment.
	(oil) well [wel]	Ölquelle	
	native ['neɪtɪv] *(n; adj)*	Ur(einwohner/in); eingeboren, einheimisch	The ~ people of Australia have lived there for 20,000 years.
	regional ['ri:dʒənl]	regional	There are ~ differences in the way people speak.
	°corporation [ˌkɔ:pə'reɪʃn]	Verwaltung	
	company ['kʌmpəni]	Firma, Gesellschaft	My uncle works for an oil ~ in Scotland.
	at (the age of) 39	mit 39, im Alter von 39 Jahren	
	president [⚠ *stress:* 'prezɪdənt]	Präsident/in	
	complete [kəm'pli:t]	vollständig, völlig	I'm sorry. I ~*ly* forgot that it's your birthday today. verb: (to) complete – adjective: *complete*
	(to) joke [dʒəʊk]	witzeln, scherzen	noun: joke – verb: *(to) joke*
	sleeping-bag ['sli:pɪŋ bæg]	Schlafsack	
	equipment *(no pl)* [ɪ'kwɪpmənt]	Ausrüstung	⚠ *Without 'a/an':* I need new sports *equipment*. (... *eine* neue Sport*ausrüstung*.)
	(to) teach sb. a lesson	jm. eine Lektion erteilen	If you do that again, you won't get any birthday presents. That *will* ~ *you a lesson*.
	(to) go for a ride	eine Spazierfahrt machen; herumfahren	Where are we going? – I don't know yet. We*'re* just *going for a* ~.
	(to) **matter** ['mætə]	von Bedeutung sein, etwas ausmachen	Sorry, I forgot the potatoes. *Does* it ~? – No, it *doesn't* ~. We can have bread instead.
	cold [kəʊld]	Kälte; Erkältung	adjective: cold – noun: *cold* ▸◂ hot *(adj)*/heat *(n)* ⚠ Ich *bin (schwer) erkältet.* = I*'ve got a (bad) cold.*

	(to) **rise** [raɪz], **rose** [rəʊz], **risen** ['rɪzn]	aufgehen *(Sonne, Mond)*; (an-, auf-) steigen	The sun ~*s* in the east. Prices *have risen* 10%.
p.31	spark [spɑːk]	Funke	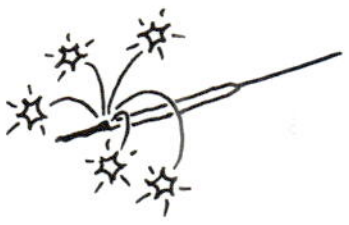 *sparks*
	leaf [liːf], *pl* **leaves** [liːvz]	Blatt *(an Pflanzen)*	In the fall, the *leaves* fall to the ground. ⚠ ein *Blatt* Papier = a *piece of* paper
	(to) **pour** [pɔː]	gießen, schütten; einschenken	 *(to) pour*
	flat (-tt-) *(adj)* [flæt]	flach, eben	The countryside is very ~. There are no mountains. ⚠ *flat* = **1.** *(n)* Wohnung; **2.** *(adj)* flach, eben
	frozen ['frəʊzn]	zugefroren; tiefgefroren	They only sell ~ food or food in tins here.
	(to) **freeze** [friːz], **froze** [frəʊz], **frozen** ['frəʊzn]	(ge)frieren; einfrieren	Rivers and lakes sometimes ~ in winter. It*'s freezing* outside. (= It's very cold outside.)
	(to) **put** sth. **up** (-tt-)	etwas aufstellen/errichten/aufhängen	The tent was new, so we needed 3 hours to ~ it *up*. We saw a note on the board. Mr Jones *had* ~ it *up*.
	(to) **melt** [melt]	schmelzen	The sun came out and the snow began to ~. (to) **melt** – sch**mel**zen ⧓ (to) freeze
	(to) **hang** [hæŋ], **hung** [hʌŋ], **hung**	hängen, aufhängen	Please ~ your coat over the chair. A photo of Alaska *hung* on the wall.
	(to) **tear** sth. **(off)** [teə], **tore** [tɔː], **torn** [tɔːn]	etwas (ab)reißen; etwas zerreißen	Fill in the form below, ~ it *off*, and send it back to us. The dog *tore* the newspaper into little pieces.
	flame [fleɪm]	Flamme	*flames* 
	edge [edʒ]	Rand, Kante	Put your cup in the middle of the table, not on the ~.
	thirst [θɜːst]	Durst	adjective: thirsty – noun: *thirst* ⚠ Ich *habe Durst.* = I*'m thirsty.*
	(to) **survive** [sə'vaɪv]	überleben	Three people ~*d* the accident, two people died.
	track [træk]	Spur, Fährte	Look at those ~*s* in the snow. I think that was a bear.
	movement ['muːvmənt]	Bewegung	I think my leg is broken. Every ~ hurts. verb: (to) move – noun: *movement*
p.32	**statement** ['steɪtmənt]	Aussage(satz)	

TIPP

Kenntnisse aus anderen Fremdsprachen nutzen

Ist dir schon einmal aufgefallen, wie ähnlich manche Wörter im Englischen, Französischen und Lateinischen sind?
Wenn du also ein unbekanntes Wort siehst, überleg erstmal, ob du es vielleicht schon aus einer anderen Sprache kennst.

Aber Vorsicht bei der Schreibung, z.B. engl. *exa̲mple* – frz. *exe̲mple*.

Englisch	Französisch	Latein
animal	**animal**	**animal**
(to) **celebrate**	**célébrer**	**celebrare**
community	**communauté**	**communitas**
(to) **complete**	**compléter**	**complere**
colour	**couleur**	**color**
difficult	**difficile**	**difficilis**
example	**exemple**	**exemplum**
family	**famille**	**familia**
hour	**heure**	**hora**
language	**langage**	**lingua**
(to) **offer**	**offrir**	**offerre**
opinion	**opinion**	**opinio**
(to) **protect**	**protéger**	**protegere**
progress	**progrès**	**progressus**

p.33 **How to use a dictionary**

headword ['hedwɜːd]	Stichwort	
translation [træns'leɪʃn]	Übersetzung	
(to) **translate (into)** [træns'leɪt]	übersetzen (in)	We had to ~ the text from English *into* German.

(to) **pronounce** [prəˈnaʊns]	aussprechen	(to) say How do you ~ this word?
pronunciation [prəˌnʌnsiˈeɪʃn]	Aussprache	⚠ verb: *(to) pronounce* – noun: *pronunciation*
(to) **underline** [ˌʌndəˈlaɪn]	unterstreichen	In the sentence 'I'm not late!' the word 'not' is ~*d*.
bracket [ˈbrækɪt]	Klammer *(in einem Text)*	(These words are in ~*s*.)

AE pronunciation – BE pronunciation

	American English		British English	
ask, last, dances	[æ]	[æsk, læst, dæns]	[ɑː]	[ɑːsk, lɑːst, dɑːns]
new, Tuesday, stupid	[uː]	[nuː, ˈtuːzdi, ˈstuːpɪd]	[juː]	[njuː, ˈtjuːzdi, ˈstjuːpɪd]
bottle, hot, forgot	[ɑː]	[ˈbɑːtl, hɑːt, fəˈgɑːt]	[ɒ]	[ˈbɒtl, hɒt, fəˈgɒt]

- In American English you can usually hear the 'r' in words like *here, more, shirt, farm*.
- The 't' in words like *city, better, motor* sounds more like a 'd' in American English.

▶▶▶ Unit 3: In Search of Colonial Virginia

pp.36/37	in search of [sɜːtʃ]	auf der Suche nach	Don has gone to Scotland *in ~ of* the Loch Ness Monster.
	colonial [kəˈləʊniəl]	kolonial, Kolonial-	
	colony [ˈkɒləni]	Kolonie	Australia was once a British ~. ⚠ stress: *colony* [ˈkɒləni] – *colonial* [kəˈləʊniəl]
	colonist [ˈkɒlənɪst]	Kolonist/in; Siedler/in	
	store [stɔː]	Geschäft, Laden	In British English only big shops are called *'stores'*. ⚠ department *store* = Kaufhaus
	°blacksmith shop [ˈblæksmɪθ ˌʃɒp]	Schmiedewerkstatt	
	living [ˈlɪvɪŋ]	lebend	▸◂ dead ⚠ – before a noun: *living* My favourite *living* writer is Stephen King. – after a verb like *be*: *alive* Is she still *alive*?
	(to) **join** sb. [dʒɔɪn]	sich jm. anschließen; mitmachen	We're going to the cinema. Do you want to ~ us? *(to) join* = **1.** beitreten, eintreten in *(einen Klub usw.)*; **2.** sich anschließen; mitmachen
	shoemaker [ˈʃuːˌmeɪkə]	Schuhmacher/in	a person who makes shoes
	wedding [ˈwedɪŋ]	Hochzeit	When are they getting married? When is the ~?

a *wedding* cake

descendant (of) [dɪˈsendənt]	Nachkomme (von)	He says he's a ~ of an 18th-century Russian prince.
ancestor [ˈænsestə]	Vorfahre	He says one of his ~*s* was a Russian prince.
(to) **march** [mɑːtʃ]	marschieren	Ordinary people walk, soldiers ~.
liberty [ˈlɪbəti]	Freiheit	New York's most famous statue is the Statue of L~.
(to) be good	gültig sein	This ticket *is* ~ for a month. = You can use it for a month.
°grove [grəʊv]	Wäldchen	
plantation [plænˈteɪʃn]	Plantage	
master [ˈmɑːstə]	Herr *(eines Sklaven/ einer Sklavin)*	a man who has slaves
the Capitol [ˈkæpɪtl]	das Kapitol *(Sitz der gesetzgebenden Versammlung)*	
governor [ˈgʌvənə]	Gouverneur/in	the 'boss' of a state or colony
courthouse [ˈkɔːthaʊs]	Gerichtsgebäude	
°green	Grünfläche, (Dorf-)Platz	
greeting [ˈgriːtɪŋ]	Gruß, Begrüßung	He said nothing as a ~, he didn't even look up.
entry [ˈentri]	Einsendung, Beitrag *(zu einem Wettbewerb)*	There were over 600 *entries* for our competition. *entry* = **1.** Eintrag; **2.** Einsendung
foreground [ˈfɔːgraʊnd]	Vordergrund	In this photo, you can see Dan better. He's in the ~,
background [ˈbækgraʊnd]	Hintergrund	and in the ~ you can see part of his house.

p.38/A1	°sis *(infml)*	= *sister*	
	family tree [ˌfæməli ˈtriː]	(Familien-)Stammbaum	
	program [ˈprəʊɡræm]	(Computer-)Programm	⚠ *AE* program – *BE* program<u>me</u> ◁ *Programm, Sendung*; *BE* program ◁ *Computerprogramm*
	printout [ˈprɪntaʊt]	Ausdruck	Make a ~ of the text, then turn the computer off.
	(to) **print** [prɪnt]	(ab)drucken	This book *was ~ed* by a company in Berlin.
	printer [ˈprɪntə]	Drucker	*printer* = **1.** a person; **2.** a machine
	great-aunt	Großtante	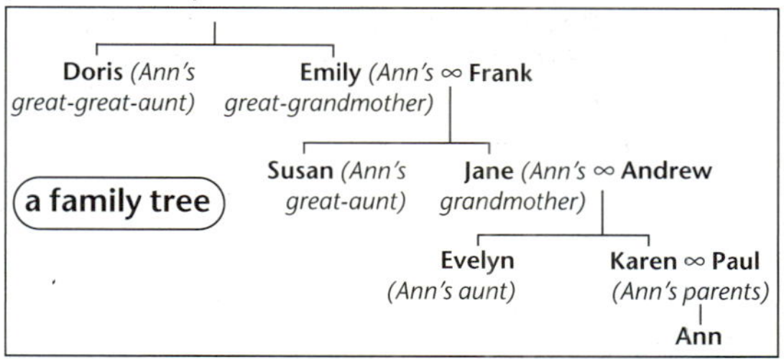
	great-great-aunt	Urgroßtante	
	great-grandmother	Urgroßmutter	
	°like [laɪk] *(infml)*	also, irgendwie	
	honour *(BE)*, honor *(AE)* [ˈɒnə]	Ehre	⚠ The *'h'* isn't pronounced: *a<u>n</u> honour* [ən‿ˈɒnə], *a<u>n</u> hour* [ən‿ˈaʊə]
	majesty [⚠ *stress:* ˈmædʒəsti]	Majestät	
	(to) check sb./sth. out *(infml)*	jn./etwas überprüfen, mehr über jn./etwas herausfinden	
A2	tobacco [təˈbækəʊ]	Tabak	⚠ spelling: *t<u>o</u>bacco*
	°planter [ˈplɑːntə]	Pflanzer/in; Plantagenbesitzer/in	
	Declaration of Independence [ˌdekləˈreɪʃn‿əv‿ˌɪndɪˈpendəns]	Unabhängigkeitserklärung *(der ehemals 13 britischen Kolonien in Nordamerika)*	The (American) ~ *of* ~ was signed on July 4th, 1776.
	declaration [ˌdekləˈreɪʃn]	Erklärung, Verkündung, Bekanntgabe	⚠ *explanation* = Erklärung, Erläuterung; *declaration* = Erklärung, Verkündung
	(to) **declare** [dɪˈkleə]	erklären, verkünden	⚠ stress: *(to) declare* [dɪˈkleə] – *declaration* [ˌdekləˈreɪʃn] — declare – erklären
	general [⚠ *stress:* ˈdʒenrəl]	General/in	
	it says	es heißt; hier steht	*It* ~ in the paper that they've found the thief.
	(to) **reply (to)** [rɪˈplaɪ]	antworten (auf), beantworten; erwidern	(to) answer
p.39/A3	the day (that) …	der Tag, an dem …	I'll never forget ~ ~ we met.
	°I will die a free man before … *(fml)*	Ich will lieber als freier Mann sterben, ehe …	
	war [wɔː]	Krieg	
	speech bubble [ˈspiːtʃ ˌbʌbl]	Sprechblase	What people say in cartoons and comics appears in ~ ~s. 
p.40/A4	(to) **drop** sb. **(-pp-)** [drɒp]	*(einen Fahrgast)* absetzen	Can you ~ me at Phil's house on your way home? *(to) drop* = **1.** fallen lassen; **2.** absetzen
	simple [ˈsɪmpl]	einfach	I did the work quickly because it was so ~. Although she is rich, she always wears ~ clothes.
	(to) come sb.'s way	jm. entgegenkommen	(to) come towards sb.
	(to) go sb.'s way	in die gleiche Richtung wie jd. gehen	(to) go the same way as sb.
	quarter [ˈkwɔːtə]	(Stadt-)Viertel, Quartier	
	pretty *(adv)* [ˈprɪti] *(infml)*	ziemlich	*pretty* = **1.** *(adj)* hübsch; **2.** *(adv)* ziemlich
	furniture *(no pl)* [ˈfɜːnɪtʃə]	Möbel	Can you help me to move the ~ / this piece of ~? ⚠ Die *Möbel <u>sind</u>* neu. = The *furniture <u>is</u>* new. *(Never:* The ~~furnitures are~~ new.)

Unit 3

p.41/A5	(to) **take a look (at)**	einen Blick werfen (auf)	(to) have a look (at)

Phrases with *(to) have* and *(to) take*

(to) **have/take a bath**	ein Bad nehmen	Do you **have/take a bath** every day?
(to) **have/take a shower**	(sich) duschen	I **have/take a shower** before I go to bed.
(to) **have/take a break**	eine Pause machen	That's enough for now. Let's **have/take a break**.
(to) **have/take a holiday**	(einen) Urlaub machen	When are you going to **have/take a holiday**?
(to) **have a listen**	es (sich) (mal) anhören	Tom recorded the song. Let's **have a listen** (to it).
(to) **have/take a guess**	(mal) raten	I don't know the answer, but I'll **have/take a guess**.
(to) **have a try**	es (mal) versuchen	Let me **have a try** on your skateboard.
(to) **have a game**	(etwas) spielen	We've practised enough now. Let's **have a game**.

	terror ['terə]	Terror; Entsetzen, Schrecken	English tests always fill me with ~.
	right *(n)* [raɪt]	Recht	What gives you the ~ to say we can't do that? ⚠ *Recht haben = (to) be right*
	property ['prɒpəti]	Eigentum, (Immobilien-)Besitz	the things that belong to sb. She's very rich. She has a lot of ~ in London.
	crop [krɒp]	(Feld-)Frucht; Ernte	what is grown in a garden or on a farm We had a good ~ of apples last year.
	(to) **grow** [grəʊ]	*(Getreide usw.)* anbauen, anpflanzen	We have a garden now and ~ our own vegetables. ⚠ *(to) grow* = **1.** wachsen; **2.** anbauen, anpflanzen
	for sale [seɪl]	zum Verkauf; zu verkaufen	
	corn [kɔːn]	*(AE:)* Mais; *(BE:)* Korn, Getreide	*corn (AE)*   *corn (BE)*
	skilled [skɪld]	Fach-; gelernte(r); geschickt	*S~* workers find jobs much more easily than *un~* ones.
	fear (of) [fɪə]	Furcht, Angst (vor)	Which is worse – ~ *of* flying or ~ *of* falling? ⚠ *Angst haben vor = to be afraid/frightened of*
	(to) separate ['sepəreɪt]	(sich) trennen	The baby lion *was ~d* from its mother and sold to a zoo.
	16-hour day	16-Stunden-Tag	

'Number + hyphen + noun'

a **16-hour** day	ein 16-Stunden-Tag
a **12-hour** flight	ein 12-stündiger Flug, ein 12-Stunden-Flug
a **24-hour** supermarket	ein Supermarkt, der 24 Stunden („rund um die Uhr") geöffnet ist
a **2-week** holiday/visit	ein zweiwöchiger Urlaub/Besuch
a **6-month** break	eine sechsmonatige Pause
a **2-year** period	ein Zeitraum von zwei Jahren
a **30-dollar** ticket	eine 30-Dollar-Karte, eine Karte für 30 Dollar

⚠ Number + hyphen[1] + **singular noun**: *a 16-**hour** day* (not: *a 16-~~hours~~ day*)

[1]hyphen ['haɪfn] *Bindestrich*

	style [staɪl]	Stil	What ~ of jacket are you looking for?
	typical (of) ['tɪpɪkl]	typisch (für)	Dan arrived 10 minutes late. That's ~ *of* him. ⚠ *Not: ~~typical for~~*
P 2	(to) **book** [bʊk]	buchen, reservieren	noun: book ('Buch') – verb: *(to) book* ('buchen')
	(to) **press** [pres]	drücken	The boy *~ed* his nose against the glass.
P 4	(to) tie sb./sth. up [ˌtaɪ‿'ʌp]	jn./etwas festbinden	Let's ~ the dog *up*, so that it can't run away.
P 6	**death** [deθ]	Tod	verb: (to) die – adjective: dead – noun: *death*
P 9	°tavern ['tævn]	Schenke	
	archaeology [⚠ *stress:* ˌɑːki'ɒlədʒi]	Archäologie	person: *archaeologist* – subject: *archaeology*
P 10	crossword ['krɒswɜːd]	Kreuzworträtsel	
	cigarette [ˌsɪgə'ret]	Zigarette	
P 11	**missing** ['mɪsɪŋ]	fehlend	
	(to) colonize ['kɒlənaɪz]	kolonisieren	
	historian [hɪ'stɔːriən]	Historiker/in	
	historical [hɪ'stɒrɪkl]	historisch, alt	The most important ~ building here is the church. It's 700 years old.
	document [⚠ *stress:* 'dɒkjumənt]	Dokument, Urkunde	

historical – historisch

The Drinking Cup

p.46	pirate [⚠ *stress:* 'paɪrət]	Pirat/in	
	bay [beɪ]	Bucht	part of the sea with land on three sides 
	(to) **go** cold/white/…	kalt/weiß/… werden	When they told him the news, his face *went* white.

German 'werden'

(to) **become** (to) **get**	The most important English ways of saying 'werden' are *(to) get* and *(to) become.* *(to) get* is used more in informal English.	(to) **become/get** | **angry/tired/nervous/old/…** **cold/windy/dark/…** **boring/funny/more interesting/…**
	⚠ With nouns, only *(to) **become*** is used: She **became a doctor/a football fan/…**	
(to) **go**	*(to) **go*** is often used with colours.	(to) **go red/brown/white/black/…**
	*(to) **go*** is also used when something changes for the worse.	(to) **go hard** *(bread)*/**bad** *(fish, eggs, cheese)*

	°convoy [⚠ *stress:* 'kɒnvɔɪ]	Konvoi	
	skeleton [⚠ *stress:* 'skelɪtn]	Skelett	
	beard [bɪəd]	Bart	a man with a ~ 
	°cannon [⚠ *stress:* 'kænən], *pl* cannon *or* cannons	Kanone	
	shot [ʃɒt]	Schuss	
	(to) **shoot** [ʃuːt], **shot** [ʃɒt], **shot** [ʃɒt]	(er-, an)schießen	The men had guns, but they *didn't* ~. noun: *shot* – verb: *(to) shoot*
	warning (to sb.**)** ['wɔːnɪŋ]	Warnung	After the accident we drove more slowly. It was a ~ *to* us.
	profit [⚠ *stress:* 'prɒfɪt]	Gewinn, Profit	How much ~ did you make? – I made a ~ of $20.
p. 47	devil ['devl]	Teufel	
	hell [hel]	(die) Hölle	
	(to) **murder** ['mɜːdə]	(er)morden	(to) kill
	murder *(n)* ['mɜːdə]	Mord	⚠ *murder (n)* = Mord (*not:* ~~Mörder~~)
	murderer ['mɜːdərə]	Mörder/in	*murderer (n)* = Mörder/in
	memory ['meməri]	Gedächtnis; Erinnerung; Gedenken	I've got a bad ~. I can never remember people's names. What *memories* do you have of your childhood? They put up a statue *in ~ of* the town's most famous writer. (= zum Gedenken an)
	°skull [skʌl]	Schädel	
	gladly *(adv)* ['glædli]	gern; freudig	'No problem,' he said. 'For you I'll do it ~.' 'Look, this is my prize!' Ann said ~.
	(to) **attack** [ə'tæk]	angreifen	verb: *(to) attack* – (to) attack –
	attack [ə'tæk]	Angriff	noun: *attack* attackieren
	goods *(pl)* [gʊdz]	Waren, Güter	things that are produced for sale
	trade [treɪd]	Handel	the activity of buying and selling
	battle ['bætl]	Schlacht, Kampf	How many soldiers were killed in the ~?
p.48	**as**	da, weil	*As* it was raining, we couldn't play outside.

as

as *(conj)*:		**as** *(prep)*: *as* a child — *als* Kind
1. *as* you all know	*wie* ihr alle wisst	**as … as:**
2. *as* she left *(= when)*	*als* sie ging	*as* fast *as* a horse — *so* schnell *wie* ein Pferd
3. *as* it was raining *(= because)*	*weil* es regnete	

sword [sɔːd]	Schwert	⚠ The *'w'* isn't pronounced: *sword* [sɔːd] 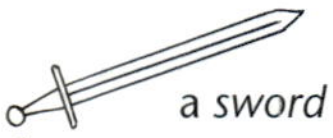 *a sword*
throat [θrəʊt]	Kehle, Hals	① *neck* [nek]  ② *throat*

(to) **fall asleep** [ə'sli:p] (to) **be asleep**	einschlafen schlafen	My grandad always *falls* ~ in front of the TV.

German 'schlafen'

People normally use *(to) be asleep* – not *(to) sleep* – to express the idea that someone is in a state[1] of sleep.

[1]state *Zustand*

Why didn't you answer the phone?
– I **was asleep**. (*Not:* I ~~was sleeping~~.)

⚠ **schlafen gehen** = (to) **go to bed**

gone [gɒn] *(adj)*	weg, fort	⚠ Be careful with *gone*: – *(to) be gone* = weg sein, fort sein: Where's Pete? – He*'s* (= He *is*) *gone*. – If you want to say where someone has gone, you use *have/has gone*: Where's Pete? – He *has gone* home.
believable [bɪ'li:vəbl] **unbelievable** [ˌʌnbɪ'li:vəbl]	glaubhaft unglaublich	It sounds a very strange story. Do you think it's ~? I don't believe it. = I find it ~. verb: (to) belie**ve** – adjective: belie**v**able

p.49

How to organize information

(to) **organize** ['ɔ:gənaɪz]	ordnen, einteilen	
task [tɑ:sk]	Aufgabe	a piece of work that has to be done
source [sɔ:s]	*(Informations-, Text-)* Quelle	The Internet is a useful ~ of information. Oil is a ~ of energy.
(to) **repair** [rɪ'peə]	reparieren, ausbessern	This road is terrible. When are they going to ~ it? repair – reparieren
(to) **escape (from** sb./sth.) [ɪ'skeɪp]	fliehen (vor jm. / aus etwas); entkommen	A lion *has ~d from* its cage. The police couldn't catch the thief – he *~d* in a fast sports car. What happens if you press the *escape* key (= Taste)?

punishment ['pʌnɪʃmənt]	Strafe, Bestrafung	What is the right ~ for a child who steals?
(to) **punish** ['pʌnɪʃ]	bestrafen	When you did something wrong as a child, how *were* you *~ed*?
(to) **do the cooking**/ (to) **do the cleaning**	kochen/sauber machen *(= das Kochen/Saubermachen übernehmen)*	Mum and Dad both work at home: one *~es the cooking*, the other *~es the cleaning*. ⚠ das Mittagessen *kochen* = *(to) cook/make* lunch Kaffee *kochen* = *(to) make* coffee
(to) set sb. free (-tt-) [ˌset 'fri:], set, set	jn. befreien	(to) give sb. his or her liberty
hut [hʌt]	Hütte	They spent the night on the mountain in a mountain ~.
°runaway ['rʌnəweɪ]	Ausreißer/in	
(to) **summarize** ['sʌməraɪz]	zusammenfassen	(to) say something in a few words Right, before we finish, let's quickly ~ what has been decided.
summary (of) ['sʌməri]	Zusammenfassung (von)	What happens in the film? Can you give me a quick ~?
(to) order ['ɔ:də]	ordnen	*(to) order* = **1.** bestellen; **2.** ordnen

TIPP

'Alphabetical sentences' – a game Hier eine Idee für ein Spiel zu zweit oder in der Gruppe (das *DICTIONARY* auf den Seiten 166–192 kann hilfreich sein):

- **Variante 1 – „ABC-Sätze“:** Jeder versucht, in einem festgelegten Zeitraum möglichst viele Sätze wie *Andrew buys cheap drinks every Friday.* oder *Kids love making noise on pavements.* zu bilden.

  Jeder richtige Satz bringt so viele Punkte, wie der Satz Wörter hat.

- **Variante 2 – „AAA-Sätze“:** Hierbei geht es um Sätze aus Wörtern mit demselben Anfangsbuchstaben (ein oder zwei nicht passende Wörter sind erlaubt). Beispiele: *Allen and Amy are almost always against all the alternatives.* oder *For fine frozen fish ask funny Fred.*

▶▶▶ Unit 4: New York – Gateway to America

pp.50/51	gateway (to) ['geɪtweɪ]	Tor(weg), Zugang (zu)	Dover is Britain's ~ to Europe.
	immigrant [⚠ *stress:* 'ɪmɪgrənt]	Einwanderer/Einwanderin, Immigrant/in	
	(to) immigrate (to) ['ɪmɪgreɪt]	einwandern, immigrieren (in *ein Land*)	(to) come to a country to live there
	immigration (to) [ˌɪmɪ'greɪʃn]	Einwanderung, Immigration (in, nach)	
	process [⚠ *stress:* 'prəʊses]	Vorgang, Verfahren, Prozess	
	great	groß, bedeutend, wichtig	

German 'groß'

large – big:	***large*** is mainly used for things; ***big*** is used for things and people.	We've got a **big/large** house near Ashton. What's the **biggest/largest** ethnic group in Bradford? Lord Nelson was not a very **big** man.
tall:	***tall*** *(groß, hoch)* is used to talk about the height[1] of people and things. [1]height [haɪt] *Höhe, Größe*	Is Janet **taller** than Karen? How **tall** is Nelson's Column?
huge:	*sehr groß, riesig*	Have you seen their new house? It's **huge**!
great:	1. *großartig, toll*	▷ **Great**! No homework today. We had a **great** time at the party. The music was **great**.
	2. *bedeutend, wichtig, berühmt*	▷ Do you know the CD '**Greatest** Rap Hits'? Who was the world's **greatest** pirate?
	3. *groß, beträchtlich*	▷ The children were in **great** danger. A **great** number of people arrived late.

	political [pə'lɪtɪkl]	politisch	
	persecution [ˌpɜːsɪ'kjuːʃn]	Verfolgung *(aus politischen, religiösen oder ethnischen Gründen)*	
	hunger ['hʌŋgə]	Hunger	adjective: hungry – noun: *hunger* ⚠ Ich *habe Hunger.* = *I'm hungry.*
	poverty ['pɒvəti]	(die) Armut	adjective: poor – noun: *poverty*
	marital status [ˌmærɪtl 'steɪtəs]	Familienstand	
	Jewish ['dʒuːɪʃ]	jüdisch	
	Jew [dʒuː]	Jude/Jüdin	
	single ['sɪŋgl]	ledig, allein stehend	Marital status: ❑ single ❑ married ❑ divorced
	(to) **fill** sth. **in** [ˌfɪl‿'ɪn]	etwas ausfüllen *(Formular usw.)*	*Fill* ~ the form and sign it, please. ⚠ *(to) fill in* = **1.** ausfüllen; **2.** einsetzen
p.52/A1	over time	über die Jahre; im Laufe der Zeit	It's interesting to watch how a baby changes and develops ~ ~.
	view (of/over) [vjuː]	Aussicht, Blick (auf/über)	This postcard shows a ~ *of* the beach. From the tower there's a lovely ~ *over* the city.
	view (about/on)	Meinung (über/zu)	What's your ~ *on* this? Do you agree with me?
	review [rɪ'vjuː]	*(Buch-, Film-)*Besprechung, Rezension	The film we saw last night got a good ~ in the paper.
	°bar mitzvah [bɑː 'mɪtsvə]	*(die)* Bar-Mizwa *(Aufnahme in die jüdische Gemeinde, vergleichbar mit Konfirmation und Firmung)*	
	(to) mail [meɪl] *(besonders AE)*	abschicken, einwerfen, zur Post bringen	(to) send by post
	(to) recite [rɪ'saɪt]	rezitieren, vortragen	Learn the poem so that you can ~ it to the class.
	Hebrew ['hiːbruː]	hebräisch; Hebräisch	
	°Torah ['tɔːrə]	*(die)* Thora *(das gesammelte jüdische Gesetz)*	
	Say. *(AE, infml)*	He! / Hör mal!	*Say,* what about an Indian meal tonight?
	honey ['hʌni]	Honig; *(infml auch:)* Schatz, Schätzchen	

	prayer [preə] (to) **pray** [preɪ] shawl [ʃɔːl]	Gebet beten Schultertuch	a *scarf*  a *shawl* 
A2	**cafeteria** [⚠ *stress:* ˌkæfəˈtɪəriə]	Kantine, Selbstbedienungsrestaurant	
	(to) **pass** sth. [pɑːs]	etwas (herüber)reichen	Can you ~ me the salt, please?
	sugar [ˈʃʊgə]	Zucker	Tea with milk and ~? – Just milk, please.
	(to) **taste** [teɪst]	schmecken	⚠ After verbs like *(to) taste, (to) smell, (to) sound* you use an adjective, not an adverb: This cheese *tastes terrible*. (*not:* ~~tastes terribly~~)
	°performing arts [pəˌfɔːmɪŋ‿ˈɑːts]	darstellende Künste *(Schauspiel- u. Tanzkünste)*	
	as well as [əz ˈwel‿əz]	und auch, ebenso wie	Michael's parents give him anything he wants. He's got his own television *as ~ as* his own computer.
	race [reɪs]	Rasse	⚠ *race* = **1.** Rennen, Wettlauf; **2.** Rasse
	°borough [*BE:* ˈbʌrə, *AE:* ˈbɜːrəʊ]	(Stadt-)Bezirk	
	twice [twaɪs]	zweimal	two – twice

once – twice – three times

once = *einmal*	I've only been to London **once**, and that was a long time ago.
twice = *zweimal*	I've seen the show **twice**, I don't want to see it again.
three times = *dreimal*	We went to the theatre **three times** last month.

	in general [ˈdʒenrəl]	im Allgemeinen	*In ~*, men are taller than women.
	specific [spəˈsɪfɪk]	bestimmte(r, s), spezifische(r, s)	◂▸ general specific – spezifisch
p.53/A3	subway [ˈsʌbweɪ] *(AE)*	U-Bahn	= *BE* underground

AE vocabulary – BE vocabulary

AE	BE		AE	BE	
apartment [əˈpɑːtmənt]	**flat**	Wohnung	**grade**	**class/form**	Klasse(nstufe)
bathroom/ restroom	**toilet**	Toilette	**I guess**	**I suppose/ I guess**	ich nehme an
bathroom	bathroom	Bad(ezimmer)	**mom**	**mum**	Mama, Mutti
(to) **date** sb./ **go out with** sb.	(to) **go out with** sb.	mit jm. ausgehen	**movie, film**	**film, movie**	Film
elevator [ˈelɪveɪtə]	**lift**	Fahrstuhl, Aufzug	**movie theater**	**cinema**	Kino
fall	**autumn**	Herbst	**neat**	**very nice**	toll, klasse
first floor	**ground floor**	Erdgeschoss	**sidewalk**	**pavement**	Bürgersteig
from … through/ from … to	**from … to**	von … bis	**sled**	**sledge**	Schlitten
			student	**pupil, student**	Schüler/in
			student	student	Student/in
			vacation	**holiday(s)**	Ferien, Urlaub
			Z [ziː]	**Z** [zed]	Z *(Buchstabe)*

°uptown [ˈʌptaʊn] *(AE)*	*der Norden Manhattans/ in den Norden Manhattans*	
°downtown [ˈdaʊntaʊn] *(AE)*	*der Süden Manhattans/ in den Süden Manhattans*	

***Why (not)* + infinitive**

You can use *Why not* + **infinitive** to make suggestions:	I don't know what to do. – **Why not write** to your friends in Germany? (= Why don't you write …?) What shall we do tonight? – **Why not go** to the cinema? (= Why don't we go …?)
You can use *Why* + **infinitive** if you think something is not necessary[1] or not sensible:	**Why pay** more at other shops? We have the cheapest clothes in town. *Warum in anderen Geschäften mehr bezahlen? …* **Why be** bored at home? Join our club and enjoy yourself! *Warum/Wozu sich zu Hause langweilen? …*

[1] necessary [ˈnesəsəri] *nötig, notwendig*

actually [ˈæktʃʊəli]	wirklich, tatsächlich, eigentlich	in fact, really

	(to) **be made up of** [ˌmeɪd‿ˈʌp‿əv]	bestehen aus	A football team *is ~ up of* 11 players.
	up to	bis (zu)	Read ~ ~ page 6, please. This bus can carry ~ ~ 80 passengers.
p.54/A4	weird [wɪəd] *(infml)*	verrückt, komisch	strange
	good looks [ˌgʊd ˈlʊks]	gutes Aussehen	She's so beautiful. I wish I had her *good ~*.
	too bad *(infml)*	ein Jammer; schade (, dass)	It's *too ~* you couldn't come to the party last weekend.
	(to) **make a speech** [spiːtʃ]	eine Rede halten, einen Vortrag halten	When Glen came back from Space Camp, he had to *make a ~* about space travel at school.
	someday [ˈsʌmdeɪ]	irgendwann, eines Tages	at some time in the future
	(to) **accept** [əkˈsept]	annehmen, akzeptieren	How many people *have ~ed* your invitation to the party? – 16 are coming.
	so far [ˈsəʊ fɑː]	bis hierher, bis jetzt	Is the film good? – *So ~* it's been OK.
	(to) come of age [ˌkʌm‿əv‿ˈeɪdʒ]	mündig/volljährig werden; kein Kind mehr sein	In Germany a lot of teenagers have *coming-of-~* ceremonies like 'Jugendweihe'.
	confirmation [⚠ *stress:* ˌkɒnfəˈmeɪʃn]	Konfirmation *(Aufnahme evangelischer Christen in die Gemeinde)*	
A5	**wide** [waɪd]	breit; *(Augen)* weit geöffnet	▸◂ narrow The captain's eyes were ~ with fear when he saw the pirate's ship.
	microphone [ˈmaɪkrəfəʊn]	Mikrofon	*a microphone* 
	Ladies and gentlemen [ˌleɪdiz‿ən ˈdʒentlmən]	Meine (sehr geehrten) Damen und Herren	
	attention [əˈtenʃn]	Aufmerksamkeit	'Your ~, please' is a polite way of saying 'Hey, listen!' 
P3	out of town	außerhalb (der Stadt)	She works in the city centre but lives *out of ~* in a village.
	finally [ˈfaɪnəli]	abschließend, zum Schluss; schließlich, endlich	We visited Boston, Detroit, Chicago and ~ Denver. We waited a long time and ~ (= at last) the train arrived.
P4	skyscraper [ˈskaɪskreɪpə]	Wolkenkratzer	*skyscrapers* 
P7	**by now**	inzwischen	Where's Sue? She should have arrived ~ ~.
[P8]	*punch-line* [ˈpʌntʃlaɪn]	*Pointe (Ende eines Witzes)*	
	scene [siːn]	*Szene*	
	millionaire [ˌmɪljəˈneə]	*Millionär/in*	
P9	diagram [⚠ *stress:* ˈdaɪəgræm]	Diagramm	
P10	**male** [meɪl]	männlich	*male* ♂
	female [ˈfiːmeɪl]	weiblich	*female* ♀

A Knight in New York

Das *VOCABULARY* enthält nicht alle neuen Wörter und Wendungen, die in *A Knight in New York* vorkommen. Du weißt ja inzwischen, wie man die Bedeutung neuer Wörter erschließen kann (vgl. dazu auch *Understanding new words* auf S. 63 oben). Wenn du doch einmal nicht weiterkommst, schlag in einem Wörterbuch nach oder frag deinen Lehrer oder deine Lehrerin.

p.59	°knight [naɪt]	Ritter	
	title [ˈtaɪtl]	Titel; Überschrift	
	(to) **take place**	stattfinden (⚠ *nicht:* ~~Platz nehmen~~)	Our next school trip *will take ~* in two months. ⚠ *Platz nehmen = (to) take a seat, (to) sit down*
	(to) line up [ˌlaɪn‿ˈʌp] *(besonders AE)*	sich anstellen *(in einer Schlange)*	You have to go in one after another, so *~ up*, please.

	heart [hɑːt]	Herz	a *heart* 
	nowhere ['nəʊweə]	nirgendwo, nirgendwohin	You can find this animal in Australia, and ~ else. Where are you going? – *Nowhere.* ▸◂ somewhere
p.60	(to) **get** *(infml)*	verstehen	Ed told a joke, but I *didn't* ~ it.
	challenge ['tʃæləndʒ]	Herausforderung, Aufgabe	I climb mountains because they're a ~.
	digit ['dɪdʒɪt]	Ziffer	All US phone numbers have 7 ~*s*.
	painting ['peɪntɪŋ]	Gemälde, Bild; Malerei	a *painting* by a boy of his mother 
	(to) **paint** [peɪnt]	malen, anstreichen	
	(to) **rent** [rent]	mieten, leihen	He hasn't bought his flat, he ~*s* it.
	°riddle ['rɪdl]	Rätsel	
	neighbour *(BE)* / **neighbor** *(AE)* ['neɪbə]	Nachbar/in	Our ~*s* phoned the police because our party was too loud.
	(to) **keep (on)** doing sth.	etwas weiter tun; etwas wiederholt tun	(to) continue doing sth.; (to) do sth. again and again  *Keep smiling!*

(to) keep

Here's your pen. – Oh, you can **keep** it. I've got another one.	... Du kannst ihn **behalten**. ...
Butter **is** best **kept** in the fridge.	Butter **bewahrt** man am besten im Kühlschrank **auf**.
Many Inuit want to **keep** their traditions **alive**.	... ihre Traditionen **am Leben erhalten**.
I'm afraid of dogs, so **keep** Lulu **away** from me.	... , also **halt** Lulu von mir **fern**.
Keep going till you get to the traffic lights.	**Geh (immer) weiter**, bis du an die Ampel kommst.
Don't keep asking silly questions.	**Stell nicht dauernd/immer wieder** dumme Fragen.

p. 61	°dudes [*BE:* djuːdz, *AE:* duːdz] *(AE, infml)*	*etwa:* Typen	
	°plaque [plæk]	Gedenktafel	
p. 62	(to) **pass** a test [pɑːs]	einen Test bestehen	

(to) pass

I **pass** the church on my way to school.	Ich **komme** an der Kirche **vorbei** ...
Could you **pass** the butter, please?	Könntest du bitte die Butter **herüberreichen**?
I've done enough work, I'm sure **I'll pass** my maths test.	... ich **bestehe** meinen Mathematiktest.
The holidays **passed** much too quickly.	Die Ferien **gingen** viel zu schnell **vorüber**.

No way! [ˌnəʊ 'weɪ] *(infml)*	Auf keinen Fall! / Kommt nicht infrage!	You want me to let you have my new car for a trip to the disco? *No* ~!
How do you know?	Woher weißt du das?	
scene [siːn]	Szene	

p. 63 **How to use a dictionary**

possible ['pɒsəbl]	möglich	I'll send some money as soon as ~.
possibly ['pɒsəbli]	vielleicht, möglicherweise	Ray phoned to say he would ~ be late.

TIPP **Vier Augen sehen mehr als zwei – Wiederholung in Partnerarbeit**

Wiederhole doch mal mit einem Partner/einer Partnerin:

- Jeder von euch fertigt Skizzen zu ausgewählten Wortfeldern – ohne Beschriftung. Dann tauscht ihr die Skizzen und versucht, sie zu beschriften.
- Danach seht ihr euch die Skizzen gemeinsam an: Vielleicht fallen euch zu zweit noch weitere Dinge ein, die ihr ergänzen könnt – vier Augen sehen mehr als zwei.

▶▶▶ Unit 5: Nebraska – the Middle of Nowhere?

pp.64/65	the middle of nowhere *(infml)*	*etwa:* das Ende der Welt	
	locker ['lɒkə]	Schließfach; Spind	
	schedule [*BE:* 'ʃedjuːl, *AE:* 'skedʒəl]	Zeitplan; *(AE auch:)* Stundenplan, Fahrplan	= *BE* timetable
	weight [weɪt]	Gewicht	You must eat less if you want to lose ~.
	study hall ['stʌdi hɔːl] *(AE)*	*Freistunde zur Erledigung von Hausaufgaben*	
	algebra ['ældʒɪbrə]	Algebra	
	physical science [ˌfɪzɪkl 'saɪəns]	Naturwissenschaft	
	computer application [ˌæplɪ'keɪʃn]	Informatik *(Schulfach)*; Computeranwendung	
	°grading system ['greɪdɪŋ sɪstəm]	Benotungssystem, Bewertungssystem	
	grade [greɪd] *(besonders AE)*	(Schul-)Note, Zensur	= *BE* mark
	excellent [⚠ *stress:* 'eksələnt]	ausgezeichnet, hervorragend	very good — excellent – exzellent
	average *(n; adj)* ['ævərɪdʒ]	Durchschnitt; durchschnittlich, Durchschnitts-	The ~ of 5, 6 and 10 is 7. The ~ time the students needed was 15 minutes.
	poor [pʊə]	schlecht, schwach, mangelhaft	*poor* = **1.** arm; **2.** schlecht, schwach
	failure *(n)* ['feɪljə]	*etwa:* nicht bestanden (*wörtlich:* Misserfolg, Scheitern, Versagen)	
	comment (on/about) [⚠ *stress:* 'kɒment]	Kommentar, Bemerkung (zu)	
	surprising [sə'praɪzɪŋ]	erstaunlich, überraschend	This surprises me a lot. = I find this very ~. ⚠ *surprising* = überraschend; *surprised* = überrascht
p.66/A1	(to) take a quiz [kwɪz] *(AE)*	einen Test machen/schreiben	= *BE* (to) do/take a test
	soy bean ['sɔɪ biːn]	Sojabohne	
	(to) **avoid** sth./sb. [ə'vɔɪd]	etw. vermeiden; jn. meiden, jm. ausweichen/aus dem Weg gehen	If you take this road, you can ~ some of the traffic. ⚠ *(es) vermeiden, etwas zu tun = (to) avoid doing sth.* I saw that stupid Peter but *~ed meeting* him.
	unlike *(prep)* [ˌʌn'laɪk]	anders als, im Gegensatz zu	My brother loves football. *U~* him, I really hate it.
	shopping mall [mɔːl, *BE auch:* mæl]	Einkaufszentrum	shopping centre with lots of different shops

German 'nächste': *nearest – next*		
nearest *is used for place:*	The **nearest** bus stop is just round the corner.	Die **nächste (= nächstgelegene)** Bushaltestelle ist gleich um die Ecke.
next *is used for time:*	We have to get off at the **next** stop.	Wir müssen an der **nächsten (= nächstfolgenden)** Haltestelle aussteigen.

A2	**kind of** quickly *(infml)*	irgendwie schnell, etwas schnell	He isn't really fat, he's ~ *of* not thin. The food wasn't brilliant, but it was ~ *of* OK.
	How did you do?	Wie hats geklappt? / Wie hast du abgeschnitten?	*How did you* ~ in the race? – Quite well: I came in fourth.
	examination, exam [ɪgˌzæmɪ'neɪʃn, ɪg'zæm]	Prüfung, Examen	All students have to take an ~ at the end of the semester. ⚠ *not:* (to) ~~make an exam~~ examination – Examen
	(to) **fail (an exam)** [feɪl]	(eine Prüfung) nicht bestehen, (bei einer Prüfung) durchfallen	(to) fail – durchfallen
	note [nəʊt]	Kurznachricht; Zettel	I haven't got time for a letter, so this is just a short ~. ⚠ *note* = **1.** Notiz; **2.** Anmerkung, Hinweis; **3.** Kurznachricht, Zettel

False friends

(to) **become** = *werden*	• *bekommen* = (to) **get**	**menu** = *Speisekarte*	• *(Tages-)Menü* = **dish of the day**
brave = *mutig*	• *brav* = **good**	**murder** = *Mord*	• *Mörder* = **murderer**
bright = *hell*	• *breit* = **wide**	**note** = *Notiz; Zettel*	• *(Zeugnis-) Note* = **mark** *(BE)*, **grade**
cake = *Kuchen*	• *Keks* = **biscuit** *(BE)*	**notice** = *Anschlag, Mitteilung*	• *Notiz* = **note**
chips = *Pommes frites*	• *(Kartoffel-) Chips* = **crisps** *(BE)*	**strong** = *stark*	• *streng* = **strict**
floor = *Fußboden; Stockwerk*	• *Flur* = **hall**	(to) **take place** = *stattfinden*	• *Platz nehmen* = (to) **take a seat**, (to) **sit down**
high school = *Oberschule*	• *Hochschule* = **college, university**		

	On seeing this *(fml)*, Debbie asked …	Als Debbie das sah, fragte sie …	*O~ seeing* the sea … = When I (we/they …) saw the sea … / When I (we/they …) see the sea …
p.67/A3	formal ['fɔːml]	förmlich, formell	'Hi' is a less ~ word for 'hello'. ▸◂ informal
	by speaking quickly	indem ich/sie/… schnell sprach; durch schnelles Sprechen	I found out the phone number ~ *looking* in the phone book.
A4	**including** *(prep)* [ɪn'kluːdɪŋ]	einschließlich	Five of my friends came, so we were six, ~ me. verb: (to) include – preposition: *including*
	however [haʊ'evə]	jedoch, aber	Everyone played well. *H~*, we still lost the game. ⚠ *however* is more formal than *but*. It is usually separated by a comma from the rest of the sentence.
	truck [trʌk]	Lastwagen, Lkw	a *truck* 
	(to) **found** [faʊnd]	gründen	to ~ a new chess club = to start a new chess club ⚠ *(to) found – founded – founded* = gründen *(to) find – found – found* = finden
	drunk driving [ˌdrʌŋk 'draɪvɪŋ] *(AE)*, drink-driving *(BE)*	Alkohol am Steuer, Trunkenheit am Steuer	
	(to) drink and drive	unter Alkoholeinfluss Auto fahren	
	by its shorter **name**	unter seinem/ihrem kürzeren Namen	Allen Stewart Konigsberger is better known ~ *his stage name* 'Woody Allen'.
	°halfway house [ˌhɑːfweɪ 'haʊs]	*Einrichtung für den offenen Strafvollzug*	
	prison ['prɪzn]	Gefängnis	Three men escaped from ~ last night. The police are looking for them. ⚠ *No article:* Ihr Mann ist *im (= in dem) Gefängnis.* = Her husband is *in prison.*
	mad (at/with sb.) **(-dd-)** [mæd] *(besonders AE, infml)*	wütend (auf jn.)	He sure was ~ (= angry) when she hit him. ⚠ *mad* = **1.** *(BE)* wahnsinnig, verrückt; **2.** wütend
	aim [eɪm]	Ziel	What is your ~ in life? – To be happy.
	pill [pɪl]	Tablette, Pille	
	(to) **warn** sb. (**about** sth.) [wɔːn]	jn. (vor etwas) warnen	I fell on those stairs. – Well, I *~ed* you *about* them. ⚠ *jn. davor warnen, etwas zu tun* = *(to) warn sb. not to do sth.*: My parents *~ed me not to walk* home alone. verb: *(to) warn* – noun: warning
p.68/A5	(to) say grace [greɪs]	das Tischgebet sprechen	⚠ *(to) say a prayer* = ein Gebet sprechen *(to) say grace* = das Tischgebet sprechen
	(to) direct [də'rekt]	leiten *(Chor, Orchester)*	
	I understand	soweit ich weiß	as far as I know
	(to) **lie (to** sb.) [laɪ] (⚠ *-ing form:* lying)	(jn. an-, be)lügen	(to) say sth. that isn't true ⚠ *(to) lie – lied – lied* = *lügen* *(to) lie – lay – lain* = *liegen*

	lie [laɪ]	Lüge	
	(to) **tell** (sb.) **lies**	(jn. an-, be)lügen	(to) lie (to sb.)
	over (to)	herüber, hinüber (nach)	Do you want to come ~ *to* my house tonight?
	(to) **work** sth. **out**	etwas ausarbeiten, etwas herausfinden	You can ~ *out* the answer by adding all the numbers.
A6	(to) **hurry** ['hʌri]	sich beeilen; eilen	We'll have to ~ or we'll be late.
	Hurry up.	Beeil dich!	verb: *(to) hurry* – noun: hurry
	off [ɒf]	weg, los	He went ~ without saying another word.
	What's the matter? ['mætə]	Was ist denn (los)?	What's wrong?
	(to) **react (to)** [ri:'ækt]	reagieren (auf)	How *did* your parents ~ *to* your holiday plans?
	reaction (to) [⚠ *stress:* ri:'ækʃn]	Reaktion (auf)	How did they react? = What was their ~?
p.69/A7	**though** [ðəʊ]	obwohl	= although
	contract [⚠ *stress:* 'kɒntrækt]	Vertrag	The company gave me a ~ to work for them for three years.
	(to) **nod** (-dd-) [nɒd]	nicken (mit)	She didn't actually say 'yes', she just ~*ded* her head.
	health [helθ]	Gesundheit	noun: *health* – adjective: healthy
	influence (on) ['ɪnfluəns]	Einfluss (auf)	The Beatles had a strong ~ *on* modern music.
	(to) accept a ride (from sb.) [ək'sept]	ein Mitfahrangebot annehmen (von jm.); bei jm. (im Auto) mitfahren	
	(to) **arrange** [ə'reɪndʒ]	arrangieren, sorgen für; vereinbaren	Jessica's mum ~*d* a party for her birthday. We ~*d* to meet at six o'clock in front of the school. (to) **arrange** – **arrang**ieren
	transportation [,trænspɔ:'teɪʃn]	Beförderung, Transport; *(AE auch:)* Verkehrsmittel	The ~ of slaves from Africa to the British colonies in North America began in 1619.
	calm [kɑ:m]	ruhig, still	quiet, not excited: a ~ person, a ~ sea
	(to) **go on**	(an)dauern; vor sich gehen, im Gange sein	(to) last: How long *has* this situation *been* ~*ing* ~? (to) happen: A party *was* ~*ing* ~ in the next room.
	we **ought to** … ['ɔ:t tə]	wir sollten/müssten (eigentlich)	You ~ *to* go now. = You should go now. You ~*n't to* eat so much. You'll get fat.

ought to – should

It's cold outside. You **ought to** put/**should** put on a coat.	solltest
You **oughtn't to** talk/**shouldn't** talk so loudly. You'll wake up the baby.	solltest nicht
We left early, so we **ought to** have/**should** have enough time.	müssten eigentlich
It's not far from here. It **oughtn't to** take/**shouldn't** take long to get there.	dürfte eigentlich nicht

	(to) **get along (with** sb.)	(mit jm.) auskommen, sich (mit jm.) verstehen	They ~ *along with* each other very well. They're good friends.
P1	**several** ['sevrəl]	mehrere, verschiedene	some, but not a lot My parents have got ~ books about the USA.
	farming ['fɑ:mɪŋ]	Landwirtschaft, Ackerbau	
P3	**drug** [drʌg]	Droge, Rauschgift; Medikament	Heroin ['herəʊɪn] and cocaine [kəʊ'keɪn] are hard ~*s*. He has to take ~*s* for his heart problem.
	prairie [⚠ *stress:* 'preəri]	Prärie, Grasebene	
	telemarketing [,teli'mɑ:kɪtɪŋ]	Telemarketing, Telefonverkauf	
P5	tornado, *pl* tornadoes [tɔ:'neɪdəʊ]	Tornado, Wirbelsturm	
	instead of *(prep)* [ɪn'sted‿əv]	(an)statt, anstelle (von)	Why don't you help me ~ *of* just sitting there? ⚠ *instead (adv) = stattdessen, dafür*
	the Midwest [,mɪd'west]	der mittlere Westen *(der USA)*	the northern central (*not:* western) part of the USA
	season [⚠ *stress:* 'si:zn]	Saison, Jahreszeit	Which is your favourite ~? – Spring.
	(to) **go for a picnic**	einen Picknickausflug machen	
	public [⚠ *stress:* 'pʌblɪk]	öffentlich	Where's the nearest ~ telephone?

P 7	**necessary** ['nesəsri]	notwendig, nötig	Food is ~ for life.
P 8	mobile (phone) [⚠ *stress:* 'məʊbaɪl]	Mobiltelefon, Handy	⚠ German: 'Handy' = English: *mobile (phone)* (*not:* ~~handy~~)
[P 9]	*(to) remind sb. of sth.* [rɪ'maɪnd]	*jn. an etwas erinnern*	
P 11	**synonym** [⚠ *stress:* 'sɪnənɪm]	Synonym, bedeutungsähnliches Wort	The adjectives 'simple' and 'easy' are ~*s*.
	(to) take it in turns	sich abwechseln	We both want to use the computer, so we'll have to *take it ~ ~*. You first or me first? ⚠ *It's my turn.* = Ich bin an der Reihe.
P 13	impression (of) [ɪm'preʃn]	Eindruck (von)	What ~ do you have *of* this song? How does it sound?
	aspect [⚠ *stress:* 'æspekt]	Aspekt, Gesichtspunkt, Seite	You should study every ~ of the subject.

I Heard the Weirdest Rumor

> Das *VOCABULARY* enthält nicht alle neuen Wörter, die in *I Heard the Weirdest Rumor* vorkommen. Du wirst den Text aber trotzdem verstehen (vgl. *Understanding new words* auf S. 63 oben). Wenn nötig, schlag in einem Wörterbuch nach.

p.74	rumour ['ru:mə] *(BE)*, rumor *(AE)*	Gerücht	Don't tell anyone, but I heard a ~ that Jessica is going out with Daniel.
	adapted from [ə'dæptɪd]	eine Bearbeitung von, frei nach	The film is ~ *from* a successful play.
	author ['ɔ:θə]	Autor/in	the ~ of a story = the person who wrote it
	beef [bi:f]	Rindfleisch	meat from a cow or bull
	misfit ['mɪsfɪt]	Außenseiter/in	Nobody understands me. I'm a total ~.
	°nerd [nɜ:d] *(infml)*	Langweiler/in, Streber/in	
	(to) **defend** [dɪ'fend]	verteidigen	The Indians ~*ed* their village against the soldiers. ◂▸ (to) attack
	sincere [sɪn'sɪə]	aufrichtig	Mike always says what he really feels or believes. He's completely ~.
	sweet [swi:t]	süß	There's too much sugar in this tea. It's too ~.
p.75	(to) **realize** ['rɪəlaɪz]	erkennen; sich klar machen; einsehen, merken	I'*ve* just ~*d* that I've left my dictionary at home.

German '(sich) merken'

Morgen gibt es keinen Sportunterricht. Bitte **merkt** euch das. (= daran denken)	There's no sport tomorrow. Please **remember.**
Plötzlich **merkte** ich, dass ich die Adresse vergessen hatte. (= sich geistig bewusst werden)	I suddenly **realized** that I had forgotten the address.
Hast du **gemerkt**, wie groß seine Füße sind? (= mit den Sinnen wahrnehmen)	**Have** you **noticed** how big his feet are?

	reputation [ˌrepju'teɪʃn]	Ruf, Ansehen	
	(to) **judge (by/from)** [dʒʌdʒ]	beurteilen, einschätzen (nach, aufgrund)	You shouldn't ~ people *by* their clothes.
	(to) **pay attention (to sb./sth.)** [ə'tenʃn]	jn./etwas beachten; aufpassen (auf etwas), aufmerksam sein	I like him a lot, but I don't think he likes me: he never *pays* any ~ *to* me. If you want to get good marks, you must *pay ~ to* your teacher.
p.76	**relationship** [rɪ'leɪʃnʃɪp]	Beziehung	
	arrow ['ærəʊ]	Pfeil	*arrows* 
	feelings **towards** sb.	Gefühle für jn. / gegenüber jm.	*towards* = **1.** auf … zu, in Richtung …; **2.** gegenüber
	behaviour *(BE)* / **behavior** *(AE)* **(towards** sb.) [bɪ'heɪvjə]	Benehmen, Verhalten (gegenüber jm.)	Tom's ~ *towards* me has changed. He is acting very strangely.
	among [ə'mʌŋ]	unter, zwischen *(mehreren Personen oder Dingen)*	 *among* the boys  *between* the boys

p.77 **How to brainstorm**

(to) brainstorm ['breɪnstɔ:m]	(ein) Brainstorming machen	(to) collect lots of ideas
creative [⚠ *stress:* kri'eɪtɪv]	kreativ, schöpferisch	
virtual ['vɜ:tʃuəl]	virtuell *(nicht echt, aber echt erscheinend)*	

everybody ... they

In the examples on the right it is unimportant or unclear whether *everybody, anybody* etc. means a man or a woman. You can use *they, them, their* to avoid complicated[1] expressions like *he or she, him or her, his or her.*

[1]complicated ['kɒmplɪkeɪtɪd] *kompliziert*

Everybody can come if **they** *(= he or she)* have time.
If **anybody** phones, tell **them** *(= him or her)* I'll be back at 7.
Someone has parked **their** car *(= his or her car)* in front of our garage.

(to) pool [pu:l]	zusammenlegen, bündeln	(to) put together
(to) **share (with)** [ʃeə]	teilen (mit); gemeinsam haben/nutzen	I haven't got my own room. I ~ a room *with* my sister.
(to) structure ['strʌktʃə]	strukturieren	

TIPP

Gut gereimt ist halb gelernt!

Mit diesem Spiel könnt ihr – zu zweit oder in der Gruppe – „alte" Vokabeln (und ihre Aussprache und Schreibung) wiederholen:

Ihr gebt abwechselnd ein Wort vor. Jeder versucht dann, in einem festgelegten Zeitraum möglichst viele Reimwörter zu finden.

Vorgabe	Reimwörter
took	*book, cook, look, shook, ...*
you	*blue, too, two, who, zoo, ...*
eat	*feet, heat, meat, ...*
cake	*break, lake, make, take, ...*
me	*sea, see, tree, we, ...*

▶▶▶ Unit 6: Dreamland California

pp.78/79

collage [*BE:* 'kɒlɑ:ʒ, *AE:* kə'lɑ:ʒ]	Collage	

p.80/A1

desert ['dezət]	Wüste	
temperature [⚠ *stress:* 'temprətʃə]	Temperatur	
134° F (= 134 degrees Fahrenheit) [dɪˌgri:z 'færənhaɪt]	134 Grad Fahrenheit	⚠ You write: *134° F*, *57° C* — You say: *134 degrees Fahrenheit*, *57 degrees Celsius*
57° C (= 57 degrees Celsius) [dɪˌgri:z 'selsiəs]	57 Grad Celsius	Water freezes at 0° C (or 32° F). (= ... at zero degrees Celsius)
twice **an** hour	zweimal pro Stunde, in der Stunde	I get £5 pocket money *a* week.
°sequoia [sɪ'kwɔɪə], °redwood ['redwʊd]	Mammutbaum	
275 ft (= 275 feet) [fi:t]	275 Fuß *(1 Fuß = ca. 30 cm)*	My dad is 6 *ft* (= 6 *feet*) tall.
inch [ɪntʃ]	Zoll *(= 2,54 cm)*	about two and a half centimetres
every ten years	alle zehn Jahre	again after each ten years
°Jurassic [dʒu'ræsɪk]	jurassisch, Jura- *(aus der Jurazeit vor ca. 180 Millionen Jahren)*	
deep [di:p]	tief	How ~ is the water at this end of the pool? – 3 metres.
earthquake ['ɜ:θkweɪk]	Erdbeben	The ~ destroyed a lot of buildings and killed hundreds of people.
speed limit ['spi:d lɪmɪt]	Geschwindigkeitsbegrenzung, Geschwindigkeitsbeschränkung	30

	least [li:st]	am wenigsten	a little, less, ~ ⧓ most
	historic [hɪ'stɒrɪk]	historisch (= geschichtlich bedeutsam)	The fall of the Berlin Wall in 1989 was a(n) ~ event for Germany and the world. ⚠ *historical* = historisch, alt, aus der Geschichte: *historical* documents
	°gold rush ['gəʊld rʌʃ]	Goldrausch	
	°gold-mining town ['gəʊld,maɪnɪŋ ,taʊn]	Goldgräberstadt	
p.81/A2	**power** ['paʊə]	Kraft, Macht	The US President has more ~ than the British King or Queen.
	soap [səʊp]	Seife	a piece of *soap* 
	special effects [,speʃl_ɪ'fekts]	Spezialeffekte *(in Filmen)*	
	°wildly popular *(infml)*	wahnsinnig beliebt	
	since *(adv)*	seitdem	She moved to Sheffield last April and has ~ got a job as a teacher.
	°silicon valley [,sɪlɪkən 'væli]	„Silicium-Tal" *(Gebiet nahe San Francisco, in dem sich viele Elektronik- u. Computerfirmen angesiedelt haben)*	
	(to) **be worth** [wɜ:θ]	wert sein	How much *is* that famous painting ~? – Millions.
	nail polish ['neɪl ,pɒlɪʃ] *(AE)*, nail varnish ['neɪl ,vɑ:nɪʃ] *(BE)*	Nagellack	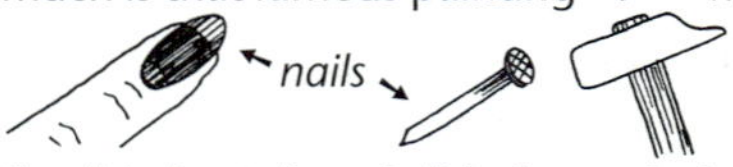 ⚠ *nail polish* ['pɒlɪʃ] – *Polish* ['pəʊlɪʃ] *(polnisch)*
	crazy (about sth./sb.**)** ['kreɪzi]	verrückt (nach etwas/jm.)	You want to go out in this rain? You must be ~. Jim loves old motorbikes. In fact, he's ~ *about* them.
	(to) **borrow** sth. ['bɒrəʊ]	sich etwas (aus)leihen, etwas entleihen	Can I ~ your dictionary, please? You'll get it back in a minute.
	candy ['kændi] *(AE)*	Bonbon; Süßigkeiten	
	(to) **come true**	wahr werden, sich bewahrheiten	*Will* my dream ~ *true*? I hope so.
	(to) **make** sth. **up**	sich etwas ausdenken, etwas erfinden	Tell the class a story. It can be a story that you*'ve made* ~.
p.82/A3	(to) **regret (-tt-)** [rɪ'gret]	bedauern, bereuen	(to) wish that you hadn't done something. Dad hates his new car. He ~*s* buying it. (= Er bereut, es gekauft zu haben. / …, dass er es gekauft hat.)
	laundry ['lɔ:ndri]	Wäscherei	
	math [mæθ] *(AE)*	Mathematik	= *BE* maths
	computer science [kəm,pju:tə 'saɪəns]	Informatik	
A4	siren [⚠ *stress:* 'saɪrən]	Sirene	
	explosion [⚠ *stress:* ɪk'spləʊʒn]	Explosion	
p.83/A5	**holiday**	Feiertag, freier Tag	Christmas Day is a ~ in most countries. public ~ = gesetzlicher Feiertag
	Buddhist [⚠ *stress:* 'bʊdɪst]	Buddhist, Buddhistin	
	envelope ['envələʊp]	(Brief-)Umschlag	I want to send this birthday card I've made to my cousin, but I haven't got a big enough ~.
	°firecracker ['faɪəkrækə]	Knallkörper	
	°evil spirits [,i:vl 'spɪrɪts]	böse Geister	
	generation [,dʒenə'reɪʃn]	Generation	The older ~ is often more conservative [kən'sɜ:vətɪv] than the younger ~.
	advert ['ædvɜ:t], *(infml auch:)* **ad** [æd]	Reklame, Annonce, Anzeige	On Saturdays the paper is full of ~*s*.
	cap [kæp]	(Schirm-)Mütze, Kappe	
P 1	statistics *(pl)* [stə'tɪstɪks]	Statistik(en)	
	per [pɜ:]	pro	50 miles ~ hour = 50 miles an hour

[P 2]	*seashore* ['siːʃɔː]	*(Meeres-)Ufer, Küste*	
	lighthouse ['laɪthaʊs]	*Leuchtturm*	
	feature ['fiːtʃə]	*Merkmal*	
P 3	**indoors** [ˌɪn'dɔːz]	drinnen, im Haus; nach drinnen	
	outdoors [ˌaʊt'dɔːz]	draußen, im Freien; nach draußen	
P 5	**cent (¢)** [sent]	Cent	There are 100 ~s in a dollar.
P 8	(to) border (on) ['bɔːdə]	(an)grenzen (an)	noun: border – verb: *(to) border*
	nature [⚠ *stress:* 'neɪtʃə]	Natur	⚠ No article: *Nature* is the mother of life.
	mixed bag [ˌmɪkst 'bæg]	bunte Mischung	
	dice, *pl* dice [daɪs]	Würfel	*one dice*   *two dice* ⚠ würfeln = (to) throw the *dice* eine Sechs würfeln = (to) throw a six
P 9	(to) **make money**	(viel) Geld verdienen	I want to ~ lots of *money* and get really rich.
P 10	compound ['kɒmpaʊnd]	zusammengesetzte(r, s); Kompositum	The ~ noun 'bathroom' is made up of the two parts 'bath' and 'room'.
	hyphen ['haɪfn]	Bindestrich	
	combination [ˌkɒmbɪ'neɪʃn]	Kombination, Verbindung	
P 11	(to) stress [stres]	betonen	noun: stress – verb: *(to) stress*

Next Month ... Hollywood

> Das *VOCABULARY* enthält nicht alle neuen Wörter, die in *Next Month ... Hollywood* vorkommen. Du wirst den Text aber trotzdem verstehen (vgl. *Understanding new words* auf S. 63 oben). Wenn nötig, schlag in einem Wörterbuch nach.

p.88	talent [⚠ *stress:* 'tælənt]	Talent, Begabung	
	°bitch [bɪtʃ]	Miststück (*wörtlich:* Hündin)	
p. 89	reliable [rɪ'laɪəbl]	zuverlässig, verlässlich	Tom's car is not very ~. There's always something wrong with it.
	in sight [saɪt]	in Sicht(weite)	
	audience ['ɔːdɪəns]	Zuschauer/innen, Zuhörer/innen, Publikum	the people who are watching a show, film, play, TV programme, or listening to a radio programme
p.90	(to) **make it** *(infml)*	es schaffen, Erfolg haben	Cathy *will* never ~ *it* as a singer. She has no talent.
	stomach ['stʌmək]	Magen, Bauch	

p.91 How to give a presentation

°nugget ['nʌgɪt]	Goldklumpen	
(to) **make sure** [ʃʊə]	sich vergewissern; darauf achten/dafür sorgen (, dass)	(to) check Please *make* ~ that you close the door when you leave the room.
OHP (overhead projector) [ˌəʊvəhed prə'dʒektə]	Tageslichtprojektor	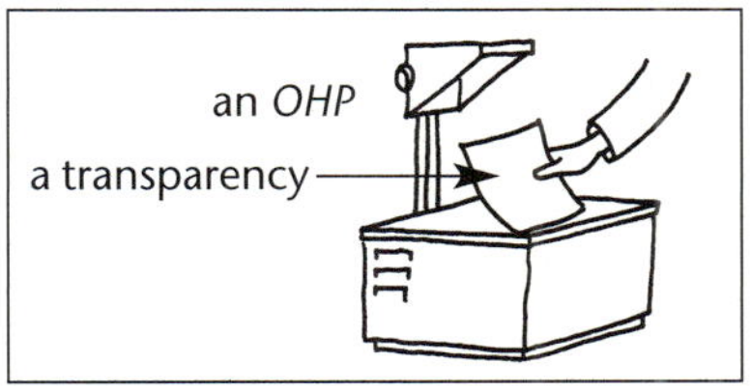
handout ['hændaʊt]	Arbeitsblatt, Informationsblatt, Handout	
quotation (by sb./**from** a book, play, etc.) [kwəʊ'teɪʃn]	Zitat, Ausspruch (von jm./aus einem Buch, Stück usw.)	'Time is money' is a famous ~ *by* Benjamin Franklin. 'God is love' is a ~ *from* the Bible ['baɪbl].
(to) **keep quiet about** sth.	etwas für sich behalten, etwas geheim halten	(to) keep sth. secret; (to) say nothing about sth.
(to) **keep quiet**	still sein	The children were told to ~ *quiet*.
(to) **spread, spread, spread** [spred]	(sich) ausbreiten, (sich) verbreiten	The fire quickly ~ to all parts of the building.
(to) **breathe** (in/out) [briːð]	(ein-/aus)atmen	*B~ in* through your nose and *out* through your mouth.

DICTIONARY Alphabetical list of words

Das *DICTIONARY* enthält den Wortschatz der Bände 1 bis 4.

° – Wörter, die mit einem kleinen Kringel (°) markiert sind, gehören nicht zum Lernwortschatz.
* – Unregelmäßige Verben sind mit einem Stern (*) gekennzeichnet (vgl. *Irregular verbs*, S. 198/199).

Abkürzungen

jm. = jemandem	sb. = somebody/someone *(jemand)*	*pl = plural*
jn. = jemanden	sth. = something *(etwas)*	*no pl = no plural*
AE = American English	*infml = informal* (umgangssprachlich, informell)	
BE = British English	*fml = formal* (förmlich, formell)	

A

a, an [ə, ən] ein, eine • **twice an hour** zweimal pro Stunde / in der Stunde

abbey ['æbi] Abtei

abbreviation [əˌbri:vi'eɪʃn] Abkürzung

able ['eɪbl]: **be able to do sth.** etwas tun können; fähig sein etwas zu tun

about [ə'baʊt] **1.** *(adv)* ungefähr; **2.** *(adv)* unterwegs; **3.** *(prep)* über; wegen • **It's about Mrs McCann.** Es ist wegen Mrs McCann. • **a question about your book** eine Frage über dein Buch/zu deinem Buch • **this book is about** dieses Buch handelt von • **dream/hear/know about** träumen/hören/wissen von • **tell about** erzählen von, berichten über • **think about** halten von, denken über **What about a calendar?** Wie wärs mit einem Kalender? **What about Jenny?** Was ist mit Jenny? / Und Jenny? • **What was funny about the docks?** Was war komisch an den Docks?

above [ə'bʌv] **1.** *(adv)* oben; **2.** *(prep)* über, oberhalb (von)

abroad [ə'brɔ:d] ins Ausland; im Ausland

°**absence (of)** ['æbsəns] Abwesenheit, Fehlen (von)

accept [ək'sept] annehmen, akzeptieren • **accept a ride (from sb.)** ein Mitfahrangebot annehmen (von jm.); bei jm. (im Auto) mitfahren

accident ['æksɪdənt] **1.** Unfall; **2.** Zufall • **by accident** zufällig, versehentlich

°**accomplish** [ə'kʌmplɪʃ] erreichen, schaffen

achievement [ə'tʃi:vmənt] Leistung, Errungenschaft

acid rain [ˌæsɪd 'reɪn] saurer Regen

across [ə'krɒs] **1.** *(prep)* (quer) über, durch; **2.** *(adv)* hinüber, herüber

act [ækt] **1.** handeln, sich verhalten; **2.** spielen, schauspielern **act out** vorspielen **3.** Nummer, Akt

°**action** ['ækʃn] Handlung, Tat

activity [æk'tɪvəti] Aktivität, Tätigkeit

actor ['æktə] Schauspieler **actress** ['æktrəs] Schauspielerin

actually ['æktʃuəli] wirklich, tatsächlich, eigentlich

ad [æd] *(infml)* Reklame, Annonce, Anzeige

AD [ˌeɪ'di:]: **70 AD** 70 n. Chr.

adapted from [ə'dæptɪd] eine Bearbeitung von, frei nach

add [æd] addieren, hinzufügen, ergänzen

address [ə'dres] Adresse, Anschrift

adopt [ə'dɒpt] adoptieren, die Patenschaft übernehmen für

advantage (over sb./sth.) [əd'vɑ:ntɪdʒ] Vorteil (gegenüber jm./etwas) • **at an advantage** im Vorteil

adventure [əd'ventʃə] Abenteuer

advert ['ædvɜ:t], *(infml auch:)* **ad** [æd] Reklame, Annonce, Anzeige

aerobics [eə'rəʊbɪks] Aerobic

afraid [ə'freɪd]: **be afraid (of)** sich fürchten (vor), Angst haben (vor) • **I'm afraid** leider

Afro-Caribbean [ˌæfrəʊ kærə'bi:ən] Afro-Karibe/Afro-Karibin *(Schwarze/r karibischer Herkunft)*

after ['ɑ:ftə] **1.** *(prep)* nach **after that** danach • **look after sb.** sich um jn. kümmern, auf jn. aufpassen • **run after sb.** hinter jm. herrennen **2.** *(conj)* nachdem

afternoon [ˌɑ:ftə'nu:n] Nachmittag • **Good afternoon.** Guten Tag. *(nachmittags)* • **in the afternoon(s)** am Nachmittag, nachmittags • **that afternoon** an jenem Nachmittag • **this afternoon** heute Nachmittag • **tomorrow afternoon** morgen Nachmittag

afterwards ['ɑ:ftəwədz] danach

again [ə'gen] wieder, noch einmal • **again and again** immer wieder

against [ə'genst] gegen

age [eɪdʒ] Alter • **at (the age of) 39** mit 39, im Alter von 39 Jahren • **come of age** mündig/volljährig werden; kein Kind mehr sein • **for ages** *(infml)* eine Ewigkeit (lang), ewig

agent ['eɪdʒənt] Agent/in

ago [ə'gəʊ]: **a long time ago** vor langer Zeit • **a minute/week ago** vor einer Minute/Woche

agree [ə'gri:] sich einigen, beschließen • **agree with sb.** mit jm. übereinstimmen; jm. zustimmen

ahead [ə'hed]: **be ahead (of sb.)** führen, in Führung liegen (vor jm.); jm. voraus sein

aim [eɪm] Ziel

air [eə] Luft • **in the open air** im Freien

airport ['eəpɔ:t] Flughafen

°**airstrip** ['eəstrɪp] Start- und Landebahn

album ['ælbəm] Album

alcohol ['ælkəhɒl] Alkohol

algebra ['ældʒɪbrə] Algebra

alive [ə'laɪv]: **be alive** leben, am Leben sein

all [ɔ:l] alle; alles • **all in all** alles in allem • **all the kids** alle Kinder • **all day/morning/summer** den ganzen Tag/Morgen/Sommer (lang) • **all the time/money/food** die ganze Zeit (lang)/das ganze Geld/Essen **all alone** ganz allein • **all around ...** überall in ... • **all over the world** auf der ganzen Welt, überall auf der Welt • **all right** gut, in Ordnung • **all wet** ganz nass, völlig nass **first of all** zuallererst

°**all-terrain vehicle (ATV)** [ˌɔ:ltəˌreɪn 'vi:əkl] Geländewagen

alligator ['ælɪgeɪtə] Alligator

allowed [ə'laʊd]: **be allowed to do sth.** etwas tun dürfen

almost ['ɔ:lməʊst] fast, beinahe

alone [ə'ləʊn] allein

along [ə'lɒŋ]: **1.** *(prep)* **along the street** entlang der Straße, die Straße entlang **2.** *(adv)* **(go/drive/move) along** weiter..., vorwärts...; dahin... • **get along (with sb.)** (mit jm.) auskommen, sich (mit jm.) verstehen

alphabet ['ælfəbet] Alphabet °**alphabetical** [ˌælfə'betɪkl] alphabetisch

already [ɔ:l'redi] schon, bereits

also ['ɔ:lsəʊ] auch

alternative *(n; adj)* [ɔ:l'tɜ:nətɪv] 1. Alternative; 2. Alternativ-

although [ɔ:l'ðəʊ] obwohl

always ['ɔ:lweɪz] immer

am [ˌeɪ_'em] … Uhr morgens/vormittags

ambulance ['æmbjələns] Krankenwagen

American *(n; adj)* [ə'merɪkən] 1. Amerikaner/in; 2. amerikanisch • **American football** Football

among [ə'mʌŋ] unter, zwischen *(mehreren Personen oder Dingen)*

an [ən] ein, eine • **twice an hour** zweimal pro Stunde / in der Stunde

ancestor ['ænsestə] Vorfahre

and [ənd, *betont:* ænd] und **And so on.** Und so weiter. **nice and warm/dry/…** schön warm/trocken/…

angry (with) ['æŋgri] böse, zornig, wütend (auf)

animal ['ænɪml] Tier

anonymous [ə'nɒnɪməs] anonym

anorak ['ænəræk] Anorak

another [ə'nʌðə] ein(e) andere(r, s); noch ein(e) • **one another** einander, sich (gegenseitig)

answer *(v; n)* ['ɑ:nsə] 1. antworten; beantworten • **answering machine** Anrufbeantworter 2. **answer (to)** Antwort (auf)

anti-(racist) ['ænti] anti-(rassistisch) • **anticlockwise** [ˌænti'klɒkwaɪz] entgegen dem Uhrzeigersinn

°**anxious** ['æŋkʃəs] besorgt

any ['eni] jede(r/s) (beliebige) **not … any** kein(e) • **not (…) any more** nicht mehr • **any?** (irgend)welche?

anybody ['enibɒdi] jede(r) (beliebige) • **not … anybody** niemand • **anybody?** (irgend)jemand?

anyone ['eniwʌn] jede(r) (beliebige) • **not … anyone** niemand • **anyone?** (irgend)jemand?

anything ['eniθɪŋ] irgendetwas (beliebiges) • **not … anything** nichts • **anything?** (irgend)etwas?

anyway ['eniweɪ] 1. jedenfalls, wie dem auch sei; 2. außerdem, und überhaupt; 3. sowieso; 4. trotzdem

anywhere ['enɪweə] irgendwo, irgendwohin • **not … anywhere** nirgendwo, nirgendwohin

°**apart from** [ə'pɑ:t] außer, abgesehen von

apartment [ə'pɑ:tmənt] *(AE)* Wohnung

appear [ə'pɪə] erscheinen, auftauchen

apple ['æpl] Apfel

April ['eɪprəl] April

archaeologist [ˌɑ:kɪ'ɒlədʒɪst] Archäologe/Archäologin

archaeology [ˌɑ:ki'ɒlədʒi] Archäologie

are [ə, *betont:* ɑ:] bist; sind; seid **How much are …?** Was kosten …? / Wie viel kosten …?

area ['eəriə] Bereich; Gebiet, Gegend

argue (with sb. about sth.) ['ɑ:gju:] sich (mit jm. über/wegen etwas) streiten, zanken **argument** ['ɑ:gjumənt] Argument, Begründung; Streit

arm [ɑ:m] Arm

around [ə'raʊnd] um … herum; in … umher • **all around …** überall in … • **around Ashton** in Ashton umher, durch Ashton **be around** *(infml)* in der Nähe sein, da sein • **Look around (you).** Sieh dich um. • **run around** umher-, herumrennen **stand around** herumstehen

arrange [ə'reɪndʒ] 1. (an)ordnen; 2. arrangieren, sorgen für; vereinbaren

°**arrest** [ə'rest] verhaften

arrival [ə'raɪvl] Ankunft • **arrive** [ə'raɪv] ankommen, eintreffen

°**arrogant** ['ærəgənt] überheblich, arrogant

arrow ['ærəʊ] Pfeil

art [ɑ:t] Kunst

article ['ɑ:tɪkl] Artikel

as [əz, *betont:* æz] 1. *(conj)* da, weil; 2. *(conj)* als, während • **as you know** wie du weißt • **as if** als ob • **as soon as** sobald 2. *(prep)* **as a child** als Kind 3. *(adv)* **as in London** wie in London • **as quick as** so schnell wie • **as bad as this** so schlimm, so schlecht • **as well as** und auch, ebenso wie

Asia ['eɪʃə, 'eɪʒə] Asien • **Asian** *(adj; n)* ['eɪʃn, 'eɪʒn] asiatisch; Asiat/in

ask [ɑ:sk] fragen • **ask sb. for sth.** jn. um etwas bitten • **ask questions** Fragen stellen • **ask sb. the way** jn. nach dem Weg fragen

asleep [ə'sli:p]: **be asleep** schlafen • **fall asleep** einschlafen

aspect ['æspekt] Aspekt, Gesichtspunkt, Seite

assembly [ə'sembli] Schulversammlung *(oft mit Andacht)* **assembly hall** Aula

assistant [ə'sɪstənt] 1. Assistent/in; 2. Verkäufer/in; 3. stellvertretende(r, s)

astronaut ['æstrənɔ:t] Astronaut/Astronautin

at [ət, *betont:* æt] an, bei • **at a travel agent's** in einem Reisebüro • **at all times** immer, jederzeit • **at Christmas** an/zu Weihnachten • **at dinner** beim Abendessen • **at first** zuerst, anfangs, am Anfang • **at home** zu Hause, daheim • **at Kingsway High School** an/auf der Kingsway High School • **at last** schließlich, endlich • **at least** wenigstens, mindestens; zumindest • **at lunch-time** zur Mittagszeit, mittags • **at night** nachts, in der Nacht • **at once** sofort, (so)gleich • **at school** in der Schule • **at sea** auf See **at six** um sechs • **at that time** damals, zu jener/dieser Zeit **at (the age of) 39** mit 39, im Alter von 39 Jahren • **at the door** an der Tür • **at the end** am Ende, am Schluss • **at the front** vorn • **at the moment** im Moment, gerade, zurzeit **at the restaurant** im Restaurant • **at the same time** zur gleichen Zeit • **at the top (of)** oben, am oberen Ende, an der Spitze (von) • **at the weekend** am Wochenende • **at weekends** an Wochenenden • **at work** bei der Arbeit, am Arbeitsplatz

athlete ['æθli:t] Athlet/in, Sportler/in • **athletics** [æθ'letɪks] Leichtathletik

atlas ['ætləs] Atlas

attack *(n; v)* [ə'tæk] 1. angreifen; 2. Angriff

attention [ə'tenʃn] Aufmerksamkeit • **pay attention (to sb./sth.)** jn./etwas beachten; aufpassen (auf etwas), aufmerksam sein

attitude (towards) ['ætɪtju:d] Haltung (gegenüber), Einstellung (zu)

attraction [ə'trækʃn] Attraktion, Anziehungspunkt

au pair [ˌəʊ 'peə] Aupairmädchen, Aupairjunge

audience ['ɔ:diəns] Zuschauer/innen, Zuhörer/innen, Publikum

°**audio** ['ɔ:dɪəʊ] Audio-

August ['ɔ:gəst] August

aunt [ɑ:nt] Tante

authentic [ɔ:'θentɪk] authentisch

author ['ɔ:θə] Autor, Autorin

automatic *(adj)* [ˌɔ:tə'mætɪk] automatisch • **automatically** *(adv)* automatisch

autumn ['ɔ:təm] Herbst

avenue ['ævənju:] Allee, Boulevard

average *(n; adj)* ['ævərɪdʒ] 1. Durchschnitt; 2. durchschnittlich, Durchschnitts-

°**aviation** [ˌeɪvi'eɪʃn] Luftfahrt

avoid sth./sb. [ə'vɔɪd] etw. vermeiden; jn. meiden, jm. ausweichen/aus dem Weg gehen

away [ə'weɪ] weg, fort

awesome ['ɔ:səm] *(AE, infml)* großartig, klasse

B

back *(n; adv)* [bæk] 1. Rücken; Rückseite, hinterer Teil • **at the back of the book** hinten im Buch 2. zurück • **Get back!** (Geh/Tritt) Zurück! • **sit back** sich zurücklehnen • **back in Chester** daheim in Chester

background ['bækgraʊnd] Hintergrund

bacon ['beɪkən] Schinkenspeck

bad [bæd] schlecht, schlimm **be bad at sth.** schlecht in etwas sein; etwas schlecht können **too bad** *(infml)* ein Jammer; schade (, dass) • **Bad luck.** Pech (gehabt)! • **do badly (in)** schlecht sein (in), schlecht abschneiden (in)

badminton ['bædmɪntən] Badminton, Federball

bag [bæg] Tasche, Beutel, Tüte; Sack • **mixed bag** bunte Mischung

°**bagel** ['beɪgl] *ringförmiges Hefegebäck*

°**baggage** ['bægɪdʒ] Gepäck

bake [beɪk] backen

°**bald eagle** [ˌbɔːld_'iːgl] Weißkopf-Seeadler

ball [bɔːl] Ball

banana [bə'nɑːnə] Banane

band [bænd] Band, (Musik-)Gruppe • **band practice** Orchesterprobe

bang [bæŋ] Knall

Bangladeshi [ˌbæŋglə'deʃi] Bangale/Bangalin *(jd. aus Bangladesch)*

°**banjo** ['bændʒəʊ] Banjo

bank [bæŋk] **1.** Bank, Sparkasse **bottle bank** Altglascontainer **2.** (Fluss-)Ufer

°**bar mitzvah** [bɑː 'mɪtsvə] *(die) Bar-Mizwa (Aufnahme in die jüdische Gemeinde, vergleichbar mit Konfirmation und Firmung)*

barbecue ['bɑːbɪkjuː] Grillparty

°**barrio** ['bæriəʊ] *(AE) überwiegend spanischsprachiges Stadtviertel in amerikanischen Städten*

baseball ['beɪsbɔːl] Baseball

based on ['beɪst_ɒn] basierend auf

basket ['bɑːskɪt] Korb

basketball ['bɑːskɪtbɔːl] Basketball

bath [bɑːθ] Bad • **have/take a bath** ein Bad nehmen, *(in der Wanne)* baden • **bathhouse** Badehaus • **bathroom** [*BE:* 'bɑːθruːm, *AE:* 'bæθruːm] Badezimmer; *(AE auch:)* Toilette *(in einem Privathaus)*

battle ['bætl] Schlacht, Kampf

bay [beɪ] Bucht

BC [ˌbiː'siː]: **70 BC** 70 v. Chr.

be* [bi, *betont:* biː] sein • **be called** heißen, genannt werden **be cold** frieren • **be in trouble** in Schwierigkeiten sein; Ärger kriegen • **be late** zu spät sein/kommen • **be on holiday** in Urlaub sein; Ferien haben/machen • **be right** Recht haben **be wrong** **1.** sich irren, Unrecht haben; **2.** nicht in Ordnung sein, nicht stimmen

beach [biːtʃ] Strand • **on the beach** am Strand

bean [biːn] Bohne

bear [beə] Bär

beard [bɪəd] Bart

beat* [biːt] besiegen; schlagen **beat sb. up** jn. zusammenschlagen

beautiful ['bjuːtɪfl] (wunder-)schön

because [bɪ'kɒz] weil • **that's because** das kommt daher, weil **because of** wegen

become* [bɪ'kʌm] werden

bed [bed] Bett

bedroom ['bedruːm] Schlafzimmer

beef [biːf] Rindfleisch

been [biːn, bɪn]: **I've been to ...** Ich war (schon mal) in ... / Ich bin (schon) in ... gewesen.

before [bɪ'fɔː] **1.** *(prep)* vor **before that** vorher, davor, zuvor **2.** *(conj)* bevor, ehe; **3.** *(adv)* vorher; vorher schon mal • **the night/week/... before** in der Nacht/Woche/... zuvor

begin* **(-nn-)** [bɪ'gɪn] beginnen, anfangen (mit) • **beginning** Anfang, Beginn • **at the beginning** am Anfang

behaviour *(BE)* / **behavior** *(AE)* **(towards sb.)** [bɪ'heɪvjə] Benehmen, Verhalten (gegenüber jm.)

behind [bɪ'haɪnd] hinter

believable [bɪ'liːvəbl] glaubhaft

believe (in) [bɪ'liːv] glauben (an) **believe one's eyes** seinen Augen trauen

bell [bel] Glocke, Klingel

°**belly-dancer** ['belidɑːnsə] Bauchtänzer/in

belong to [bɪ'lɒŋ] gehören (zu)

below [bɪ'ləʊ] **1.** *(adv)* unten; **2.** *(prep)* unter, unterhalb (von)

bench [bentʃ] Bank *(zum Sitzen)*

best [best]: **(the) best** (der/die/das) beste ...; am besten

bet* **(-tt-)** [bet] wetten

better (than) ['betə] besser (als)

between [bɪ'twiːn] zwischen

beyond [bɪ'jɒnd] über ... hinaus, jenseits (von)

bicycle ['baɪsɪkl] Fahrrad

°**bid** [bɪd] Gebot

big **(-gg-)** [bɪg] groß

bike [baɪk] Fahrrad • **ride a bike** Rad fahren • **bike ride** Radfahrt, Radtour

bikini [bɪ'kiːni] Bikini

billion ['bɪljən] Milliarde(n)

bin [bɪn] Papierkorb, Mülleimer

bingo ['bɪŋgəʊ] Bingo

biology [baɪ'ɒlədʒi] Biologie

bird [bɜːd] Vogel

biro ['baɪrəʊ] Kugelschreiber

birth [bɜːθ] Geburt • **date of birth** Geburtsdatum • **place of birth** Geburtsort

birthday ['bɜːθdeɪ] Geburtstag **birthday card** Geburtstagskarte **Happy birthday!** Herzlichen Glückwunsch zum Geburtstag! **It's my birthday next week.** Ich habe nächste Woche Geburtstag. • **When's your birthday?** Wann hast du Geburtstag?

biscuit ['bɪskɪt] Keks, Plätzchen

bit: **a bit** [ə 'bɪt] ein bisschen, etwas

°**bitch** [bɪtʃ] Miststück *(wörtlich:* Hündin)

black *(adj; n)* [blæk] **1.** schwarz; **2.** Schwarze(r)

°**blacksmith shop** ['blæksmɪθ ˌʃɒp] Schmiedewerkstatt

°**blindfold sb.** ['blaɪndfəʊld] jm. die Augen verbinden • **Somebody is blindfolded.** Jemandem sind die Augen verbunden.

°**blizzard** ['blɪzəd] Schneesturm

block [blɒk] (Häuser-, Wohn-)Block

blond [blɒnd] blond

blood [blʌd] Blut

blouse [blaʊz] Bluse

blow* [bləʊ] wehen, blasen

°**blubber** ['blʌbə] (Walfisch-)Speck

blue [bluː] blau

blush [blʌʃ] rot werden, erröten

board *(n; v)* [bɔːd] **1.** Brett; (Wand-)Tafel • **board-game** Brettspiel • **notice board** Anschlagtafel, schwarzes Brett °**2.** Spielbrett; **3. on board (the ship)** an Bord (des Schiffes) **go on board** an Bord gehen **4. board a plane/ship** an Bord eines Flugzeugs/Schiffes gehen

boat [bəʊt] Boot, Schiff

body ['bɒdi] Körper • **body language** Körpersprache

°**bold print** [ˌbəʊld 'prɪnt] Fettdruck

bomb [bɒm] Bombe

bone [bəʊn] Knochen

book *(n; v)* [bʊk] **1.** Buch • **bookshop** Buchhandlung, Buchladen • **bookshelf** ['bʊkʃelf], *pl* **bookshelves** ['bʊkʃelvz] Bücherregal • **exercise book** Heft, Schulheft **2.** buchen, reservieren

border *(n; v)* ['bɔːdə] **1.** Grenze °**border patrol** ['bɔːdə pəˌtrəʊl] Grenzpolizei **2. border (on)** (an)grenzen (an)

bored [bɔːd]: **be/feel bored** gelangweilt sein, sich langweilen **boring** ['bɔːrɪŋ] langweilig

born [bɔːn]: **be born** geboren sein/werden

°**borough** [*BE:* 'bʌrə, *AE:* 'bɜːrəʊ] (Stadt-)Bezirk

borrow ['bɒrəʊ] entleihen, sich (aus)leihen

boss [bɒs] *(infml)* Boss, Chef/in

both [bəʊθ] beide, beides **both of you** alle beide; ihr beide

bottle ['bɒtl] Flasche • **a bottle of ...** eine Flasche ... • **bottle bank** ['bɒtl bæŋk] Altglascontainer

bottom ['bɒtəm] Boden *(eines Gefäßes usw.)*; unteres Ende **bottom row** untere Reihe

boutique [buː'tiːk] Boutique
bowling ['bəʊlɪŋ] Bowling
box [bɒks] Kasten, Kiste • **a box of chocolates** eine Schachtel Pralinen
boy [bɔɪ] Junge • °**boy scout** [*BE:* ˌbɔɪ 'skaʊt, *AE:* 'bɔɪ ˌskaʊt] Pfadfinder (spielen)
boyfriend ['bɔɪfrend] (fester) Freund
bracket ['brækɪt] Klammer *(in einem Text)*
brain [breɪn] Gehirn • **brainstorm** ['breɪnstɔːm] (ein) Brainstorming machen
brave [breɪv] tapfer, mutig
bread *(no pl)* [bred] Brot
break [breɪk] Pause • **have/take a break** eine Pause machen
break* [breɪk] (zer)brechen; kaputtmachen; kaputtgehen **break loose (from)** sich losreißen, sich lösen (von)
breakfast ['brekfəst] Frühstück **at breakfast** beim Frühstück **for breakfast** zum Frühstück **have breakfast** frühstücken
breathe (in/out) [briːð] (ein-/aus)atmen
bridge [brɪdʒ] Brücke
briefing ['briːfɪŋ] Einsatzbesprechung
bright [braɪt] leuchtend, hell **brightness** ['braɪtnəs] Helligkeit, *(das)* Leuchten
brilliant ['brɪliənt] toll, glänzend, großartig
bring* [brɪŋ] (mit-, her)bringen
British ['brɪtɪʃ] britisch • **He's/She's British.** Er ist Brite./Sie ist Britin. • **the British** die Briten
Briton ['brɪtn] Britannier *(keltische Urbevölkerung Großbritanniens)*
brochure [*BE:* 'brəʊʃə, *AE:* brəʊ'ʃʊr] Prospekt, Broschüre
broken *(adj)* ['brəʊkən] gebrochen; zerbrochen
brother ['brʌðə] Bruder
brown [braʊn] braun
brush *(n; v)* [brʌʃ] **1.** (Haar-)Bürste; **2.** bürsten • **brush your teeth** sich die Zähne putzen
Buddhist ['bʊdɪst] Buddhist/in
budgie ['bʌdʒi] Wellensittich
°**buffet** ['bʊfeɪ] Büfett
build* [bɪld] bauen • **builder** Bauarbeiter/in
building ['bɪldɪŋ] Gebäude
bull [bʊl] Bulle, Stier
bulldozer ['bʊldəʊzə] Planierraupe, Bulldozer
°**bulletin board** ['bʊlətɪn ˌbɔːd] *(AE)* Anschlagtafel, schwarzes Brett
°**buoy** [bɔɪ] Boje
burglar ['bɜːglə] Einbrecher/in
burn [bɜːn] (ver)brennen; anbrennen lassen
bus [bʌs] Bus • **on the bus** im Bus • **bus stop** Bushaltestelle
business ['bɪznəs] Unternehmen, Geschäft(e)
busy ['bɪzi] beschäftigt; belebt, verkehrsreich, hektisch
but [bət, *betont:* bʌt] aber °**nothing but** nichts als; nur
butcher ['bʊtʃə] Fleischer/in, Metzger/in, Schlachter/in
butter ['bʌtə] Butter
button ['bʌtn] Knopf
buy* [baɪ] kaufen
by [baɪ] **1.** von; durch • **by accident** zufällig, versehentlich **by its shorter name** unter seinem/ihrem kürzeren Namen **What do you mean by that?** Was verstehst du darunter? **by speaking quickly** indem ich/sie/... schnell sprach; durch schnelles Sprechen
2. an, neben; (nahe) bei • **by the way** übrigens, nebenbei (bemerkt)
3. by bike/car/... mit dem Rad/Auto/... • **take sb. by the hand** jn. an die Hand nehmen
4. by 31st May bis spätestens 31. Mai • **by now** inzwischen
Bye bye! [baɪ 'baɪ] Tschüs!

C

c. (= circa) ['sɜːkə] ca. (= zirka)
cable ['keɪbl] Kabel
café ['kæfeɪ] (kleines) Restaurant, Imbissstube; Café
cafeteria [ˌkæfə'tɪəriə] Kantine, Selbstbedienungsrestaurant
cage [keɪdʒ] Käfig
cake [keɪk] Kuchen, Torte
calendar ['kælɪndə] Kalender
call *(v; n)* [kɔːl] **1.** nennen; rufen; anrufen; aufrufen • **call for help** um Hilfe rufen • **What do you call this?** Wie nennt man dies? • °**call off** abbrechen, beenden, absagen • **call out** rufen, schreien • **call sb. (stupid) names** jn. verspotten, jn. beschimpfen • **called** mit (dem) Namen • **be called** heißen, genannt werden **caller** Anrufer/in
2. (An-)Ruf
calm [kɑːm] ruhig, still
camcorder ['kæmkɔːdə] Camcorder *(Videokamera mit eingebauter Abspielfunktion)*
camera ['kæmərə] Kamera, Fotoapparat
camp (Trainings-, Zelt-)Lager **camp-site** ['kæmpsaɪt] Campingplatz, Zeltplatz
can [kæn] Dose, Büchse
can [kən, *betont:* kæn] **1.** können; **2.** dürfen • **you can't** [kɑːnt] (= **cannot**) ['kænɒt] du kannst nicht / darfst nicht
canal [kə'næl] Kanal
candle ['kændl] Kerze
candy ['kændi] *(AE)* Bonbon; Süßigkeiten
°**cannon** ['kænən], *pl* **cannon** *or* **cannons** Kanone
canteen [kæn'tiːn] Kantine, Schulmensa
canyon ['kænjən] Cañon, Schlucht
cap [kæp] (Schirm-)Mütze, Kappe
capital ['kæpɪtl] Hauptstadt
Capitol ['kæpɪtl]: **the Capitol** das Kapitol *(Sitz der gesetzgebenden Versammlung)*
captain ['kæptɪn] Kapitän/in
caption ['kæpʃn] Bildunterschrift
°**capture** ['kæptʃə] gefangen nehmen
car [kɑː] Auto
card [kɑːd] Karte
°**cardboard** ['kɑːdbɔːd] Pappe, Karton
care (about) [keə] **1.** sich kümmern (um), wichtig nehmen **I don't care.** Das ist mir egal. **Who cares?** *etwa:* Wen interessiert das? / Ist doch egal! °**2. take care of** sich kümmern um
careful *(adj)* ['keəfl] **1.** vorsichtig; **2.** sorgfältig • **carefully** *(adv)* ['keəfəli] **1.** vorsichtig; **2.** sorgfältig
°**caribou** ['kærɪbuː], *pl* **caribou** *or* **caribous** Karibu *(nordamerikanische Rentierart)*
carpenter ['kɑːpəntə] Zimmermann, Tischler/in
carry ['kæri] **1.** tragen; **2.** befördern, transportieren
cart [kɑːt] Karren, Wagen
carton ['kɑːtn] Karton, (Milch-, Saft-)Packung
cartoon [kɑː'tuːn] Zeichentrickfilm; Cartoon, Bilderwitz
cashier [kæ'ʃɪə] Kassierer/in
cassette [kə'set] Cassette **cassette recorder** Cassettenrecorder
castle ['kɑːsl] Burg, Schloss
cat [kæt] Katze, Kater
catch* [kætʃ] fangen; erwischen **catch a train/bus** einen Zug/Bus nehmen, erreichen
cathedral [kə'θiːdrəl] Kathedrale, Dom
cause [kɔːz] verursachen
CD [ˌsiː'diː] CD • **CD player** CD-Spieler • **CD-ROM** [ˌsiːdiː'rɒm] CD-ROM *(nur lesbare, nicht überschreibbare Computer-CD)*
ceiling ['siːlɪŋ] Decke *(eines Zimmers)*
celebrate ['selɪbreɪt] feiern **celebration** [ˌselɪ'breɪʃn] (Gedenk-)Feier
Celsius: 57° C (= 57 degrees Celsius) [dɪˌgriːz 'selsiəs] 57 Grad Celsius
Celtic ['keltɪk] keltisch; Keltisch
cent (¢) [sent] Cent
°**center island** [ˌsentər_'aɪlənd] *(AE)* Mittelstreifen
centimetre ['sentɪmiːtə] Zentimeter
central ['sentrəl] Zentral-, Mittel-
centre ['sentə] Zentrum; Mitte
century ['sentʃəri] Jahrhundert

ceremony ['serəməni] Zeremonie; Feier(lichkeit)
chain [tʃeɪn] Kette
chair [tʃeə] Stuhl
challenge ['tʃæləndʒ] Herausforderung, Aufgabe
champion ['tʃæmpiən] Wettkampfsieger/in, Champion, Meister/in • **championship** ['tʃæmpiənʃɪp] Meisterschaft
chance [tʃɑːns] Chance, Gelegenheit
change *(v; n)* [tʃeɪndʒ] **1.** ändern **change into** (ver)ändern, umwandeln in; sich verändern in, werden zu • **change (trains)** umsteigen
2. *(Geld)* wechseln, umtauschen
3. wechseln *(Kleidung)*; sich umziehen • **changing room** Umkleideraum
4. (Ver-)Änderung, Wechsel
channel ['tʃænl] Kanal
chaos ['keɪɒs] Chaos
character ['kærəktə] Charakter; Person, Figur *(in Roman, Film)*
charm [tʃɑːm] Charme
°**chart** [tʃɑːt] Tabelle
chase sb. (away) [tʃeɪs] jn. (weg-)jagen
cheap [tʃiːp] billig, preiswert
check [tʃek] (über)prüfen, kontrollieren • **check in** einchecken *(Flughafen)*; sich anmelden, sich eintragen *(Hotel)* **check sb./sth. out** *(infml)* jn./etwas überprüfen, mehr über jn./etwas herausfinden
cheer [tʃɪə] jubeln, Beifall klatschen
cheese [tʃiːz] Käse
chemistry ['kemɪstri] Chemie
chess [tʃes] Schach
chicken ['tʃɪkɪn] Huhn; (Brat-)Hähnchen
°**chief** [tʃiːf] Häuptling
child [tʃaɪld], *pl* **children** ['tʃɪldrən] Kind • **childhood** ['tʃaɪldhʊd] Kindheit
Chinese *(adj; n)* [ˌtʃaɪ'niːz] chinesisch; Chinesisch; Chinese/Chinesin
chips *(pl)* [tʃɪps] Pommes frites
chocolate ['tʃɒklət] **1.** Schokolade; **2.** Praline
choice [tʃɔɪs] (Aus-)Wahl
choir ['kwaɪə] Chor
choose* [tʃuːz] aussuchen, (aus-)wählen
Christ [kraɪst] Christus • **Christian** *(adj; n)* ['krɪstʃən] christlich; Christ/in
Christmas ['krɪsməs] Weihnachten • **at Christmas** an/zu Weihnachten • **for Christmas** zu Weihnachten
church [tʃɜːtʃ] Kirche
cigarette [ˌsɪgə'ret] Zigarette
cinema ['sɪnəmə] Kino
circus ['sɜːkəs] **1.** Zirkus; **2.** (runder) Platz *(in einer Stadt)*
city ['sɪti] Stadt, Großstadt
clap **(-pp-)** [klæp] (Beifall) klatschen
class [klɑːs] Klasse, Kurs • **in class** in der Klasse, im Unterricht • °**classmate** ['klɑːsmeɪt] Klassenkamerad/in, Mitschüler/in • **classroom** Klassenzimmer • **classroom phrases** *Redewendungen für das Klassenzimmer; Unterrichtssprache*
classical ['klæsɪkl] klassisch
clause [klɔːz] (Teil-, Glied-)Satz **main clause** Hauptsatz
clean *(adj; v)* [kliːn] **1.** sauber; **2.** sauber machen • **cleaner** Raumpfleger/in, Putzhilfe
clear *(adj)* [klɪə] klar, deutlich **clearly** *(adv)* ['klɪəli] eindeutig, klar
clever ['klevə] schlau, klug **cleverness** ['klevənəs] Klugheit, Cleverness
cliff [klɪf] Klippe
climb [klaɪm] klettern; hinaufklettern (auf)
clique [kliːk] Clique, Freundeskreis
cloakroom ['kləʊkruːm] Garderobe
clock [klɒk] (Wand-, Stand-, Turm-)Uhr • **clockwise** ['klɒkwaɪz] im Uhrzeigersinn
close [kləʊz] schließen, zumachen
close (to) [kləʊs] nahe (bei, an) **work closely with sb.** ['kləʊsli] eng mit jm. zusammenarbeiten
clothes *(pl)* [kləʊðz, kləʊz] Kleidung, „Klamotten"
cloud [klaʊd] Wolke • **cloudy** ['klaʊdi] bewölkt, wolkig
clown [klaʊn] Clown
club [klʌb] Klub; Verein
clue [kluː] Hinweis, Anhaltspunkt **clueless** ahnungslos; ratlos
coach [kəʊtʃ] **1.** Reisebus; **2.** Trainer/in
coast [kəʊst] Küste • **on the coast** an der Küste
coat [kəʊt] Mantel
cocoa ['kəʊkəʊ] Kakao
code [kəʊd] (Geheim-)Kode
coffee ['kɒfi] Kaffee • **coffee shop** Kaffeestube, Café
coin [kɔɪn] Münze
cola ['kəʊlə] Cola
cold *(adj; n)* [kəʊld] **1.** kalt • **be/feel cold** frieren • **I was/felt cold.** Mir war kalt.
2. Kälte; Erkältung • **I've got a cold.** Ich bin erkältet.
collage [*BE:* 'kɒlɑːʒ, *AE:* kə'lɑːʒ] Collage
collect [kə'lekt] (ein)sammeln **collection** [kə'lekʃn] Sammlung
college ['kɒlɪdʒ] Hochschule, Fachschule
colonial [kə'ləʊniəl] kolonial, Kolonial- • **colonist** ['kɒlənɪst] Kolonist/in; Siedler/in • **colonize** ['kɒlənaɪz] kolonisieren **colony** ['kɒləni] Kolonie
colour *(n; v)* ['kʌlə] **1.** Farbe **What colour is it?** Welche Farbe hat es (er, sie)? • °**colourful** ['kʌləfl] bunt, farbenprächtig °**2.** bunt anmalen
column ['kɒləm] **1.** Säule; °**2.** Spalte
comb *(n; v)* [kəʊm] **1.** Kamm; **2.** kämmen • **Comb your hair.** Kämm dich.
combination [ˌkɒmbɪ'neɪʃn] Kombination, Verbindung **combine** [kəm'baɪn] kombinieren, verbinden
come* [kʌm] kommen • **Come here.** Komm her. • **come in** hereinkommen • **come (in) third** als Dritter ins Ziel kommen; Dritter werden • **come of age** mündig/volljährig werden; kein Kind mehr sein • **Come on.** Komm schon! Los, komm! **come sb.'s way** jm. entgegenkommen • **come true** wahr werden, sich bewahrheiten
comic ['kɒmɪk] Comic-Heft
comment (on/about) ['kɒment] Kommentar, Bemerkung (zu)
common ['kɒmən]**: have sth. in common** etwas miteinander gemein haben
communication [kəˌmjuːnɪ'keɪʃn] Kommunikation
community [kə'mjuːnəti] Gemeinde, Gemeinschaft
company ['kʌmpəni] Firma, Gesellschaft
compare (to, with) [kəm'peə] vergleichen (mit) • °**make comparisons** [kəm'pærɪsnz] Vergleiche anstellen, vergleichen
competition [ˌkɒmpə'tɪʃn] Wettbewerb, Wettkampf
complain (to sb. about sth.) [kəm'pleɪn] sich (bei jm. über etwas) beschweren, beklagen
complete *(v; adj)* [kəm'pliːt] **1.** vervollständigen, ergänzen; **2.** vollständig, völlig
complex ['kɒmpleks] (Gebäude-)Komplex
compound ['kɒmpaʊnd] Kompositum; zusammengesetzte(r, s)
°**compound** ['kɒmpaʊnd] umzäuntes Gelände
computer [kəm'pjuːtə] Computer, Rechner • **computer application** Informatik *(Schulfach)*; Computeranwendung **computer science** Informatik
concert ['kɒnsət] Konzert
conclusion [kən'kluːʒn] Schluss(folgerung), Abschluss
°**confident** ['kɒnfɪdənt] zuversichtlich
confirmation [ˌkɒnfə'meɪʃn] Konfirmation *(Aufnahme evangelischer Christen in die Gemeinde)*
connect (to/with) [kə'nekt] verbinden (mit)
construction [kən'strʌkʃn] Konstruktion
contact sb. ['kɒntækt] sich mit jm. in Verbindung setzen; mit jm. Kontakt aufnehmen
context ['kɒntekst] Zusammenhang, Kontext

continue [kən'tɪnjuː] weitergehen/-reden/-machen, weiter (tun); fortsetzen, fortfahren (mit)
contract ['kɒntrækt] Vertrag
control [kən'trəʊl] Kontrolle; *hier:* Kontrollzentrum
conversation [ˌkɒnvə'seɪʃn] Gespräch, Unterhaltung
°**convoy** ['kɒnvɔɪ] Konvoi
cook *(v; n)* [kʊk] **1.** kochen, zubereiten; **2.** Koch, Köchin
cooker ['kʊkə] Herd
cool [kuːl] **1.** kühl; **2.** cool, scharf, stark
copy *(v; n)* ['kɒpi] **1.** übertragen, kopieren, abschreiben; **2.** Kopie, Abschrift
corn [kɔːn] *(AE:)* Mais; *(BE:)* Korn, Getreide
corner ['kɔːnə] Ecke • **on the corner** an der Ecke
cornflakes ['kɔːnfleɪks] Cornflakes
Cornish ['kɔːnɪʃ] kornisch *(aus Cornwall, zu Cornwall gehörig)*
°**corporation** [ˌkɔːpə'reɪʃn] Verwaltung
correct *(v; adj)* [kə'rekt] **1.** verbessern, korrigieren; **2.** richtig, korrekt
corridor ['kɒrɪdɔː] Gang, Korridor
cost* *(v; n)* [kɒst] **1.** kosten; **2.** Kosten
costume ['kɒstjuːm] Kostüm, Verkleidung
could [kəd, *betont:* kʊd] **1.** konnte(n); **2.** könnte(n)
counsellor ['kaʊnsələ] (*AE auch:* **counselor**) Berater/in
count [kaʊnt] zählen
°**counter** ['kaʊntə] Theke
country ['kʌntri] Land • **in the country** auf dem Land
country singer *(amerik.)* Volksmusiksänger/in
countryside ['kʌntrɪsaɪd] Landschaft, (ländliche) Gegend
county ['kaʊnti] Grafschaft, Verwaltungsbezirk
course [kɔːs] Kurs, Lehrgang
course: of course [əv 'kɔːs] natürlich, selbstverständlich
courthouse ['kɔːthaʊs] Gerichtsgebäude
cousin ['kʌzn] Cousin/Cousine
cover ['kʌvə] **1.** bedecken, zudecken; beziehen, überziehen; °**2. take cover** Schutz suchen
cow [kaʊ] Kuh
Crack! [kræk] Knacks!
crash [kræʃ] **1.** krachen • **crash (into)** zusammenstoßen (mit), hineinfahren (in)
2. abstürzen *(Computer)*
crazy (about sth./sb.) ['kreɪzi] verrückt (nach etwas/jm.)
°**cream** [kriːm] Sahne
creative [kri'eɪtɪv] kreativ, schöpferisch
°**credit** ['kredɪt] Punkt(e) *(für den High School- oder College-Abschluss)*
crew [kruː] Crew, Besatzung, Mannschaft *(eines Schiffs, Flugzeugs)*
cricket ['krɪkɪt] Kricket
crime [kraɪm] Verbrechen; Kriminalität
crisps [krɪsps] Kartoffelchips
crop [krɒp] (Feld-)Frucht; Ernte
cross [krɒs] überqueren; (sich) kreuzen • **cross out** ausstreichen, durchstreichen
crossword ['krɒswɜːd] Kreuzworträtsel
crowd [kraʊd] **1.** (Menschen-) Menge; °**2. crowd around** sich drängen/scharen um
crown [kraʊn] krönen
°**cruise** [kruːz] *(AE)* herumfahren, spazieren fahren *(ohne festes Ziel)*
cry *(v; n)* [kraɪ] **1.** weinen; schreien; **2.** Schrei, Ruf
culture ['kʌltʃə] Kultur
cup [kʌp] Tasse • **a cup of tea** eine Tasse Tee
cupboard ['kʌbəd] Schrank
curry ['kʌri] *scharfes, mit Curry gewürztes Gericht*
customer ['kʌstəmə] Kunde, Kundin
cut* **(-tt-)** [kʌt] (aus)schneiden
cut off abschneiden; *hier:* amputieren • **cut out** ausschneiden • **cut up** zerschneiden, in Stücke schneiden
cute [kjuːt] *(infml)* niedlich, süß
cycle ['saɪkl] Rad fahren • **cycling** *(das)* Radfahren • **cycle lane, cycle track** ['saɪkl leɪn, 'saɪkl træk] Radweg • **cyclist** ['saɪklɪst] Radfahrer/in

D

dad [dæd] Vati, Papa; Vater
°**damage** ['dæmɪdʒ] Schaden, Schäden
dance *(v; n)* [dɑːns] **1.** tanzen
dancing *(das)* Tanzen • **dancer** Tänzer/in
2. Tanz
danger ['deɪndʒə] Gefahr • **put sb. in danger** jn. in Gefahr bringen • **dangerous** ['deɪndʒərəs] gefährlich
dark [dɑːk] dunkel • **darkness** ['dɑːknəs] Dunkelheit
darling ['dɑːlɪŋ] Liebling, Schatz
date [deɪt] **1.** Datum • **date of birth** Geburtsdatum • **What's the date?** Welches Datum haben wir?
2. go on a date (with sb.) *(AE)* mit jm. (aus)gehen • **make a date (with sb.)** *(AE)* sich (mit jm.) *(zum Ausgehen)* verabreden
3. date sb. *(AE)* mit jm. (aus-) gehen
daughter ['dɔːtə] Tochter
day [deɪ] Tag • **day of the week** Wochentag • **in the old days** in alten Zeiten, früher • **one day** eines Tages • **that day** an jenem Tag • **the day (that) ...** der Tag, an dem ... • **the next day** der nächste Tag; am nächsten Tag • **dish of the day** Tagesmenü
dead [ded] tot
dear [dɪə] Liebling, Schatz
Dear Katrin and Julia Liebe Katrin, liebe Julia • **Dear Sir or Madam** Sehr geehrte Damen und Herren
death [deθ] Tod
December [dɪ'sembə] Dezember
decide (on) [dɪ'saɪd] sich entscheiden (für), beschließen
decision [dɪ'sɪʒn] Entscheidung
make a decision eine Entscheidung treffen/fällen
deck [dek] Deck
declaration [ˌdeklə'reɪʃn] Erklärung, Verkündung, Bekanntgabe
Declaration of Independence Unabhängigkeitserklärung *(der ehemals 13 britischen Kolonien in Nordamerika)* • **declare** [dɪ'kleə] erklären, verkünden
deep [diːp] tief
deer, *pl* **deer** [dɪə] Reh, Hirsch
°**defeat** [dɪ'fiːt] besiegen
defend [dɪ'fend] verteidigen
°**definite** ['defɪnət] bestimmt, festgelegt, definitiv
°**definition** [ˌdefɪ'nɪʃn] Definition
degree [dɪˌgriː] Grad • **134° F (= 134 degrees Fahrenheit)** [dɪˌgriːz 'færənhaɪt] 134 Grad Fahrenheit • **57° C (= 57 degrees Celsius)** [dɪˌgriːz 'selsiəs] 57 Grad Celsius
delay [dɪ'leɪ] Verzögerung
delicious [dɪ'lɪʃəs] lecker, köstlich
demonstration [ˌdemən'streɪʃn] Demonstration
°**deny** [dɪ'naɪ] ablehnen, zurückweisen
department store [dɪ'pɑːtmənt stɔː] Kaufhaus
departure [dɪ'pɑːtʃə] Abfahrt, Abreise
descendant (of) [dɪ'sendənt] Nachkomme (von)
describe [dɪ'skraɪb] beschreiben
description [dɪ'skrɪpʃn] Beschreibung
desert ['dezət] Wüste
design *(v; n)* [dɪ'zaɪn] **1.** entwerfen, konstruieren; **2.** Entwurf; Design, Gestaltung, Konstruktion • **Design and Technology** Design und Technologie/Technik *(engl. Schulfach)*
desire [dɪ'zaɪə] Wunsch, Verlangen
desk [desk] **1.** Schreibtisch, Schülertisch; **2.** *(Informations-)* Schalter
destroy [dɪ'strɔɪ] zerstören, vernichten
detail ['diːteɪl] Detail, Einzelheit
°**detective** [dɪ'tektɪv] Detektiv
develop (from ... into) [dɪ'veləp] entwickeln; sich entwickeln (aus ... zu) • **developer** [dɪ'veləpə] Entwickler/in • **development** [dɪ'veləpmənt] Entwicklung

devil ['devl] Teufel
diagram ['daɪəgræm] Diagramm
dialogue ['daɪəlɒg] Dialog
diary ['daɪəri] Tagebuch; Terminkalender
dice, *pl* **dice** [daɪs] Würfel
throw the dice würfeln
dictionary ['dɪkʃənri] Wörterbuch, *(alphabet.)* Wörterverzeichnis
die (of) [daɪ] sterben (an)
difference ['dɪfrəns] Unterschied
a software with a difference eine etwas andere Software; eine Software, die mal was anderes ist • **different (from)** ['dɪfrənt] anders (als); verschieden, unterschiedlich; andere(r, s)
difficult ['dɪfɪkəlt] schwierig, schwer
dig* (up) **(-gg-)** [dɪg] (aus-, um)graben
digit ['dɪdʒɪt] Ziffer
° **dining room** ['daɪnɪŋ ruːm] Esszimmer
dinner ['dɪnə] Abendessen
at dinner beim Abendessen
for dinner zum Abendessen
have dinner Abendbrot essen
direct [də'rekt] leiten *(Chor, Orchester)*
directions *(pl)* [də'rekʃnz] Anweisung(en)
director [də'rektə] Regisseur/in
dirty ['dɜːti] schmutzig
disabled [dɪs'eɪbld] (körper)behindert
disadvantage [ˌdɪsəd'vɑːntɪdʒ] Nachteil • **at a disadvantage** im Nachteil
disagree (with) [ˌdɪsə'griː] anderer Meinung sein (als), nicht übereinstimmen (mit)
disappear [ˌdɪsə'pɪə] verschwinden
disappointed (with sb., with/ about sth.) [ˌdɪsə'pɔɪntɪd] enttäuscht (von jm./etwas)
° **disaster** [dɪ'zɑːstə] Katastrophe, Unglück
disc [dɪsk] Scheibe • **disc jockey** ['dɪsk dʒɒki] Diskjockey
disco ['dɪskəʊ] Disko
discover [dɪ'skʌvə] entdecken; herausfinden, feststellen • **discovery** [dɪ'skʌvəri] Entdeckung
discuss [dɪ'skʌs] besprechen, diskutieren über • **discussion** [dɪ'skʌʃn] Diskussion
° **disease** [dɪ'ziːz] Krankheit
° **disguised**: **disguised voice** [dɪsˌgaɪzd 'vɔɪs] verstellte Stimme
dish [dɪʃ] Schale, Schüssel, Platte
dish of the day Tagesmenü
dishes *(pl)* Geschirr • **wash the dishes** das Geschirr abwaschen
divorced [dɪ'vɔːst] geschieden
DJ [ˌdiː'dʒeɪ], **disc jockey** ['dɪsk dʒɒki] Diskjockey
do* [duː] tun, machen • **do so** es/das tun • **do well/badly (in)** gut/schlecht sein (in), gut/schlecht abschneiden (in)
How did you do? Wie hats geklappt? / Wie hast du abgeschnitten? • **do a test** *(BE)* einen Test/eine Prüfung machen
do your homework die Hausaufgabe(n) machen, Schularbeiten machen • **do jobs** Arbeiten/Aufträge erledigen • **do sport(s)** Sport treiben • **do sums** rechnen • **do the cooking/cleaning** kochen/sauber machen *(= das Kochen/Saubermachen übernehmen)* • **do the shopping** Einkäufe machen/erledigen, einkaufen
dock [dɒk] Dock, Anlegestelle
doctor ['dɒktə] Arzt/Ärztin; Doktor
document ['dɒkjumənt] Dokument, Urkunde
dog [dɒg] Hund
dollar ($) ['dɒlə] Dollar *(US-Währung)*
dolphin ['dɒlfɪn] Delphin
door [dɔː] Tür • **at the door** an der Tür • **front door** [ˌfrʌnt 'dɔː] Wohnungstür, Haustür
doorbell ['dɔːbel] Türklingel
ring the doorbell (an der Tür) klingeln
° **double** ['dʌbl] verdoppeln
down [daʊn] hinunter, herunter, nach unten • **down south** unten im Süden • **down the tree** den Baum hinunter • **put down** hinstellen, hinlegen • **sit down** sich hinsetzen • **throw down** auf den Boden werfen • **write down** aufschreiben, notieren
upside down [ˌʌpsaɪd 'daʊn] verkehrt herum, auf dem Kopf
downstairs [ˌdaʊn'steəz] nach unten; unten
° **downtown** [ˌdaʊn'taʊn] Stadtzentrum, Innenstadt • °**downtown** ['daʊntaʊn] *(AE)* *der Süden Manhattans / in den Süden Manhattans*
Dr = Doctor ['dɒktə] Dr. = Doktor
drama ['drɑːmə] Drama, Schauspiel
draw* [drɔː] zeichnen
°**drawing** ['drɔːɪŋ] Zeichnung
dream *(n; v)* [driːm] **1.** Traum
dreamland Traumland
2. dream (about/of) träumen (von)
dress [dres] Kleid
° **dress** [dres] sich kleiden, sich anziehen • °**dress up** [ˌdres_'ʌp] (sich) verkleiden
dressed [drest]: **be dressed**
1. angezogen sein; **2. be dressed in sth.** etwas tragen, anhaben • **get dressed** sich anziehen
drink* *(v; n)* [drɪŋk] **1.** trinken
drink to sb./sth. auf jn./etwas trinken • **drink and drive** unter Alkoholeinfluss Auto fahren • **drink-driving** *(BE)* Alkohol am Steuer, Trunkenheit am Steuer
2. Getränk
drive* *(v; n)* [draɪv] **1.** *(ein Auto, einen Bus)* fahren • °**drive sb. away** jn. vertreiben, wegjagen
drive off wegfahren • **drive on** weiterfahren • **driver** Fahrer/in
2. (Auto-)Fahrt
drop **(-pp-)** [drɒp] fallen lassen
drop sb. *(einen Fahrgast)* absetzen
drug [drʌg] Droge, Rauschgift; Medikament
° **drugstore** ['drʌgstɔː] *(AE)* *Laden mit Imbiss*
drum [drʌm] Trommel; Schlagzeug • **play the drums** Schlagzeug spielen
drunk [drʌŋk]: **drunk driving** [ˌdrʌŋk 'draɪvɪŋ] *(AE)* Alkohol am Steuer, Trunkenheit am Steuer
dry [draɪ] trocken
duck [dʌk] Ente
° **duck (down)** [dʌk] sich ducken
° **dudes** [*BE:* djuːdz, *AE:* duːdz] *(AE, infml)* *etwa:* Typen
dump [dʌmp] Müllkippe
during *(prep)* ['djʊərɪŋ] während
° **dust** [dʌst] Staub

E

each [iːtʃ] jeder, jede, jedes (einzelne) • **each other** einander, sich (gegenseitig)
ear [ɪə] Ohr
early ['ɜːli] früh; zu früh
earth [ɜːθ] Erde • **on earth** auf der Erde
earthquake ['ɜːθkweɪk] Erdbeben
east [iːst] östlich; (nach) Osten
eastbound ['iːstbaʊnd] Richtung Osten • **eastern** ['iːstən] östlich, Ost- • °**Eastern Time** östliche Zeit *(Zeitzone an der Atlantikküste der USA)*
easy ['iːzi] leicht, einfach
eat* [iːt] essen
° **ecosystem** ['iːkəʊˌsɪstəm] Ökosystem
edge [edʒ] Rand, Kante
education [ˌedʒu'keɪʃn] (Schul-, Aus-)Bildung; Erziehung
e.g. [ˌiː 'dʒiː] z. B. (zum Beispiel)
egg [eg] Ei
either ['aɪðə, 'iːðə]: **not (…) either** auch nicht; auch kein
electric [ɪ'lektrɪk] elektrisch
electrician [ɪˌlek'trɪʃn] Elektriker/in
electronic [ɪˌlek'trɒnɪk] elektronisch
° **element** ['elɪmənt] Element
elephant ['elɪfənt] Elefant
elevator ['elɪveɪtə] *(AE)* Fahrstuhl, Aufzug
else [els]: **anyone/anything else** sonst (noch) jemand / sonst (noch) etwas • **anywhere else** sonst (noch) irgendwo(hin)
everyone/everything else alle anderen / alles andere • **everywhere else** überall sonst
someone/something else

(noch) jemand anderes / (noch) etwas anderes • **somewhere else** woanders(hin), sonst irgendwo(hin) • **who/what/where/why/... else?** wer/was/wo/warum/... sonst (noch)?
e-mail ['i:meɪl] E-Mail, elektronische Post
embarrass sb. [ɪm'bærəs] jn. in Verlegenheit bringen
°**emerald** ['emərəld] Smaragd; Smaragdgrün
emergency [i'mɜ:dʒənsi] Notfall
empire ['empaɪə] Reich, Weltreich
empty ['empti] leer
encounter [ɪn'kaʊntə] Begegnung
encyclopedia [ɪn,saɪklə'pi:dɪə] Enzyklopädie, Lexikon
end *(v; n)* [end] **1.** enden; beenden; **2.** Ende, Schluss • **at the end** am Ende, am Schluss **in the end** schließlich, am Ende, zum Schluss • **endless** endlos
ending ['endɪŋ] Ende, Schluss; Endung • **happy ending** Happy End
energy ['enədʒi] Energie
engine ['endʒɪn] Motor, Maschine
engineer [,endʒɪ'nɪə] Ingenieur, Ingenieurin, Techniker/in
England ['ɪŋglənd] England
English ['ɪŋglɪʃ] englisch; Englisch • **He's/She's English.** Er ist Engländer. / Sie ist Engländerin. • **in English** auf Englisch **What's this in English?** Wie heißt das auf Englisch? °**English-speaking** Englisch sprechend, englischsprachig
enjoy [ɪn'dʒɔɪ] mögen, genießen, gern haben/tun • **Enjoy yourself!** Viel Spaß! / Amüsier dich gut!
enough [ɪ'nʌf] genug
enter ['entə] betreten; einreisen in
entrance ['entrəns] Eingang
entry ['entri] **1.** Eintrag, Eintragung *(in einem Tagebuch/Wörterbuch)*; **2.** Einsendung, Beitrag *(zu einem Wettbewerb)*
envelope ['envələʊp] (Brief-)Umschlag
environment [ɪn'vaɪrənmənt] Umwelt, Umgebung • **environment-friendly** umweltfreundlich
equipment *(no pl)* [ɪ'kwɪpmənt] Ausrüstung
°**eraser** [*BE:* ɪ'reɪzə, *AE:* ɪ'reɪsə] *(AE)* Radiergummi
escape (from sb./sth.) [ɪ'skeɪp] fliehen (vor jm. / aus etwas); entkommen
Eskimo ['eskɪməʊ] Eskimo
especially [ɪ'speʃli] besonders, insbesondere
etc. [et'setərə] usw.
ethnic ['eθnɪk] ethnisch, Volks-
euro (€) ['jʊərəʊ] Euro *(europäische Währungseinheit)*
Europe ['jʊərəp] Europa
even ['i:vn] sogar, selbst • **even better/worse/taller** (sogar) noch besser/schlechter/größer **even if** selbst wenn, auch wenn °**even though** obwohl, auch wenn • °**Should he even ask?** Sollte er überhaupt fragen?
evening ['i:vnɪŋ] Abend • **Good evening.** Guten Abend. • **in the evening(s)** am Abend, abends • **this evening** heute Abend • **tomorrow evening** morgen Abend
event [ɪ'vent] Ereignis; Veranstaltung • **sporting event** Sportveranstaltung, Sportwettkampf
ever ['evə] je, jemals, schon mal **the best festival ever** das beste Fest, das es je gegeben hat
every ['evri] jede, jeder, jedes **every ten years** alle zehn Jahre
everybody ['evribɒdi] jeder, alle
everyday *(adj)* ['evrideɪ] Alltags-; alltäglich
everyone ['evriwʌn] jeder, alle
everything ['evriθɪŋ] alles
everywhere ['evriweə] überall
°**evil spirits** [,i:vl 'spɪrɪts] böse Geister
exact *(adj)* [ɪg'zækt] genau **exactly** *(adv)* [ɪg'zæktli] genau
exam(ination) [ɪg'zæm, ɪg,zæmɪ'neɪʃn] Prüfung, Examen **fail an exam** eine Prüfung nicht bestehen, bei einer Prüfung durchfallen • **take an exam** eine Prüfung ablegen, machen
example [ɪg'zɑ:mpl] Beispiel **for example** zum Beispiel
excellent ['eksələnt] ausgezeichnet, hervorragend
except *(prep)* [ɪk'sept] außer °**exception** [ɪk'sepʃn] Ausnahme
°**exchange rate** [ɪks'tʃeɪndʒ reɪt] Wechselkurs
excited (about) [ɪk'saɪtɪd] aufgeregt (wegen, über) **exciting** [ɪk'saɪtɪŋ] aufregend, spannend
excuse *(n; v)* **1.** [ɪk'skju:s] Ausrede, Entschuldigung; **2. Excuse me.** [ɪk'skju:z] Entschuldigung./ Entschuldigen Sie.
execute ['eksɪkju:t] hinrichten
exercise ['eksəsaɪz] **1.** Übung **exercise book** Übungsheft, Schulheft **2.** *(no pl)* (körperliche) Bewegung, Training, Gymnastik
°**exit** ['eksɪt] Ausfahrt, Abfahrt
expect [ɪk'spekt] erwarten, annehmen, vermuten
expensive [ɪk'spensɪv] teuer
experience *(n; v)* [ɪk'spɪərɪəns] **1.** Erlebnis, Erfahrung; **2.** erfahren, erleben
experiment [ɪk'sperɪmənt] Experiment • °**experimental prototype community** [ɪk,sperɪmentl ,prəʊtətaɪp kə'mju:nəti] *etwa:* experimentelle Mustergemeinde
expert ['ekspɜ:t] Experte, Expertin, Fachmann, Fachfrau
explain sth. to sb. [ɪk'spleɪn] jm. etwas erklären, erläutern **explanation** [,eksplə'neɪʃn] Erklärung
exploration [,eksplə'reɪʃn] Erforschung, Erkundung • **explore** [ɪk'splɔ:] erforschen, erkunden
explosion [ɪk'spləʊʒn] Explosion
°**express** [ɪk'spres] ausdrücken, äußern • **expression** [ɪk'spreʃn] Ausdruck
extra ['ekstrə] zusätzlich, Extra-
°**extract (from)** ['ekstrækt] Auszug, Ausschnitt (aus) *(einem Film, Buch)*
eye [aɪ] Auge

F

face [feɪs] Gesicht
fact [fækt] Tatsache, Fakt • **in fact** eigentlich, genau gesagt; in Wirklichkeit
factory ['fæktri] Fabrik
°**fade in/out** [,feɪd_'ɪn/'aʊt] ein-/ausblenden
Fahrenheit: 134° F (= 134 degrees Fahrenheit) [dɪ,gri:z 'færənhaɪt] 134 Grad Fahrenheit
fail (an exam) [feɪl] (eine Prüfung) nicht bestehen, (bei einer Prüfung) durchfallen • **failure** *(n)* ['feɪljə] *etwa:* nicht bestanden (*wörtlich:* Misserfolg, Scheitern, Versagen)
fair [feə] fair, gerecht
faithfully ['feɪθfəli]: **Yours faithfully** Mit freundlichen Grüßen / Hochachtungsvoll
fall* [fɔ:l] fallen • **fall asleep** einschlafen • **fall in love (with sb./sth.)** sich verlieben (in jn./etwas)
fall [fɔ:l] *(AE)* Herbst
°**falls** *(pl)* [fɔ:lz] Wasserfall
false [fɔ:ls] falsch, unecht
family ['fæməli] Familie • °**family member** Familienangehörige(r) • **family name** Familienname, Nachname • **family tree** (Familien-)Stammbaum
famous (for) ['feɪməs] berühmt (für, wegen)
fan [fæn] Fan
fantastic [fæn'tæstɪk] fantastisch, toll
far [fɑ:] weit (entfernt) • **so far** ['səʊ fɑ:] bis hierher, bis jetzt
farm *(n; v)* [fɑ:m] **1.** Bauernhof, Farm • **farmer** Bauer/Bäuerin, Landwirt/in **2.** Landwirtschaft betreiben; *(Land)* bebauen, bewirtschaften **farming** Landwirtschaft, Ackerbau
farther ['fɑ:ðə] weiter (entfernt)
farthest ['fɑ:ðɪst] am weitesten (entfernt)

fashion ['fæʃn] Mode • °**fashionable** ['fæʃnəbl] modisch, elegant
fast *(adj; adv)* [fɑːst] schnell
fat **(-tt-)** [fæt] dick
father ['fɑːðə] Vater
fault [fɔːlt] **1.** Schuld; Fehler; °**2.** Verwerfung, Graben
favourite ['feɪvərɪt] Favorit/in; Lieblings-
fax [fæks] (Tele-)Fax • **fax machine** Faxgerät
fear (of) [fɪə] Furcht, Angst (vor)
°**feast** [fiːst] Fest
February ['februəri] Februar
fed up [ˌfed‿'ʌp]: **be fed up (with)** die Nase voll haben (von), satt haben • **get fed up (with)** die Nase voll haben (von), satt haben/bekommen
feed* [fiːd] füttern • **feeding times** Fütterungszeiten
feel* [fiːl] fühlen; sich fühlen **How do you feel about ...?** Was denkst du über ...? / Was hältst du von ...? • **feel bored** sich langweilen • **feel cold** frieren • **I felt cold/hot.** Mir war kalt/heiß. • **feel sorry for sb.** jn. bedauern • **feeling** Gefühl • **feelings towards sb.** Gefühle für jn. / gegenüber jm.
feet [fiːt] *pl von „foot"*
felt-tip ['felttɪp] Filzstift
female ['fiːmeɪl] weiblich
fence [fens] Zaun
ferry ['feri] Fähre
festival ['festɪvl] Fest, Festival
fetch (from) [fetʃ] holen, abholen (von)
few [fjuː] wenige • **a few** ein paar, einige
°**fiddle** ['fɪdl] Geige, Fidel
field [fiːld] Feld, Wiese, Weide **in the field** auf dem Feld, der Wiese, der Weide
fight* (against) sb./sth. [faɪt] jn./etwas bekämpfen, gegen jn./etwas kämpfen
figure ['fɪgə] Gestalt, Figur
file [faɪl] (Computer-)Datei, Ordner
fill (with) [fɪl] füllen (mit) • **fill in** **1.** einsetzen; **2.** ausfüllen *(Formular usw.)* • **fill up with** auffüllen mit, tanken
film *(n; v)* [fɪlm] **1.** Film; **2.** filmen
finally ['faɪnəli] abschließend, zum Schluss; schließlich, endlich
find* [faɪnd] finden; suchen **find out** herausfinden
fine [faɪn] gut, fein, schön • **I'm fine.** Mir gehts gut. / Es geht mir gut.
finger ['fɪŋgə] Finger
finish ['fɪnɪʃ] beenden, zu Ende machen; enden • **finished** fertig, vollendet
fire ['faɪə] Feuer, Brand • **on fire** in Brand • **fire brigade** ['faɪə brɪˌgeɪd] Feuerwehr • °**firecracker** Knallkörper • **firework** Feuerwerkskörper • **fireworks** *(pl)* Feuerwerk
first [fɜːst] **1.** erste(r, s) • **first floor** *(BE:)* erster Stock; *(AE:)* Erdgeschoss • **first language** Muttersprache • **first name** Vorname
2. zuerst, als Erstes, erstens **first of all** zuallererst • **at first** zuerst, anfangs, am Anfang **firstly; ...** erstens, ...
°**3.** zum ersten Mal, das erste Mal • **The first time he saw Mark's room ...** Als er Marks Zimmer das erste Mal sah, ...
fish *(n; v)* [fɪʃ] **1.** *(pl* **fish***)* Fisch **fish finger** Fischstäbchen **fisherman** ['fɪʃəmən], *pl* **fishermen** ['fɪʃəmən] Fischer
2. fischen, angeln • **fishing** *(das)* Angeln • **fishing village** Fischerdorf
fit **(-tt-)** [fɪt] *(in der Größe)* passen
fitness ['fɪtnəs] Fitness
fix [fɪks] reparieren, in Ordnung bringen
flag [flæg] Fahne, Flagge
flame [fleɪm] Flamme
flash [flæʃ] aufleuchten, blinken °**flashlight** ['flæʃlaɪt] *(AE)* Taschenlampe
flat **(-tt-)** [flæt] flach, eben
flat [flæt] Wohnung • **in the flats** *hier:* in unserem Wohnblock
fleet [fliːt] Flotte
flight [flaɪt] Flug
float [fləʊt] **1.** *(auf dem Wasser)* schwimmen, treiben; °**2.** schweben, gleiten
floor [flɔː] **1.** Fußboden; **2.** Stock(werk) • **first floor** *(BE:)* erster Stock; *(AE:)* Erdgeschoss • **ground floor** *(BE)* Erdgeschoss • **on the first floor/ground floor** im ersten Stock/Erdgeschoss
°**flow** [fləʊ] fließen
°**flower** ['flaʊə] Blume
fly* [flaɪ] fliegen
focus on grammar/on words ['fəʊkəs] *etwa:* Blickpunkt „Grammatik"/„Wörter"
°**folk music** ['fəʊk mjuːzɪk] Volksmusik
follow ['fɒləʊ] folgen; verfolgen **following** folgend • **the following** das Folgende
food [fuːd] Essen; Lebensmittel; Futter
foot [fʊt], *pl* **feet** [fiːt] **1.** Fuß; **2.** Fuß *(Längenmaß; 1 Fuß = ca. 30 cm)*
football ['fʊtbɔːl] Fußball *(AE auch* = American football)
for [fə, *betont:* fɔː] für • **for breakfast/lunch/dinner** zum Frühstück/Mittagessen/Abendessen • **for Christmas** zu Weihnachten • **for example** zum Beispiel • **for sale** zum Verkauf; zu verkaufen • **for other reasons** aus anderen Gründen • **for the first time** zum ersten Mal • **for ages** *(infml)* eine Ewigkeit (lang), ewig • **for a few seconds** einige Sekunden (lang); seit einigen Sekunden • **for a long time** seit langem; lange Zeit **for an hour** seit einer Stunde; eine Stunde lang • **for hours/weeks** stundenlang/wochenlang
forecast ['fɔːkɑːst] Vorhersage, Voraussage
foreground ['fɔːgraʊnd] Vordergrund
foreign ['fɒrən] ausländisch, fremd • **foreigner** ['fɒrənə] Ausländer/in, Fremde(r)
forest ['fɒrɪst] Wald
°**forever** [fə'revə] für immer, ewig
forget* **(-tt-)** [fə'get] vergessen
fork [fɔːk] Gabel
form [fɔːm] **1.** *(englische)* (Schul-)Klasse; **2.** Form; **3.** Formular, Vordruck; **4.** (sich) bilden, formen
formal ['fɔːml] förmlich, formell
fort [fɔːt] Fort
fortunately ['fɔːtʃnətli] glücklicherweise
°**fortune** ['fɔːtʃuːn] Glück °**fortune-teller** Wahrsager/in
forward(s) ['fɔːwədz] vorwärts, nach vorn • **look forward to sth.** sich auf etwas freuen
foul [faʊl] Foul, Regelverstoß
found [faʊnd] gründen
frantic ['fræntɪk] verzweifelt, aufgeregt, in Panik
free [friː] **1.** kostenlos; **2.** frei **free time** Freizeit, freie Zeit
°**freeway** ['friːweɪ] *(AE)* Autobahn
freeze* [friːz] (ge)frieren; einfrieren • **freeze-dried** ['friːzdraɪd] gefriergetrocknet
French [frentʃ] französisch; Französisch • °**French fries** *(pl,* *[BE:* ˌfrentʃ 'fraɪz, *AE:* 'frentʃ ˌfraɪz] *(AE)* Pommes frites
fresh [freʃ] frisch; neu
Friday ['fraɪdeɪ, 'fraɪdi] Freitag
fridge [frɪdʒ] Kühlschrank
friend [frend] Freund/in • **be friends with sb.** mit jm. befreundet sein • **make friends (with sb.)** Freunde finden, sich anfreunden (mit jm.)
friendly ['frendli] freundlich, nett **friendliness** ['frendlɪnəs] Freundlichkeit
°**fries: French fries** *(pl)* [*BE:* ˌfrentʃ 'fraɪz, *AE:* 'frentʃ ˌfraɪz] *(AE)* Pommes frites
frighten ['fraɪtn] ängstigen, erschrecken • **be frightened (of)** ['fraɪtnd] Angst haben (vor) sich fürchten (vor)
from [frəm, *betont:* frɒm] aus; von **I'm from ...** Ich bin aus ... / Ich komme aus ... • **from Monday to Friday** von Montag bis Freitag • **from ... through** *(AE)* von ... bis (einschließlich) **from side to side** von einer Seite auf die andere
front [frʌnt] Vorderseite, vorderer Teil • **at the front** vorn • **in**

front of vor • **front door** [ˌfrʌnt ˈdɔː] Wohnungstür, Haustür

°**frontier** [ˈfrʌntɪə, frʌnˈtɪə] Grenze, Grenzland

frozen *(adj)* [ˈfrəʊzn] zugefroren; tiefgefroren

fruit [fruːt] Obst, Früchte; Frucht

full (of) [fʊl] voll (mit/von) **work full-time** ganztags arbeiten, als Vollzeitkraft beschäftigt sein

fun [fʌn] Spaß • **have fun** Spaß haben, sich amüsieren **Have fun!** Viel Spaß! **Shopping is (great) fun.** Einkaufen macht (viel/großen) Spaß. • **make fun of sb./sth.** sich über jn./etwas lustig machen • **funny** [ˈfʌni] witzig, komisch, merkwürdig

furniture *(no pl)* [ˈfɜːnɪtʃə] Möbel

future [ˈfjuːtʃə] **1.** Zukunft; **2.** zukünftige(r, s)

G

gadget [ˈgædʒɪt] Gerät, Apparat

game [geɪm] Spiel • **have a game** (etwas) spielen

gang [gæŋ] Bande, Gang, Truppe

°**gap** [gæp] Lücke

garage [ˈgærɪdʒ] Garage

°**garbage** [ˈgɑːbɪdʒ] *(AE)* Müll, Abfall • °**garbage dump** [ˈgɑːbɪdʒ ˌdʌmp] *(AE)* Müllhalde, -kippe

garden [ˈgɑːdn] Garten

garlic [ˈgɑːlɪk] Knoblauch

°**gas** [gæs] *(AE)* Benzin

gate [geɪt] **1.** Tor, Pforte; **2.** Flugsteig

gateway (to) [ˈgeɪtweɪ] Tor(weg), Zugang (zu)

Gee, … [dʒiː] *(AE, infml)* Mensch, …! / Mann, …! *(Ausruf)*

general [ˈdʒenrəl] General/in

general [ˈdʒenrəl] allgemeine(r, s), generelle(r, s) • **in general** im Allgemeinen

generation [ˌdʒenəˈreɪʃn] Generation

genuine [ˈdʒenjuɪn] echt

gentleman: Ladies and gentlemen [ˌleɪdiz‿ən ˈdʒentlmən] Meine (sehr geehrten) Damen und Herren

geography [dʒiˈɒgrəfi] Geographie, Erdkunde

German [ˈdʒɜːmən] deutsch; Deutsch; Deutsche(r)

Germany [ˈdʒɜːməni] Deutschland

get* **(-tt-)** [get] **1.** bekommen, kriegen • **get a friendly welcome** freundlich empfangen werden • **get time off** frei bekommen, Urlaub bekommen **2.** *(infml)* verstehen **3.** holen, besorgen **4.** gelangen, (hin)kommen **Get back!** (Geh/Tritt) Zurück! **5.** bringen, befördern • **get sb. into trouble** jn. in Schwierigkeiten bringen **6. get angry, cold, …** wütend, kalt, … werden • **get along (with sb.)** (mit jm.) auskommen, sich (mit jm.) verstehen **get dressed** sich anziehen **get fed up (with sth.)** etwas satt haben/bekommen; die Nase voll haben (von etwas) • **get in** einsteigen • **get in(to) a car/taxi** in ein Auto/Taxi einsteigen **get lost** sich verlaufen • **get married (to sb.)** (sich ver)heiraten (mit jm.), (jn.) heiraten **get off** aussteigen • **get off a bus/train/bike** aus einem Bus/Zug aussteigen; von einem Fahrrad absteigen • **get on a bus/train/bike** in einen Bus/Zug einsteigen; auf ein Fahrrad aufsteigen • **get out of a car/taxi** aus einem Auto/Taxi aussteigen • **get ready** sich bereitmachen, sich fertig machen **get sth. right/wrong** etwas richtig/falsch machen • **get through** durchkommen, Verbindung bekommen *(am Telefon)* • **get to know** kennen lernen • **get up** aufstehen

ghost [gəʊst] Geist, Gespenst **ghost town** Geisterstadt

giant [ˈdʒaɪənt] riesig, gigantisch

gift [gɪft] Geschenk, Gabe

giraffe [dʒəˈrɑːf] Giraffe

girl [gɜːl] Mädchen

girlfriend [ˈgɜːlfrend] (feste) Freundin

give* [gɪv] geben • **give a talk (on)** einen Vortrag/eine Rede halten (über) • **give sb. a friendly welcome** jn. freundlich empfangen • **give sb. $3 off** jm. eine Ermäßigung von 3 Dollar geben • **Give Susan my love.** Grüß Susan von mir. **give sth. up** etwas aufgeben

glacier [*BE:* ˈglæsiə, *AE:* ˈgleɪʃə] Gletscher

glad (-dd-) [glæd]: **be glad (about)** froh sein, sich freuen (über) • **gladly** *(adv)* gern; freudig

glamour [ˈglæmə] Glanz • **glamorous** [ˈglæmərəs] glanzvoll

glass [glɑːs] Glas

°**glee** [gliː] Freude

glove [glʌv] Handschuh

°**glue** [gluː] Klebstoff

go* [gəʊ] **1.** gehen; fahren; **2.** (hin)gehören, (hin)kommen; **3. go cold/white/…** kalt/weiß/… werden • **Let's go.** Auf gehts! • **go away** verreisen **go climbing/surfing/swimming** klettern/wellenreiten/schwimmen gehen • **go shopping/go to the shops** einkaufen gehen • **go a long way** viel erreichen, viel bewirken **go for a walk** einen Spaziergang machen • **go for a picnic** einen Picknickausflug machen **go for a ride** eine Spazierfahrt machen; herumfahren • **go for help** Hilfe holen gehen • **go in** hineingehen • **go on** °**1.** weitergehen; **2.** weitermachen; **3.** fortfahren, weiterreden; **4.** angehen *(Licht)*; **5.** (an)dauern; vor sich gehen, im Gange sein • **go on a date (with sb.)** *(AE)* mit jm. (aus)gehen • **go on a trip** einen Ausflug/eine Reise machen • **go on board** an Bord gehen • **go on holiday** in Urlaub fahren; Ferien machen **go out** **1.** ausgehen, weggehen; **2.** ausfahren, auslaufen; **3.** ausgehen *(Licht)* • **go sb.'s way** in die gleiche Richtung wie jd. gehen • **go under** untergehen **go up** steigen, in die Höhe gehen • **go with** gehören zu, passen zu • **I'm going to phone.** Ich werde anrufen. / Ich habe vor anzurufen.

goal [gəʊl] Tor *(im Sport)*

god, God [gɒd] Gott • **goddess** [ˈgɒdes] Göttin

°**goggles** *(pl)* [ˈgɒglz] Schutzbrille

gold [gəʊld] Gold • **golden** [ˈgəʊldən] golden • **goldfish,** *pl* **goldfish** Goldfisch • °**gold rush** [ˈgəʊld rʌʃ] Goldrausch °**gold-mining town** Goldgräberstadt

golf [gɒlf] Golf

gone *(adj)* [gɒn] weg, fort

good [gʊd] **1.** gut • **Good luck.** Viel Glück. • **Good morning/afternoon/evening/night.** Guten Morgen/Tag/Abend/Gute Nacht. • **Goodbye.** [ˌgʊdˈbaɪ] Auf Wiedersehen. **be good at sth.** gut in etwas sein; etwas gut können • **good-looking** gut aussehend • **be no good** zu nichts zu gebrauchen sein, nichts taugen **2.** artig, brav; **3. be good** gültig sein *(Fahrkarte usw.)*

goods *(pl)* [gʊdz] Waren, Güter

governor [ˈgʌvənə] Gouverneur/in

grace [greɪs]: **say grace** das Tischgebet sprechen

grade [greɪd] **1.** *(AE)* (Schul-)Klasse, Jahrgangsstufe; **2.** *(besonders AE)* (Schul-)Note, Zensur • °**grading system** Benotungssystem, Bewertungssystem

graffiti *(pl)* [grəˈfiːti] Graffiti *(Wandkritzeleien)*

grammar [ˈgræmə] Grammatik

grand- [ˈgræn-]: **grandad** Opa °**grandchild** Enkel/in • **grandfather** Großvater • **grandma** Oma • **grandmother** Großmutter • **grandpa** Opa **grandparents** Großeltern

grape [greɪp] Weintraube

grapefruit, *pl* **grapefruit** [ˈgreɪpfruːt] Grapefruit

grateful [ˈgreɪtfəl]: **be grateful (to sb.)** (jm.) dankbar sein

grave [greɪv] Grab

gravity ['grævəti] Schwerkraft
gravy ['greɪvi] (Braten-)Soße
great [greɪt] 1. großartig, toll **look great** toll aussehen 2. groß, bedeutend, wichtig; 3. groß, beträchtlich • **great-aunt/great-uncle** Großtante/Großonkel • **great-grandfather/great-grandmother** Urgroßvater/Urgroßmutter **great-great-aunt/great-great-uncle** Urgroßtante/Urgroßonkel
green [gri:n] 1. grün; °2. Grünfläche, (Dorf-)Platz
greeting ['gri:tɪŋ] Gruß, Begrüßung
grey [greɪ] grau
grim *(adj)* [grɪm] grimmig **grimly** *(adv)* grimmig
°**grizzly bear** ['grɪzli beə] Grislibär
ground [graʊnd] (Erd-)Boden **ground floor** *(BE)* Erdgeschoss
group *(n; v)* [gru:p] 1. Gruppe **a group of girls** eine Gruppe (von) Mädchen • **in groups of four** in Vierergruppen 2. gruppieren, zu Gruppen zusammenstellen
°**grove** [grəʊv] Wäldchen
grow* [grəʊ] 1. wachsen **grow up** aufwachsen; erwachsen werden 2. *(Getreide usw.)* anbauen, anpflanzen
guess [ges] raten, erraten • **I guess** *(besonders AE)* ich nehme an, ich denke • **have/take a guess** (mal) raten
guest [gest] Gast
guide *(v; n)* [gaɪd] 1. führen, lenken, leiten; 2. (Fremden-)Führer/in, Reiseleiter/in **guidebook** Reiseführer
guitar [gɪ'tɑ:] Gitarre • **play the guitar** Gitarre spielen
gun [gʌn] Schusswaffe
guy [gaɪ] *(infml)* Typ, Kerl **guys** *(AE, infml)* Leute
gym [dʒɪm] Sport-, Turnhalle

H

hair *(no pl)* [heə] Haar, Haare **Comb your hair.** Kämm dich.
half [hɑ:f], *pl* **halves** [hɑ:vz] Hälfte • **pay half** die Hälfte bezahlen • **a year and a half** eineinhalb Jahre, anderthalb Jahre • **the first half** die erste Hälfte/Halbzeit • **half-time** [ˌhɑ:f'taɪm] Halbzeitpause **half an hour/mile** eine halbe Stunde/Meile • **half past eight** halb neun (8.30/20.30)
°**halfway house** [ˌhɑ:fweɪ 'haʊs] *Einrichtung für den offenen Strafvollzug*
hall [hɔ:l] Halle, Saal; Flur, Diele
hamburger ['hæmbɜ:gə] Hamburger
hamster ['hæmstə] Hamster
hand [hænd] Hand • **handbag** Handtasche • **handbook** Handbuch • **handout** Arbeitsblatt, Informationsblatt, Handout
°**handle** ['hændl] Griff
handsome ['hænsəm] gut aussehend
hang* [hæŋ] hängen, aufhängen **Hang in there!** *(AE, infml)* Halte durch!
°**Hanukkah** ['hɑ:nəkə] *jüdisches Fest im Dezember*
happen (to sb.) ['hæpən] (jm.) geschehen, passieren • **What's happening?** Was ist los? / Was geht hier vor?
happy ['hæpi] glücklich, froh **Happy birthday!** Herzlichen Glückwunsch zum Geburtstag! **happy ending** Happy End **happiness** Glück
harbour ['hɑ:bə] Hafen
hard [hɑ:d] 1. *(adj)* hart; schwierig, schwer; 2. *(adv)* heftig, kräftig, sehr • **try hard** sich sehr bemühen, sich anstrengen **work hard at sth.** hart an/für etwas arbeiten
hardly ['hɑ:dli] kaum
°**harpoon** [hɑ:'pu:n] Harpune
hat [hæt] Hut
hate [heɪt] hassen, gar nicht mögen • **hate shopping** gar nicht gern einkaufen gehen
have* [hæv] haben • **have breakfast/lunch/dinner** frühstücken/Mittag essen/Abendbrot essen • **have a bath** ein Bad nehmen, *(in der Wanne)* baden • **have a break** eine Pause machen • **have a cola/a hamburger** eine Cola trinken/einen Hamburger essen **have a game** (etwas) spielen **have a guess** (mal) raten **have a holiday** (einen) Urlaub machen • **have a listen** es (sich) (mal) anhören • **have a shower** (sich) duschen • **have a look at** ansehen, einen Blick werfen auf • **have a party** eine Party veranstalten, feiern • **have a try** es (mal) versuchen • **have fun** Spaß haben, sich amüsieren • **Have a nice weekend.** Schönes Wochenende. • **have sth. in common** etwas miteinander gemein haben
have got* haben, besitzen **have got to do sth.** etwas tun müssen
have* to do sth. ['hæf tə, 'hæv tə] etwas tun müssen
he [hi, *betont:* hi:] er
head [hed] Kopf • **headless** ohne Kopf
heading ['hedɪŋ] Überschrift
headline ['hedlaɪn] Schlagzeile
headteacher [ˌhed'ti:tʃə] Schulleiter/in
headword ['hedwɜ:d] Stichwort
health [helθ] Gesundheit **healthy** ['helθɪ] gesund
hear* [hɪə] hören
heart [hɑ:t] Herz • °**learn sth. by heart** etwas auswendig lernen
°**heartland** ['hɑ:tlænd]: **America's heartland** *der durch die Landwirtschaft geprägte Mittlere Westen der USA*
heat [hi:t] Hitze • **in this heat** bei dieser Hitze
heavy ['hevi] schwer *(von Gewicht)*
Hebrew ['hi:bru:] hebräisch; Hebräisch
helicopter ['helɪkɒptə] Hubschrauber, Helikopter
hell [hel] (die) Hölle
Hello. [hə'ləʊ] Hallo. / Guten Tag. **Say hello to …** Grüß …
helmet ['helmɪt] Helm • **put on a helmet** einen Helm aufsetzen **take off a helmet** einen Helm absetzen
help *(v; n)* [help] 1. helfen **Help yourself.** Greif zu! / Bedien dich! • **May I help you?** Sie wünschen? 2. Hilfe • **shout for help** um Hilfe rufen • **with the help of** mithilfe (von)
her [hə, *betont:* hɜ:] 1. ihr, ihre; 2. sie; ihr
herd [hɜ:d] 1. Herde *(z.B. Kühe)*, Herden-; °2. treiben, zusammenpferchen
here [hɪə] hier; hierher • **Here you are.** Hier bitte. Bitte sehr.
hero ['hɪərəʊ], *pl* **heroes** ['hɪərəʊz] Held, Heldin; Idol, Vorbild
hers [hɜ:z] ihre(r, s)
herself [hə'self, *betont:* hɜ:'self] sich (selbst); selbst, selber
hide* [haɪd] (sich) verstecken; verbergen
high [haɪ] hoch • **high school** (US) *Gesamtschule mit den Klassen 7–12 für 13- bis 18-Jährige*
hill [hɪl] Hügel, Berg • **hilly** ['hɪli] hügelig
him [hɪm] ihn; ihm
himself [hɪm'self] sich (selbst); selbst, selber
Hindu *(adj; n)* [ˌhɪn'du:] Hindu-; Hindu
his [hɪz] 1. sein, seine; 2. seine(r, s)
Hispanic *(n; adj)* [hɪ'spænɪk] Hispano-Amerikaner/in *(Einwanderer aus Lateinamerika und dessen/deren Nachkommen)*; hispanisch
historian [hɪ'stɔ:riən] Historiker/Historikerin
history ['hɪstri] Geschichte, Vergangenheit • **historic** [hɪ'stɒrɪk] historisch (= geschichtlich bedeutsam) • **historical** [hɪ'stɒrɪkl] historisch, alt
hit [hɪt] Hit
hit* sb./sth. (-tt-) [hɪt] jn./etwas anfahren; gegen etwas stoßen; jn./etwas schlagen, treffen
hobby ['hɒbi] Hobby

hockey ['hɒki] Hockey
hold* [həʊld] **1.** (fest)halten; **2.** veranstalten, abhalten **hold on (to)** sich festhalten (an) • °**hold up** hochhalten
hole [həʊl] Loch
holiday ['hɒlədeɪ] **1.** Feiertag, freier Tag • **public holiday** gesetzlicher Feiertag **2. holiday(s)** Ferien, Urlaub **be/go on holiday** in Urlaub sein/fahren; Ferien haben/machen • **have/take a holiday** (einen) Urlaub machen **holidaymaker** Urlauber/in °**holiday spirit** [ˌhɒlədeɪ 'spɪrɪt] Urlaubsstimmung
home [həʊm] **1.** Heim, Zuhause; Heimat; Heimat-; **2.** nach Hause **at home** zu Hause, daheim **We're home.** Wir sind (wieder) zu Hause. **homeless** obdachlos **homelessness** Obdachlosigkeit
homepage ['həʊmpeɪdʒ] Homepage *(Einstiegs- u. Informationsseite von Firmen/Institutionen im Internet)*
homework *(no pl)* ['həʊmwɜːk] Hausaufgabe(n) • **do your homework** die Hausaufgabe(n) machen
honey ['hʌni] Honig; *(infml auch:)* Schatz, Schätzchen
honour *(BE)* / **honor** *(AE)* ['ɒnə] Ehre
hope *(n; v)* [həʊp] **1.** Hoffnung **hopeless** hoffnungslos, aussichtslos **2. hope (for)** hoffen (auf)
horrible ['hɒrəbl] scheußlich, grauenhaft, furchtbar
horse [hɔːs] Pferd
hospital ['hɒspɪtl] Krankenhaus
hot (-tt-) [hɒt] heiß • **hot dog** ['hɒt dɒg] Hotdog
hotel [həʊ'tel] Hotel • **stay at a hotel** in einem Hotel übernachten
hour ['aʊə] Stunde • **a 16-hour day** ein 16-Stunden-Tag • **a 24-hour supermarket** ein Supermarkt, der 24 Stunden („rund um die Uhr") geöffnet ist **for an hour** eine Stunde lang; seit einer Stunde • **for hours** stundenlang • **half an hour** eine halbe Stunde
house [haʊs] Haus
household ['haʊshəʊld] Haushalt; Haushalts-
°**hover** ['hɒvə] schweben (lassen)
how [haʊ] wie • **How are you?** Wie geht es dir/euch/Ihnen? **How did they like it?** Wie gefiel es ihnen? / Wie fanden sie es? **How did you do?** Wie bist du vorangekommen? • **how many?** wie viele? • **how much?** wie viel? • **How much is/are …?** Was kostet/kosten …? / Wie viel kostet/kosten …? **how to do sth.** wie man etwas tun kann/soll • **How do you know?** Woher weißt du das?
however [haʊ'evə] jedoch, aber
huge [hjuːdʒ] sehr groß, riesig
hundred ['hʌndrəd] hundert **hundreds of thousands (of)** Hunderttausende (von)
hunger ['hʌŋgə] Hunger • **hungry** ['hʌŋgri] hungrig • **be hungry** hungrig sein, Hunger haben
hunt (for) [hʌnt] jagen (nach); Jagd machen (auf), suchen
hurricane ['hʌrɪkən] Hurrikan, Orkan
hurry ['hʌri] **1.** sich beeilen; eilen **Hurry up.** Beeil dich! / Mach schnell! **2. be in a hurry** in Eile sein, es eilig haben
hurt* [hɜːt] **1.** verletzen; wehtun **She wasn't hurt.** Sie war/wurde nicht verletzt. **2.** schaden, schädigen
husband ['hʌzbənd] Ehemann
hut [hʌt] Hütte
hyphen ['haɪfn] Bindestrich

I

I [aɪ] ich • **I'm fine.** Mir gehts gut. / Es geht mir gut. • **I'm afraid** leider
ice [aɪs] Eis • **ice-cream** (Speise-)Eis • **ice-hockey** ['aɪs hɒki] Eishockey • **ice skating** ['aɪs skeɪtɪŋ] *(das)* Eislaufen
idea [aɪ'dɪə] **1.** Idee, Einfall; **2. idea (of)** Vorstellung (von)
if [ɪf] **1.** wenn, falls • **even if** selbst wenn, auch wenn **2.** ob • **as if** als ob
ill [ɪl] krank • **illness** ['ɪlnəs] Krankheit
imaginary [ɪ'mædʒɪnəri] imaginär *(nur in der Vorstellung vorhanden, nicht wirklich)*
imagine sth. [ɪ'mædʒɪn] sich etwas vorstellen • **imagination** [ɪˌmædʒɪ'neɪʃn] Vorstellungskraft, Fantasie
immigrant ['ɪmɪgrənt] Einwanderer/Einwanderin, Immigrant/in **immigrate (to)** ['ɪmɪgreɪt] einwandern, immigrieren (in *ein Land*) • **immigration (to)** [ˌɪmɪ'greɪʃn] Einwanderung, Immigration (in, nach)
important (to) [ɪm'pɔːtnt] wichtig (für)
impression (of) [ɪm'preʃn] Eindruck (von)
°**improve** [ɪm'pruːv] verbessern
in [ɪn] in • **in 1645** (im Jahre) 1645 • **(just) in time** (gerade) rechtzeitig • **in bad weather** bei schlechtem Wetter • °**in different ways** auf verschiedene Weise(n) • **in English** auf Englisch • **in fact** eigentlich, genau gesagt; in Wirklichkeit **in front of** vor • **in general** im Allgemeinen • **in memory of** zum Gedenken an • **in my opinion** meiner Meinung nach **in November** im November **in order to do sth.** um etwas zu tun • **in search of** auf der Suche nach • **in the country** auf dem Land • **in the end** schließlich, am Ende, zum Schluss • **in the field** auf dem Feld/der Wiese/der Weide • **in the morning(s)/afternoon(s)/evening(s)** am Morgen, morgens/am Nachmittag, nachmittags/am Abend, abends **in the old days** in alten Zeiten, früher • **in the open air** im Freien • **in the photo/picture** auf dem Foto/Bild • **in the sky** am Himmel • **in the street** auf der Straße • **in the world** auf der Welt • **in this heat** bei dieser Hitze • **in there** dort drinnen • **go/come in** hineingehen/hereinkommen • **work in television** beim Fernsehen arbeiten
inch [ɪntʃ] Zoll *(= 2,54 cm)*
°**incident** ['ɪnsɪdənt] Zwischenfall
include [ɪn'kluːd] (mit) einschließen, enthalten • **including** *(prep)* [ɪn'kluːdɪŋ] einschließlich
independence [ˌɪndɪ'pendəns] Unabhängigkeit
Indian *(adj; n)* ['ɪndiən] **1.** indisch; Inder/in; **2.** indianisch; Indianer/in
indoors [ˌɪn'dɔːz] drinnen, im Haus; nach drinnen, ins Haus
°**industrialist** [ɪn'dʌstriəlɪst] Industrielle(r)
industry ['ɪndəstri] Industrie
influence (on) ['ɪnfluəns] Einfluss (auf)
informal [ɪn'fɔːml] informell, nicht förmlich; umgangssprachlich
information *(no pl)* [ˌɪnfə'meɪʃn] Information(en); Auskunft, Auskünfte • **information desk** Informationsschalter
injury ['ɪndʒəri] Verletzung
inline skating ['ɪnlaɪn skeɪtɪŋ] *(das)* Inlineskating
inside [ˌɪn'saɪd] **1.** *(prep)* innerhalb, im Innern (von); in (… hinein); **2.** *(adv)* drinnen; nach drinnen
inspector [ɪn'spektə] *etwa:* Polizeiinspektor/in
instead *(adv)* [ɪn'sted] stattdessen, dafür • **instead of** *(prep)* [ɪn'sted‿əv] (an)statt, anstelle (von)
instruction [ɪn'strʌkʃn] Anweisung, Anleitung
instrument ['ɪnstrəmənt] Instrument
intelligent [ɪn'telɪdʒənt] intelligent, klug
interactive [ˌɪntər'æktɪv] interaktiv
interest sb. in sth. ['ɪntrəst] jn. an/für etwas interessieren • **be interested (in)** ['ɪntrəstɪd] interessiert sein (an), sich interessieren (für) • **interesting** ['ɪntrəstɪŋ] interessant

international [ˌɪntəˈnæʃnəl] international

Internet [ˈɪntənet] Internet • **on the Internet** im Internet

° **interpreter** [ɪnˈtɜːprɪtə] Dolmetscher/in

interrupt [ˌɪntəˈrʌpt] unterbrechen

° **interstate** [ˌɪntəˈsteɪt] *(AE)* Fernstraße, Autobahn

interview *(v; n)* [ˈɪntəvjuː] **1.** befragen, interviewen; **2.** Interview

into [ˈɪntə, *betont:* ˈɪntuː] in (… hinein)

introduce sb. to sb. [ˌɪntrəˈdjuːs] jn. jm. (anderen) vorstellen, jn. mit jm. bekannt machen
introduction (to) [ˌɪntrəˈdʌkʃn] **1.** Einführung (in), Einleitung; **2.** Vorstellung *(von Personen)*

Inuit, *pl* **Inuit** *or* **Inuits** [ˈɪnuɪt, ˈɪnjuɪt] Inuit, Eskimo

° **Inupiaq** [ɪˈnuːpiæk] *Sprache der Inupiat*

° **Inupiat** [ɪˈnuːpiæt] *im Norden und Nordwesten Alaskas lebendes Inuit-Volk*

invent [ɪnˈvent] erfinden • **invention** [ɪnˈvenʃn] Erfindung
inventor [ɪnˈventə] Erfinder/in

invitation [ˌɪnvɪˈteɪʃn] Einladung
invite [ɪnˈvaɪt] *(Gäste)* einladen

Irish [ˈaɪrɪʃ] irisch, Irisch

irregular [ɪˈregjələ] unregelmäßig

is [ɪz] ist • **How much is …?** Was kostet …? / Wie viel kostet …? • **the felt-tip is 65p** der Filzstift kostet 65 Pence

island [ˈaɪlənd] Insel

issue [ˈɪʃuː] **1.** (Streit-)Frage, Thema, Angelegenheit; °**2.** Ausgabe *(einer Zeitschrift)*

it [ɪt] es *(bei Sachen und Tieren auch:* er, sie) • **It's me – Sita.** Ich bin es – Sita. • **its** [ɪts] sein, seine *(bei Sachen und Tieren auch:* ihr, ihre)

itself [ɪtˈself] sich (selbst); selbst, selber

J

jacket [ˈdʒækɪt] Jacke; Jackett, Sakko

January [ˈdʒænjuəri] Januar

jar [dʒɑː] Glas, Topf

jazz [dʒæz] Jazz

jealous (of) [ˈdʒeləs] neidisch (auf); eifersüchtig (auf)

jeans *(pl)* [dʒiːnz] Jeans

° **jerk** [dʒɜːk] *(infml)* Blödmann, Trottel

Jew [dʒuː] Jude/Jüdin • **Jewish** [ˈdʒuːɪʃ] jüdisch

job [dʒɒb] Beruf, Arbeit, Job; Aufgabe • **do jobs** Arbeiten/Aufträge erledigen • **jobless** arbeitslos, ohne Arbeit

jogging [ˈdʒɒgɪŋ] *(das)* Joggen, Jogging

join [dʒɔɪn] beitreten, eintreten in *(einen Klub usw.)* • **join sb.** sich jm. anschließen; mitmachen
°**join together** miteinander verbinden

joke *(n; v)* [dʒəʊk] **1.** Witz; **2.** witzeln, scherzen

journey [ˈdʒɜːni] Reise, Fahrt, Weg

judge (by/from) [dʒʌdʒ] beurteilen, einschätzen (nach, aufgrund)

judo [ˈdʒuːdəʊ] Judo

juice [dʒuːs] Saft

July [dʒuˈlaɪ] Juli

jump [dʒʌmp] springen

June [dʒuːn] Juni

junior [ˈdʒuːniə] Junioren-, Jugend-

° **Jurassic** [dʒuˈræsɪk] jurassisch, Jura- *(aus der Jurazeit vor ca. 180 Millionen Jahren)*

just [dʒʌst] **1.** nur, bloß • **I'm just looking.** Ich sehe mich nur um. • **Just a moment!** Einen Moment mal (eben)! • **just after/before 10.30** kurz nach/vor 10.30
2. einfach • **Just imagine.** Stell dir (nur) mal vor!
3. gerade (eben), soeben • **just in time** (gerade) rechtzeitig
just then genau in dem Moment; gerade dann
4. just as tired (as you are) genauso müde (wie du) • **just like** genau wie

K

karaoke [ˌkærəˈəʊkeɪ] Karaoke

kayaking [ˈkaɪækɪŋ] *(das)* Kajakfahren

keep* [kiːp] (be)halten; aufbewahren, aufheben • **keep (on) doing sth.** etwas weiter tun; etwas wiederholt tun • **Don't keep asking.** Frag nicht dauernd/immer wieder. • **keep alive** am Leben erhalten
keep sb./sth. away (from) jn./etwas fern halten (von) • **keep quiet** still sein • **keep quiet about sth.** etwas für sich behalten, etwas geheim halten

ketchup [ˈketʃəp] Ketschup

key [kiː] Schlüssel

kick [kɪk] treten (gegen)

kid [kɪd] Kind, Jugendliche(r)

kidnap (-pp-) [ˈkɪdnæp] entführen, kidnappen

kill [kɪl] töten • **killer** Killer/in, Mörder/in • **killing** Tötung

kilo [ˈkiːləʊ] Kilo(gramm)
2 kilos of meat 2 Kilo Fleisch

kilometre [ˈkɪləmiːtə] Kilometer

kind [kaɪnd] freundlich, gütig, nett

kind (of) [kaɪnd] Art • **What kind of …?** Was für ein/e …?
kind of quickly *(infml)* irgendwie schnell, etwas schnell

kindergarten [ˈkɪndəgɑːtn] Kindergarten; Vorschule

king [kɪŋ] König

kiss [kɪs] küssen

kitchen [ˈkɪtʃɪn] Küche

kite [kaɪt] Drachen • °**fly a kite** einen Drachen steigen lassen

knife [naɪf], *pl* **knives** [naɪvz] Messer

° **knight** [naɪt] Ritter

° **knock** [nɒk] klopfen

know* [nəʊ] **1.** wissen • **I don't know.** Ich weiß (es) nicht. **How do you know?** Woher weißt du das? • **you know** weißt du; nämlich
2. kennen • **get to know** kennen lernen • **known as** bekannt als

L

° **label** [ˈleɪbl] beschriften, etikettieren; benennen, mit einem Namen versehen

° **labour** *(BE)* / **labor** *(AE)* [ˈleɪbə] Arbeit

° **ladder** [ˈlædə] *(die)* Leiter

lady [ˈleɪdi] Dame • **ladies** meine Damen • **Ladies and gentlemen** Meine (sehr geehrten) Damen und Herren

lake [leɪk] (Binnen-)See

lamb [læm] Lamm

lamp [læmp] Lampe

land *(n; v)* [lænd] **1.** Land, Grund und Boden; **2.** landen *(Flugzeug)*, anlegen *(Schiff)*

language [ˈlæŋgwɪdʒ] Sprache
first language Muttersprache

large [lɑːdʒ] groß

laser [ˈleɪzə] Laser

last [lɑːst] **1.** (an-, fort)dauern; **2.** halten *(Obst, Gemüse usw.)*

last [lɑːst] **1.** letzte(r, s) • **last year** letztes Jahr/im letzten Jahr
2. zuletzt, das letzte Mal • **at last** schließlich, endlich

late [leɪt] spät; zu spät • **be late** zu spät sein/kommen • **I'm late for school.** Ich komme zu spät zur Schule. • **sleep late** lange schlafen • **later** später

Latin [ˈlætɪn] Latein

laugh [lɑːf] lachen • **laugh at** lachen über; auslachen

launch *(v; n)* [lɔːntʃ] **1.** *(ins All)* (ab)schießen; **2.** Start, Abschuss
°**launch pad** [ˈlɔːntʃ pæd] Abschussrampe

laundry [ˈlɔːndri] Wäscherei

° **lavender** [ˈlævəndə] Lavendel; Lavendelblau

lazy [ˈleɪzi] faul, träge

lead* [liːd] führen, leiten
leader (An-)Führer/in

leaf [liːf], *pl* **leaves** [liːvz] Blatt *(an Pflanzen)*

learn [lɜːn] lernen • °**learn by heart** auswendig lernen
learn about etwas erfahren über/von, etwas herausfinden über

least [liːst] am wenigsten • **at least** wenigstens, mindestens; zumindest

leave* [liːv] **1.** weggehen, abfahren; **2.** (zurück)lassen, hinterlassen; verlassen • **leave a message** eine Nachricht hinterlassen • °**leave room** Platz lassen • **leave school** von der Schule abgehen • **leave sth. out** etwas auslassen, weglassen
left [left] nach links; linke(r, s) **on the left** links, auf der linken Seite • **to the left** links, auf der linken Seite, zur Linken
leg [leg] Bein
lemonade [ˌlemə'neɪd] Limonade
less [les] weniger
lesson ['lesn] Unterrichtsstunde **lessons** *(pl)* Unterricht **teach sb. a lesson** jm. eine Lektion erteilen
let* sb. do sth. **(-tt-)** [let] jm. erlauben, etwas zu tun; jn. etwas tun lassen • **Let's …** Lass(t) uns … • **Let's swap.** Lass uns tauschen. / Tauschen wir. **Let's go.** Auf gehts!
letter ['letə] **1.** Buchstabe; **2. letter (to)** Brief (an)
lettuce ['letɪs] (Kopf-)Salat
liberty ['lɪbəti] Freiheit
librarian [laɪ'breəriən] Bibliothekar/in • **library** ['laɪbrəri] Bibliothek, Bücherei
lie* [laɪ] liegen
lie *(n; v)* [laɪ] **1.** Lüge • **tell (sb.) lies** (jn. an-, be)lügen **2. lie (to sb.)** (jn. an-, be)lügen
life [laɪf], *pl* **lives** [laɪvz] (das) Leben • **lifeless** leblos • °**life-size** lebensgroß
lift [lɪft] (an-, hoch)heben
lift [lɪft] Lift, Aufzug, Fahrstuhl
light* *(v; n)* [laɪt] **1.** anzünden; **2.** Licht, Lampe
like *(conj)* [laɪk] *(infml)* als ob
like [laɪk] **1.** wie • **What's … like?** Wie ist …? • **blouses like this** solche Blusen • **Start like this** Fang so an • **like that** so °**2.** *(infml)* also, irgendwie
like [laɪk] mögen, gern haben **How did they like …?** Wie gefiel ihnen …? / Wie fanden sie …? • **like shopping** gern einkaufen gehen • **I'd like (= I would like)** Ich hätte gern / Ich möchte gern • **I'd like to go.** Ich würde gern/möchte gehen.
limit: **speed limit** ['spiːd lɪmɪt] Geschwindigkeitsbegrenzung, Geschwindigkeitsbeschränkung
line [laɪn] **1.** Zeile; **2.** (U-Bahn-) Linie
line up [ˌlaɪn_'ʌp] *(besonders AE)* sich anstellen *(in einer Schlange)*
link *(v; n)* [lɪŋk] **1.** verbinden, verknüpfen; **2.** Verbindung **linking word** Bindewort
lion ['laɪən] Löwe
list *(v; n)* [lɪst] **1.** auflisten, aufzählen; **2.** Liste
listen ['lɪsn] zuhören; horchen **listen for sth.** auf etwas horchen, auf etwas achten • **listen to sb./sth.** jm. zuhören / sich etwas anhören • **listener** Zuhörer/in • **have a listen** es (sich) (mal) anhören
litre ['liːtə] Liter • **2 litres of milk** 2 Liter Milch
little ['lɪtl] **1.** klein, jung; **2.** wenig **a little** ein bisschen, ein wenig
live [lɪv] leben, wohnen; *(Patient usw.)* am Leben bleiben, überleben • **living** ['lɪvɪŋ] lebend **living-history museum** Freilichtmuseum *(mit kostümierten Fremdenführern, historischen Aufführungen usw.)*
live [laɪv] live, direkt
lives [laɪvz] *pl von „life"*
living-room ['lɪvɪŋruːm] Wohnzimmer
load [ləʊd] (auf-, ein)laden; beladen
local ['ləʊkl] **1.** örtlich, Lokal-; am/vom Ort; °**2.** Einheimische(r)
lock [lɒk] abschließen, zuschließen
locker ['lɒkə] Schließfach; Spind
logbook ['lɒgbʊk] Logbuch *(Schiffstagebuch)*
Londoner ['lʌndənə] Londoner/in
lonely ['ləʊnli] einsam • **loneliness** ['ləʊnlɪnəs] Einsamkeit
long [lɒŋ] lang • **a long way** ein weiter Weg; weit (entfernt) **a minute longer** noch eine Minute
look *(v; n)* [lʊk] **1.** schauen, sehen • **I'm just looking.** Ich sehe mich nur um. • **Look.** Pass auf. / Hör mal. • **Look out!** Pass auf! / Vorsicht! • **look at** anschauen, ansehen • **Look at the board.** Sieh an die Tafel. **Look at the picture.** Sieh dir das Bild an. • **look after sb.** sich um jn. kümmern, auf jn. aufpassen • **look for** suchen **look forward to sth.** sich auf etwas freuen • **look round** sich umsehen • **look through sth.** etwas durchsehen, durchsuchen • **look sth. up** etwas nachschlagen, etwas heraussuchen **2.** aussehen • **look great** toll aussehen • **look like** aussehen wie • **Does this shirt look good on me?** Steht mir dieses Hemd? **3.** Blick • **have/take a look (at)** einen Blick werfen (auf), ansehen **4. good looks** gutes Aussehen
loose [luːs] locker, lose • **break loose (from)** sich losreißen, sich lösen (von)
lose* [luːz] verlieren • **loser** Verlierer/in
lost *(adj)* [lɒst] verloren • °**lost-property office** ['prɒpəti] Fundbüro • **get lost** sich verlaufen
lot [lɒt]: **a lot (of)** eine Menge, viel, viele • **lots (of)** eine Menge, viel, viele • **like sb. a lot** jn. sehr mögen
loud [laʊd] laut
love *(v; n)* [lʌv] **1.** lieben, sehr mögen • **love shopping** sehr gern einkaufen gehen • **lover** Liebhaber/in **2.** Liebe • **Love, …** Viele liebe Grüße (von) … • **fall in love (with sb./sth.)** sich verlieben (in jn./etwas) • **Give Susan my love.** Grüß Susan von mir.
love [lʌv] null *(Tennis)*
lovely ['lʌvli] schön, herrlich, hübsch
°low [ləʊ] niedrig
lower ['ləʊə] herab-, hinablassen
luck [lʌk]: **Good luck.** Viel Glück. **Bad luck.** Pech (gehabt)! **You're lucky.** ['lʌki] Du hast Glück. / Du bist gut dran. **lucky day** Glückstag
°lunar ['luːnə] Mond-
lunch [lʌntʃ] Mittagessen • **for lunch** zum Mittagessen • **have lunch** Mittag essen • **at lunchtime** mittags, zur Mittagszeit

M

machine [mə'ʃiːn] Maschine, Gerät; *(Getränke- usw.)*Automat
mad **(-dd-)** [mæd] verrückt, wahnsinnig • **mad (at/with sb.)** *(besonders AE, infml)* wütend (auf jn.)
Madam ['mædəm]: **Dear Sir or Madam** Sehr geehrte Damen und Herren
made [meɪd]: **be made of** aus (gemacht) sein • **be made up of** bestehen aus
magazine [ˌmægə'ziːn] Zeitschrift
magic *(adj; n)* ['mædʒɪk] magisch, Zauber-; Magie, Zauberkunst
°magnitude ['mægnɪtjuːd] Stärke
mail [meɪl] *(besonders AE)* abschicken, einwerfen, zur Post bringen • °**mailbox** ['meɪlbɒks] *(AE)* Briefkasten
main [meɪn] Haupt- • **main clause** Hauptsatz • **mainly** ['meɪnli] hauptsächlich
majesty ['mædʒəsti] Majestät
make* [meɪk] machen, bilden, bauen; zubereiten • **make it** *(infml)* es schaffen, Erfolg haben **be made of** aus (gemacht) sein **be made up of** bestehen aus **make sb. do sth.** jn. dazu bringen, etwas zu tun; jn. zwingen, etwas zu tun • **make sb. sth.** jn. zu etwas machen • **make sth. sth.** etwas zu etwas *(anderem)* machen • **make a date (with sb.)** *(AE)* sich (mit jm.) *(zum Ausgehen)* verabreden **make a decision** eine Entscheidung treffen/fällen • **make a speech** eine Rede/einen Vortrag halten • °**make comparisons** Vergleiche anstellen, vergleichen • **make friends (with sb.)** Freunde finden, sich anfreunden (mit jm.) • **make fun**

of sb./sth. sich über jn./etwas lustig machen • **make money** (viel) Geld verdienen • **make notes** sich Notizen machen **make sure** sich vergewissern; darauf achten/dafür sorgen (, dass) • **make trouble** Ärger/Schwierigkeiten machen, bereiten • **make sth. up** sich etwas ausdenken, etwas erfinden

make-up ['meɪkʌp] Make-up

male [meɪl] männlich

mama [mə'mɑ:] Mama

man [mæn], *pl* **men** [men] Mann

°**manager** ['mænɪdʒə] Geschäftsführer/in, Manager/in

°**mandolin** [,mændə'lɪn] Mandoline

manual ['mænjuəl] Handbuch

many ['meni] viele • **how many?** wie viele?

map [mæp] Landkarte, Stadtplan

march [mɑ:tʃ] marschieren

March [mɑ:tʃ] März

marital status [,mærɪtl 'steɪtəs] Familienstand

mark [mɑ:k] *(BE)* (Schul-)Note, Zensur

market ['mɑ:kɪt] Markt

marmalade ['mɑ:məleɪd] (Orangen-)Marmelade

marriage ['mærɪdʒ] Ehe; Hochzeit

marry ['mæri] heiraten • **married (to)** ['mærid] verheiratet (mit) • **get married (to sb.)** (sich ver)heiraten (mit jm.), (jn.) heiraten

mask [mɑ:sk] Maske

master ['mɑ:stə] Herr *(eines Sklaven/einer Sklavin)*

match *(n; v)* [mætʃ] **1.** Spiel, Wettkampf; **2.** Streichholz; **3.** zuordnen

mate [meɪt] Kumpel, Kamerad

material [mə'tɪəriəl] Material, Stoff

maths [mæθs] *(BE)* / **math** [mæθ] *(AE)* Mathematik

matter *(v; n)* ['mætə] **1.** von Bedeutung sein, etwas ausmachen; **2. What's the matter?** Was ist denn (los)?

May [meɪ] Mai

may [meɪ] dürfen • **May I help you?** Sie wünschen?

may [meɪ]: **he may be the best ...** er ist vielleicht der beste ...

maybe ['meɪbi] vielleicht

mayday ['meɪdeɪ] SOS-Ruf, Maydaysignal

maze [meɪz] Irrgarten, Labyrinth

me [mi, *betont:* mi:] mir; mich **It's me – Sita.** Ich bin es – Sita. **Me too.** Ich auch.

meal [mi:l] Mahlzeit, Essen

mean* [mi:n] **1.** meinen (= sagen wollen) • **What do you mean by that?** Was verstehst du darunter?
2. bedeuten • **mean something to sb.** jm. etwas bedeuten • **The name means nothing to me.** Der Name sagt mir nichts. / Ich kenne den Namen nicht. • **meaning** ['mi:nɪŋ] Bedeutung

meanwhile ['mi:nwaɪl] inzwischen, währenddessen

meat [mi:t] Fleisch

medicine ['medɪsn, 'medsn] Medizin, Arznei

meet* [mi:t] **1.** sich treffen; *jn.* treffen • **Nice to meet you.** Freut mich, euch (dich/Sie) kennen zu lernen. • **meeting** Versammlung, Besprechung, Treffen
2. meet sb. jn. abholen

mega ['megə] mega-; Mega-

melt [melt] schmelzen

member (of) ['membə] Mitglied (in, von)

°**memorial** [mə'mɔ:riəl] Gedenk-

memory ['meməri] Gedächtnis; Erinnerung; Gedenken • **in memory of** zum Gedenken an

men [men] *pl von „man"*

mention ['menʃn] erwähnen, nennen

menu ['menju:] Speisekarte; (Computer-)Menü

message ['mesɪdʒ] Nachricht **leave a message** eine Nachricht hinterlassen

metal ['metl] Metall

method ['meθəd] Methode

metre ['mi:tə] Meter

mice [maɪs] *pl von „mouse"*

microchip ['maɪkrəʊtʃɪp] Mikrochip

microphone ['maɪkrəfəʊn] Mikrofon

microwave ['maɪkrəweɪv] Mikrowelle, Mikrowellengerät

midday [,mɪd'deɪ] Mittags-; Mittagszeit

middle ['mɪdl] Mitte • **middle row** mittlere Reihe • **the middle of nowhere** *(infml) etwa:* das Ende der Welt

midnight ['mɪdnaɪt] Mitternacht

Midwest [,mɪd'west]: **the Midwest** der mittlere Westen *(der USA)*

might [maɪt]: **You might be right.** Du könntest (vielleicht) Recht haben.

mile [maɪl] Meile *(= ca. 1,6 km)*

milk [mɪlk] Milch • **milk shake** Milkshake • °**Milky Way** [,mɪlki 'weɪ] Milchstraße

million ['mɪljən] Million

°**mime** [maɪm] vorspielen, pantomimisch darstellen • **mime group** Pantomimengruppe

°**mind** [maɪnd] Geist, Verstand

°**Mind the spelling.** [maɪnd] Gib Acht auf die Schreibung.

mine [maɪn] Bergwerk

mine [maɪn] meine(r, s)

mineral water ['mɪnərəl wɔ:tə] Mineralwasser

minority [maɪ'nɒrəti] Minderheit

minute ['mɪnɪt] Minute • **a minute longer** noch eine Minute

mirror ['mɪrə] Spiegel

miserable ['mɪzrəbl] unglücklich, elend; erbärmlich, armselig

misfit ['mɪsfɪt] Außenseiter/in

miss [mɪs] *etwa:* mein Fräulein *(höfliche, nur noch selten gebrauchte Anrede)* • **Miss ...** Fräulein/Frau ... *(unverheiratet)*

miss [mɪs] vermissen; verpassen, verfehlen • **be missing** fehlen **missing** fehlend

mission ['mɪʃn] Einsatz, Mission; *hier:* Weltraumflug

mistake [mɪ'steɪk] Fehler, Irrtum

°**mixed** [mɪkst] gemischt **mixed bag** bunte Mischung

°**mix up** [,mɪks_'ʌp] durcheinander bringen • °**mixed up** durcheinander

mobile (phone) [,məʊbaɪl 'fəʊn] Mobiltelefon, Handy

°**mockingbird** ['mɒkɪŋbɜ:d] Spottdrossel

model ['mɒdl] **1.** Modell, Modell-; **2.** Model, Mannequin

modern ['mɒdən] modern

mom [mɒm] *(AE)* Mutti, Mama; Mutter

moment ['məʊmənt] Moment, Augenblick • **at the moment** im Moment, gerade, zurzeit **Just a moment!** Einen Moment mal (eben)!

Monday ['mʌndeɪ, 'mʌndi] Montag

money ['mʌni] Geld • **make money** (viel) Geld verdienen °**money matters** **1.** Geldangelegenheiten; **2.** Geld ist wichtig

monitor ['mɒnɪtə] Bildschirm, Monitor

monkey ['mʌŋki] Affe

monster ['mɒnstə] Monster, Ungeheuer

month [mʌnθ] Monat • **a 6-month break** eine sechsmonatige Pause

mood [mu:d] Laune, Stimmung **be in a bad mood** in schlechter Stimmung sein, schlechte Laune haben • **be in a good mood** in guter Stimmung sein, gute Laune haben

moon [mu:n] Mond

°**moose**, *pl* **moose** [mu:s] *(amerikanischer)* Elch

more [mɔ:] mehr, weitere • **more and more** immer mehr • **one more** noch ein(e), ein(e) weitere(r, s) • **no more school** keine Schule mehr • **no more than** nicht mehr als • **not (...) any more** nicht mehr • **more expensive (than)** teurer (als)

morning ['mɔ:nɪŋ] Morgen, Vormittag • **Good morning.** Guten Morgen. / Guten Tag. *(vormittags)* • **in the morning(s)** am Morgen, morgens **this morning** heute Morgen **tomorrow morning** morgen früh, morgen Vormittag

most [məʊst] (der/die/das) meiste ...; am meisten • **most kids/cars/...** die meisten Kinder/Autos/... • **(the) most important** (der/die/das) wichtigste ...; am wichtigsten

°**mostly** ['məʊstli] hauptsächlich
motel [məʊ'tel] Motel
mother ['mʌðə] Mutter
motor ['məʊtə] Motor • **motorbike** ['məʊtəbaɪk] Motorrad
motorcyclist ['məʊtəsaɪklɪst] Motorradfahrer/in
mountain ['maʊntən] Berg
mouse [maʊs], *pl* **mice** [maɪs] Maus
mouth [maʊθ] Mund
move [mu:v] **1.** (sich) bewegen °**Move your counter.** Zieh deinen Spielstein. • **movement** ['mu:vmənt] Bewegung **2.** (um)ziehen • **move in** einziehen
3. on the move unterwegs, auf Achse
movie ['mu:vi] *(besonders AE)* Film • **movie theater** ['mu:vi ˌθɪətə] *(AE)* Kino
Mr ['mɪstə] Herr …
Mrs ['mɪsɪz] Frau … *(verheiratet)*
Ms Morrison [mɪz, məz] Frau Morrison
much [mʌtʃ] **1.** viel • **How much?** Wie viel? • **How much is/are …?** Was kostet/kosten …? Wie viel kostet/kosten …?
2. *(adv)* sehr, viel
mum [mʌm] Mutti, Mama; Mutter
murder *(n; v)* ['mɜ:də] **1.** Mord; **2.** (er)morden • **murderer** ['mɜ:dərə] Mörder/in
museum [mju'zɪəm] Museum
music ['mju:zɪk] Musik
musical ['mju:zɪkl] Musik-, musikalisch
Muslim *(adj; n)* ['mʊzlɪm, 'mʌzlɪm] moslemisch; Moslem
must [məst, *betont:* mʌst] müssen
mustn't ['mʌsnt] nicht dürfen
my [maɪ] mein, meine • **My name is …** Mein Name ist …/ Ich heiße …
myself [maɪ'self] mir/mich (selbst); selbst, selber
mystery *(n; adj)* ['mɪstri] Rätsel; rätselhafte(r, s)

N

nail [neɪl] Nagel • **nail polish** ['neɪl ˌpɒlɪʃ] *(AE)* / **nail varnish** ['neɪl ˌvɑ:nɪʃ] *(BE)* Nagellack
name [neɪm] Name • **My name is …** Mein Name ist … / Ich heiße … • **What's your name?** Wie heißt du? • **first name** Vorname • **by its shorter name** unter seinem/ihrem kürzeren Namen
narrow ['nærəʊ] schmal, eng
nation ['neɪʃn] Nation, Volk
national ['næʃnəl] national
nationality [ˌnæʃə'næləti] Staatsangehörigkeit, Nationalität
native *(n; adj)* ['neɪtɪv] **1.** Ur(einwohner/in); **2.** eingeboren, einheimisch • **Native American** amerikanische(r) Ureinwohner/in, Indianer/in
nature ['neɪtʃə] Natur
°**natural disaster** [ˌnætʃrəl dɪ'zɑ:stə] Naturkatastrophe
near (to) [nɪə] in der Nähe von, nahe (bei) • **near there** dort in der Nähe; nicht weit von dort
nearly ['nɪəli] fast, beinahe
neat [ni:t] *(AE, infml)* toll, prima, klasse
necessary ['nesəsri] notwendig, nötig
neck [nek] Hals
need [ni:d] brauchen, benötigen
need to do tun müssen
needn't nicht brauchen, nicht müssen
negative ['negətɪv] negativ
neighbour *(BE)* / **neighbor** *(AE)* ['neɪbə] Nachbar/in • °**neighbourhood** *(BE)* / **neighborhood** *(AE)* ['neɪbəhʊd] Nachbarschaft
°**neither … nor** ['naɪðə/'ni:ðə … 'nɔ:] weder … noch
°**nerd** [nɜ:d] *(infml)* Langweiler/in, Streber/in
nervous ['nɜ:vəs] nervös, aufgeregt
net [net] Netz • **network** ['netwɜ:k] (Wörter-)Netz, „Wörterspinne"
never ['nevə] nie, niemals
new [nju:] neu • **New Year** Neujahr • °**New Year's Eve** [ˌnju: jɪəz_'i:v] Silvester
news *(no pl)* [nju:z] Nachricht(en), Neuigkeit(en)
newspaper ['nju:speɪpə] Zeitung • **newsreader** ['nju:zˌri:də] Nachrichtensprecher/in
next [nekst] **1.** nächste(r, s) *(zeitlich; Reihenfolge)* • **next Monday** (am) nächsten Montag
next week nächste Woche, in der nächsten Woche • **the next day** der nächste Tag; am nächsten Tag
2. als Nächstes
next to ['nekst tə] neben
nice [naɪs] schön, nett • **Nice to meet you.** Freut mich, Sie (dich/euch) kennen zu lernen.
°**nigger** ['nɪgə] *grobes Schimpfwort für einen Schwarzen/eine Schwarze*
night [naɪt] Nacht, (später) Abend • **at night** in der Nacht, nachts • **that night** in jener Nacht • **from morning till night** von morgens bis abends, von früh bis spät
nil [nɪl] null • **one nil to Kingsway** eins zu null für Kingsway
no [nəʊ] **1.** nein; **2.** kein, keine
no more school keine Schule mehr • **no more than** nicht mehr als • **no one** ['nəʊ_wʌn] niemand • **No way!** [ˌnəʊ 'weɪ] *(infml)* Auf keinen Fall! / Kommt nicht infrage! • °**no whit** [nəʊ 'wɪt] kein bisschen
nobody ['nəʊbədi] niemand
nod (-dd-) [nɒd] nicken (mit)
noise [nɔɪz] Geräusch; Lärm
noisy ['nɔɪzi] laut, lärmend
°**nominate** ['nɒmɪneɪt] nominieren, vorschlagen
none [nʌn] keine(r, s)
north [nɔ:θ] nördlich; (nach) Norden • **northbound** ['nɔ:θbaʊnd] Richtung Norden
northern ['nɔ:ðən] nördlich, Nord- • **north-east** [ˌnɔ:θ'i:st] nordöstlich; (nach) Nordosten
north-west [ˌnɔ:θ'west] nordwestlich; (nach) Nordwesten
nose [nəʊz] Nase
not [nɒt] nicht • **I'm not German.** Ich bin kein Deutscher/ keine Deutsche. • **not (…) any more** nicht mehr • **not (…) either** ['aɪðə, 'i:ðə] auch nicht; auch kein • **not really** eigentlich nicht • **not … until/till** erst (um) • **not (…) yet** noch nicht
note [nəʊt] **1.** Notiz; Kurznachricht; Zettel; Anmerkung, Hinweis • **make notes** sich Notizen machen • **take notes** sich Notizen machen, mitschreiben
°**2. note sth. down** etwas aufschreiben, notieren
nothing ['nʌθɪŋ] nichts
°**nothing but** nichts als, nur
notice *(v; n)* ['nəʊtɪs] **1.** (be)merken; **2.** Anschlag, Mitteilung
notice board ['nəʊtɪs bɔ:d] Anschlagtafel, schwarzes Brett
nought [nɔ:t] null
November [nəʊ'vembə] November
now [naʊ] nun, jetzt • **by now** inzwischen • **right now** im Moment, jetzt gerade • °**Now that …** Jetzt, wo … / Jetzt, da … • **Now what?** Was nun?
nowhere ['nəʊweə] nirgendwo, nirgendwohin • **the middle of nowhere** *(infml)* *etwa:* das Ende der Welt
nuclear ['nju:kliə] nuklear, Kern-, Atom- • **nuclear power station** [ˌnju:kliə 'paʊə steɪʃn] Atom-, Kernkraftwerk
°**nugget** ['nʌgɪt] Goldklumpen
number ['nʌmbə] Zahl, Ziffer
a small number of children eine kleine Anzahl Kinder/von Kindern
nurse [nɜ:s] Krankenschwester, Krankenpfleger
nylon ['naɪlɒn] Nylon

O

object ['ɒbdʒɪkt] Gegenstand
ocean ['əʊʃn] Ozean
o'clock [ə'klɒk]: **six o'clock** sechs Uhr
October [ɒk'təʊbə] Oktober
Odd word out [ˌɒd wɜ:d_'aʊt] *etwa:* Das unpassende Wort raus

of [əv, *betont:* ɒv] von • **a picture of Chester** ein Bild von Chester • **a group of girls** eine Gruppe (von) Mädchen **a small number of children** eine kleine Anzahl Kinder/von Kindern • **in groups of four** in Vierergruppen • **one of you** eine/r von euch • **both of you** alle beide; ihr beide • **the two of them** die beiden; alle beide **the name of the street** der Name der Straße • **the city of Glasgow** die Stadt Glasgow **2 kilos of meat** 2 Kilo Fleisch **2 litres of milk** 2 Liter Milch **a piece of** ein Stück • **a lot of/lots of** eine Menge, viel, viele **think of** halten von, denken über • **of course** natürlich, selbstverständlich

off [ɒf] 1. aus; von (… herunter/hinunter); 2. weg, los • **be off** aus(geschaltet) sein • **give sb. $3 off** jm. eine Ermäßigung von 3 Dollar geben • **take off** 1. ausziehen *(Kleidung)*; 2. starten, abfliegen, abheben *(Flugzeug)* • **turn off the light** das Licht ausschalten

offer ['ɒfə] bieten, anbieten

office ['ɒfɪs] Büro

officer ['ɒfɪsə] Offizier/in **police officer** Polizist/in, Polizeibeamte(r)/Polizeibeamtin

often ['ɒfn] oft

OHP (overhead projector) [ˌəʊvəhed prə'dʒektə] Tageslichtprojektor

oil [ɔɪl] Öl • **oil rig** ['ɔɪl rɪg] (Öl-)Bohrinsel • **oil well** ['ɔɪl wel] Ölquelle

old [əʊld] alt • **16-year-old** 16-jährige(r, s) • **in the old days** in alten Zeiten, früher

oldie ['əʊldi] Oldie

olive ['ɒlɪv] Olive; Oliven-

Olympic Games [əˌlɪmpɪk 'geɪmz] Olympische Spiele

on [ɒn] 1. auf • **report/show/film on** Reportage/Show/Film über • **on your own** allein, selbstständig • **on board the ship** an Bord des Schiffes • **on fire** in Brand • **on the beach/coast** am Strand/an der Küste **on the corner** an der Ecke **on the bus/train/plane** im Bus/Zug/Flugzeug • **on the floor** auf dem Fußboden • **on the first floor** im ersten Stock **on the Internet** im Internet **on the left** links, auf der linken Seite • **on the move** unterwegs, auf Achse • **on the phone** am Telefon • **on the radio/on TV** im Radio/im Fernsehen • **on the right** rechts, auf der rechten Seite • **on the River Elbe** an der Elbe • **on the show** in der Show/Sendung • **on the wall** an der Wand • **on 12th January** am 12. Januar • **on Monday** am Montag • **on Mondays** montags, jeden Montag • **on top (of sth.)** oben, obendrauf (auf etwas) • **on top of that** außerdem; darüber hinaus • **On seeing this, Debbie asked …** *(fml)* Als Debbie das sah, fragte sie … • **be on** an sein, laufen *(Fernseher, Licht usw.)* • **turn on the light** das Licht einschalten 2. weiter- • **straight on** geradeaus weiter • **on and on** immer weiter • **and so on** und so weiter • **go on** fortfahren, weitermachen; weiterreden **walk/drive/sail on** weitergehen/weiterfahren/weitersegeln

once [wʌns] einmal; einst • **at once** sofort, (so)gleich

one [wʌn] 1. eins • **one more** noch ein(e), ein(e) weitere(r, s) **one of you** eine/r von euch **one morning/day** eines Morgens/Tages • **a yellow one** ein gelber, eine gelbe, ein gelbes **the yellow ones** die gelben **which one/ones** welche(r, s)/welche 2. man • **one's** sein/e • **no one** niemand • **one another** einander, sich (gegenseitig)

oneself [wʌn'self] sich (selbst)

onion ['ʌnjən] Zwiebel

only ['əʊnli] nur, bloß; erst • **the only …** der/die/das einzige …

onto ['ɒntə, *betont:* 'ɒntu:] auf (… hinauf)

open *(v; adj)* ['əʊpən] 1. öffnen, aufmachen; sich öffnen; eröffnen; 2. geöffnet, offen

operate (on sb.) ['ɒpəreɪt] (jn.) operieren • **operating room** Operationssaal • **operation** [ˌɒpə'reɪʃn] Operation *(auch medizinisch)*

opinion (of) [ə'pɪnjən] Meinung (von, zu) • **in my opinion** meiner Meinung nach

opposite *(prep; n)* ['ɒpəzɪt] 1. gegenüber (von); 2. Gegenteil

°**optimist** ['ɒptɪmɪst] Optimist/in

or [ɔ:] oder

orange ['ɒrɪndʒ] Orange, Apfelsine • **orange juice** Orangensaft

°**orbit** ['ɔ:bɪt] (Erd-, Mond-) Umlaufbahn

orchestra ['ɔ:kɪstrə] Orchester

order ['ɔ:də] bestellen • **order** *(v; n)* ['ɔ:də] 1. ordnen; 2. Reihenfolge; (An-)Ordnung

order ['ɔ:də]: **in order to do sth.** um etwas zu tun

ordinary ['ɔ:dnəri] gewöhnlich, normal

organize ['ɔ:gənaɪz] 1. organisieren, veranstalten • **organizer** ['ɔ:gənaɪzə] Organisator/in 2. ordnen, einteilen

origin ['ɒrɪdʒɪn] Herkunft, Ursprung, Entstehung • **original** [ə'rɪdʒənl] Original-

Oscar ['ɒskə] Oscar *(Filmpreis)*

other ['ʌðə] andere • **the other** der/die/das andere, die anderen **each other** einander, sich (gegenseitig)

ought: **we ought to …** ['ɔ:t tə] wir sollten/müssten (eigentlich)

our ['aʊə] unser, unsere

ours ['aʊəz] unsere(r, s)

ourselves [aʊə'selvz] uns (selbst); selbst, selber

out [aʊt] hinaus, heraus; draußen **out there** dort draußen • **be out** 1. weg sein, nicht da sein; °2. ausgeschieden sein • **run out** knapp werden, zu Ende gehen, ausgehen • **I've run out of money.** Mir ist das Geld ausgegangen. • **out of …** aus … (heraus/hinaus) • **9 out of 11** 9 von 11 • °**out of cardboard** aus Pappe, aus Karton **out of town** außerhalb (der Stadt) • **out of work** arbeitslos

outdoors [ˌaʊt'dɔ:z] draußen, im Freien; nach draußen, ins Freie

outside [ˌaʊt'saɪd] 1. *(prep)* außerhalb (von); aus (… heraus); 2. *(adv)* draußen; nach draußen

oval ['əʊvl] oval

oven ['ʌvn] Backofen

over ['əʊvə] 1. über, oberhalb von • **all over the world** auf der ganzen Welt, überall auf der Welt • **over there** dort drüben, da drüben • **over time** über die Jahre; im Laufe der Zeit **over (to)** herüber, hinüber (nach) 2. über, mehr als 3. **be over** vorbei sein, zu Ende sein

overhead projector [ˌəʊvəhed prə'dʒektə] Tageslichtprojektor

overtake* [ˌəʊvə'teɪk] überholen

overwhelm [ˌəʊvə'welm] überwältigen

own [əʊn]: **your own bike** dein/Ihr/euer eigenes Fahrrad • **on your own** allein, selbstständig

owner ['əʊnə] Besitzer/in

P

pack [pæk] packen, einpacken

°**pack** [pæk] Rudel *(Wölfe, Hunde)*

packet ['pækɪt] Paket, Päckchen; Packung, Tüte

page [peɪdʒ] (Buch-, Heft-)Seite **Open your books at page 5.** Schlagt Seite 5 auf. • **on page 25** auf Seite 25

paint [peɪnt] malen, anstreichen **painting** ['peɪntɪŋ] Gemälde, Bild; Malerei

pair (of) [peə] Paar

Pakistani [ˌpɑ:kɪ'stɑ:ni] Pakistani, Pakistaner/in

palace ['pæləs] Palast, Schloss

panic *(n; v)* ['pænɪk] 1. Panik; 2. in Panik geraten

°**pants** *(pl)* [pænts] *(AE)* Hose

papa [pə'pɑ:] Papa

paper ['peɪpə] **1.** Papier; **2.** Zeitung
°**parachute** ['pærəʃu:t] Fallschirm
parade [pə'reɪd] Parade, Umzug
paradise ['pærədaɪs] Paradies
paragraph ['pærəgrɑ:f] Absatz, Abschnitt
paramedic [,pærə'medɪk] Sanitäter/in
parent ['peərənt] Elternteil *(Vater oder Mutter)* • **parents** Eltern
park [pɑ:k] Park
parliament ['pɑ:ləmənt] Parlament
part [pɑ:t] Teil
partner ['pɑ:tnə] Partner/in
party ['pɑ:ti] Party, Feier • **have a party** eine Party veranstalten, feiern
pass [pɑ:s] **1.** überholen; vorbeigehen, vorbeifahren an; **2.** vergehen, vorübergehen *(Zeit)*; **3. pass sth.** etwas (herüber)reichen; **4. pass a test** einen Test bestehen
pass [pɑ:s] Pass, Ballabgabe
passage ['pæsɪdʒ] Abschnitt, Passage
passenger ['pæsɪndʒə] Passagier/in, Fahrgast
passport ['pɑ:spɔ:t] (Reise-)Pass
past [pɑ:st] **1.** *(n)* Vergangenheit; **2.** *(prep; adv)* vorbei, vorüber (an) • **half past eight** halb neun (8.30/20.30) • **quarter past eight** Viertel nach acht (8.15/20.15)
path [pɑ:θ] Pfad, Weg
patient ['peɪʃnt] Patient/in
pavement ['peɪvmənt] **1.** *(BE)* Fußweg, Gehweg; **2.** *(AE)* Fahrbahn
pay* (for) [peɪ] bezahlen • **pay half** die Hälfte bezahlen • **pay attention (to sb./sth.)** jn./etwas beachten; aufpassen (auf etwas), aufmerksam sein • **payment** ['peɪmənt] (Be-)Zahlung
PE [,pi:_'i:] **(Physical Education** [,fɪzɪkəl_edʒu'keɪʃn]) Turnen, Sport(unterricht) *(in der Regel in der Halle)*
pea [pi:] Erbse
°**peace** [pi:s] Frieden
peanut ['pi:nʌt] Erdnuss
pen [pen] Füller, Kugelschreiber °**pen-friend** ['penfrend] Brieffreund/in
penalty ['penəlti] Strafe, Strafstoß
pence (p) *(pl)* [pens, pi:] Pence
pencil ['pensl] Bleistift
pencil-case ['penslkeɪs] Federmäppchen
°**pen-friend** ['penfrend] Brieffreund/in
penguin ['peŋgwɪn] Pinguin
penny ['peni] *kleinste britische Münze*
people ['pi:pl] **1.** *(pl)* Leute, Menschen; **2.** Volk
per [pɜ:] pro • **per cent (%)** [pə'sent] Prozent
perfect ['pɜ:fɪkt] perfekt, einwandfrei, vollkommen; ideal
°**performing arts** [pə,fɔ:mɪŋ_'ɑ:ts] darstellende Künste *(Schauspiel- u. Tanzkünste)*
perfume ['pɜ:fju:m] Parfüm
perhaps [pə'hæps] vielleicht
period ['pɪəriəd] **1.** Zeitdauer, Periode; **2.** Unterrichtsstunde
persecution [,pɜ:sɪ'kju:ʃn] Verfolgung *(aus politischen, religiösen oder ethnischen Gründen)*
person ['pɜ:sn] Person
persuade sb. (to do sth.) [pə'sweɪd] jn. überzeugen/überreden (etwas zu tun)
°**pessimist** ['pesɪmɪst] Pessimist/in
pet [pet] Haustier • **pet mouse** zahme Maus
phone *(v; n)* [fəʊn] **1.** anrufen; **2.** Telefon • **on the phone** am Telefon • **phone number** Telefonnummer • **phone box** *(BE)* / °**phone booth** [*BE:* 'fəʊn ,bu:ð, *AE:* 'fəʊn ,bu:θ] *(AE)* Telefonzelle
photo ['fəʊtəʊ] Foto • **in the photo** auf dem Foto • **take photos** Fotos machen, fotografieren
phrase [freɪz] Ausdruck, (Rede-)Wendung
physical ['fɪzɪkl]: **Physical Education** Turnen, Sport(unterricht) *(in der Regel in der Halle)* **physical science** Naturwissenschaft
physics *(no pl)* ['fɪzɪks] Physik
piano [pi'ænəʊ] Klavier • **play the piano** Klavier spielen
°**pick** [pɪk] pflücken
pick up [,pɪk_'ʌp] abholen, mitnehmen; aufheben
picnic ['pɪknɪk] Picknick • **have a picnic** ein Picknick machen
picture ['pɪktʃə] Bild • **in the picture** auf dem Bild
piece: **a piece of** [ə 'pi:s_əv] ein Stück
pig [pɪg] Schwein
pigeon ['pɪdʒɪn] Taube
°**pilgrim** ['pɪlgrɪm] Pilger/in
pill [pɪl] Tablette, Pille
pilot ['paɪlət] Pilot, Pilotin
pink [pɪŋk] pink, rosa
pipe [paɪp] Pfeife
pipeline ['paɪplaɪn] Pipeline *(Rohrleitung für Gas/Erdöl)*
pirate ['paɪrət] Pirat/in
pizza ['pi:tsə] Pizza
place [pleɪs] Ort, Platz, Stelle **place of birth** Geburtsort • **in Nancy's place** an Nancys Stelle **take place** stattfinden • **take third place** den dritten Platz belegen
plan *(v; n)* [plæn] **1. (-nn-)** planen • **planner** Planer/in **2.** Plan
plane [pleɪn] Flugzeug • **plane ticket** Flugschein, Flugticket
planet ['plænɪt] Planet • **planetary** ['plænətri] Planeten-
plant *(n; v)* [plɑ:nt] **1.** Pflanze; **2.** (ein)pflanzen • °**planter** Pflanzer/in; Plantagenbesitzer/in
plantation [plæn'teɪʃn] Plantage
°**plaque** [plæk] Gedenktafel
plastic ['plæstɪk] Plastik, Kunststoff
plate [pleɪt] Teller
platform ['plætfɔ:m] Bahnsteig, Gleis
play *(v; n)* [pleɪ] **1.** spielen • **play a cassette (to sb.)** (jm.) eine Cassette vorspielen • **play the drums/the piano** Schlagzeug/Klavier spielen • **play a team** gegen eine Mannschaft spielen **play a trick on sb.** jm. einen Streich spielen • **player** Spieler/in **2.** Spiel; Theaterstück
playground ['pleɪgraʊnd] Schulhof; Spielplatz
please [pli:z] bitte *(in Fragen und Aufforderungen)*
pleased [pli:zd] erfreut, froh **be pleased (with/about)** sich freuen (über), zufrieden sein (mit)
plenty (of) ['plenti] eine Menge, viel(e)
plug [plʌg] Stecker
pm [,pi:_'em] ... Uhr nachmittags/abends
pocket ['pɒkɪt] Tasche *(an einem Kleidungsstück)* • **pocket money** Taschengeld
poem ['pəʊɪm] Gedicht
point *(n; v)* [pɔɪnt] **1.** Punkt; **2. 10.4 (ten point four)** 10,4 (zehn Komma vier); **3. point (at/to)** zeigen, deuten (auf) **point sth. at sb.** etwas auf jn. richten
°**poke out** [,pəʊk_'aʊt] herausstrecken
°**pole** [pəʊl] Stange, Pfahl, Mast
police *(pl)* [pə'li:s] Polizei • **policeman/policewoman** Polizist/Polizistin • **police officer** Polizeibeamte(r)/Polizeibeamtin, Polizist/in • **police station** Polizeiwache, Polizeirevier
polish: **nail polish** *(AE)* ['neɪl ,pɒlɪʃ] Nagellack
polite [pə'laɪt] höflich
political [pə'lɪtɪkl] politisch
pollute [pə'lu:t] *(die Umwelt)* verschmutzen • **pollution** [pə'lu:ʃn] (Umwelt-)Verschmutzung
pool *(v; n)* [pu:l] **1.** zusammenlegen, bündeln; **2.** Fonds, „Topf"; Pool • **swimming-pool** Schwimmbecken
poor [pɔ:, pʊə] **1.** arm • **poor things** die Armen • **poor Trundle** der arme Trundle **poor you** du Arme/r, du Ärmste/r **2.** schlecht, schwach, mangelhaft
pop [pɒp] Pop(musik)
popcorn ['pɒpkɔ:n] Popcorn
popular (with) ['pɒpjələ] beliebt (bei)
population [,pɒpju'leɪʃn] Bevölkerung, Einwohner(zahl)

positive ['pɒzətɪv] positiv
possible ['pɒsəbl] möglich
possibly ['pɒsəbli] vielleicht, möglicherweise
post [pəʊst] Post(sendungen) **post office** Postamt • **postbox** Briefkasten • **postcard** Postkarte
poster ['pəʊstə] Poster
pot [pɒt] Topf, Kochtopf
potato, *pl* **potatoes** [pə'teɪtəʊ] Kartoffel
pound (£) [paʊnd] Pfund *(britische Währung)*
pound against [paʊnd] klatschen gegen
pour [pɔː] gießen, schütten; einschenken
poverty ['pɒvəti] (die) Armut
°**powder** ['paʊdə] Pulver
power ['paʊə] **1.** Kraft, Macht; **2.** Strom, Energie • **power station** Kraftwerk, Elektrizitätswerk
practice *(no pl)* ['præktɪs] Praxis, Übung(en) • **band practice** Orchesterprobe
practise ['præktɪs] üben, trainieren
prairie ['preəri] Prärie, Grasebene
pray [preɪ] beten • **prayer** [preə] Gebet
°**preach** [priːtʃ] predigen
prefer sth. (to) **(-rr-)** [prɪ'fɜː] etwas lieber haben/tun (als), etwas *(einer anderen Sache)* vorziehen • **prefer to do sth.** etwas lieber tun
prefix ['priːfɪks] Vorsilbe
prepare (for) [prɪ'peə] (sich) vorbereiten (auf); *(Mahlzeit)* zubereiten
present ['preznt] **1.** Gegenwart; **2.** Geschenk
present sth. (to sb.) [prɪ'zent] (jm.) etwas präsentieren, zeigen, vorstellen • **presenter** [prɪ'zentə] Moderator/in **presentation** [ˌprezn'teɪʃn] Präsentation, Darbietung, Vorstellung
president ['prezɪdənt] Präsident/Präsidentin
press [pres] drücken
pretty *(adj; adv)* ['prɪti] **1.** hübsch; **2.** *(infml)* ziemlich
price [praɪs] (Kauf-)Preis
prince [prɪns] Prinz
print [prɪnt] **1.** (ab)drucken **printer** ['prɪntə] Drucker **printout** ['prɪntaʊt] Ausdruck °**2. bold print** [ˌbəʊld 'prɪnt] Fettdruck
prison ['prɪzn] Gefängnis
prize [praɪz] Preis, Gewinn
probably ['prɒbəbli] wahrscheinlich
problem ['prɒbləm] Problem
process ['prəʊses] Vorgang, Verfahren, Prozess
produce [prə'djuːs] produzieren, erzeugen, herstellen
professor [prə'fesə] Professor/in
profit ['prɒfɪt] Gewinn, Profit
program ['prəʊgræm] **1.** *(AE, BE)* (Computer-)Programm; **2.** *(AE)* Programm, (Radio-, Fernseh-) Sendung
programme ['prəʊgræm] *(BE)* Programm, (Radio-, Fernseh-) Sendung
progress *(no pl)* ['prəʊgres] Fortschritt(e)
project ['prɒdʒekt] Projekt
promise ['prɒmɪs] versprechen
pronounce [prə'naʊns] aussprechen • **pronunciation** [prəˌnʌnsi'eɪʃn] Aussprache
proof *(no pl)* [pruːf] Beweis(e), Nachweis(e)
properly ['prɒpəli] richtig, ordentlich, sachgemäß
property ['prɒpəti] Eigentum, (Immobilien-)Besitz
protect sb. (from sth.) [prə'tekt] jn. (be)schützen (vor etwas)
proud (of) [praʊd] stolz (auf)
°**prove** [pruːv] beweisen
public ['pʌblɪk] öffentlich **public holiday** gesetzlicher Feiertag
°**publish** ['pʌblɪʃ] veröffentlichen
pull [pʊl] ziehen
pullover ['pʊləʊvə] Pullover
°**pumpkin pie** [ˌpʌmkɪn 'paɪ] Kürbiskuchen
punish ['pʌnɪʃ] bestrafen **punishment** ['pʌnɪʃmənt] Strafe, Bestrafung
pupil ['pjuːpl] Schüler/in
purse [pɜːs] Portmonee, Geldbeutel
push [pʊʃ] drücken, schieben, stoßen
put* **(-tt-)** [pʊt] legen, stellen, *(etwas wohin)* tun • **put down** **1.** hinstellen, hinlegen, aus der Hand legen; °**2.** anzahlen • **put the phone down** den Hörer auflegen • **put in** einsetzen, einfügen, hineintun • **put on** anziehen *(Kleidung)*; aufsetzen *(Helm)* • **put up** aufstellen, errichten, aufhängen • **put up one's hand** sich melden

Q

quarter ['kwɔːtə] Viertel; (Stadt-) Viertel, Quartier • **quarter past eight** [ˌkwɔːtə pɑːst_'eɪt] Viertel nach acht (8.15/20.15) **quarter to nine** [ˌkwɔːtə tə 'naɪn] Viertel vor neun (8.45/20.45)
quarterback ['kwɔːtəbæk] Quarterback *(American football)*
queen [kwiːn] Königin
question ['kwestʃn] Frage • **ask questions** Fragen stellen
questionnaire [ˌkwestʃə'neə] Fragebogen
quick *(adj)* [kwɪk] schnell **quickly** *(adv)* ['kwɪkli] schnell
quiet ['kwaɪət] ruhig, leise, still **keep quiet** still sein • **keep quiet about sth.** etwas für sich behalten, etwas geheim halten
quite [kwaɪt] ziemlich; ganz
quiz, *pl* **quizzes** [kwɪz] **1.** Quiz, Ratespiel; **2.** *(AE)* Test • **take a quiz** *(AE)* einen Test machen/schreiben
quotation (by sb./from a book, play) [kwəʊ'teɪʃn] Zitat, Ausspruch (von jm./aus einem Buch, Stück)

R

rabbit ['ræbɪt] Kaninchen
race [reɪs] Rennen, (Wett-)Lauf **racing** ['reɪsɪŋ] Rennsport
race [reɪs] Rasse • **racism** ['reɪsɪzəm] Rassismus • **racist** *(n; adj)* ['reɪsɪst] **1.** Rassist/in; **2.** rassistisch
radar ['reɪdɑː] Radar
radio ['reɪdiəʊ] **1.** Radio • **on the radio** im Radio • °**work in radio** beim Rundfunk arbeiten °**radio play** Hörspiel • °**radio station** Radiosender, Rundfunksender **2.** Funk; Funkgerät
railway ['reɪlweɪ] Eisenbahn
rain *(v; n)* [reɪn] **1.** regnen; **2.** Regen • **acid rain** [ˌæsɪd 'reɪn] saurer Regen • **rainy** ['reɪni] regnerisch
range [reɪndʒ] (Berg-, Felsen-) Kette
rap [ræp] Rap *(rhythmischer Sprechgesang)*
°**rape** [reɪp] Vergewaltigung
°**rather** ['rɑːðə] lieber
rattle ['rætl] rütteln; klappern
°**rattlesnake** ['rætlsneɪk] Klapperschlange
RE [ˌɑːr_'iː] **(Religious Education)** [rɪˌlɪdʒəs_edʒu'keɪʃn] Religion(sunterricht)
reach [riːtʃ] erreichen
react (to) [riː'ækt] reagieren (auf) **reaction (to)** [riː'ækʃn] Reaktion (auf)
read* [riːd] lesen • **read sth. out** etwas vorlesen • **read sth. to sb.** jm. etwas vorlesen **reader** Leser/in
ready ['redi] bereit, fertig • **get ready** sich bereitmachen, sich fertig machen
real *(adj)* [rɪəl] echt, wirklich **really** *(adv)* ['rɪəli] wirklich **not really** eigentlich nicht **real exciting** *(adv)* ['riːəl] *(AE, infml)* wirklich aufregend, echt aufregend
realize ['rɪəlaɪz] erkennen; sich klar machen; einsehen, merken
reason (for .../why ...) ['riːzn] Grund, Begründung (für .../dafür, dass ...) • **for other reasons** aus anderen Gründen
recess ['riːses, rɪ'ses] *(AE)* Pause *(zwischen Schulstunden)*
recite [rɪ'saɪt] rezitieren, vortragen
°**recognize** ['rekəgnaɪz] (wieder) erkennen

record [rɪ'kɔːd] aufnehmen, aufzeichnen *(auf Band)*
record ['rekɔːd] Schallplatte
recycle [ˌriː'saɪkl] wieder verwerten, wieder aufbereiten • **recycling** [ˌriː'saɪklɪŋ] Wiederverwertung, Wiederaufbereitung
red (-dd-) [red] rot
°**redwood** ['redwʊd] Mammutbaum
refer to (-rr-) [rɪ'fɜː] sich beziehen auf
regional ['riːdʒənl] regional
regret (-tt-) [rɪ'gret] bedauern, bereuen
regular ['regjələ] regelmäßig; regulär, Regel-
rehearsal [rɪ'hɜːsl] Probe *(Theater, Film)*
relationship [rɪ'leɪʃnʃɪp] Beziehung
relative ['relətɪv] Verwandte(r)
relax [rɪ'læks] (sich) entspannen, sich ausruhen
reliable [rɪ'laɪəbl] zuverlässig, verlässlich
religion [rɪ'lɪdʒn] Religion
religious [rɪ'lɪdʒəs] religiös, Religions- • **Religious Education** [rɪˌlɪdʒəs_ edʒu'keɪʃn] Religion(sunterricht)
remains *(pl)* [rɪ'meɪnz] (Über-)Reste
remember sth. [rɪ'membə] sich an etwas erinnern; an etwas denken, sich etwas merken
rent [rent] mieten, leihen
repair [rɪ'peə] reparieren, ausbessern
°**repeat** [rɪ'piːt] wiederholen
°**replace sth. (with)** [rɪ'pleɪs] etwas ersetzen (durch)
reply (to) [rɪ'plaɪ] antworten (auf), beantworten; erwidern
report *(v; n)* [rɪ'pɔːt] **1.** berichten, melden • **reporter** Reporter/in **2. report (on)** Bericht, Reportage (über)
reputation [ˌrepju'teɪʃn] Ruf, Ansehen
request [rɪ'kwest] Bitte, Wunsch
rescue ['reskjuː] retten; befreien
°**reservation** [ˌrezə'veɪʃn] Reservat, Reservation *(den Indianern vorbehaltenes Gebiet)*
rest (of) [rest] Rest
°**rest** [rest] (sich aus)ruhen
restaurant ['restrɒnt] Restaurant **at the restaurant** im Restaurant
restroom ['restruːm] *(AE)* *(öffentliche)* Toilette
result [rɪ'zʌlt] Ergebnis, Resultat **as a result** als Ergebnis, als Resultat
retell* [ˌriː'tel] nacherzählen
return *(v; n)* [rɪ'tɜːn] **1.** zurückkehren; zurücksenden, zurückbringen; **2.** Rückkehr, Wiederkehr
review [rɪ'vjuː] *(Buch-, Film-)*Besprechung, Rezension
revision [rɪ'vɪʒn] Wiederholung *(des Lernstoffs)*
revolution [ˌrevə'luːʃn] Revolution
rice [raɪs] Reis
rich [rɪtʃ] reich
°**riddle** ['rɪdl] Rätsel
ride* *(v; n)* [raɪd] **1.** reiten; **2.** fahren mit • **ride a bike** Rad fahren • **Let's ride our bikes to school.** Lass(t) uns mit dem Rad zur Schule fahren. • **rider** Reiter/in; (Fahrrad-, Motorrad-)Fahrer/in • **riding** *(das)* Reiten, Reitsport
3. Fahrt; Spazierfahrt, Ausflug **bike ride** Radfahrt, Radtour **go for a ride** eine Spazierfahrt machen; herumfahren
rig [rɪg] Bohrinsel, Förderturm
right [raɪt] **1.** richtig • **get sth. right** etwas richtig machen **my watch is right** meine Uhr geht richtig • **You're right.** Du hast Recht. / Stimmt. **Right, Debbie?** Nicht wahr, Debbie? • **Right.** Gut. / In Ordnung. • **all right** gut, in Ordnung
2. nach rechts; rechte(r, s) • **on the right** rechts, auf der rechten Seite • **to the right** rechts, auf der rechten Seite, zur Rechten
3. ganz, völlig; genau, direkt; gerade • **right now** im Moment, jetzt gerade
4. *(n)* Recht
ring* [rɪŋ] klingeln, läuten **ring the doorbell** (an der Tür) klingeln
rise* [raɪz] aufgehen *(Sonne, Mond)*; (an-, auf)steigen
rival ['raɪvl] Rivale, Rivalin; Konkurrent, Konkurrentin
river ['rɪvə] Fluss • **on the River Elbe** an der Elbe
road [rəʊd] Straße, Landstraße **road sign** Verkehrszeichen
rob (-bb-) [rɒb] be-, ausrauben
°**robe** [rəʊb] Gewand
robot ['rəʊbɒt] Roboter
rock [rɒk] Fels, Felsen
rocket ['rɒkɪt] Rakete
role [rəʊl] Rolle • **role-play** ['rəʊl pleɪ] Rollenspiel
Roman *(adj; n)* ['rəʊmən] römisch; Römer/in
roof [ruːf] Dach
room [ruːm] Zimmer, Raum
rope [rəʊp] Seil
rose [rəʊz] Rose
round [raʊnd] **1.** rund; **2.** um … (herum) • **look round** sich umsehen • **the wrong way round** verkehrt herum
route [ruːt] Route, Strecke
row [rəʊ]: **top/middle/bottom row** obere/mittlere/untere Reihe
rub (-bb-) [rʌb] (ein)reiben
rubber ['rʌbə] Radiergummi
rubbish ['rʌbɪʃ] **1.** Abfall, Müll **rubbish dump** Müllhalde, Müllkippe
2. *(infml)* Quatsch, Blödsinn
rucksack ['rʌksæk] Rucksack
rude (to sb.) [ruːd] unhöflich, grob (zu jm.)
rugby ['rʌgbi] Rugby
rule *(v; n)* [ruːl] **1.** (be)herrschen, regieren; **2.** Regel, Vorschrift
ruler ['ruːlə] Lineal
rumour *(BE)* / **rumor** *(AE)* ['ruːmə] Gerücht
run* **(-nn-)** [rʌn] **1.** laufen, rennen • **run around** umherrennen, herumrennen • **runner** Läufer/in • **running** *(das)* Laufen
2. verkehren, fahren *(Zug, Bus)*
3. leiten, betreiben, (durch-)führen, veranstalten
4. run out knapp werden, zu Ende gehen, ausgehen • **I've run out of money.** Mir ist das Geld ausgegangen.
°**runaway** ['rʌnəweɪ] Ausreißer/in

S

sad (-dd-) [sæd] traurig • **sadness** ['sædnəs] Traurigkeit
safe (from) [seɪf] sicher (vor), gefahrlos • **safety** ['seɪfti] Sicherheit
sail [seɪl] segeln • **sailing** *(das)* Segeln • **sailor** ['seɪlə] Seemann, Matrose
salad ['sæləd] Salat *(als Gericht oder Beilage)*
sale [seɪl]: **for sale** zum Verkauf; zu verkaufen
salt [sɒlt] Salz
same [seɪm]: **the same (as)** der-/die-/dasselbe, dieselben (wie) **the same thing** der-, die-, dasselbe
sanctuary ['sæŋktʃuəri] (Natur-, Tier-, Vogel-)Schutzgebiet
sandal ['sændl] Sandale
sandwich ['sænwɪdʒ] *(zusammengeklapptes)* belegtes Brot, Sandwich
satellite ['sætəlaɪt] Satellit
Saturday ['sætədeɪ, 'sætədi] Samstag, Sonnabend
sauce [sɔːs] Soße
sausage ['sɒsɪdʒ] (Brat-, Bock-)Würstchen, Wurst
save [seɪv] **1.** sparen; **2. save sb. from sth.** jn. vor etwas retten **save the day** die Situation retten, der Retter sein *(in einer bestimmten Situation)*
say* [seɪ] sagen • **it says** es heißt; hier steht • **Say.** *(AE, infml)* He! / Hör mal! • **Say hello to …** Grüß … • **say so** es/das sagen • **say grace** das Tischgebet sprechen
scan (-nn-) [skæn] *(einen Text)* überfliegen *(um bestimmte Informationen zu finden)*
scare [skeə] erschrecken, Angst machen • **be scared (about; of)** [skeəd] Angst haben (wegen; vor) • **scary** ['skeəri] unheimlich, gruselig

D

scarf [skɑ:f], *pl* **scarves** [skɑ:vz] Schal

scene [si:n] Szene

schedule [*BE:* 'ʃedju:l, *AE:* 'skedʒəl] Zeitplan; *(AE auch:)* Stundenplan, Fahrplan

scholarship ['skɒləʃɪp] Stipendium • **win a scholarship** ein Stipendium bekommen

school [sku:l] Schule • **at school** in der Schule • **leave school** von der Schule abgehen **start school** eingeschult werden • **school bag** Schultasche **school subject** ['sku:l ˌsʌbdʒɪkt] Schulfach

science ['saɪəns] (Natur-)Wissenschaft • **scientist** ['saɪəntɪst] Wissenschaftler/in

° **scissors** *(pl)* ['sɪzəz] (eine) Schere

score *(v; n)* [skɔ:] **1.** *(einen Treffer)* erzielen, *(ein Tor)* schießen; **2.** Spielstand, (Spiel-)Ergebnis, Punktestand

scrambled egg(s) [ˌskræmbld 'eg(z)] Rührei, Rühreier

scrapbook ['skræpbʊk] Sammelalbum

scream *(v; n)* [skri:m] **1.** schreien, kreischen; **2.** Schrei, Aufschrei

screen [skri:n] Bildschirm; Leinwand

script [skrɪpt] Drehbuch

sea [si:] Meer, *(die)* See • **at sea** auf See

sea lion ['si: laɪən] Seelöwe

seal [si:l] Robbe, Seehund

search [sɜ:tʃ] Suche, Durchsuchung • **in search of** auf der Suche nach • **search engine** Suchmaschine

season ['si:zn] Saison, Jahreszeit

seat [si:t] Sitzplatz • **take a seat** Platz nehmen

second ['sekənd] zweite(r, s) **secondly, …** zweitens …

second ['sekənd] Sekunde

secret *(adj; n)* ['si:krət] geheim; Geheimnis

secretary ['sekrətri] Sekretär/in

° **section** ['sekʃn] Abschnitt, Teil

see* [si:] sehen • **see the sights** sich die Sehenswürdigkeiten ansehen • **See, …** Siehst du, … **See you.** Tschüs. / Bis bald. / Bis dann. • **I see!** Ich verstehe! / Aha! / Ach so! • **you see** weißt du, nämlich
2. besuchen, aufsuchen

seem (to be/do) [si:m] (zu sein/tun) scheinen

sell* [sel] verkaufen

semester [sɪ'mestə] *(besonders AE)* Semester, (Studien-)Halbjahr

senator ['senətə] Senator/in

send* (to) [send] schicken, senden (an) • **send in** einschicken, einreichen

sensible ['sensəbl] vernünftig

sentence ['sentəns] Satz

separate ['sepəreɪt] (sich) trennen

September [sep'tembə] September

° **sequoia** [sɪ'kwɔɪə] Mammutbaum

serious ['sɪəriəs] ernst(haft) • **be serious about sth.** etwas ernst nehmen

service ['sɜ:vɪs] Dienst, Service

set* sb. free (-tt-) [ˌset 'fri:] jn. befreien

° **set** [set] *hier:* eingearbeitet, eingelassen

° **settler** ['setlə] Siedler/in

several ['sevrəl] mehrere, verschiedene

shadow ['ʃædəʊ] Schatten

shake* [ʃeɪk] zittern; schütteln

shall [ʃæl, ʃəl]: **Shall I …?** Soll ich …?

Shalom! [*BE:* ʃæ'lɒm, *AE:* ʃæ'ləʊm] Schalom! / Frieden! *(hebräische Begrüßungs- u. Verabschiedungsformel)*

share (with) [ʃeə] teilen (mit); gemeinsam haben/nutzen

° **shaving cream** ['ʃeɪvɪŋ ˌkri:m] Rasierschaum

shawl [ʃɔ:l] Schultertuch

she [ʃi, *betont:* ʃi:] sie

sheep, *pl* **sheep** [ʃi:p] Schaf

shelf [ʃelf], *pl* **shelves** [ʃelvz] Regal

shelter (from) ['ʃeltə] Schutz (vor); Schutzraum

ship [ʃɪp] Schiff

shirt [ʃɜ:t] (Ober-)Hemd

shocked [ʃɒkt] schockiert

shoe [ʃu:] Schuh • **shoemaker** ['ʃu:ˌmeɪkə] Schuhmacher/in

shoot* [ʃu:t] (er-, an)schießen

shop *(n; v)* [ʃɒp] **1.** Laden, Geschäft • **shop assistant** Verkäufer/in
2. (-pp-) einkaufen gehen **shopping** ['ʃɒpɪŋ] *(das)* Einkaufen; Einkäufe • **shopping mall** [mɔ:l, *BE auch:* mæl] Einkaufszentrum • **go to the shops/go shopping** einkaufen gehen • **do the shopping** einkaufen, Einkäufe machen/erledigen • **like shopping** gern einkaufen gehen • **hate shopping** gar nicht gern einkaufen gehen **shopper** Käufer/in • **shoplifter** ['ʃɒplɪftə] Ladendieb/in

short [ʃɔ:t] kurz

shorts *(pl)* [ʃɔ:ts] Shorts, kurze Hose

shot [ʃɒt] Schuss

should [ʃəd, *betont:* ʃʊd]: **they should …** sie sollten …

shout (at) [ʃaʊt] rufen, (an-)schreien • **shout for help** um Hilfe rufen

show* *(v; n)* [ʃəʊ] **1.** zeigen °**In this it shows …** Darin zeigt/zeigen sich …
2. Schau, Show; Ausstellung; Vorstellung, Aufführung; (Fernseh-, Radio-)Sendung • **on the show** in der Show/Sendung

shower Dusche; Regenschauer **have/take a shower** (sich) duschen

shut* (-tt-) [ʃʌt] schließen, zumachen • **shut up** *(infml)* den Mund halten

shuttle ['ʃʌtl] Shuttle, (Weltraum-)Fähre, Transporter

shy [ʃaɪ] scheu, schüchtern

sick [sɪk] krank

side [saɪd] Seite • **from side to side** von einer Seite auf die andere

sidewalk ['saɪdwɔ:k] *(AE)* Gehweg, Fußweg

° **sigh** [saɪ] seufzen

sight [saɪt]: **in sight** in Sicht(weite)

sights *(pl)* [saɪts] Sehenswürdigkeiten • **see the sights** sich die Sehenswürdigkeiten ansehen

sign [saɪn] Schild; Zeichen **road sign** Verkehrszeichen

sign [saɪn] unterschreiben

° **silicon valley** [ˌsɪlɪkən 'væli] „Silicium-Tal" *(Gebiet nahe San Francisco, in dem sich viele Elektronik- u. Computerfirmen angesiedelt haben)*

silly ['sɪli] albern, dumm **silliness** ['sɪlɪnəs] Albernheit, Dummheit

similar (to sb./sth.) ['sɪmɪlə] (jm./einer Sache) ähnlich

simple ['sɪmpl] einfach

° **simulator** ['sɪmjuleɪtə] Simulator *(Gerät, in dem bestimmte Bedingungen wirklichkeitsgetreu nachgestellt werden)*

since [sɪns] **1.** seit • **since then** seitdem, seit damals
2. *(adv)* seitdem

sincere [sɪn'sɪə] aufrichtig **Yours sincerely, …** [sɪn'sɪəli] Mit freundlichen/herzlichen Grüßen

sing* [sɪŋ] singen • **singer** Sänger/in

single ['sɪŋgl] ledig, allein stehend

sink* [sɪŋk] sinken, untergehen

Sir [sɜ:, sə] *engl. Adelstitel*

sir [sɜ:] mein Herr *(höfliche Anrede)* • **Dear Sir or Madam** Sehr geehrte Damen und Herren

siren ['saɪrən] Sirene

° **sis** [sɪs] *(infml) = sister*

sister ['sɪstə] Schwester

sit* (-tt-) [sɪt] sitzen; sich (hin-)setzen • **sit back** sich zurücklehnen • **sit down** sich hinsetzen

site [saɪt] Ausgrabungsstätte; Bauplatz

situation [ˌsɪtʃu'eɪʃn] Situation

size [saɪz] Größe • **What size are you?** Welche Größe hast du/haben Sie?

skateboard ['skeɪtbɔ:d] Skateboard

skating ['skeɪtɪŋ] *(das)* Eislaufen

skeleton ['skelɪtn] Skelett

° **sketch** [sketʃ] skizzieren

ski [ski:] Ski laufen/fahren • **ski-lift** ['ski:lɪft] Skilift • **skiing** ['ski:ɪŋ] Skisport, *(das)* Skilaufen

skilled [skɪld] Fach-; gelernte(r); geschickt
skin [skɪn] Haut
skirt [skɜːt] Rock
°**skull** [skʌl] Schädel
sky [skaɪ] Himmel • **in the sky** am Himmel • **skyscraper** ['skaɪskreɪpə] Wolkenkratzer
slave [sleɪv] Sklave, Sklavin **slave-owner** Sklavenhalter/in
sled [sled] *(AE)* Schlitten
sledge [sledʒ] *(BE)* Schlitten
sleep* *(v; n)* [sliːp] **1.** schlafen **sleep late** lange schlafen **sleeping-bag** Schlafsack **2.** Schlaf • **sleepless** schlaflos
°**slogan** ['sləʊgən] Slogan, Werbespruch
slope [sləʊp] Hang
slow [sləʊ] langsam
small [smɔːl] klein
smell *(v; n)* [smel] **1.** riechen; **2.** Geruch
smile *(n; v)* [smaɪl] **1.** Lächeln; **2. smile (at sb.)** (jn. an)lächeln
smoke *(v; n)* [sməʊk] **1.** rauchen; **2.** Rauch
°**snake** [sneɪk] Schlange
snow [snəʊ] Schnee • °**snowmobile** ['snəʊməˌbiːl] Schneemobil
so [səʊ] **1.** deshalb, daher; also; **2.** so • **so boring** so langweilig **so far** ['səʊ fɑː] bis hierher, bis jetzt • **do so** es/das tun • **say so** es/das sagen • **I think so.** Ich glaube (ja). • **I don't think so.** Das finde/glaube ich nicht. **3. so (that)** sodass, damit
soap [səʊp] Seife
Social Studies [ˌsəʊʃl 'stʌdiz] Sozial-, Gemeinschaftskunde
sock [sɒk] Socke, Strumpf
sofa ['səʊfə] Sofa
soft [sɒft] weich
software ['sɒftweə] (Computer-)Software
solar energy [ˌsəʊlər'enədʒi] Sonnenenergie, Solarenergie **solar-powered** [ˌsəʊlə'paʊəd] mit Sonnenenergie betrieben
soldier ['səʊldʒə] Soldat/in
some [səm, *betont:* sʌm] einige, ein paar; etwas
somebody ['sʌmbədi] jemand
someday ['sʌmdeɪ] irgendwann, eines Tages
someone ['sʌmwʌn] jemand
something ['sʌmθɪŋ] etwas
sometimes ['sʌmtaɪmz] manchmal
somewhere ['sʌmweə] irgendwo(hin)
son [sʌn] Sohn
song [sɒŋ] Lied; Gesang
soon [suːn] bald • **as soon as** *(conj)* sobald
sorry ['sɒri]: **Sorry. / I'm sorry.** Entschuldigung. Tut mir Leid. **Sorry?** Wie bitte? • **feel sorry for sb.** jn. bedauern
sort (of) [sɔːt] Art, Sorte
°**soul** [səʊl] Seele

sound *(v; n)* [saʊnd] **1.** klingen, sich *(gut usw.)* anhören; **2.** Laut, Geräusch, Ton, Klang
°**sound** [saʊnd] Sund, Meerenge, Bucht
soup [suːp] Suppe
source [sɔːs] *(Informations-, Text-)*Quelle
south [saʊθ] südlich; (nach) Süden • **southbound** ['saʊθbaʊnd] Richtung Süden **southern** ['sʌðən] südlich, Süd- **south-east** [ˌsaʊθ'iːst] südöstlich; (nach) Südosten • **south-west** [ˌsaʊθ'west] südwestlich; (nach) Südwesten
souvenir [ˌsuːvə'nɪə] Souvenir, Andenken
soy bean ['sɔɪ biːn] Sojabohne
space [speɪs] (der) Weltraum; Raum, Platz • °**spacecraft** ['speɪskrɑːft] Raumschiff **spaceship** Raumschiff
Spanish ['spænɪʃ] Spanisch; spanisch
°**spare time** [ˌspeə 'taɪm] Freizeit
spark [spɑːk] Funke
speak* [spiːk] sprechen **speaker** Sprecher/in
special *(adj; n)* ['speʃl] **1.** besondere(r, s) • **special effects** Spezialeffekte *(in Filmen)* • **be special** etwas Besonderes sein **2. special (on)** Sonderprogramm, -sendung (über)
specific [spə'sɪfɪk] bestimmte(r, s), spezifische(r, s)
speech [spiːtʃ] Rede, Vortrag **make a speech** eine Rede/einen Vortrag halten • **speech bubble** ['spiːtʃ ˌbʌbl] Sprechblase
speed [spiːd] Geschwindigkeit **speed limit** Geschwindigkeitsbegrenzung, Geschwindigkeitsbeschränkung
spell [spel] buchstabieren **spelling** ['spelɪŋ] (Recht-)Schreibung, Schreibweise
spend* time/money (on) [spend] Zeit verbringen (mit) / Geld ausgeben (für)
spoon [spuːn] Löffel
sport [spɔːt] Sport, Sportart **do sport(s)** Sport treiben **sporting event** Sportveranstaltung, Sportwettkampf
spot [spɒt]: **Spot the difference.** Entdecke den Unterschied.
spray [spreɪ] Spray
spread* [spred] (sich) ausbreiten, (sich) verbreiten
spring [sprɪŋ] Frühling
square [skweə] Platz *(in einer Stadt)*
square km (sq km) [skweə] Quadratkilometer
stab (-bb-) [stæb] (zu)stechen
stadium ['steɪdɪəm] Stadion
staff room ['stɑːf ruːm] Lehrerzimmer
stage [steɪdʒ] Bühne • **put on stage** auf die Bühne bringen

stairs *(pl)* [steəz] Treppe; Treppenstufen
stall [stɔːl] Stand
stamp [stæmp] Briefmarke
stand* [stænd] stehen; sich (hin-)stellen • **stand around** herumstehen • **stand back (from)** zurücktreten (von); entfernt stehen (von)
star [stɑː] (Film-, Pop-)Star
start *(v; n)* [stɑːt] **1.** anfangen, beginnen (mit); *(Geschäft, Familie usw.)* gründen • **start a car** ein Auto anlassen, starten **start school** eingeschult werden **2.** Anfang, Beginn, Start
state [steɪt] Staat; (Bundes-)Land
statement ['steɪtmənt] Aussage(satz)
station ['steɪʃn] **1.** Bahnhof; **2.** Station • **police station** Polizeiwache, Polizeirevier **power station** Kraftwerk, Elektrizitätswerk
statistics *(pl)* [stə'tɪstɪks] Statistik(en)
statue ['stætʃuː] Statue
status: **marital status** [ˌmærɪtl 'steɪtəs] Familienstand
stay *(v; n)* [steɪ] **1.** bleiben; übernachten • **stay away from** sich fern halten von, die Finger lassen von • **stay out** wegbleiben, nicht nach Hause kommen **2. stay (with)** Aufenthalt, Besuch (bei)
steal* [stiːl] stehlen
°**steel** [stiːl] Stahl
step [step] Schritt; Stufe • **step by step** Schritt für Schritt **take a step towards sb.** einen Schritt auf jn. zugehen
stereo ['steriəʊ] Stereoanlage; Stereo
stick* [stɪk] kleben • **stick together** zusammenhalten **sticker** Sticker, Aufkleber
°**stick** [stɪk] Stock • °**stick figure** ['stɪk fɪgə] Strichmännchen
still [stɪl] **1.** (immer) noch; **2.** trotzdem, dennoch
sting* [stɪŋ] stechen
stomach ['stʌmək] Magen, Bauch
stone [stəʊn] Stein • °**Stone Age** ['stəʊn‿eɪdʒ] Steinzeit
stop *(v; n)* [stɒp] **1. (-pp-)** anhalten, stoppen; **2.** Halt; Haltestelle
store [stɔː] Geschäft, Laden **store(room)** Lager(raum)
storm [stɔːm] Sturm; Gewitter
story ['stɔːri] Geschichte, Erzählung
straight *(adj; adv)* [streɪt] gerade; gerade(wegs), direkt; geradeaus **straight on** geradeaus weiter
strange [streɪndʒ] **1.** seltsam, sonderbar; **2.** fremd • **stranger** ['streɪndʒə] Unbekannte(r), Fremde(r)
stream [striːm] Bach
street [striːt] Straße *(in einer Stadt)* • **in the street** auf der Straße • **streetball** ['striːtbɔːl]

eine Art Basketball (wird auf der Straße mit nur einem Korb gespielt) • °**streetcar** *(AE)* Straßenbahn, Tram

stress *(v; n)* [stres] **1.** betonen °**stressed syllable** betonte Silbe **2.** Betonung

strict (with sb.) [strɪkt] streng (mit/zu jm.)

string [strɪŋ] Schnur, Bindfaden

strong [strɒŋ] stark; kräftig, fest

structure ['strʌktʃə] strukturieren

student ['stju:dənt] Student/in, Schüler/in

studio ['stju:diəʊ] Studio

study ['stʌdi] studieren; lernen; sorgfältig durchlesen • **study hall** ['stʌdi hɔ:l] *(AE) Freistunde zur Erledigung von Hausaufgaben*

stuff [stʌf] *(infml)* Zeug, Kram

stupid ['stju:pɪd] blöd, dämlich

style [staɪl] Stil

subject ['sʌbdʒɪkt] **1.** Thema, Gegenstand; **2.** (Unterrichts-)Fach

subway ['sʌbweɪ] *(AE)* U-Bahn

successful [sək'sesfl] erfolgreich

°**such a place** [sʌtʃ] so ein Ort

suddenly ['sʌdnli] plötzlich, auf einmal

suffix ['sʌfɪks] Nachsilbe, Suffix

sugar ['ʃʊgə] Zucker

suggest sth. (to sb.) [sə'dʒest] (jm.) etwas vorschlagen **suggestion** [sə'dʒestʃn] Vorschlag

suit [su:t] (Herren-)Anzug; (Damen-)Kostüm

suitcase ['su:tkeɪs] Koffer

sum [sʌm] Rechenaufgabe; Summe • **do sums** rechnen

summarize ['sʌməraɪz] zusammenfassen • **summary (of)** ['sʌməri] Zusammenfassung (von)

summer ['sʌmə] Sommer • **in (the) summer** im Sommer

sun [sʌn] Sonne • **sunshine** Sonnenschein • **sunny** sonnig

Sunday ['sʌndeɪ, 'sʌndi] Sonntag

super ['su:pə] super, toll

supermarket ['su:pəmɑ:kɪt] Supermarkt

supper ['sʌpə] (warmes) Abendessen

support *(v; n)* [sə'pɔ:t] **1.** unterstützen; *(Familie usw.)* ernähren, unterhalten; **2.** Unterstützung, Beistand

suppose [sə'pəʊz] annehmen, vermuten • **be supposed to do/be** tun sollen / angeblich sein sollen

sure [ʃʊə] **1.** sicher(lich) • **Sure.** Sicher!/Natürlich!/Klar! • **make sure** sich vergewissern; darauf achten/dafür sorgen (, dass) **2.** *(infml, besonders AE)* wirklich, echt

surf [sɜ:f]: **surf the Internet/the World Wide Web** im Internet/im World Wide Web surfen **surfing** *(das)* Wellenreiten, Surfen • **go surfing** wellenreiten gehen, surfen gehen

surgeon ['sɜ:dʒən] Chirurg/in

surprise [sə'praɪz] überraschen **surprised (at/by)** überrascht (über) • **surprising** erstaunlich, überraschend

survive [sə'vaɪv] überleben

suspect ['sʌspekt] Verdächtige(r)

swap **(-pp-)** [swɒp] tauschen

sweatshirt ['swetʃɜ:t] Sweatshirt

sweet [swi:t] süß

swim* **(-mm-)** [swɪm] schwimmen • **swimming** *(das)* Schwimmen • **swimming-pool** Schwimmbad, Swimmingpool • **swimming-trunks** *(pl)* ['swɪmɪŋtrʌŋks] Badehose **swimsuit** ['swɪmsu:t] Badeanzug

sword [sɔ:d] Schwert

°**syllable** ['sɪləbl] Silbe

symbol ['sɪmbl] Symbol

synonym ['sɪnənɪm] Synonym, bedeutungsähnliches Wort

synthesizer ['sɪnθəsaɪzə] Synthesizer

system ['sɪstəm] System

T

table ['teɪbl] **1.** Tisch • **table tennis** Tischtennis **2.** Tabelle

taco ['tɑ:kəʊ] *eine Art Pfannkuchen, mit Fleisch oder Gemüse, Käse und Gewürzen gefüllt*

tail [teɪl] Schwanz

take* [teɪk] **1.** nehmen; mitnehmen; (weg)bringen • **take sb. away** *hier:* jn. abführen • **take a bath** baden, ein Bad nehmen **take a break** eine Pause machen • **take an exam** eine Prüfung ablegen, machen • **take a guess** (mal) raten • **take a holiday** (einen) Urlaub machen **take a look (at)** einen Blick werfen (auf) • **take a quiz** *(AE)* einen Test/eine Prüfung machen **take a seat** Platz nehmen **take a shower** (sich) duschen **take a step towards sb.** einen Schritt auf jn. zugehen • **take a test** *(BE)* einen Test/eine Prüfung machen • **take a walk** einen Spaziergang machen, spazieren gehen • **take notes** sich Notizen machen • **take it in turns** sich abwechseln • **take off** **1.** ausziehen *(Kleidung)*; absetzen *(Helm)*; **2.** starten, abfliegen, abheben *(Flugzeug)* • **take out** herausnehmen; ausleihen *(Bücher)* • **take photos** Fotos machen, fotografieren • **take place** stattfinden • **take third place** den dritten Platz belegen **2.** dauern; *(Zeit)* brauchen **Take a little time.** Nehmen Sie sich etwas Zeit.

talent ['tælənt] Talent, Begabung

talk *(n; v)* [tɔ:k] **1.** Vortrag, Referat, Rede; Gespräch • **give a talk (on)** einen Vortrag/eine Rede halten (über) **2. talk (to)** reden (mit), sich unterhalten (mit)

tall [tɔ:l] groß (gewachsen); hoch *(Bäume, Türme usw.)*

°**tanker** ['tæŋkə] Tanker, Tankschiff

tape [teɪp] (Ton-)Band

tartan ['tɑ:tn] Schottenstoff, Schottenmuster

task [tɑ:sk] Aufgabe

taste [teɪst] schmecken

°**tavern** ['tævn] Schenke

tax (on) [tæks] Steuer (auf)

taxi ['tæksi] Taxi

tea [ti:] Tee

teach* [ti:tʃ] unterrichten, lehren **teach sb. sth.** jm. etwas beibringen • **teach sb. a lesson** jm. eine Lektion erteilen **teacher** Lehrer/in

team [ti:m] Team, Mannschaft **team-mate** ['ti:mmeɪt] Mannschaftskamerad/in

tear [tɪə] Träne

tear* sth. (off) [teə] etwas (ab-)reißen; etwas zerreißen

technique [tek'ni:k] (Arbeits-)Verfahren, Technik, Methode

techno ['teknəʊ] Techno

technology [tek'nɒlədʒi] Technologie; Technik

teenager ['ti:neɪdʒə] Teenager, Jugendliche(r, s)

teeth [ti:θ] *pl von „tooth"*

telemarketing [ˌteli'mɑ:kɪtɪŋ] Telemarketing, Telefonverkauf

telephone ['teləfəʊn] Telefon **telephone box** Telefonzelle **telephone number** Telefonnummer

television ['telɪvɪʒn] Fernsehen; Fernsehgerät • **work in television** beim Fernsehen arbeiten

tell* [tel] **1. tell (about)** erzählen (von), berichten (über) **tell (sb.) lies** (jn. an-, be)lügen **tell sb. (not) to do sth.** jn. auffordern, etwas (nicht) zu tun; jm. sagen, dass er/sie etwas (nicht) tun soll • **tell the way (to)** den Weg (zu/nach ...) beschreiben • **Can you tell me the way to ...?** Können Sie mir sagen, wie ich zu/nach ... komme? **2.** erkennen; unterscheiden

temperature ['temprətʃə] Temperatur

tennis ['tenɪs] Tennis

tense [tens] Zeitform, Tempus

tent [tent] Zelt

term [tɜ:m] Trimester

terrible ['terəbl] schrecklich, furchtbar

°**territory** [*BE:* 'terətri, *AE:* 'terətɔ:ri] Gebiet

terror ['terə] Terror; Entsetzen, Schrecken

test *(v; n)* [test] **1.** testen, prüfen; **2.** Test, Prüfung, Klassenarbeit **do/take a test** *(BE)* einen Test/eine Prüfung machen

text [tekst] Text

than: slower than [ˈsləʊə ðən] langsamer als
thank sb. [θæŋk] **1.** jm. danken, sich bei jm. bedanken **Thank you.** Danke (schön). **thanks** danke • **Thanks a lot.** Danke vielmals. Vielen Dank. **thanks to Ben and Jenny** dank Ben und Jenny; wegen Ben und Jenny
2. thank-you *(das)* Dankeschön
° **Thanksgiving** [ˌθæŋksˈgɪvɪŋ] Erntedankfest *(amerikanischer Feiertag am vierten Donnerstag im November)*
that [ðət, *betont:* ðæt] **1.** dass **so (that)** sodass, damit **2.** der/die/das, die *(Relativpronomen)*
that [ðæt] jene(r, s); das (dort) **that afternoon/day/night** an jenem Nachmittag/Tag/in jener Nacht • **that's because** das kommt daher, weil • **that's why** deshalb, darum • **before that** vorher, davor, zuvor **like that** so
the [ðə] der, die, das; die • **the next day** der nächste Tag; am nächsten Tag • **the same** der-/die-/dasselbe, dieselben
theatre [ˈθɪətə] Theater
their [ðeə] ihr, ihre *(Plural)*
theirs [ðeəz] ihre(r, s)
them [ðəm, *betont:* ðem] sie; ihnen • **the two of them** die beiden; alle beide
° **theme park** [ˈθiːm pɑːk] *Freizeitpark mit Attraktionen zu einem bestimmten Thema*
themselves [ðəmˈselvz] sich (selbst); selbst, selber
then [ðen] **1.** dann, danach **just then** genau in dem Moment; gerade dann **2.** damals, zu der Zeit
there [ðeə] da, dort; dahin, dorthin • **in there** dort drinnen **out there** dort draußen • **near there** dort in der Nähe; nicht weit von dort • **over there** dort drüben, da drüben • **up there** dort oben (hin), da oben (hin) • **there are** es sind (vorhanden); es gibt • **there's (there is)** es ist (vorhanden); es gibt
these [ðiːz] diese, die (hier)
they [ðeɪ] **1.** sie *(Plural)*; **2.** man
thick [θɪk] dick; dicht
thief [θiːf], *pl* **thieves** [θiːvz] Dieb, Diebin
thin (-nn-) [θɪn] dünn
thing [θɪŋ] Ding, Sache • **the same thing** der-, die-, dasselbe **poor things** die Armen
think* [θɪŋk] glauben, meinen, denken • **think (about)** nachdenken (über) • **think about/of** halten von, denken über **think of** denken an, sich ausdenken
third [θɜːd] dritte(r, s) • **thirdly, ...** drittens ...
thirst [θɜːst] Durst • **thirsty** [ˈθɜːsti] durstig • **be thirsty** durstig sein, Durst haben
this [ðɪs] diese(r, s); dies (hier) **This is ...** Dies ist ... • **this morning/afternoon/evening** heute Morgen/Nachmittag/Abend • **this way 1.** hier entlang; **2.** so, auf diese Weise
those [ðəʊz] die (da), jene (dort)
though [ðəʊ] obwohl • °**even though** obwohl, auch wenn
thoughtful [ˈθɔːtfəl] aufmerksam, rücksichtsvoll; nachdenklich
thousand [ˈθaʊznd] tausend
thriller [ˈθrɪlə] Thriller, Krimi
throat [θrəʊt] Kehle, Hals
° **throne** [θrəʊn] Thron
through [θruː] durch • **from ... through** *(AE)* von ... bis (einschließlich)
throw* [θrəʊ] werfen • **throw down** auf den Boden werfen **throw a six** eine Sechs würfeln **throw the dice** würfeln
Thursday [ˈθɜːzdeɪ, ˈθɜːzdi] Donnerstag
° **tick** [tɪk] Häkchen
ticket [ˈtɪkɪt] **1.** Eintrittskarte **a 30-dollar ticket** eine 30-Dollar-Karte, eine Karte für 30 Dollar **2.** Fahrkarte, Fahrschein **ticket office** (Fahr-)Kartenschalter; Kartenvorverkaufsstelle
tidy [ˈtaɪdi] ordentlich, aufgeräumt • **tidy up** aufräumen
tie [taɪ] (zusammen)binden, (zusammen)schnüren • **tie to** (an)binden an • **tie up** festbinden
tiger [ˈtaɪgə] Tiger
tile [taɪl] **1.** Ziegel, Fliese; °**2.** fliesen, kacheln
till [tɪl] bis *(zeitlich)* • **not ... till** erst (um)
time [taɪm] **1.** Zeit • **What time is it?** Wie spät ist es? • **What time is the film?** Wann fängt der Film an? • **(just) in time** (gerade) rechtzeitig • **at all times** immer, jederzeit • **at that time** damals, zu jener/dieser Zeit • **a long time ago** vor langer Zeit • **for a long time** lange Zeit • **over time** über die Jahre; im Laufe der Zeit **get time off** frei bekommen, Urlaub bekommen • **Take a little time.** Nehmen Sie sich etwas Zeit. • **work full-time** ganztags arbeiten, als Vollzeitkraft beschäftigt sein • **feeding times** Fütterungszeiten • **free time** Freizeit, freie Zeit • °**spare time** Freizeit • **timer** Zeitmesser • **timeless** zeitlos, ewig **2. time(s)** Mal(e); -mal • **for the first time** zum ersten Mal **The first time Brian saw Mark's room ...** Als Brian Marks Zimmer das erste Mal sah, ... • **five times nought** fünf mal null
timetable [ˈtaɪmteɪbl] **1.** Stundenplan; **2.** Fahrplan
tin [tɪn] Dose, Büchse
tip [tɪp] Tipp
tired [ˈtaɪəd] müde
title [ˈtaɪtl] Titel; Überschrift
to [tə, *betont:* tuː] **1.** zu, nach **letter to** Brief an • **Welcome to ...** Willkommen in ... • **I've been to Husum.** Ich war (schon mal) in Husum. / Ich bin (schon) in Husum gewesen. • **to the left** links, auf der linken Seite, zur Linken • **to the right** rechts, auf der rechten Seite, zur Rechten • **quarter to nine** Viertel vor neun (8.45/20.45) **3.50 to 5.30** 3 Uhr 50 bis 5 Uhr 30 • **from Monday to Friday** von Montag bis Freitag • **next to** neben • **one nil to Kingsway** eins zu null für Kingsway **2.** um zu; **3. try to do sth.** versuchen etwas zu tun
toast [təʊst] Toast(brot)
tobacco [təˈbækəʊ] Tabak
today [təˈdeɪ] heute • **today's match** das heutige Spiel
together [təˈgeðə] zusammen
toilet [ˈtɔɪlət] Toilette
tomato [təˈmɑːtəʊ], *pl* **tomatoes** [təˈmɑːtəʊz] Tomate
tomorrow [təˈmɒrəʊ] morgen **tomorrow morning/afternoon/evening** morgen Vormittag/Nachmittag/Abend
° **tongue** [tʌŋ] Zunge
tonight [təˈnaɪt] heute Nacht, heute Abend
too [tuː] **1.** auch • **and on her birthday, too!** und noch dazu an ihrem Geburtstag. • **And they were pretty dresses, too.** Und schöne Kleider waren es außerdem/noch dazu. **2. too little** zu klein • **too bad** *(infml)* ein Jammer; schade (, dass)
tool [tuːl] Werkzeug • **tool box** Werkzeugkasten
tooth [tuːθ], *pl* **teeth** [tiːθ] Zahn **brush your teeth** sich die Zähne putzen
top [tɒp] Spitze, oberes Ende **at the top (of)** oben, am oberen Ende, an der Spitze (von) **top row** obere Reihe • **on top (of sth.)** oben, obendrauf (auf etwas) • **on top of that** außerdem; darüber hinaus
topic [ˈtɒpɪk] Thema, Themenbereich
° **Torah** [ˈtɔːrə] *(die)* Thora *(das gesammelte jüdische Gesetz)*
tornado, *pl* **tornadoes** [tɔːˈneɪdəʊ] Tornado, Wirbelsturm
tortoise [ˈtɔːtəs] Schildkröte
total *(n; adj)* [ˈtəʊtl] **1.** Gesamtbetrag, Summe; **2.** Gesamt-, gesamt, völlig, total
touch [tʌtʃ] berühren, anfassen
° **tough** [tʌf] hart, zäh
tour (of) [tʊə] Tour, (Rund-)Reise (durch)

tourist ['tʊərɪst] Tourist/in **tourist board** ['tʊərɪst bɔːd] Fremdenverkehrsbüro • **tourist office** Fremdenverkehrsbüro; Touristeninformation

towards [tə'wɔːdz]: **towards him** auf ihn zu, in seine Richtung **feelings towards sb.** Gefühle für jn. / gegenüber jm.

tower ['taʊə] Turm

town [taʊn] Stadt • **out of town** außerhalb (der Stadt) **town hall** [ˌtaʊn 'hɔːl] Rathaus

toy [tɔɪ] Spielzeug

track [træk] Spur, Fährte

trade [treɪd] Handel

tradition [trə'dɪʃn] Tradition

traffic ['træfɪk] Verkehr • **traffic light(s)** ['træfɪk laɪts] Verkehrsampel

tragedy ['trædʒədi] Tragödie

°**trail** [treɪl] Weg, Pfad

train [treɪn] Zug • **on the train** im Zug

train [treɪn] üben; *(jn.)* trainieren; *(jn.)* ausbilden • **trainer** ['treɪnə] Trainer/in • **training** ['treɪnɪŋ] Training, Ausbildung

tram [træm] Straßenbahn, Tram

translate (into) [træns'leɪt] übersetzen (in) • **translation** [træns'leɪʃn] Übersetzung

transparency [træns'pærənsi] Folie

transport *(no pl)* ['trænspɔːt] Transport(mittel), Verkehrsmittel

transportation [ˌtrænspɔː'teɪʃn] Beförderung, Transport; *(AE auch:)* Verkehrsmittel

travel *(v; n)* ['trævl] **1.** (-ll-) reisen **traveller** Reisende(r) **2.** (das) Reisen • **travel agent** ['trævl_ˌeɪdʒənt] Reisebürokaufmann/-kauffrau; *auch:* Reisebüro °**travelcard** *Dauerkarte für den öffentlichen Nahverkehr*

tree [triː] Baum

trend [trend] (Mode-)Trend

tribe [traɪb] (Volks-)Stamm

trick [trɪk] Trick • **play a trick on sb.** jm. einen Streich spielen

°**trick-or-treat** [ˌtrɪk_ɔː 'triːt]: **go trick-or-treating** *(AE) etwa:* einen Streich spielen, wenn es keine Süßigkeiten gibt *(Sitte an Halloween)*

trip (to) [trɪp] Ausflug, Reise (nach, zu) • **go on a trip** einen Ausflug/eine Reise machen

trouble ['trʌbl] Ärger, Schwierigkeiten • **be in trouble** in Schwierigkeiten sein; Ärger kriegen • **get sb. into trouble** jn. in Schwierigkeiten bringen **make trouble** Ärger/Schwierigkeiten machen, bereiten **trouble spot** ['trʌbl spɒt] *hier etwa:* Falle

trousers *(pl)* ['traʊzəz] (lange) Hose

truck [trʌk] Lastwagen, Lkw

true [truː] wahr • **come true** wahr werden, sich bewahrheiten

try [traɪ] **1.** versuchen, (aus)probieren • **try hard** sich sehr bemühen, sich anstrengen • **try on** anprobieren *(Kleidung)* °**try sth. on sb.** etwas an jm. ausprobieren • **try to do sth./ try and do sth.** versuchen etwas zu tun **2. have a try** es (mal) versuchen

T-shirt ['tiːʃɜːt] T-Shirt

tube [tjuːb]: **the tube** *(no pl) (infml)* die U-Bahn *(in London) (eigentlich:* Rohr, Röhre)

Tuesday ['tjuːzdeɪ, 'tjuːzdi] Dienstag

°**tundra** ['tʌndrə] Tundra *(baumlose Steppe)*

°**tune** [tjuːn] Melodie

tunnel ['tʌnl] Tunnel

°**turkey** ['tɜːki] Truthahn

Turkish ['tɜːkɪʃ] türkisch

turn *(v; n)* [tɜːn]: **1.** drehen • **turn (around)** sich umdrehen **turn right/left (into)** (nach) rechts/links abbiegen (in) **turn (a vehicle)** (ein Fahrzeug) wenden • °**turn on sb.** jn. angreifen • **turn to sb.** sich jm. zuwenden; sich an jn. wenden **2. turn on/off** ein-/ausschalten *(Licht, Gerät)* • **turn up/down** *(Radio usw.)* lauter/leiser stellen; *(Heizung usw.)* aufdrehen/niedriger stellen **3. It's my turn (to write/...)** Ich bin an der Reihe (zu schreiben/...) • **take it in turns** sich abwechseln

TV [ˌtiː'viː] Fernsehgerät; Fernsehen • **on TV** im Fernsehen **watch TV** fernsehen

twice [twaɪs] zweimal

twins [twɪnz] Zwillinge

two [tuː] zwei • **the two of them** die beiden

type (of) [taɪp] Art, Sorte, Typ

typical (of) ['tɪpɪkl] typisch (für)

U

umbrella [ʌm'brelə] Regenschirm

°**umiak** ['uːmiæk] *offenes, mit Robbenhaut bespanntes Boot*

UN [ˌjuː_'en] **(United Nations)** [juˌnaɪtɪd 'neɪʃnz] UN (Vereinte Nationen)

unbelievable [ˌʌnbɪ'liːvəbl] unglaublich

uncle ['ʌŋkl] Onkel

under ['ʌndə] unter

underground ['ʌndəgraʊnd]: **the underground** *(no pl)* die U-Bahn

underline [ˌʌndə'laɪn] unterstreichen

understand* [ˌʌndə'stænd] verstehen, begreifen • **I understand** soweit ich weiß

unfortunately [ʌn'fɔːtʃnətli] leider, unglücklicherweise

unfriendly [ˌʌn'frendli] unfreundlich

unhappy (about) [ʌn'hæpi] unglücklich, traurig (über/wegen)

unhealthy [ʌn'helθɪ] ungesund

uniform ['juːnɪfɔːm] Uniform

unimportant [ˌʌnɪm'pɔːtnt] unwichtig

unit ['juːnɪt] Kapitel, Lektion

United Nations [juˌnaɪtɪd 'neɪʃnz] **(UN)** [ˌjuː_'en] Vereinte Nationen (UN)

university [ˌjuːnɪ'vɜːsəti] Universität, Hochschule

unknown [ˌʌn'nəʊn] unbekannt

unless [ən'les] wenn ... nicht, außer wenn, sofern ... nicht

unlike *(prep)* [ˌʌn'laɪk] anders als, im Gegensatz zu

unload [ˌʌn'ləʊd] ausladen, abladen

unlucky [ʌn'lʌki] unglückselig, Unglücks-

unpack [ˌʌn'pæk] auspacken

unskilled [ˌʌn'skɪld] ungelernte(r)

untidy [ˌʌn'taɪdi] unordentlich, unaufgeräumt

until [ən'tɪl] bis • **not ... until** erst (um)

unusual [ʌn'juːʒuəl] ungewöhnlich, außergewöhnlich

up [ʌp] hinauf, herauf, nach oben • **up north** oben im Norden • **up the tree** den Baum hinauf • **up there** dort oben (hin), da oben (hin) • **up to** bis (zu) • **be up** auf(gestanden) sein

upset (about) [ˌʌp'set] aufgebracht, aufgeregt; betrübt (wegen)

upside down [ˌʌpsaɪd 'daʊn] verkehrt herum, auf dem Kopf

upstairs [ˌʌp'steəz] (nach) oben

°**uptown** ['ʌptaʊn] *(AE) der Norden Manhattans / in den Norden Manhattans*

us [əs, *betont:* ʌs] uns

use [juːz] gebrauchen, verwenden, benutzen • **use up** aufbrauchen • **user** Benutzer/in, Anwender/in

°**used**: **I used to ...** ['juːstə] Früher bin/habe ich immer ...

useful ['juːsfəl] nützlich

useless ['juːsləs] nutzlos, zu nichts nütze

usual ['juːʒuəl] gewöhnlich, üblich • **usually** ['juːʒuəli] meistens, gewöhnlich, normalerweise

V

vacation [*BE:* və'keɪʃn, *AE:* veɪ'keɪʃn] *(AE)* Urlaub, Ferien

valley ['væli] Tal

valuable ['væljuəbl] wertvoll

van [væn] Lieferwagen

varnish: **nail varnish** *(BE)* ['neɪl ˌvɑːnɪʃ] Nagellack

vegetable ['vedʒtəbl] *(ein)* Gemüse

vegetarian [ˌvedʒə'teəriən] Vegetarier, Vegetarierin

vehicle ['viːəkl] Fahrzeug

°**verse** [vɜːs] Vers

very ['veri] sehr • **very funny** sehr witzig, sehr komisch
°**victory** ['vɪktəri] Sieg
video ['vɪdiəʊ] Video • **video recorder** ['vɪdiəʊ rɪˌkɔːdə] Videorecorder
view [vjuː]: **1. view (of/over)** Aussicht, Blick (auf/über)
2. view (about/on) Meinung (über/zu)
villa ['vɪlə] Landhaus; Ferienhaus
village ['vɪlɪdʒ] Dorf
violent ['vaɪələnt] gewalttätig, gewaltsam
°**violin** [ˌvaɪə'lɪn] Violine
virtual ['vɜːtʃuəl] virtuell *(nicht echt, aber echt erscheinend)*
°**virus** ['vaɪrəs] Virus
visit *(v; n)* ['vɪzɪt] **1.** besuchen; besichtigen • **visitor** ['vɪzɪtə] Besucher/in, Gast
2. Besuch
vocabulary [və'kæbjələri] **1.** Vokabelverzeichnis, Wörterverzeichnis; **2.** Wortschatz, Vokabular
voice [vɔɪs] Stimme • °**disguised voice** [dɪsˌgaɪzd 'vɔɪs] verstellte Stimme
volleyball ['vɒlibɔːl] Volleyball
volume ['vɒljuːm] Lautstärke
volunteer [ˌvɒlən'tɪə] Freiwillige(r) **volunteer work** ehrenamtliche Arbeit *(ohne Bezahlung)*
°**vote** [vəʊt] wählen

W

wait (for) ['weɪt fɔː] warten (auf) **I can't wait (to do sth.)** Ich kann es kaum erwarten (, etwas zu tun)
waiter ['weɪtə] Kellner • **waitress** ['weɪtrəs] Kellnerin
wake up* [ˌweɪk_'ʌp] aufwachen **wake sb. (up)** jn. (auf)wecken
walk *(v; n)* [wɔːk] **1.** (zu Fuß) gehen, laufen; spazieren gehen °**walk about** herumlaufen **walk on** weitergehen • **go walking** wandern
2. Spaziergang • **go for a walk** einen Spaziergang machen **take a walk** einen Spaziergang machen, spazieren gehen
walkie-talkie [ˌwɔːki 'tɔːki] Walkie-Talkie *(tragbares Funksprechgerät)*
walkman ['wɔːkmən] Walkman
wall [wɔːl] Wand; Mauer • **on the wall** an der Wand • °**wall display** ['wɔːl dɪˌspleɪ] Wandzeitung, Wandbild
°**wallpaper** ['wɔːlpeɪpə] Tapete
want [wɒnt] (haben) wollen **I want to go.** Ich will/möchte gehen.
war [wɔː] Krieg
warm [wɔːm] warm
warn sb. (about sth.) [wɔːn] jn. (vor etwas) warnen • **warn sb. not to do sth.** jn. davor warnen, etwas zu tun; jn. ermahnen, etwas nicht zu tun **warning (to sb.)** Warnung
wash [wɒʃ] waschen • **wash the dishes** das Geschirr abwaschen
washing-machine ['wɒʃɪŋ məˌʃiːn] Waschmaschine
wasp [wɒsp] Wespe
waste (on) [weɪst] verschwenden, vergeuden (für)
watch *(n; v)* [wɒtʃ] **1.** Armbanduhr; **2.** beobachten, sich *etwas* ansehen; zuschauen • **watch out** aufpassen • **watch TV** fernsehen
water ['wɔːtə] Wasser
wave [weɪv] Welle • °**wavy lines** [ˌweɪvi 'laɪnz] Wellenlinien, Schlangenlinien
wax [wæks] Wachs
way [weɪ] **1.** Weg • **ask sb. the way** jn. nach dem Weg fragen **be in sb.'s way** jm. im Weg sein **come sb.'s way** jm. entgegenkommen • **go sb.'s way** in die gleiche Richtung wie jd. gehen **tell sb. the way (to)** jm. den Weg (zu/nach) beschreiben **Can you tell me the way to ...?** Können Sie mir sagen, wie ich zu/nach ... komme? • **on my way (to)** auf dem Weg, unterwegs (nach/zu) • **a long way** ein weiter Weg; weit (entfernt) **go a long way** viel erreichen, viel bewirken • **by the way** übrigens, nebenbei (bemerkt)
2. Richtung • **this way** hier entlang • **the wrong way** in die falsche Richtung • **the wrong way round** verkehrt herum
3. Art und Weise • **in an intelligent way** auf intelligente Weise • °**in different ways** auf verschiedene Weise(n) • **old/new ways** alte/neue Lebensweisen, Denkweisen, Bräuche **No way!** *(infml)* Auf keinen Fall! / Kommt nicht infrage! • **this way** so, auf diese Weise
we [wi, *betont:* wiː] wir
weak [wiːk] schwach
wear* [weə] tragen, anhaben *(Kleidung)*
weather ['weðə] Wetter • **in bad weather** bei schlechtem Wetter
web site ['web saɪt] *alle Seiten eines Anbieters im World Wide Web*
wedding ['wedɪŋ] Hochzeit
Wednesday ['wenzdeɪ, 'wenzdi] Mittwoch
week [wiːk] Woche • **next week** nächste Woche, in der nächsten Woche • **for weeks** wochenlang; seit Wochen **day of the week** Wochentag **a six-week trip** eine sechswöchige Reise
weekend [ˌwiːk'end] Wochenende • **at the weekend** am Wochenende • **at weekends** an Wochenenden • **Have a nice weekend.** Schönes Wochenende.
weight [weɪt] Gewicht • **weight training** Krafttraining
weird [wɪəd] *(infml)* verrückt, komisch
welcome ['welkəm] **1.** willkommen • **Welcome to ...** Willkommen in ...
2. *(v)* **welcome sb. (to)** jn. willkommen heißen (in)
3. *(n)* **get a friendly welcome** freundlich empfangen werden **give sb. a friendly welcome** jn. freundlich empfangen
well [wel] **1.** *(adj)* gesund, wohlauf; **2.** *(adv)* gut • **as well as** und auch, ebenso wie • **Well, ...** Nun, ...; Also, ... • **do well (in)** gut sein (in), gut abschneiden (in) • **You're doing well.** Du machst es gut.
well [wel]: **oil well** Ölquelle
Welsh [welʃ] Walisisch
west [west] westlich; (nach) Westen • **western** westlich, West- • **westbound** ['westbaʊnd] Richtung Westen
wet **(-tt-)** [wet] nass, feucht
whale [weɪl] Wal(fisch) **whaling** Walfang • **go whaling** auf Walfang gehen
what [wɒt] **1.** was; **2.** welche, welcher, welches • **what a ...** was für ein(e) ... • **Now what?** Was nun? • **What about a calendar?** Wie wärs mit einem Kalender? • **What about Jenny?** Was ist mit Jenny? / Und Jenny? • **What are they talking about?** Worüber reden sie? • **What colour is it?** Welche Farbe hat es (er, sie)? **What day is 1st January?** Was für ein Tag ist der 1. Januar? **What do you call this?** Wie nennt man dies? • **What's ... like?** Wie ist ...? • **What kind of ...?** Was für ein/e ...? **What size are you?** Welche Größe hast du/haben Sie? **What time is it?** Wie spät ist es? **What time is the film?** Wann fängt der Film an? • **What's the date?** Welches Datum haben wir? • **What's the matter?** Was ist denn (los)? • **What's this in English?** Wie heißt das auf Englisch? • **What's your name?** Wie heißt du? / Wie heißen Sie?
whatever [wɒt'evə] was (auch) immer
wheel [wiːl] Rad
wheelchair ['wiːltʃeə] Rollstuhl
when [wen] **1.** wann • **When is it?** Wann fängt es an? **When's your birthday?** Wann hast du Geburtstag?
2. wenn; **3.** als
whenever [wen'evə] wann (auch) immer

where [weə] wo; wohin **Where are you from?** Wo kommst du her?
wherever [weər'evə] wohin (auch) immer; wo (auch) immer
whether ['weðə] ob
which … [wɪtʃ] **1.** welche(r, s) … **which one(s)** welche(r, s); welche **2.** der/die/das, die *(Relativpronomen)*
while *(conj)* [waɪl] während
whisper ['wɪspə] flüstern
whistle ['wɪsl] pfeifen
°**whit**: **no whit** [nəʊ 'wɪt] kein bisschen
white *(adj; n)* [waɪt] **1.** weiß; **2.** Weiße/r
who [hu:] **1.** wer; **2.** wen; wem; **3.** der/die/das, die *(Relativpronomen)*
whoever [hu:'evə] wer (auch) immer, wen/wem (auch) immer
whole [həʊl] ganze(r, s), gesamte(r, s)
whose [hu:z] **1.** wessen **Whose are these (CDs)?** Wem gehören die (CDs) hier? **2.** deren, dessen *(Relativpronomen)*
why [waɪ] warum • **Why be bored?** Warum/Wozu sich (denn) langweilen? • **Why not ask …?** Warum fragst du nicht …? / Warum fragen wir nicht …? **that's why** deshalb, darum
wide [waɪd] breit; *(Augen)* weit geöffnet
wife [waɪf], *pl* **wives** [waɪvz] Ehefrau
wild [waɪld] wild • °**wildly popular** *(infml)* wahnsinnig beliebt
°**wildlife** ['waɪldlaɪf] die Tier- und Pflanzenwelt
will [wɪl]: **The world will be fantastic.** Die Welt wird fantastisch sein. • **You won't find many.** [wəʊnt] **(= You will not find many.)** Du wirst nicht viele finden. • °**I will die a free man before …** *(fml)* Ich will lieber als freier Mann sterben, ehe …
win* *(v; n)* [wɪn] **1. (-nn-)** gewinnen • **win a scholarship** ein Stipendium bekommen **winner** Gewinner/in, Sieger/in **2.** Sieg
wind [wɪnd] Wind • **windy** ['wɪndi] windig
window ['wɪndəʊ] Fenster
windsurfing ['wɪndsɜ:fɪŋ] *(das)* Windsurfen
winter ['wɪntə] Winter
°**wire** ['waɪə] (Stachel-)Draht
wish *(v; n)* [wɪʃ] **1.** wünschen; **2.** Wunsch
with [wɪð] mit (… zusammen), bei • **a software with a difference** eine etwas andere Software; eine Software, die mal was anderes ist
without [wɪ'ðaʊt] ohne
witness ['wɪtnəs] Zeuge, Zeugin
wives [waɪvz] *pl von „wife"*
wolf [wʊlf], *pl* **wolves** [wʊlvz] Wolf
woman ['wʊmən], *pl* **women** ['wɪmɪn] Frau
wonder ['wʌndə] sich fragen, gern wissen wollen
wonderful ['wʌndəfəl] wunderbar
won't [wəʊnt]: **You won't (= will not) find many.** Du wirst nicht viele finden.
wood [wʊd] Holz • °**woods** *(pl)* Wald, Wälder
word [wɜ:d] Wort • **word group** Wortgruppe • **word link** Wortverbindung • °**word order** Wortstellung
work *(v; n)* [wɜ:k] **1.** arbeiten **work full-time** ganztags arbeiten, als Vollzeitkraft beschäftigt sein • **work hard at sth.** hart an/für etwas arbeiten • **work on sth.** an etwas arbeiten **work sth. out** etwas ausarbeiten, herausfinden • **worker** Arbeiter/in **2.** funktionieren; **3.** Arbeit • **at work** bei der Arbeit, am Arbeitsplatz • **out of work** arbeitslos **work camp** Arbeitslager
world [wɜ:ld] Welt • **in the world** auf der Welt • °**out of this world** *(infml)* fantastisch **World Cup** [ˌwɜ:ld 'kʌp] Weltmeisterschaft • **World Wide Web** „weltweites Netz" *(weltweites Informationssystem im Internet)*
worried (about) ['wʌrid] beunruhigt (wegen), besorgt (wegen/um)
worry *(n; v)* ['wʌri] **1.** Sorge, Kummer; **2. worry (about)** sich Sorgen machen (wegen, um) **worry sb.** jn. beunruhigen, jm. Sorgen machen
worse [wɜ:s] schlechter, schlimmer
worst [wɜ:st]: **(the) worst** (der/die/das) schlechteste, schlimmste …; am schlechtesten, schlimmsten
worth [wɜ:θ]: **be worth** wert sein
would [wəd, *betont:* wʊd] würde, würdest, würden • **I'd (= I would) fly to …** Ich würde nach … fliegen. • **What would you like to do?** Was würdest/möchtest du gern machen? **I'd like** Ich hätte gern / Ich möchte gern • **I'd like to go.** Ich würde gern/möchte gehen.
wound [wu:nd] Wunde
Wow! [waʊ] *(infml) (Ausruf)* Mensch! / Wahnsinn!
write* (to) [raɪt] schreiben (an) **write down** aufschreiben, notieren • **write sth. out** etwas ausschreiben, etwas aufschreiben • **writer** Schreiber/in, Schriftsteller/in • **writing** Geschriebenes; (Hand-)Schrift
wrong [rɒŋ] falsch • **What's wrong?** Was ist los? • **the wrong way** in die falsche Richtung • **the wrong way round** verkehrt herum • **be wrong** **1.** sich irren, Unrecht haben; **2.** nicht in Ordnung sein, nicht stimmen • **get sth. wrong** etwas falsch machen

Y

yawn [jɔ:n] gähnen
yeah [jeə] *(infml)* ja
year [jɪə] Jahr; Jahrgangsstufe **a year and a half** eineinhalb Jahre, anderthalb Jahre • **a 2-year period** ein Zeitraum von zwei Jahren • **16-year-old** 16-jährige(r, s) • **yearbook** Jahrbuch *(einer Schule)*
yellow ['jeləʊ] gelb
yes [jes] ja
yesterday ['jestədeɪ, -di] gestern
yet [jet]: **… yet?** … schon …? **not (…) yet** noch nicht
you [ju, *betont:* ju:] **1.** du; ihr; Sie; **2.** dich/dir; euch/euch; Sie/Ihnen; **3.** man • **you know** weißt du; nämlich • **You say** Du sagst / Man sagt • **you see** weißt du, nämlich • **How are you?** Wie geht es dir? / Wie geht es euch? / Wie geht es Ihnen? • **Thank you.** Danke (schön).
young *(adj; n)* [jʌŋ] **1.** jung; **2.** *(pl)* Jungen *(eines Tieres)*
your [jɔ:] dein/deine; euer/eure; Ihr/Ihre
yours [jɔ:z] deine(r, s); eure(r, s); Ihre(r, s) • **a teacher of yours** eine/r deiner Lehrer/innen; ein/e Lehrer/in von dir
Yours [jɔ:z] dein/deine; euer/eure; Ihr/Ihre *(Briefschluss)* **Yours faithfully** ['feɪθfəli] Mit freundlichen Grüßen / Hochachtungsvoll • **Yours sincerely,** [sɪn'sɪəli] Mit freundlichen/herzlichen Grüßen
yourself [jə'self, *betont:* jɔ:'self] dir/dich (selbst); selbst, selber
yourselves [jə'selvz, *betont:* jɔ:'selvz] euch (selbst); selbst, selber
youth hostel ['ju:θ hɒstl] Jugendherberge
Yuck! [jʌk] Igitt! / Bäh!

Z

zebra ['zebrə] Zebra
zero ['zɪərəʊ] null
zoo [zu:] Zoo, Tierpark

STATES / COUNTRIES / CONTINENTS

State/Country/Continent	Adjective/Person(s) *
Africa ['æfrɪkə] *Afrika*	African ['æfrɪkən]
Alaska [ə'læskə] *Alaska*	Alaskan [ə'læskən]
America [ə'merɪkə] *Amerika*	American [ə'merɪkən]
Asia ['eɪʃə, 'eɪʒə] *Asien*	Asian ['eɪʃn, 'eɪʒn]
Australia [ɒ'streɪliə] *Australien*	Australian [ɒ'streɪliən]
Austria ['ɒstriə] *Österreich*	Austrian ['ɒstriən]
Belgium ['beldʒəm] *Belgien*	Belgian ['beldʒən]
Bosnia-Herzegovina [ˌbɒzniə ˌhɜːtsəgə'viːnə] *Bosnien-Herzegowina*	Bosnian ['bɒzniən]
(Great) Britain ['brɪtn] *Großbritannien*	British ['brɪtɪʃ]; a Briton ['brɪtn], *pl* the British
California [ˌkælɪ'fɔːniə] *Kalifornien*	Californian [ˌkælɪ'fɔːniən]
Canada ['kænədə] *Kanada*	Canadian [kə'neɪdiən]
China ['tʃaɪnə] *China*	Chinese [ˌtʃaɪ'niːz]; a Chinese, *pl* the Chinese
Colombia [kə'lʌmbiə] *Kolumbien*	Colombian [kə'lʌmbiən]
Croatia [krəʊ'eɪʃə] *Kroatien*	Croatian [krəʊ'eɪʃən]
the **Czech Republic** [ˌtʃek rɪ'pʌblɪk] *Tschechien, die Tschechische Republik*	Czech [tʃek]
Denmark ['denmɑːk] *Dänemark*	Danish ['deɪnɪʃ]; a Dane [deɪn], *pl* -s
El Salvador [el 'sælvəˌdɔː] *El Salvador*	Salvadoran [ˌsælvə'dɔːrən]
England ['ɪŋglənd] *England*	English ['ɪŋglɪʃ]; an Englishman/-woman, *pl* the English
Europe ['jʊərəp] *Europa*	European [ˌjʊərə'piːən]
Finland ['fɪnlənd] *Finnland*	Finnish ['fɪnɪʃ]; a Finn [fɪn], *pl* -s
France [frɑːns] *Frankreich*	French [frentʃ]; a Frenchman/-woman, *pl* the French
Germany ['dʒɜːməni] *Deutschland*	German ['dʒɜːmən]
Greece [griːs] *Griechenland*	Greek [griːk]
Guatemala [ˌgwɑːtə'mɑːlə] *Guatemala*	Guatemalan [ˌgwɑːtə'mɑːlən]
Hungary ['hʌŋgəri] *Ungarn*	Hungarian [hʌŋ'geəriən]
India ['ɪndiə] *Indien*	Indian ['ɪndiən]
Ireland ['aɪələnd] *Irland*	Irish ['aɪrɪʃ]; an Irishman/-woman, *pl* the Irish
Italy ['ɪtəli] *Italien*	Italian [ɪ'tæliən]
Japan [dʒə'pæn] *Japan*	Japanese [ˌdʒæpə'niːz]; a Japanese, *pl* the Japanese
Mexico ['meksɪkəʊ] *Mexiko*	Mexican ['meksɪkən]
Nebraska [nə'bræskə] *Nebraska*	Nebraskan [nə'bræskən]
the **Netherlands** ['neðələndz] *die Niederlande*	Dutch [dʌtʃ]; a Dutchman/-woman, *pl* the Dutch
Norway ['nɔːweɪ] *Norwegen*	Norwegian [nɔː'wiːdʒən]
Pakistan [ˌpɑːkɪ'stɑːn] *Pakistan*	Pakistani [ˌpɑːkɪ'stɑːni]
Panama ['pænəmɑː] *Panama*	Panamanian [ˌpænə'meɪniən]
the **Philippines** ['fɪlɪpiːnz] *die Philippinen*	Philippine ['fɪlɪpiːn]; a Filipino/-na [ˌfɪlɪ'piːnəʊ, -nə], *pl* -s
Poland ['pəʊlənd] *Polen*	Polish ['pəʊlɪʃ]; a Pole [pəʊl], *pl* -s
Portugal ['pɔːtʃʊgl] *Portugal*	Portuguese [ˌpɔːtʃʊ'giːz]; a Portuguese, *pl* the Portuguese
Puerto Rico [ˌpwɜːtəʊ 'riːkəʊ] *Puerto Rico*	Puerto Rican [ˌpwɜːtəʊ 'riːkən]
Romania [ru'meɪniə] *Rumänien*	Romanian [ru'meɪniən]
Russia ['rʌʃə] *Russland*	Russian ['rʌʃn]
Scotland ['skɒtlənd] *Schottland*	Scottish ['skɒtɪʃ]; a Scotsman/-woman *or* a Scot [skɒt], *pl* the Scottish *or* the Scots
Slovakia [sləʊ'vɑːkiə, sləʊ'vækiə] *die Slowakei*	Slovak ['sləʊvæk]
Slovenia [sləʊ'viːniə] *Slowenien*	Slovene ['sləʊviːn] *or* Slovenian [sləʊ'viːniən]
Spain [speɪn] *Spanien*	Spanish ['spænɪʃ]; a Spaniard ['spænɪəd], *pl* -s
Sweden ['swiːdn] *Schweden*	Swedish ['swiːdɪʃ]; a Swede [swiːd], *pl* -s
Switzerland ['swɪtsələnd] *die Schweiz*	Swiss [swɪs]; a Swiss, *pl* the Swiss
Turkey ['tɜːki] *die Türkei*	Turkish ['tɜːkɪʃ]; a Turk [tɜːk], *pl* -s
the **United Kingdom** (the UK) [juˌnaɪtɪd 'kɪŋdəm, ˌjuː'keɪ] *das Vereinigte Königreich*	British ['brɪtɪʃ]; a Briton ['brɪtn], *pl* the British
the **United States of America** (the USA) [juˌnaɪtɪd ˌsteɪts‿əv‿ə'merɪkə, ˌjuː‿es‿'eɪ] *die Vereinigten Staaten von Amerika*	American [ə'merɪkən] *or* US [ˌjuː‿'es]; an American, *pl* -s
Vietnam [ˌviət'næm, ˌviət'nɑːm] *Vietnam*	Vietnamese [ˌviətnə'miːz]; a Vietnamese, *pl* the Vietnamese
Virginia [və'dʒɪniə] *Virginia*	Virginian [və'dʒɪniən]
Wales [weɪlz] *Wales*	Welsh [welʃ]; a Welshman/-woman, *pl* the Welsh
Yugoslavia [ˌjuːgəʊ'slɑːviə] *Jugoslavien*	Yugoslavian [ˌjuːgəʊ'slɑːviən]; a Yugoslav ['juːgəʊslɑːv], *pl* -s

* If there is only one word in this column, it means that the form for the adjective and person(s) is the same: *Naples is an* ***Italian*** *city. / I met an* ***Italian*** *called Marco.* For the plural, add an '-s': *The* ***Italians*** *invented pizza.*

NAMES

People

Aglukark ['æglukɑ:k]
Al Pacino [ˌæl pə'tʃi:nəʊ]
Amy ['eɪmi]
Astaire [ə'steə]
Banderas [bæn'derəs]
Benjamin ['bendʒəmɪn]
Benson ['bensn]
Betsey ['betsi]
Blair [bleə]
Brian ['braɪən]
Buffy Sainte-Marie [ˌbʌfi seɪnt mə'ri:]
Butcher ['bʊtʃə]
Cameahwait ['kæmɪəweɪt]
Carnegie ['kɑ:nəgi, kɑ:'negi]
Cathy Luchetti [ˌkæθi lʊ'tʃeti]
Chang [tʃæŋ]
Charbonneau [ˌʃɑ:bə'nəʊ]
Cher [ʃeə]
Cheryl ['ʃerəl]
Chloe ['kləʊi]
Columbus [kə'lʌmbəs]
Conchita [kən'tʃi:tə, kɒn'tʃi:tə]
Countee Cullen [ˌkaʊntɪ 'kʌlən]
Daniel ['dænjəl]
Deleisha [də'li:ʃə]
Dina ['daɪnə]
Dionne Warwick [di:ˌɒn 'wɒrɪk, 'wɔ:wɪk]
Dole [dəʊl]
Donnelly ['dɒnəli]
Donovan ['dɒnəvən]
Drew Barrymore [ˌdru: 'bærimɔ:]
Dylan Thomas [ˌdɪlən 'tɒməs]
Eartha Kitt [ˌɜ:θə 'kɪt]
Edward ['edwəd]
Erica ['erɪkə]
Erwin ['ɜ:wɪn]
Estes ['estɪs]
Eve [i:v]
Filo ['faɪləʊ]
Francis ['frɑ:nsɪs]
Frederic ['fredrɪk]
Gary ['gæri]
George [dʒɔ:dʒ]
Gerald ['dʒerəld]
Geronimo [dʒə'rɒnɪməʊ]
Gershwin ['gɜ:ʃwɪn]
Ginger Rogers [ˌdʒɪndʒə 'rɒdʒəz]
Godzilla [gɒd'zɪlə]
Gomez ['gəʊmez]
Gonzales [gɒn'zɑ:lez, gən'zɑ:ləs]
Gordon ['gɔ:dn]
Grace Paley [ˌgreɪs 'peɪli]
Harriet Tubman [ˌhæriət 'tʌbmən]
Haynes [heɪnz]
Hazlewood ['heɪzlwʊd]
Hoa [hwʌ]
Howard ['haʊəd]
Ira ['aɪrə]
Irving Berlin [ˌɜ:vɪŋ bɜ:'lɪn]
Ivy ['aɪvi]
James Anderson [ˌdʒeɪmz_'ændəsən]
Jane [dʒeɪn]
Janine [dʒə'ni:n]
Jean Davies Okimoto [ˌdʒi:n ˌdeɪvɪs_əʊki'məʊtəʊ]
Jefferson ['dʒefəsən]
Jerry Yang [ˌdʒerɪ 'jæŋ]
Jim Thorpe [ˌdʒɪm 'θɔ:p]
Joe [dʒəʊ]
Jones [dʒəʊnz]
José [həʊ'zeɪ]
Joseph ['dʒəʊzɪf, 'dʒəʊsɪf]
Joshua ['dʒɒʃjuə, 'dʒɒʃuə]
Josie ['dʒəʊzi]
Julie ['dʒu:li]
Juliet ['dʒu:liət, 'dʒu:liet]
Keene [ki:n]
Keith [ki:θ]
Kimberley ['kɪmbəli]
Larry ['læri]
Laura ['lɔ:rə]
Lavell [lə'vel]
Lee [li:]
Lennon ['lenən]
Levi Strauss [ˌli:vaɪ 'straʊs]
Lew [lu:]
Lincoln ['lɪŋkən]
Liza Minelli [ˌlaɪzə mɪ'neli]
Lula ['lu:lə]
MacDuff [mək'dʌf]
Malcolm ['mælkəm]
Manford ['mænfəd]
Marcia ['mɑ:siə, 'mɑ:ʃə]
Margo ['mɑ:gəʊ]
Maria(h) [mə'ri:ə]
Marshall ['mɑ:ʃl]
Martin Luther King [ˌmɑ:tɪn ˌlu:θə 'kɪŋ]
Maynard ['meɪnɑ:d]
Melanie ['meləni]
Meriwether Lewis [ˌmerɪweðə 'lu:ɪs]
Miwok ['mi:wɒk]
Mohajer [məʊ'heɪdʒə]
Morrison ['mɒrɪsən]
Muramoto [ˌmu:rə'məʊtəʊ]
Nancy ['nænsi]
Naomi ['neɪəmi, neɪ'əʊmi]
Neil [ni:l]
Nguyen Duc [ˌŋwiən 'dʌk]
Nuss [nu:s]
Oktollik [ɒk'tɒlɪk]
Olwell ['ɒlwəl]
Omori [ə'mɔ:ri]
Paco ['pɑ:kəʊ]
Pedro ['pedrəʊ, 'peɪdrəʊ]
Phuong ['fʌəŋ]
Pinchas ['pɪntʃəz]
Pocahontas [ˌpɒkə'hɒntəs, ˌpəʊkə'hɒntəs]
Powhatan ['paʊətæn]
Ramos ['rɑ:mɒs, 'reɪmɒs]
Randolph ['rændɒlf]
Ray [reɪ]
Robert ['rɒbət]
Rodney ['rɒdni]
Rolfe [rɒlf]
Romeo ['rəʊmiəʊ]
Sacajawea [ˌsækədʒə'wi:ə]
Scooter ['sku:tə]
Serkoak ['sɜ:kəʊˌæk]
Seward ['si:wəd, 'su:əd]
Sherman ['ʃɜ:mən]
Shoshoni [ʃəʊ'ʃəʊni]
Shriver ['ʃraɪvə]
Slaight [sleɪt]
Spielberg ['spilbɜ:g]
Stark [stɑ:k]
Streeper ['stri:pə]
Sucadoha [ˌsʊkə'dəʊə]
Sue [su:]
Sullivan ['sʌlɪvən]
Suyama [su'jɑ:mə]
Suzanne [su:'zæn]
Suzanne Vega [su:ˌzæn 'vi:gə, 'veɪgə]
Swenson ['swensn]
Sylvia ['sɪlviə]
Thomas ['tɒməs]
Trevor ['trevə]
Truong ['tʃʌəŋ]
Tyler ['taɪlə]
Wagner ['wægnə]
Watson ['wɒtsn]
Wayne [weɪn]
William ['wɪljəm]

Places

A.J. Dimond High School [ˌeɪ ˌdʒeɪ 'daɪmənd]
Alabama [ˌælə'bæmə]
Alaska [ə'læskə]
Anchorage ['æŋkərɪdʒ]
Atlantic Ocean [ətˌlæntɪk_'əʊʃn]
Atqasuk ['ætkəsʊk]
Bering Sea [ˌbe(ə)rɪŋ 'si:]
Bitterroot Mountains [ˌbɪtəru:t 'maʊntɪnz]
Bodie ['bəʊdi]
Bristol ['brɪstl]
Broken Bow [ˌbrəʊkn 'bəʊ]
the Bronx [brɒnks]
Brooks Range [ˌbrʊks 'reɪndʒ]
Carter's Grove [ˌkɑ:təz 'grəʊv]
Chesapeake Bay [ˌtʃesəpi:k 'beɪ]
Chowning's Tavern [ˌtʃaʊnɪŋz 'tævən]
Chrysler Building ['kraɪzlə, 'kraɪslə ˌbɪldɪŋ]
Chugach Mountains [ˌtʃu:gætʃ 'maʊntɪnz]
Cologne [kə'ləʊn] *Köln*
Commonwealth Avenue [ˌkɒmənwelθ_'ævənju:]
Connecticut [kə'netɪkət]
Copenhagen [ˌkəʊpən'heɪgən]
Cosmic Café [ˌkɒzmɪk kæ'feɪ, 'kæfeɪ]
Dakota [də'kəʊtə]
Delaware ['deləweə]
Denali [də'nɑ:li]
Emerald Isle [ˌemrəld_'aɪl] *Grüne Insel (Irland)*
Epcot ['epkɒt]
Everglades ['evəgleɪdz]
Fiorello H. LaGuardia High School [fiəˌreləʊ_ˌeɪtʃ lə'gwɑ:diə]
Florida ['flɒrɪdə]
Franklin High School ['fræŋklɪn]
Georgia ['dʒɔ:dʒə]
Habitat ['hæbɪtæt]
Hastings ['heɪstɪŋz]
Houston ['hju:stn]
Iditarod [aɪ'dɪtərɒd]
Jacksonville ['dʒæksənvɪl]
James River [ˌdʒeɪmz 'rɪvə]
Jamestown ['dʒeɪmztaʊn]
Juneau ['dʒu:nəʊ]
Jupiter ['dʒu:pɪtə]
LaGuardia Airport [lə'gwɑ:diə]
Lincoln Center [ˌlɪŋkən 'sentə]
Los Angeles (L.A.) [lɒs_'ændʒəli:z, -lɪs]
Louisiana [luˌi:zi'ænə]
Lyceum Theater [laɪˌsi:əm 'θɪətə]
Macy's ['meɪsi:z]
Mallorca [mə'jɔ:kə]
Mars [mɑ:z]
Massachusetts [ˌmæsə'tʃu:sɪts]
Metropolitan Museum of Art [metrəˌpɒlɪtən mjuˌzɪəm_əv_'ɑ:t]
Miami [maɪ'æmi]
Milwaukee [mɪl'wɔ:ki]
Missouri [mɪ'sʊəri, mɪ'zʊəri]
Mitiwanga [ˌmɪti'wɒŋgə]
Monticello [ˌmɒntɪ'tʃeləʊ]
Moscow ['mɒskəʊ, 'mɒskaʊ] *Moskau*
Mount McKinley [ˌmaʊnt mə'kɪnli]
Mount Whitney [ˌmaʊnt 'wɪtni]
Mulberry Row [ˌmʌlbəri 'rəʊ]
Naples ['neɪplz] *Neapel*
Nebraska [nə'bræskə]

New Hampshire [ˌnjuː ˈhæmpʃə]
New Jersey [ˌnjuː ˈdʒɜːzi]
New Orleans [ˌnjuː‿ɔːˈliːnz, ˌnjuː‿ˈɔːlənz]
Nome [nəʊm]
North Carolina [ˌnɔːθ kærəˈlaɪnə]
North Platte [ˌnɔːθ ˈplæt]
O'Hare Airport [əʊˈheə]
Omaha [ˈəʊməhɑː]
Oregon [ˈɒrɪɡən]
Orlando [ɔːˈlændəʊ]
Pacific Ocean [pəˌsɪfɪk‿ˈəʊʃn]
Pennsylvania [ˌpensɪlˈveɪniə]
Phoenix [ˈfiːnɪks]
Plimoth Plantation [ˌplɪməθ plɑːnˈteɪʃn]
Plymouth Rock [ˌplɪməθ ˈrɒk]
Point Comfort [ˌpɔɪnt ˈkʌmfət]
Point Reyes [ˌpɔɪnt ˈreɪjez]
Portage Glacier [ˌpɔːtɪdʒ ˈɡlæsiə, ˈɡleɪʃə]
Prudhoe Bay [ˌpruːdəʊ ˈbeɪ]
Raleigh Tavern [ˌrɑːli, ˌrɔːli ˈtævən]
Rhode Island [ˌrəʊd‿ˈaɪlənd]
Roberto Clemente High School [rəˌbɜːtəʊ klɪˈmenti]
Rodeo Drive [rəʊˌdeɪəʊ ˈdraɪv]
San Andreas fault [ˌsæn‿ænˈdreɪəs ˈfɔːlt]
Santa Barbara [ˌsæntə ˈbɑːbrə]
Seattle [siˈætl]
Siberia [saɪˈbɪəriə]
Sitka [ˈsɪtkə]
South Carolina [ˌsaʊθ kærəˈlaɪnə]
Staten Island [ˌstætn‿ˈaɪlənd]
St. Louis [snt ˈluːɪs]
Sunset Boulevard [ˌsʌnset ˈbuːləvɑːd]
Sutter's Mill [ˌsʌtəz ˈmɪl]
Tallahassee [ˌtæləˈhæsi]
Tennessee [ˌtenəˈsiː]
Texas [ˈteksəs]
Tijuana [tɪˈwɑːnə]
Tomales Point [təˈmɑːlez]
Tomesha [tɒˈmiːʃə]
Valdez [vælˈdiːz]
Venice Beach [ˌvenɪs ˈbiːtʃ]
Virginia [vəˈdʒɪniə]
Waiilatpu [ˌwaɪɪˈlæpuː]
Williamsburg [ˈwɪljəmzbɜːɡ]
Yorktown [ˈjɔːktaʊn]

Other names

Aviation Challenge [ˌeɪviˈeɪʃn ˌtʃæləndʒ]
Exxon Valdez [ˌeksɒn vælˈdiːz]
Igaramkin [ɪˈɡæræmkən]
Nalukataq [næˈluːkæˌtek]
NASA [ˈnæsə]
Universal Studios [ˌjuːnɪvɜːsl ˈstjuːdiəʊz]
Virginia Gazette [vəˌdʒɪnjə ɡəˈzet]
Voyager [ˈvɔɪədʒə]

Bildquellen: Accent Alaska, Ken Graham Agency, Girdwood, AK (S. 92/S. 96 Susan Butcher: Frank Flavin; S. 116 r.); Action Press, Hamburg (S. 85 o.l.: Steve Granitz/Retna Pictures); AP, Frankfurt (S. 78 dune buggy; S. 111 M.l.); Archiv für Kunst und Geschichte, Berlin (S. 34 M.; S. 50 o.; S. 55 Columbus); Ardea Ltd., London (S. 112); Bavaria Bildagentur, Gauting (S. 6/7; S. 8/9; S. 11 u.; S. 27; S. 54 Chinatown; S. 62; S. 79 beach; S. 92 kids; S. 95; S. 97 o.; S. 118 o.l.; S. 201 UN Building, Times Square, World Trade Center); John Berthelot, Santa Barbara, CA (S. 7 Nr. 2); Corbis/Picture Press, Hamburg (S. 60/61 horse riding: Michael S. Yamashita; S. 60/61 Central Park aerial view; S. 79 grape harvester: Jim Sugar; S. 99 u.: Bettmann; S. 101 fort/lake : David Muench; mountains: Charles E. Rotkin; river: Richard A. Cooke; S. 118 Dylan Thomas: Hulton-Deutsch); Corel Library (S. 14 u.; S. 15 M.; S. 50/51; S. 61 o.M.; S. 70 u.; S. 72 u.; S. 73 o.; S. 78 Lake Tahoe, earthquake, Redwood Tree, grizzly, Golden Gate Bridge; S. 79 Ghost Town, Hollywood Sign, mission; S. 84 o.; S. 92 track; S. 96 o., M.; S. 97 M., u.r.; S. 99 o.; S. 100; S. 101 snake, prairie dog, buffalo; S. 105 Halloween; S. 106; S. 107; S. 201 Central Park, Statue of Liberty); Roy Corral, Eagle River, AK (S. 9 Glen; S. 24 u.; S. 26; S. 116 l.); Culver Pictures, New York (S. 121 o.r.); Deutsche Bundesbahn AG, Jet-Foto, Berlin (S. 123 o.); dpa, Frankfurt (S. 93 subway; S. 97 u.l.); Richard Estes/VAGA, NY, NY/ Marlborough Gallery, NY (S. 103); Europäisches Währungsinstitut, 1997 Europäische Zentralbank (S. 15 u.); Brian Fairlee, Woodland Hills, CA (S. 109 o.); Focus, Hamburg (S. 7 Nr. 3: Thomas Ives; S. 61 o.r.: Sebastian Hartz; S. 79 Black Youths: Paul Fusco/Magnum; S. 92 und S. 110/111: Mireille Vautier; S. 111 o.l./u.: Alon Reininger/Contact Press, NY; o.M.: Steve Smith/Wheeler Pictures; o.r.: Alex Quesada/ Matrix; M.r.: Greg Smith/ Picture Group); Das Fotoarchiv, Essen (Jochen Tack: S. 9 license plate; S. 121 o.l.; S. 201 Broadway); Kathryn Goertzen, Henderson, NE (S. 9 Nancy; S. 64 Nancy; S. 65 Nancy; S. 66; S. 68; S. 69; S. 71 u.; S. 119); Roz Goodman, Dillingham, AK (S. 24 o.); Dwight Haigh, Flagstaff, AZ (S. 7 Nr. 4, 5, 6); Laurence Harger, San Francisco, CA (S. 79 street scene); Henry Huntington, Eagle River, AK (S. 20/21; S. 23 u.); IFA Bilderteam, Taufkirchen (S. 13; S. 84 police); Image Bank, Berlin (S. 9 alligator; S. 78 in-line skater, Chinatown; S. 79 Hollywood Boulevard; S. 83 u.; S. 84 M.; S. 105 Christmas tree); International Stock, New York (S. 56 u.; S. 65 u.M.; S. 73 u.; S. 79 surfer; S. 85 l.; S. 93 mailbox; S. 104 St. Patrick's Day; S. 105 Kermit; S. 201 Rockefeller Center, Brooklyn Bridge); Keystone, Hamburg (S. 51 u.r.); Jamestown-Yorktown Foundation (S. 55 Jamestown settlement); JPL Nasa, Picture Archive (S. 14 o.); Ute Klaphake, London (S. 93 pavement, rubber); KPA, Berlin (S. 123 u.); John Lally, York (S. 93 phone); Pia Lassahn, Berlin (S. 74/75 Hintergrund); Library of Congress, Washington, D.C. (S. 49); Mauritius, Berlin (S. 8 Margo; S. 29; S. 70 M.; S. 78 Oscar; S. 79 Death Valley; S. 80 o.r./u.; S. 92 San Andreas fault; S. 101 falls; S. 92/S. 105 fireworks; S. 108 o.); Massachusetts Historical Society, Boston (S. 98); Metacreations, Carpinteria, CA (S. 81 o.l.; S. 87); Peter Newark's Western Americana, Bath (S. 34 houses, hunting; S. 35; S. 55 Inuit; S. 92 Lewis & Clark; S. 101 u.); The New York Public Library (S. 41: Arents Collection; S. 50 u.: William Williams Collection, Milstein Division of United States History, Local History and Genealogy, Astor Lenox and Tilden Foundations; S. 51 u.l.: Lewis W. Hine Collection); Okapia, Berlin (S. 25/S. 113 wolf, moose; S. 122); Otto-Versand, Hamburg (S. 93 trousers); PC Magazine, December 15, 1998 (S. 81 o.r.); Pictor, Hamburg (S. 64/65; S. 84 computer work); Private Eye, No. 954, July 1998 (S. 28 o.); Public Information Office North Slope Borough, Barrow, AK (S. 23 o.); Punch Publications Ltd., London (S. 43 l.; S. 117; S. 131); PWE Kinoarchiv, Hamburg (S. 79 E.T.; S. 92 r.); Redferns, London (S. 85 o.r.; S. 109 u.); Calvin Redmond, New York (S. 9 Joshua; S. 52; S. 54 Josh, Daniel); Reuters (S. 104 u.l.); Lonnie Schlein, New York (S. 7 Nr. 7); David Simson, UK (S. 118 o.r.); Skjold Photographs, Saint Paul, USA (S. 8 Kimberley; S. 44 o.; S. 104 l.o.; S. 105 kids); South Yorkshire Supertram Ltd., Sheffield (S. 93 tram); Space & Rocket Center, Huntsville, AL (S. 8 brochure; S. 11 o.; S. 92 Space Camp; S. 94); The Spectator, London (S. 43 r.; S. 128; S. 199); Stockfood, München (S. 12; S. 93 chips, crisps); Cristina Taccone, San Francisco (S. 9 Scott; S. 82; S. 83 o.); Tony Stone, Hamburg (S. 78 homeless man; S. 108 M.: Hulton-Getty); Transglobe, Hamburg (S. 59; S. 75 o.; S. 78 highway sign; S. 80 Sequoia sign, skull; S. 81 u.; S. 84 DJ; S. 93 rubbish; S. 94 o.l.; S. 96 flag); Vieri Tomaselli, Miami (S. 8 Conchita; S. 9 seaquarium, restaurant; S. 10); Ullstein Bilderdienst, Berlin (S. 70 o.: Camera Press Ltd.; S. 71 o.: AP; S. 118 John Lennon: Camera Press Ltd.); U.S. Department of the Interior, National Park Service, by Courtesy of the Statue of Liberty National Monument (S. 51 o.l., o.r.); David Weil, Chicago (S. 84 male nurse); Wayne L. Whitehorne, New York (S. 103 u.); Colonial Williamsburg Foundation, Williamsburg, VA (S. 36; S. 37; S. 38 Robert "King" Carter: owned by Shirley Plantation; S. 39; S. 40; S. 42; S. 44 u.); ZEFA, Düsseldorf (S. 25 o.; S. 25/S. 113 caribou, grizzly bear; S. 28)

Titelbild: Brooklyn Bridge, New York: Bavaria Bildagentur, Gauting; Central Park: Corel Library

u. = unten; o. = oben; r. = rechts; l. = links; M. = Mitte

Textquellen: S. 33/S. 63: Excerpts taken from *Das Oxford Schulwörterbuch English–German/German–English*. © Oxford University Press, 1996, 1998; S. 74–75: adapted from *I Heard The Weirdest Rumor* by Brad Slaight. © 1995 by Brad Slaight. All rights reserved; S. 88–90: adapted from *Next Month … Hollywood* by Jean Davies Okimoto. © 1993 by Jean D. Okimoto, from JOIN IN, edited by Donald R. Gallo, reprinted, abridged and adapted by permission of Jean D. Okimoto; S. 95: *Incident* from ON THESE I STAND by Countée Cullen. © 1925 by Harper & Row, Publishers, Inc., renewed 1953 by Ida M. Cullen. Reprinted by permission of Harper & Row, Publishers, Inc., New York; S. 95: *Saying Yes* by Diana Chang, taken from "Tapestry: A Multicultural Anthology". © 1993 by Globe Book Company, Paramus, New Jersey. All rights reserved; S. 95: *Science* by Gordon Nelson, taken from "African American Poetry". © 1993 by Globe Book Company, Paramus, New Jersey. All rights reserved; S. 95: *Going Into Space* by Francis Becenti, taken from "Rising Voices: Writings of Young Native Americans", Ivy Books, published by Ballantine Books. © 1992 by Arlene B. Hirschfelder und Beverly R. Singer; S. 103: *On the Subway Station* by Grace Paley. © From "New and Collected Poems" by Grace Paley, Tilbury House, Publishers, Gardiner, Maine, 1992; S. 106: *Going West* based on: *Women of the West* by Cathy Luchetti and Carol Olwell. © Antelope Island Press, Utah; S. 110–111 adapted from *Across the Wire: Life and Hard Times on the Mexican Border* by Luis Alberto Urrea. © 1993 by Luis Alberto Urrea; S. 120: Excerpt reprinted from *The Last Light Breaking: Living among Alaska's Inupiat Eskimos* by Nick Jans. © 1993, with permission of Alaska Northwest Books, an Imprint of Graphic Arts Center Publishing Company; S. 121: taken from the TV series *The Bold and the Beautiful* © Excerpt reprinted with permission of "The Bold and the Beautiful" – Bradley Bell and John F. Smith, Writers; S. 121: excerpt from Dorling Kindersley Travel Guide to New York © 1993, 1997 Dorling Kindersley Ltd., London.

Liedquellen: S. 28: *Ancestor Song* by Ulali and The Silvercloud Singers, music and text by Pura Fe, Soni, Jen, Traditional. © 1994 Corn Beans & Squash Music; S. 92: *Let's Call The Whole Thing Off* by Fred Astaire and Ginger Rogers, music by George Gershwin, text by Ira Gershwin. © Chappell & Co. Inc., Chappell & Co. GmbH, Hamburg; S. 109: *Do you know the way to San Jose?* by Dionne Warwick, music by Burt Bacharach, text by Hal David. © New-Hidden-Valley-Music Company/Casa David, Melodie der Welt J. Michel KG Musikverlag, Frankfurt a. M.; S. 109: *Don't be denied* by Neil Young, music and text by Neil Young. © Silver Fiddle, Global Musikverlag, München.

Nicht alle Copyright-Inhaber konnten ermittelt werden. Deren Urheberrechte werden hiermit vorsorglich und ausdrücklich anerkannt.

			Summary-Abschnitt
abstract noun ['æbstrækt]	abstraktes Nomen	*food, history, life, technology*	**U4**: 1a
active ['æktɪv]	Aktiv	*The man **hit** the dog.*	**U3**: 1
adjective ['ædʒɪktɪv]	Adjektiv	*good, new, red, funny, boring*	
adverb ['ædvɜ:b]	Adverb	*always, badly, here, really, today*	**U6**: 2
adverb of degree [dɪ'gri:]	Gradadverb	*very, quite, really, too*	
adverb of frequency ['fri:kwənsi]	Häufigkeitsadverb	*always, usually, often, sometimes, never*	
adverb of indefinite time [ɪnˌdefɪnət 'taɪm]	Adverb der unbestimmten Zeit	*already, always, before, ever, just, never, often, yet, not … yet*	
adverb of manner ['mænə]	Adverb der Art und Weise	*badly, happily, electronically, well*	
adverbial phrase [ædˌvɜ:biəl 'freɪz]	zusammengesetzte Adverbialbestimmung	*to the shops, in the morning, by accident, without asking*	**U6**: 2
article ['ɑ:tɪkl]	Artikel	*the, a/an*	**U4**: 1 / **U6**: 1
auxiliary [ɔ:g'zɪliəri]	Hilfsverb	*be, have, do; will, can, must, might*	
backshift of tenses ['bækʃɪft]	Verschiebung der Zeiten (in der indirekten Rede)	*Ann: 'I **am** sorry.'* ▶ *Ann said she **was** sorry.*	**U3**: 2b
comparative [kəm'pærətɪv]	Komparativ, erste Steigerungsform	*taller; more boring; more easily*	
comparison [kəm'pærɪsn]	Steigerung; Vergleich	*tall – taller – tallest* *easily – more easily – most easily*	
conditional sentence [kənˌdɪʃənl 'sentəns]	Bedingungssatz	*If it rains tomorrow, we won't go.*	**U4**: 2
conjunction [kən'dʒʌŋkʃn]	Konjunktion	*Wash your hands **before** we eat.*	
contact clause ['kɒntækt klɔ:z]	Relativsatz ohne Relativpronomen	*That's the man **we met** last week.* *The bike **I got** is great.*	
countable noun ['kaʊntəbl]	zählbares Nomen	*girl – girls, ruler – rulers*	
defining relative clause [dɪˌfaɪnɪŋ ˌrelətɪv 'klɔ:z]	bestimmender/notwendiger Relativsatz	*That's the girl **who helped me**.* *The car **that hit the tree** was red.*	
definite article ['defɪnət]	bestimmter Artikel	*the*	**U4**: 1
direct speech [ˌdaɪrekt 'spi:tʃ]	direkte Rede, wörtliche Rede	*Ann said, **'I'm sorry.'***	**U3**: 2
emphasizing pronoun [ˌemfəsaɪzɪŋ 'prəʊnaʊn]	verstärkendes Pronomen	*I did it **myself**.*	
full verb [ˌfʊl 'vɜ:b]	Vollverb (= Wortart)	*go, dance, play, sit, work*	
future ['fju:tʃə]	Futur, Zukunft		
gerund ['dʒerənd]	Gerundium	*I like **dancing**. **Dancing** is fun.*	**U5**: 1
***going to*-future**	Futur mit *going to*	***I'm going to watch** TV tonight.*	**U3**: 1
***if*-clause** ['ɪf klɔ:z]	Nebensatz mit „if", „if"-Satz	***If it rains tomorrow**, we won't go.*	**U4**: 2
imperative [ɪm'perətɪv]	Imperativ (Befehlsform)	***Open** your books. **Don't talk**.*	**U3**: 2c
indefinite article [ɪn'defɪnət]	unbestimmter Artikel	*a/an*	**U6**: 1
indirect speech [ˌɪndɪrekt 'spi:tʃ]	indirekte Rede, nicht wörtliche Rede	*Ann said **(that) she was sorry**.* *Do you know **where Ken is**?*	**U3**: 2
infinitive [ɪn'fɪnətɪv]	Infinitiv	*(to) open, (to) see, (to) hear*	**U1**: 1/3/ **U2**: 2/ **U4**: 3
***-ing* form** ['ɪŋ fɔ:m]	*-ing*-Form des Verbs	*going, dancing, playing, sitting*	**U5**: 1
irregular verb [ɪ'regjələ]	unregelmäßiges Verb	*(to) go – went – gone*	
main clause [ˌmeɪn 'klɔ:z]	Hauptsatz	*If it rains tomorrow, **we won't go**.*	**U4**: 2
main verb [ˌmeɪn 'vɜ:b]	Hauptverb, Vollverb	*I can **dance**. We didn't **play**.*	
material noun [mə'tɪəriəl]	Stoffbezeichnung	*air, bread, coffee, water*	**U4**: 1a
modal auxiliary [ˌməʊdl‿ɔ:g'zɪliəri]	modales Hilfsverb, Modalverb	*can, could, may, must, needn't, should, would*	**U4**: 3
negative statement [ˌnegətɪv 'steɪtmənt]	verneinter Aussagesatz	*I'm not ten. I haven't got a sister.* *I don't like pop songs.*	
noun [naʊn]	Nomen, Substantiv	*Glen, Amy, girl, brother, time*	
object ['ɒbdʒɪkt]	Objekt	*Scott is writing **a letter**.*	**U1**: 1/3/ **U2**: 2g
object question	Objektfrage, Frage nach dem Objekt	*Who do they help?* *What did you eat?*	**U6**: 3
passive ['pæsɪv]	Passiv	*The dog **was hit** (by the man).*	**U3**: 1
past [pɑ:st]	Vergangenheit		
past participle [ˌpɑ:st 'pɑ:tɪsɪpl]	Partizip Perfekt	*climbed, saved, stopped, tidied, bought, fallen, gone, written*	**U2**: 1/ **U4**: 2b/3
past perfect [ˌpɑ:st 'pɜ:fɪkt]	Plusquamperfekt, Vorvergangenheit	*Mike was late because he **had missed** the bus.*	**U2**: 1/ **U3**: 1/ **U4**: 2b
past perfect progressive [ˌpɑ:st ˌpɜ:fɪkt prə'gresɪv]	Verlaufsform des *past perfect*	*Liz **had been waiting** for one hour when Pete arrived.*	**U2**: 1b/ **U3**: 1

			Summary-Abschnitt
past progressive [ˌpɑːst prəˈgresɪv]	Verlaufsform der Vergangenheit	*I **was washing** my hair at 8 o'clock yesterday evening.*	U3: 1
personal pronoun [ˌpɜːsnəl ˈprəʊnaʊn]	Personalpronomen (persönliches Fürwort)	*I, you, he, she, it, we, they, me, you, him, her, us, them*	
plural [ˈplʊərəl]	Plural, Mehrzahl		
positive statement [ˌpɒzətɪv ˈsteɪtmənt]	bejahter Aussagesatz	*I'm 14. I've got a sister. I like pop songs.*	
possessive determiner [pəˌzesɪv dɪˈtɜːmɪnə]	Possessivbegleiter (besitzanzeigender Begleiter)	*my, your, his, her, its, our, their*	
possessive pronoun [pəˌzesɪv ˈprəʊnaʊn]	Possessivpronomen	*mine, yours, his, hers, ours, theirs*	U5: 2
prefix [ˈpriːfɪks]	Vorsilbe, Präfix	*in-, un-, dis-*	
preposition [ˌprepəˈzɪʃn]	Präposition	*after, at, in, next to, on, to, under*	U5: 1
present [ˈpreznt]	Präsens, Gegenwart		
present perfect [ˌpreznt ˈpɜːfɪkt]	*present perfect* (Perfekt)	*I've **packed** my bag. **Have** you **packed** yours? – Yes, I **have**. Liz **has known** Megan for years.*	U3: 1
present perfect progressive [ˌpreznt ˌpɜːfɪkt prəˈgresɪv]	Verlaufsform des *present perfect*	*Liz **has been waiting** for one hour.*	U3: 1
present progressive [ˌpreznt prəˈgresɪv]	Verlaufsform der Gegenwart	*Scott **is writing** a letter. **I'm leaving** Germany tomorrow.*	U1: 2 / U3: 1
pronoun [ˈprəʊnaʊn]	Pronomen		
prop-word [ˈprɒpwɜːd]	Stützwort	*I've got three dogs, a black **one** and two brown **ones**.*	
quantifier [ˈkwɒntɪfaɪə]	Mengenbezeichnung	*some, any; much, many; a little, a few*	
question [ˈkwestʃən]	Frage(satz)		U3: 2c / U6: 3
question tag [ˈkwestʃən tæg]	Frageanhängsel	*Ann lives in Chester, **doesn't she?** But she isn't British, **is she?***	
question word [ˈkwestʃən wɜːd]	Fragewort	*who?, what?, when?, where?, why?, how?*	
reflexive pronoun [rɪˌfleksɪv ˈprəʊnaʊn]	Reflexivpronomen	*myself, yourself, him-/her-/itself, ourselves, yourselves, themselves*	
regular verb [ˈregjələ]	regelmäßiges Verb	*(to) help – helped – helped*	
relative clause [ˌrelətɪv ˈklɔːz]	Relativsatz	*That's the girl **who helped me**. The car **that hit the tree** was red.*	
relative pronoun [ˌrelətɪv ˈprəʊnaʊn]	Relativpronomen	*who, that, which, whose*	
reporting verb [rɪˌpɔːtɪŋ ˈvɜːb]	Verb des Berichtens	*(to) tell, (to) say, (to) think*	U3: 2a
***s*-genitive** [ˈes ˌdʒenətɪv]	*s*-Genitiv	***Sue's** brother; **my sister's** name*	U5: 2
simple past [ˌsɪmpl ˈpɑːst]	einfache Form der Vergangenheit	*I **didn't go** to school yesterday. I **stayed** at home. **Did** you **go**?*	U3: 1
simple present [ˌsɪmpl ˈpreznt]	einfache Form der Gegenwart	*I **start** school at 8.45 every day. When **do** you **start** school?*	U3: 1
singular [ˈsɪŋgjələ]	Singular, Einzahl		
sub-clause [ˈsʌbklɔːz], **subordinate clause** [səˌbɔːdɪnət ˈklɔːz]	Nebensatz	***If it rains**, we won't go. I can't come **because I'm ill**.*	
subject [ˈsʌbdʒɪkt]	Subjekt	***My dog** is black. **His name** is Tim.*	
subject question	Subjektfrage, Frage nach dem Subjekt	*Who helped you? What woke you up?*	U6: 3
suffix [ˈsʌfɪks]	Nachsilbe, Suffix	*-er, -ion, -ly*	
superlative [suːˈpɜːlətɪv]	Superlativ, höchste Steigerungsform	*tallest; most boring; most easily*	
tense [tens]	(grammatische) Zeitform, Tempus		U3: 1/2b
uncountable noun [ʌnˈkaʊntəbl]	nicht zählbares Nomen	*music, water, butter, money, homework, information*	
verb [vɜːb]	Verb	*count, hear, open, rain, see*	
verb of perception [pəˈsepʃn]	Verb der Wahrnehmung	*(to) watch, (to) listen, (to) see, (to) hear*	U1: 3
***will*-future**	Futur mit *will*	***I'll be** 15 next week. I'm thirsty. – **I'll get** you a drink.*	U3: 1
word order [ˈwɜːd_ɔːdə]	Wortstellung		U3: 2c / U6: 2/3
yes/no question	Entscheidungsfrage	*Are you German? Do you like music?*	U3: 2c

IRREGULAR VERBS

Infinitive	Simple past	Past participle	
(to) **be**	**was/were**	**been**	sein
(to) **beat**	**beat**	**beaten**	schlagen; besiegen
(to) **become**	**became**	**become**	werden
(to) **begin**	**began**	**begun**	beginnen, anfangen (mit)
(to) **bet**	**bet**	**bet**	wetten
(to) **blow**	**blew**	**blown**	wehen, blasen
(to) **break** [eɪ]	**broke**	**broken**	(zer)brechen; kaputtgehen
(to) **bring**	**brought**	**brought**	(mit-, her)bringen
(to) **build**	**built**	**built**	bauen
(to) **buy**	**bought**	**bought**	kaufen
(to) **catch**	**caught**	**caught**	fangen; erwischen
(to) **choose** [uː]	**chose** [əʊ]	**chosen** [əʊ]	(aus)wählen, aussuchen
(to) **come**	**came**	**come**	kommen
(to) **cost**	**cost**	**cost**	kosten
(to) **cut**	**cut**	**cut**	(aus)schneiden
(to) **dig**	**dug**	**dug**	(aus-, um)graben
(to) **do**	**did**	**done** [ʌ]	tun, machen
(to) **draw**	**drew**	**drawn**	zeichnen
(to) **drink**	**drank**	**drunk**	trinken
(to) **drive** [aɪ]	**drove**	**driven** [ɪ]	*(ein Auto, einen Bus usw.)* fahren
(to) **eat**	**ate** [et, eɪt]	**eaten**	essen
(to) **fall**	**fell**	**fallen**	(hin)fallen
(to) **feed**	**fed**	**fed**	füttern
(to) **feel**	**felt**	**felt**	fühlen; sich fühlen
(to) **fight**	**fought**	**fought**	(be)kämpfen
(to) **find**	**found**	**found**	finden
(to) **fly**	**flew**	**flown**	fliegen
(to) **forget**	**forgot**	**forgotten**	vergessen
(to) **freeze**	**froze**	**frozen**	(ge)frieren; einfrieren
(to) **get**	**got**	**got**	bekommen; holen, besorgen; gelangen, hinkommen; werden
(to) **give**	**gave**	**given**	geben
(to) **go**	**went**	**gone** [ɒ]	gehen; fahren; werden
(to) **grow**	**grew**	**grown**	wachsen; anbauen, anpflanzen
(to) **hang**	**hung**	**hung**	hängen, aufhängen
(to) **have (have got)**	**had**	**had**	haben
(to) **hear** [ɪə]	**heard** [ɜː]	**heard** [ɜː]	hören
(to) **hide**	**hid**	**hidden**	(sich) verstecken
(to) **hit**	**hit**	**hit**	schlagen, treffen
(to) **hold**	**held**	**held**	(fest)halten; veranstalten, abhalten
(to) **hurt**	**hurt**	**hurt**	verletzen, wehtun; schaden, schädigen
(to) **keep**	**kept**	**kept**	(be-, ein-, er)halten; aufbewahren, aufheben
(to) **know** [nəʊ]	**knew** [njuː]	**known** [nəʊn]	wissen; kennen
(to) **lead**	**led**	**led**	führen, leiten
(to) **leave**	**left**	**left**	(zurück)lassen; verlassen; weggehen, abfahren
(to) **let**	**let**	**let**	(zu)lassen, erlauben
(to) **lie** [aɪ]	**lay** [eɪ]	**lain** [eɪ]	liegen
(to) **light**	**lit**	**lit**	anzünden
(to) **lose** [uː]	**lost** [ɒ]	**lost** [ɒ]	verlieren
(to) **make**	**made**	**made**	machen
(to) **mean** [iː]	**meant** [e]	**meant** [e]	bedeuten; meinen, sagen wollen
(to) **meet**	**met**	**met**	(sich) treffen; abholen
(to) **overtake**	**overtook**	**overtaken**	überholen
(to) **pay**	**paid**	**paid**	bezahlen
(to) **put**	**put**	**put**	legen, stellen, *(wohin)* tun
(to) **read** [iː]	**read** [e]	**read** [e]	lesen
(to) **retell**	**retold**	**retold**	nacherzählen
(to) **ride**	**rode**	**ridden**	reiten; *(Rad)* fahren
(to) **ring**	**rang**	**rung**	klingeln, läuten; anrufen
(to) **rise** [aɪ]	**rose**	**risen** [ɪ]	aufgehen *(Sonne)*; (an-, auf)steigen
(to) **run**	**ran**	**run**	laufen; verkehren; (durch)führen
(to) **say** [eɪ]	**said** [e]	**said** [e]	sagen

Infinitive	Simple past	Past participle	
(to) see	saw	seen	sehen; besuchen
(to) sell	sold	sold	verkaufen
(to) send	sent	sent	schicken, senden
(to) set free	set free	set free	befreien
(to) shake	shook	shaken	zittern; schütteln
(to) shoot	shot	shot	(er-, an)schießen
(to) show [əʊ]	showed [əʊ]	shown [əʊ]	zeigen
(to) shut	shut	shut	schließen, zumachen
(to) sing	sang	sung	singen
(to) sink	sank	sunk	sinken; versenken
(to) sit	sat	sat	sitzen; sich setzen
(to) sleep	slept	slept	schlafen
(to) speak	spoke	spoken	sprechen
(to) spend	spent	spent	*(Zeit)* verbringen; *(Geld)* ausgeben
(to) spread [e]	spread [e]	spread [e]	(sich) ausbreiten, (sich) verbreiten
(to) stand	stood	stood	stehen; sich (hin)stellen
(to) steal	stole	stolen	stehlen
(to) stick	stuck	stuck	kleben
(to) sting	stung	stung	stechen
(to) swim	swam	swum	schwimmen
(to) take	took	taken	(mit)nehmen; (weg)bringen; dauern
(to) teach	taught	taught	unterrichten, lehren
(to) tear [eə]	tore	torn	reißen; zerreißen
(to) tell	told	told	erzählen, berichten; erkennen
(to) think	thought	thought	(nach)denken; glauben, meinen
(to) throw	threw	thrown	werfen
(to) understand	understood	understood	verstehen, begreifen
(to) wake up	woke up	woken up	aufwachen; (auf)wecken
(to) wear [eə]	wore	worn	tragen, anhaben
(to) win	won [ʌ]	won [ʌ]	gewinnen
(to) write	wrote	written	schreiben

'Stop talking now, class.'

◦ USEFUL PHRASES FOR DISCUSSIONS IN THE CLASSROOM

Giving an opinion / Asking for an opinion	**Eine Meinung äußern / Nach einer Meinung fragen**
In my opinion, …	Meiner Meinung nach … / Meines Erachtens …
I think/feel/find/suppose (that) …	Ich glaube/meine/finde/nehme an, (dass) …
Well, if you ask me, …	Also wenn du mich fragst, …
What do you think about …?	Was hältst du von … ? / Was meinst du zu …?
How do you feel about this?	Was hältst du davon?
What's your opinion on this?	Was ist deine Meinung dazu?
Saying what you think is probably true	**Sagen, was vermutlich der Fall ist**
Perhaps/Maybe he is lonely/…	Vielleicht ist er einsam/…
He may/might be lonely.	Er ist vielleicht einsam/könnte vielleicht einsam sein.
He may/might have been lonely.	Er ist vielleicht einsam gewesen. / Er war vielleicht einsam.
He is probably lonely.	Er ist wahrscheinlich einsam.
Agreeing / Disagreeing	**Zustimmen / Widersprechen**
I think you are right/wrong.	Ich finde, du hast Recht/nicht Recht.
That's (quite) right.	Das ist (ganz) richtig.
I agree completely.	Ich bin ganz deiner Meinung.
I'm of the same opinion (as Alina).	Ich bin derselben Meinung (wie Alina).
Yes, but …	Ja, aber …
I can see your point, but …	Ich verstehe dein Argument, aber …
No, I (completely) disagree with you.	Nein, das sehe ich (ganz) anders.
That can't be right.	Das kann nicht stimmen.
Never!	Nie im Leben!
Making suggestions	**Vorschläge machen**
How about …? / What about …?	Wie wäre es mit …? / Was hältst du von …?
Let's …	Lass(t) uns …
Couldn't we …?	Könnten wir nicht …?
Why don't you …?	Könntest du nicht …? / Wie wäre es, wenn du …?
Comparing and contrasting	**Gemeinsamkeiten und Unterschiede herausstellen**
… is (much) bigger than …	… ist (viel) größer als …
… is (not) as big as …	… ist (nicht) so groß wie …
Unlike …/In contrast to …	Im Gegensatz/Unterschied zu …
A is hot, while B is cold.	A ist heiß, während/wohingegen B kalt ist.
Asking for clarification / Clarifying	**Um Klärung bitten / Etwas erklären**
Could you explain that (again), please?	Könntest du/Könnten Sie das bitte (noch einmal) erklären?
Sorry, what do you mean by that?	Entschuldigung, was meinst du damit?
I didn't quite follow that. Do you mean …?	Ich habe das nicht ganz verstanden. Meinst du …?
I mean …	Ich meine … / Ich will sagen …
Well, what I am trying to say is this: …	Also, was ich sagen will, ist Folgendes: …
Let me put it like this: …	Lass es mich mal so sagen/ausdrücken: …
Praising and criticizing other students	**Mitschüler/innen loben und kritisieren**
Well done.	(Das hast du/habt ihr) gut gemacht.
Your … was really good/nice/excellent/super/…	Dein(e) … war wirklich gut/prima/toll/super/…
I (really) liked your transparencies/handouts.	Deine Folien/Handouts haben mir (wirklich) gefallen.
You could have spoken more clearly.	Du hättest deutlicher sprechen können.
He should have written the words on the board.	Er hätte die Wörter an die Tafel schreiben sollen.
Starting and finishing a presentation	**Eine Präsentation einleiten und beenden**
In this talk we're going to discuss/show/…	In diesem Referat sprechen wir über/zeigen wir/…
We'd like to talk about …	Wir möchten/werden über … sprechen.
First/Next/Now we're going to …	Zuerst/Als Nächstes/Jetzt werden wir …
In conclusion/Finally, we'd like to …	Abschließend/Zum Schluss möchten wir …